Intimate Letters

Intimate Letters

LEOŠ JANÁČEK
TO KAMILA STÖSSLOVÁ

edited and translated by

John Tyrrell

PRINCETON UNIVERSITY PRESS
PRINCETON, NEW JERSEY

First published in the United States of America by
Princeton University Press
41 William Street, Princeton, New Jersey 08540

Published in Great Britain
by Faber and Faber Limited
3 Queen Square, London, WC1N 3AU

Original Czech text transcribed and edited by
Svatava Přibáňová as *Hádanka života: dopisy Leoše Janáčka Kamile Stösslové*
(Brno, Opus musicum, 1990) © Opus musicum and Svatava Přibáňová 1990
Translated by permission of DILIA, Prague

Typography by Humphrey Stone
Photoset by Parker Typesetting Service, Leicester
Printed in England by Clays Ltd, St Ives plc

Library of Congress Cataloging-in-Publication Data

Janáček, Leoš, 1854–1928.
[Correspondence. English. Selections]
Intimate letters, Leoš Janáček to Kamila Stösslová / edited and
translated by John Tyrrell.
p. cm.
Includes bibliographical references (p.) and index.
ISBN 0–691–03648–9 (cloth)
1. Janáček, Leoš, 1854–1928—Correspondence. 2. Stösslová,
Kamila, 1891–1935—Correspondence. 3. Composers—Czechoslovakia—
Correspondence. I. Stösslová, Kamila, 1891–1935. II. Tyrrell,
John. III. Title.
ML410.J18A4 1994
780'.92—dc20
[B]
93–38365
CIP
MN

2 4 6 8 10 9 7 5 3 1

TO SVATAVA PŘIBÁŇOVÁ
JANA KUCHTOVÁ
AND JIM FRIEDMAN

Contents

List of Plates

32 Pastel study of Janáček by his friend František Ondrúšek (1926).
33 Bookplate made for Janáček by Eduard Milén (1924).
34 Janáček on his return from England (1926)
35 Janáček notating the waves in Flushing, Holland (1926).
36 Otto and Rudolf Stössel aged four and seven (1920).
37 František Dvořák's *Dallying Cherubs*, which Janáček bought from the Stössels in 1927.

Plates 1–4, 11–12, 18–19, 22–6, 28, 30, 32–3 and 36 and the facsimiles on pp. 36, 77, 148, 243 and 251 appeared in the original Czech edition by Svatava Přibáňová: *Hádanka života* (Brno, Opus musicum, 1990)

Plates 7 and 27 were first published in Jaroslav Procházka: *Lašské kořeny života i díla Leoše Janáčka* (Okresní a místní rada osvětová, Frýdek-Místek, 1948); Plates 8 and 13 in Jak. Balhar: *Průvodce Lázněmi Luhačovicemi na Moravě a 75 výletů do okolí* (F. Hložek, Luhačovice, revised 3/1914); Plates 14, 16 and 17 in Jakub Balhar et al: *Lázně Luhačovice 1902–1927* [Luhačovice, 1927]; Plate 35 in *Listy Hudební matice*, v (1926), supplement 24.

The facsimile on p. 4 and remaining plates appear by kind permission of the following: Music Division of the Moravian Regional Museum, Brno (Plates 5–6, 9–10, 15, 20–1, 34 and 37), Brno Regional Archive (Plate 31), private collection (Plate 29).

Preface and Acknowledgements

For many years Janáček's letters to Kamila Stösslová were subject to a taboo. It was known that the Czech composer had maintained a close friendship with a woman half his age who had apparently inspired many of the works of his late years. But the exact nature of the relationship remained unclear. Speculation about it began during the composer's lifetime – he died in 1928 at the age of seventy-four – and has continued ever since, fuelled by the knowledge that some seven hundred letters from Janáček to Stösslová survived, and that these were not generally accessible. Fragments of them, usually describing Janáček's works, had crept out, but about the bulk of them there was tantalizing silence.

After Stösslová's early death in 1935, and shortly before the outbreak of the Second World War when her husband fled to Switzerland, Professor Vladimír Helfert acquired the letters for the Masaryk University of Brno. Piety to the memory of Janáček's widow, who survived until 1938, was a key factor in the decision by Helfert and his successors in the Music Division of the Moravian Regional Museum to restrict access. It was not until 1990 that Dr Svatava Přibáňová, then chief Janáček scholar of the museum, was able, with active encouragement by the publisher Opus musicum, to bring about a change of policy and publish the letters in their entirety. (Dr Přibáňová's description of the history of the letters is given in Appendix 1.) The significance of Dr Přibáňová's volume cannot be overstated. This is by far the most important source for the understanding of Janáček's emotional and creative life in the last twelve years of his life – the period in which he became famous and in which he composed his greatest works. The fact that this source has been suppressed for so long has meant that biographers have been working on incomplete and misleading information for this period of Janáček's life, and only now is a proper perspective on it possible. Quite apart from their musicological and biographical significance these letters are valuable as being the most beautiful and self-revealing ever written by Janáček. He was always a gifted and imaginative letter writer but these letters go to the heart of his inner life. And within them, they contain a great love story.

The Czech edition that Dr Přibáňová published in 1990 is the basis
for the present English edition, which has been made with the whole-
hearted support and co-operation of Dr Přibáňová, her publisher Dr
Eva Drlíková of Opus musicum, and Dr Jiří Sehnal, the present
director of the Music History Division of the Moravian Regional
Museum. The Czech edition is a complete one, containing all that has
survived, including the empty envelopes and miscellaneous fragments. While Janáček scholars will naturally wish to read the letters
in the original language, it was felt that this English edition could be
directed towards a general public that is becoming more and more
interested in the composer. I have therefore prepared an edition
which is significantly different from the Czech one in several respects.
First, it is not complete. I have made cuts (described below) both to
enhance the narrative force of the story, and at the same time to bring
the material (some 200,000 words in the original) down to a commer-
cially viable length while allowing room for other features such as the
inclusion of more letters from Kamila Stösslová (the Czech edition
includes a few in the footnotes). Second, I have introduced linking
commentaries to bridge many of the gaps, especially in the earlier part
of the correspondence – by the last two years such a commentary
becomes increasingly redundant. In the first Czech edition, Dr Přibáňová was scrupulously careful to let the letters speak for themselves, and not to impose her own interpretation on them. Her
footnotes, while providing a vast amount of relevant information, are
equally self-effacing. A similar feat, however, is impossible with a
translation. A translator is constantly needing to make choices in
ambiguous readings and to propose a clear view of what is being
expressed. I have therefore needed to go further than Dr Přibáňová
and make guesses and hypotheses, as will be evident from my commentary and footnotes.

As stated above, I have made cuts in the material, thereby reducing
the overall total by about a quarter. I have done so mostly at the
expense of the letters from the first nine years of the relationship.
These make up roughly half the total material, which has now been
reduced to half again, both by excluding many letters and by cutting
others. This material is notably less interesting than that of the final
two years: formal letters setting up and acknowledging meetings,
letters discussing the household provisions with which the Stössels
supplied the Janáčeks in the difficult last years of the war, and other
trivia. I hope, nevertheless, to have left enough to give the reader a
flavour of the earlier part of the relationship, and to have included all
the letters that chart the different stages in its development. Naturally

I have also tried to include those letters in which Janáček discusses his own works or which shed light on his personality, views and interests. From April 1927, when the relationship took a deep and serious turn, about eighty per cent of the material has been retained. Cuts have been made where Janáček is repetitive (he was by then writing almost every day – sometimes several times a day – and understandably repeated himself); his comments on letters from Stösslová which have not survived, where his words are thus unintelligible without more context, have also been omitted. My cuts are shown exclusively with square brackets [...].

My cuts are not the only ones. It is clear that Stösslová herself burnt some of Janáček's letters (often leaving the empty envelopes as proof of their former existence), tore off single leaves of bifolia, cut out certain parts of letters with scissors, or blotted out particular words, presumably because she felt they were indecorous (with the loss of possibly decorous material on the other side). (For further details see Glossary: 'omissions, crossings out'.) These cuts are indicated < >, usually with some indication of how much is missing. Words and phrases left after such interventions and which are too incomplete to make sense have been omitted editorially, though a few tantalizing fragments have been left in.

Stösslová's own letters suffered a much worse fate. She was in any case a far less active correspondent than Janáček, but almost all the letters from the later years were burnt by Janáček on her instructions: he frequently, and tearfully, chronicled the burning (see Glossary: 'burning of letters').

After giving some indication of Janáček's usual practice, salutations and sign-offs are mostly omitted from the earlier letters. When the correspondence became more intimate in April 1927, Janáček varies his salutations and sign-offs, so most of these are given.

Dates and dating have been standardized. Janáček usually put the place and date at the end of the letter. For convenience this has been moved to the top, in a standardized form. Double dates usually indicate a later, dated, postscript or continuation of the letter the next day. Enough dates have been left in the body of the letter to show what parts were written when and a line space added to clarify temporal breaks in writing. Stösslová seldom dated her letters though most are possible to date from postmarks on the envelopes, which Janáček carefully preserved. All dates given for her letters should be regarded as being derived from this method or, where postmarks are illegible, from internal evidence.

The numbering of Janáček's letters established by Dr Přibáňová has been retained, both for ease in referring to the Czech edition, and to give the reader some indication of what has been omitted from the English edition. References (in footnotes and commentary) to letters reproduced in full only in the Czech edition are given by preceding the number with an asterisk (e.g. *9).

I have tried to preserve Janáček's idiosyncratic paragraphing. Some letters have tiny 'paragraphs' (e.g. 625), and in others there are for whole pages without paragraph breaks. Where my paragraphing differs from that of the Czech edition, which sometimes smooths out such differences, it reflects that of Janáček's original manuscript. I have also taken the opportunity of restoring a handful of short passages inadvertently omitted from the Czech edition (e.g. in 516).

Where Janáček's spelling of names is incorrect, I have corrected it without comment. He frequently wrote local variants for 'Hukvaldy' ('Pod Hukvaldy', 'Ukvaldy'); these have been standardized to Hukvaldy. I have retained the various abbreviations he used for his wife's name and given the full version as he wrote it ('Zdenka') rather than the correct Czech version ('Zdeňka').

Janáček's references to currency have been standardized to 'K' (*Krone, koruna* = crown) up to 1918 and Kč (*Koruna československá* = Czechoslovak crown) from 1919, always placed before the digits (Janáček usually wrote it afterwards). The prewar parity of £1 = K 24.02 ($1 = K 4.93) proved impossible to maintain after 1918. By January 1920 the new Czechoslovak currency was worth only a tenth of its former value, reaching a low at the end of 1921 of £1 = Kč 419 ($1 = Kč 104.0). Stringent measures during 1922, however, meant that by January 1923 a stable rate of £1 = Kč 160 ($1 = Kč 34.4) was established which, with little variation, lasted until 1931.

The letters, after the initial rather formal ones that Janáček wrote, come in a direct, informal style. I have approximated this by using contractions (I am = I'm), but I have not endeavoured to represent in English the somewhat old-fashioned and dialect expressions which Janáček occasionally used. Idiosyncratic word order (much freer in Czech anyway) is only occasionally imitated, but all typographical emphases (usually underlining, shown here by italics) and quotation marks have been retained. Additional emphases (e.g. Janáček's double underlining) is shown by underlining (e.g. 703). Where possible I have attempted to reproduce Janáček's punctuation, except where there are grammatical differences between Czech and English (in the use, for instance, of the comma).

A far greater problem for the translator is posed by Kamila Stösslová's letters, which are the letters of a poorly educated woman, not used to expressing herself in writing. There seemed little point in introducing wrong spellings to reflect her spelling of Czech; I have however left her rudimentary, often comma-less, punctuation to approximate this aspect of her style. Even so, the reader should be aware that the letters still sound more literate in translation than in the original.

English usage has been maintained for Czech titles of works (their original-language titles can be found after the English title in the index, listed under author, composer, etc). Names of journals, periodicals etc. are left untranslated. Names of Czech buildings and institutions are given in English if a standard, accepted translation exists (e.g. the Prague National Theatre, Brno Organ School); others (e.g. Hudební matice, Besední dům) are left in Czech, usually with a translation or explanation supplied at the first occurrence.

While most names, terms and works are explained in footnotes as they come, more persistent references, including some general topics, are discussed in the Glossary. The reader may also find it useful to refer to the Diary of Meetings.

The staff of the Music History Division of the Moravian Regional Museum have been as helpful as always, and in particular I am grateful to the director, Dr Jiří Sehnal, for access to all the material I have used, and to Dr Jaroslava Procházková, now in charge of the Janáček archive, who located many stray documents and helped solve several puzzles in the footnotes. Kamila Stösslová's surviving son, Mr Otto Stössel, has kindly allowed me to publish his mother's letters. Ruth Thackeray smoothed the many rough edges in my manuscript and helped me solve all sorts of difficult questions. I am grateful to my editors at Faber and Faber for their enthusiastic and efficient handling of my manuscript, and in particular to my copy editor, Ingrid Grimes. I would also like to acknowledge most warmly help from the following friends and colleagues: Dr Jindra Bártova, Dr Glen Bauer, Dr Jarmil Burghauser, Dr Eva Drlíková, Dr Richard Klos, Ing. Václav Křepelka, Dr Jitka Ludvová, Dr Alena Němcová, Mr Brad Robinson, Mr Nigel Simeone, Dr Miloš Štědroň, Mr Václav Štěpán, CSc, Mr Heinz Stolba, Dr Charles Süsskind, Mr Colin Tindley, Miss Audrey Twine.

I have had the great advantage not only of being able to work from Dr Přibáňová's transcriptions of these letters, but also from her exemplary footnotes based on a lifetime's work in the Janáček archives. Many of her footnotes have been taken over wholesale; in other cases I have expanded them or made additional ones to help both the English reader and a more general public. I have not attempted to signal responsibility for each footnote (or part of it). Those consulting the Czech edition will see my debt, though even this is misleading since Dr Přibáňová continued to give expert help, and to answer many of my supplementary questions. I have also had the benefit of Dr Přibáňová's transcriptions of some of the letters written by Kamila Stösslová, either reprinted in Dr Přibáňová's footnotes, or in manuscript.

This book would not to have come about without the help of two further friends. Dr Jana Kuchtová, a lecturer in English at Masaryk University, Brno, patiently went through all my translations, corrected my many errors, made many excellent suggestions that I seized on with gratitude and gave imaginative advice for dealing with difficult passages. Finally Jim Friedman sat for hours with me, dictionaries and thesauruses in hand, debating the nuances of individual words and phrases. Many of the more ingenious and pleasing solutions are his. He has read several versions of the manuscript and in long discussions contributed to its pacing, shaping and character. By dedicating the book to these friends I wish to show my appreciation of their help and share credit with them in bringing to the English-reading public one of the most remarkable and touching collections of letters ever bequeathed by a composer to future generations.

JOHN TYRRELL
Nottingham, 20 April 1993

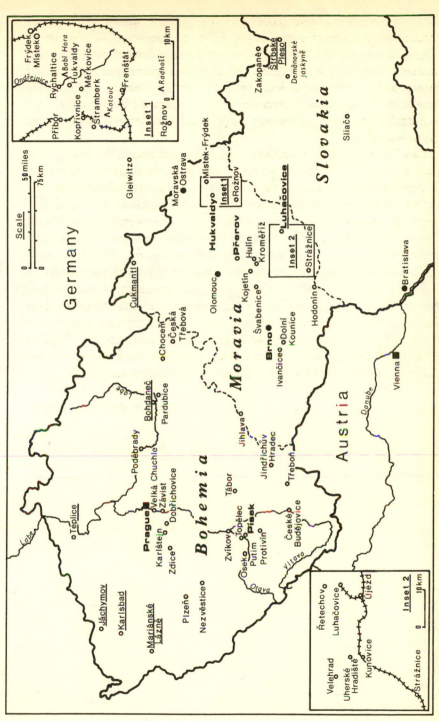

Map of Bohemia and Moravia in 1918, showing towns and other geographical features mentioned in the text. The names of towns and villages of particular importance to Janáček are set in bold; the names of spa towns are underlined. *Drawn by Marion Hubbard*

Inset 1

Frýdek
Místek
Ondřeinice
Rychaltice
Babí Hora
Hukvaldy
Měřkovice
Příbor
Kopřivnice
Štramberk
Frenštát
Kotouč
Rožnov 0
Radhošť
0   10 km

Inset 1 (main map)

Mistek-Frýdek
Hukvaldy
Rožnov

Inset 2 (main map)

Luhačovice
Strážnice

Inset 2

Řetechov
Luhačovice
Újezd
Velehrad
Uherské
Hradiště
Kunovice
Strážnice
0   10 km

Germany

Gleiwitz

Moravská
Ostrava

Čukmantl

Choceň
Česká
Třebová

Olomouc

Přerov
Hulín
Kojetín
Kroměříž

Švabenice

Dolní
Kounice

Brno
Ivančice

Hodonín

Bratislava

Jihlava

Jindřichův
Hradec

Třeboň

Slovakia

Zakopané
Štrbské
Pleso
Demänovské
jaskyně

Sliač

Vienna

Austria

Danube

Vltava

Otava

Elbe

Labe

Bohemia
Moravia

Jáchymov
Karlsbad

Mariánské
Lázně

Plzeň
Nezvěstice

Teplice

Poděbrady

Bohdaneč
Pardubice

Velká Chuchle
Závist
Dobřichovice

Prague
Karlštejn
Zdice

Zvíkov
Topělec
Oseko
Putim
Písek
Protivín

České
Budějovice

Tábor

Scale

0   50 miles
0   75 km

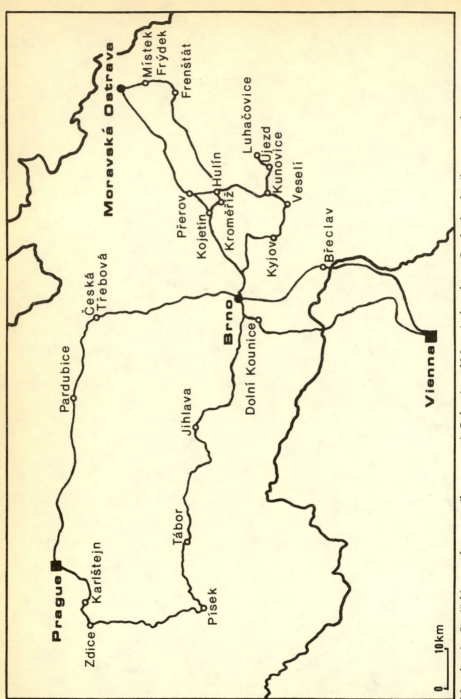

Map showing Janáček's most frequent railway routes in Bohemia and Moravia, based on a Czechoslovak railway map of 1919.
Drawn by Marion Hubbard

THE LETTERS

1 Luhačovice, 16 July 1917

Dear Madam

Accept these few roses as a token of my unbounded esteem for you. You are so lovely in character and appearance that in your company one's spirits are lifted; you breathe warm-heartedness, you look on the world with such kindness that one wants to do only good and pleasant things for you in return. You will not believe how glad I am that I have met you.

Happy you! All the more painfully I feel my own desolation and bitter fate.

Always think well of me – just as you will always stay in my memory.

Heartily devoted to you

Leoš Janáček

According to Janáček's later reminiscences, his first meeting with Kamila Stösslová at Luhačovice in 1917 was somewhere above the Slovácká búda (a well-known wine bar), where she sat down on the grass 'like an exhausted little bird who doesn't yet know how to fly' (320). The meeting must have taken place shortly after Janáček arrived (on 3 July 1917)[1] since by 8 July 1917 he had already jotted down – in his usual way – a fragment of her speech in his diary (see Facsimile, p.4). He had not quite got her name right, however. The speech fragment 'Dovolíte prosím' ['Please allow me'] is attributed to 'pí. C' ['Mrs C.'] and indeed his first letter to her above was addressed to 'Mrs Camilla Stößlová'.

Almost every summer from 1903 onwards Janáček spent a few weeks in this Moravian spa town. He always came alone, chiefly for his health, taking the waters and many long walks in the surrounding countryside. Spa holidays were popular at the time, especially in the landlocked Czech regions of the Habsburg Empire. Although Janáček occasionally went to other spas such as Bohdaneč and Teplice, he was particularly attached to Luhačovice because it was nearer Brno and because it attracted mostly Czechs (Germans patronized better-established spa resorts such as Karlsbad). In Janáček's

---

1 List of visitors to the spa, quoted in Štědroň 1939, 23, gives his date of arrival.

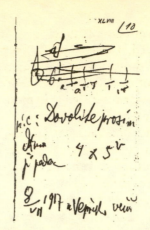

recollection from 1925, he appears to have started up the conversation himself (320). This is corroborated by Stösslová's chance remark (20 January 1925, p.63) that she 'didn't want to speak to him', which is perhaps not surprising if the letter of 6 June 1925 is an accurate reflection of his opening conversational gambit. By the time of their meeting, a year after the successful Prague première of his opera *Jenůfa* in 1916, Janáček was something more than a local celebrity and well on his way to becoming known internationally.

The Stössels seemed a happy young couple with two little boys, Rudolf (born 1913) and Otto (born 1916). Possibly David Stössel's army service meant he could be at Luhačovice only part of the time, leaving Kamila to her own devices, and giving Janáček the opportunity for walks and conversations with her alone over the following week. He mentions these in his next communication written on the back of a photograph taken of him at Luhačovice (see Plate 4):

2   Luhačovice, 24 July 1917

Dear Madam
   We used to walk together, people envied us – and yet you only talked about your family happiness – and I about my unhappiness.
   Keep well
   Leoš Janáček

In Janáček's recollections five years later, Mrs Stösslová talked about her sorrow too: 'Tears ran down your cheeks when you remembered your husband in those beautiful days in Luhačovice' (195). Janáček probably presented this inscribed photograph as a farewell token, leaving soon afterwards – he had been there for three weeks. On his return to Brno he wrote again:

[4]

3 Brno, 30 July 1917

Dear Madam

I hope you have both got home safely!

When the train moved, I cried bitterly to myself, and then in a lonely mood was lost in thought – until my arrival in Brno.

But it was so pleasant in your company. You are both such good and happy people. The warmth of your happiness touched me. It was my nicest stay in Luhačovice.

We await you for certain on Saturday [4 August].

Give my greetings to your husband, I hope he brings you [in] as cheerful [a mood] as you used to be at Luhačovice. So reply with a few words: let me make a writer of you.

With sincere respects, yours devotedly
Leoš Janáček

Perhaps surprising was the fact that Janáček had extended an invitation to the Stössels to meet his wife. Mrs Stösslová's reply, with a promptness altogether uncharacteristic, was on behalf of both herself and her husband David, known as 'Dori'; the use of their first names suggests the friendly terms which the relationship had reached, and also the discrepancy in ages: at sixty-three Janáček was a generation older than Mrs Stösslová (twenty-five) and her husband (twenty-seven).[1]

Kamila Stösslová to Leoš Janáček, Přerov, 31 July 1917

Thank you for your letter. We've arrived safely and I hope that we'll come on Saturday. Everybody's surprised how well I look and how dark I am. I have to go to Vienna tomorrow so I don't know I'm also quite missing Luhačovice but what's to be done since everyone has to return to his occupation.

I greet you both affectionately.
Kamila and Dori

4 [undated, postmarked Brno, 2 August 1917]

The apricots on the tree are waiting for you, as are the pickled gherkins – and antiques! No use talking. I'll wait at the station.

With regards to your husband, devotedly
Leoš Janáček

1 Kamila Stösslová [née Neumannová], was born on 12 September 1891, at Putim, near Písek, Bohemia; David Stössel was born on 6 November 1889 at Strážnice, Moravia. They were married on 5 May 1912.

It is, however, from Mrs Janáčková that we know most about the beginnings of the friendship. Her memoirs, from 1935 (posthumously edited 1939) and thus some eighteen years after the event, need to be treated with caution, but there is no reason to doubt her generally positive impression of this period. Her relationship with her husband had never been easy, and in 1916 had been stretched to breaking point by his ostentatious affair with the Kostelnička from the Prague *Jenůfa*, Gabriela Horvátová (see Glossary). Mrs Janáčková had feared that Mrs Horvátová would join Janáček in Luhačovice; Janáček's friendship instead with a pleasant young couple, seemingly devoted to one another, was evidently a great relief, though his invitation meant a postponement of Mrs Janáčková's planned trip to Hukvaldy.

Zdenka Janáčková: *My Life* (1935)

[...] We didn't write to one another. Just once he sent me a message through a former pupil not to worry about provisions, because he had made an 'acquaintance in flour' in Luhačovice. From the same messenger I also learnt that Mrs Horvátová was not in Luhačovice. That was news! My husband in Luhačovice alone and taking care of provisions for our household! [...]

As early as ten in the morning a carriage clattered up in front of the garden, Leoš leapt out of it beaming, and at once began telling me merrily that he'd travelled first thing by the early morning express, and that in Luhačovice he'd met a young married couple.

'They really love one another.'

He pulled out a photograph and gave it to me. A young woman, brunette, evidently a second edition of Mrs Horvátová, except much younger, about twenty-five years old, in a *dirndl* or something peculiar – at that time [i.e. during the war] many women wore these sorts of fantasies on national costumes; they were meant to show the intensely patriotic feeling of the wearer. My instinct clearly told me:

'Mrs Horvátová has fallen off his shovel, now this one takes over.'

But my reason objected that I was wrong, that this lady was surely too young. And furthermore my husband continually related how much the couple loved one another, how delightful they were, until suddenly he blurted out:

'You know, I've invited them, they're coming on Saturday [4 August].'

I was surprised by Leoš's liveliness, his kindliness to me, and because he was again inviting guests to visit us.

'But I'd wanted to go away.'

'Oh no, you can't, you must be here, I've told her about you, she wants to meet you.'

[6]

How could I go when such things were happening? I thought hard how I would entertain these two: at this time there was everywhere a terrible shortage of provisions. I had my work cut out, but on Saturday, when my husband went to meet the guests at the station, I was decently prepared. I received them on the veranda. I was surprised to see two decidedly Jewish types. Especially Mr Stössel, although he was in soldier's uniform, looked very much like a red-haired Polish Jew. Of course I didn't let on at all myself, but I was most surprised at Leoš. The wife apologized profusely that she was putting me out, but my husband apparently wouldn't have it otherwise and definitely wanted the two of us to get to know one another. I thought she was quite nice: young, cheerful, one could have a really good talk with her, she was always laughing. She was of medium height, dark, curly-haired like a Gypsy woman, with great black, seemingly bulging eyes, an 'ox-eyed Hera' like Mrs Horvátová – with heavy eyebrows, a sensuous mouth. The voice was unpleasant, shrill, strident. Her husband was sturdy, much taller than Leoš, with reddish blonde hair, but with a pleasing appearance and very nice manners. She was called Kamila, he David. He dealt in antiques. My husband had suggested that I sell him my china, but I refused. Both promised the whole time that they would look out for provisions for us, Mr Stössel was in the army in Přerov and knew how to come by them. His wife lived there too, they rented a house there, they had one little son with them, the second was with the wife's parents in Písek.[1] One thing was certain was that they brought action and laughter into our sad quietness. We had tea in the garden, Leoš beamed, and busily waited on her, Mr Stössel was overjoyed at his wife's success. She began to pick apricots. She stood on the ladder, Leoš looked at her enthusiastically from below, not caring that people from the opposite windows were looking on curiously to see what was going on at our place. They slept the night downstairs with me,[2] in the morning they went to see friends and arrived back only at teatime. She again saw to it that there was lots of commotion and fuss until, late in the evening, someone from the military hospital next door told her off for carrying on like that at night. Only then did she quieten down. I had to show them that china of mine. Mr Stössel made it clear that it wasn't worth much until I said to him that it wasn't for sale since the pieces were family

1 Přerov is in Moravia, 82 km north-east of Brno; Písek, where the couple moved in April 1919, is in southern Bohemia.
2 From the summer of 1916 the Janáčeks slept apart, she in their little villa in the grounds of the Organ School, and he in his upstairs study in the Organ School (Janáčková 1939, 122).

[7]

heirlooms. She, however, was always enthusiastic, she liked many things at our place and Leoš would most gladly have given her the lot if they hadn't been mine. When I saw that, and she was in ecstasies about one old folk plate, I gave it to her. Straightaway she promised me a morning jacket in return.

When in the evening my husband went upstairs to sleep, the three of us remained sitting around and chatting. She soon turned the conversation to Mrs Horvátová. She knew about everything; Leoš, she said, had confided everything in her, and apparently also complained about my not having understood his friendship. In reply Mrs Stösslová had told him it was difficult for her to make a judgement when she didn't know me. That was the reason why he invited her to see me. So this was it, then: my husband made this young person, whom he'd just met, the judge in our affairs. Fine, I went along with that too. I told her how I saw it. She readily felt sorry for me, she showed friendly concern, she was full of understanding, so much so that Mářa [Marie Stejskalová, the Janáčeks' maid] and I later said to one another that it was probably good my husband brought her to us, because she understands me and could have a good effect on him. That she really did have a big influence on Leoš was something I found out very soon. Her husband left for Přerov on Monday [6 August]; she, however, was persuaded by my husband to stay longer with us until I left for Hukvaldy because we'd be going the same way as far as Přerov. It wasn't pleasant for me, but I had to appear to welcome this proposal. And then on Monday morning when, out of boredom, Mrs Stösslová was looking over the photographs hanging in my husband's study and came across the unhappy picture of Mrs Horvátová that she herself had christened 'Angel of Peace', I said to her:

'You can see for yourself, I think, how I feel when I have to look at this here for days on end.'

'Wait a moment, I'll fix it.'

She went straight into the garden to my husband, spoke with him for a moment, rushed back and laughed:

'He gave me that picture because it's not important to him any more.'

Together we took down the picture of Mrs Horvátová and Mrs Stösslová took it back with her to Přerov. What I, our friends and lawyers couldn't manage was achieved in a trice by this clever, cheerful little Jewess. In this way she very much won me over. After that I rather liked her. When later I travelled with her in the train, we had quite a lot of time for chatting and so I got to know her well and her circumstances. She was a Czech Jew, her father[1] had been first a butcher in Písek, then he traded in horses. Mr Stössel was domiciled in Lwów through his father,[2] but his mother lived in Strážnice, so he spoke Czech, though worse than his wife. After the take-over [i.e. the creation of an independent Czechoslovakia in 1918] he was to have been deported from the Republic as a foreign subject, but my husband saw to it that he wasn't expelled.[3] In the war they lived a 'Tschacherl'[4] life, he lent money to officers, which is why he had good connections. Although clever, his wife was not particularly intelligent. She told me she didn't like going to school and didn't like learning. That was certainly true because her letters were full of spelling mistakes. In music she was totally ignorant, knowing almost nothing about composers. She called Leoš's pieces 'those notes of yours', and hadn't heard of Wagner. In literature it wasn't any better. Once she wrote to Leoš: 'Send me something to read that's not too long, a love story with a happy ending.'[5] She gained my husband's favour through her cheerfulness, laughter, temperament, Gypsy-like appearance and buxom body, perhaps also because she reminded him of Mrs Horvátová, although she had none of that woman's demonic qualities or artfulness. She was natural, sometimes even uninhibited. One couldn't really say that she won my husband over, for she didn't try to. He himself had begun to send her bouquets and letters in Luhačovice: it seems that it was more Mr Stössel with his fine business flair who realized the value of this well-known composer's fondness. She herself was completely unimpressed by my husband's fame, and also by his person: sometimes she laid into him quite sharply and other times he was ridiculous in her eyes. On that journey we got very friendly. I felt I had no option when I saw how desperately Leoš wanted this friendship. I said to myself that she could be a good support for me against Mrs Horvátová. In Přerov we warmly said goodbye to one another. Her husband came to meet her at the station, and brought me the promised morning jacket. I went on further to Hukvaldy. [...]

1 Adolf Neumann (1864–1942).
2 David Stössel's father Marcus Stössel (1851–99), came from Lwów (then Lemberg in Austrian Galicia and from 1918 to 1939 part of Poland).
3 See 605.
4 Mrs Janáčková uses the demeaning diminutive of a Viennese dialect word with its intimations of cheap retailing bordering on black marketeering.
5 Janáček attempted to send her something along these lines (see 37).

5 Brno, 7 August 1917

Dear Madam

After your departure and that of my wife it is empty here.

You are a dear child who has already suffered but nevertheless does not know the world and its evils. You want to live only by goodness and love in the family. You are cheerful, just occasionally lonely. Stay like that: for your tender little soul it is quite enough. More – and your body would not take it. You must learn to control yourself, not give in so boundlessly to feeling.

Give vent to it also in a different direction; read prudently and observe life about you carefully.

[...]

So I've preached a sermon to you and that was because I would always like to see you healthy, beautiful and happy.

Greet your husband and write what your journey was like. I'll come on Sunday [12 August] then. [...]

The protective tone that Janáček adopted so soon in the correspondence was one that continued, and intensified, right through to the end. Janáček's next letter was the first in which he wrote about his compositions. The phrase '*that* Gypsy love' suggests that he had already mentioned his plan to compose *The Diary of One who Disappeared* (this is his earliest reference anywhere to the work, based on poems which had appeared in *Lidové noviny* in May 1916); the 'Luhačovice mood' hints at connections between the work and Mrs Stösslová.

6 Brno, 10 August 1917

Those postcards of yours! They're like speech without speaking, like a song without words.

[...]

Will you believe that I've not yet got out of the house? In the morning I potter around in the garden; regularly in the afternoon a few motifs occur to me for those beautiful little poems about that Gypsy love.[1] Perhaps a nice little musical romance will come out of it – and a tiny bit of the Luhačovice mood would be in it. [...]

1 This is accurately reflected by the first sketches for *The Diary of One who Disappeared*: the earliest date, 9 August, can be found in no.3; three more numbers (8, 6 and 11) are dated 11, 12 and 19 August respectively.

Stösslová, however, seldom showed any interest in Janáček's works and instead the acquaintance was kept going on a rather more mundane basis. As Mrs Janáčková explained (see p.9), David Stössel's military connections in Přerov gave him access to goods in short supply during the war. Correspondence over provisions killed two birds with one stone. Mrs Janáčková was glad to have her household supplies supplemented and Janáček discovered a way of maintaining a correspondence with a woman of no intellectual pretensions. The following excerpts are typical of the main thrust of his letters during the next few weeks. 'Thanks for the bread; I now know that I won't die of hunger' (*7: postmarked Brno, 11 August 1917). 'I'm finishing your loaf of bread. From Tuesday I won't have any more. How can you help me? With a loaf? I don't want to give you trouble and effort rolling it out. So a little flour? How to get it here? Once I sent a few plums by registered express post and they were stolen. Would you like perhaps to come to Brno?' (*13: Brno, 24 August 1917). 'And remember some butter for us? And semolina flour.[1] All of course on a strict account. I finished eating the loaf today. [...] Zdenka is returning from Hukvaldy at the end of the month. Perhaps she could take a few small provisions from you on her journey via Přerov?' (*15: 26 August 1917). By 2 September 1917 (*18) Janáček was asking about the prices of geese in Přerov, whether Stösslová could have one prepared for him to take back with him, and for flour and butter. Many of the goods arrived via military personnel and the correspondence makes reference to 'soldiers' and other messengers turning up unexpectedly with goods for the Janáčeks.

The visit to Přerov which Janáček had mentioned in his letter of 7 August duly took place on Sunday, 12 August. He went without Zdenka, since she was still away in Hukvaldy.

8 Brno, 13 August 1917

Dear Madam

On my return the first thought was to remember you and your 'informal' household – dear and heartfelt in every aspect. It seems to me how with this visit the beautiful days of the holiday were brought to an end; and I am so sad about it.

Well, life isn't all fun.

[...]

Tomorrow I go on further [he sent a card two days later from the Bohemian spa town of Bohdaneč, *9], but believe me I travel like an exhausted volcano. Greet your good fellow – your husband. I would give him my legs, if he could take some fifteen–twenty years from me. This business is also barter – only it cannot be carried out.

---

1 The coarsest grade of flour used by Czechs not simply for making semolina pudding, but in porridge, dumplings, cakes, etc.

Keep healthy both of you – I like you both so much – and remember me too with a little love.

With respects, yours devotedly
Leoš Janáček

Another trip to Přerov took place the next month (8 September), this time with Zdenka.

Zdenka Janáčková: *My Life* (1935)

[...] Soon afterwards she invited both of us to Přerov. At Dýma[1] in Brno my husband bought her a little knitted silver bag as a present, like those much in fashion at the time. We were royally entertained at their place, they had a larder crammed full, some Italian woman cooked for them. When Leoš produced his present for Mrs Kamila, they wouldn't accept it and refused it so persistently that we had to take the bag back home. On the whole they did us many more favours at first than we did for them. Mr Stössel sent flour to us via soldiers, his wife corresponded in a friendly fashion with me, and irreproachably with my husband. [...]

22   Brno, 9 September 1917

Do excuse that we dropped in on you. I wanted to make a trip to you, in Přerov, to tear myself away from work, but my wife also wanted to go and see you. So I went along with her wishes. I just regret that I could not pay you back adequately, that it worked out so badly for me. [...]

A trip to Prague the next month to see *Jenůfa* also went awry. Whether the offered reason for refusal (David Stössel's military commitments) was genuine is hard to tell: it was the first of many invitations which were not taken up.

25   Brno, 4 October 1917

Dear Madam!
No, I am not angry. I haven't been angry for ages.
Two nice seats were prepared for you, nos. 17 and 18. Who can

---

1 A small shop selling pipes and tobacco (*dým* = smoke) and evidently a few other goods. Its location near the station suggests that the bag may have been a last-minute idea.

account for military whim? It's too bad that I had just left the hotel when you telephoned. We could at least then have had a chat.

[...] I wouldn't have travelled to Prague had I foreseen that something would happen to your husband to prevent your coming. But it's happened. Even so my trip and presence in Prague was important and necessary.

So I am not angry; do be good enough to write.

Today, 4 October, a lovely loaf of bread arrived from Písek from you. I cut myself a slice at once – the crust. Excellent. We thank you for it.

Do, now, come to Brno. Do you have your boy with you? So you will bring him.

I greet you both. In [the midst of] serious work[1] I am really a different person from that carefree fellow in Luhačovice. [...]

Undeterred by this non-attendance, Janáček immediately issued another invitation (*26: 7 October 1917), this time to Brno to attend a 'nice concert of the Prague National Theatre' (which included a performance of Janáček's prelude to *Jenůfa*, 'Jealousy'). It was not seriously considered by the Stössels. Next it was Janáček who was unable to accept an invitation to visit Přerov as he needed to be in Prague (*33: 30 November 1917). After that Janáček suggested that the two families should see in the New Year together: 'We would spend New Year's Eve and New Year's Day together in Brno. Do you agree to that? I expect your husband will have these days free. Take a rest then at our place, as it suits you. Today Zdenka and I settled it and I am writing to you immediately' (*35: 19 December 1917). Once again the invitation was not taken up. That no offence was given is evident from Janáček's next letter, with its more personal tone and ambitions:

36 Brno, 30 December 1917

I laughed heartily at your card today – until I had a fit of coughing.

Even if I had such a delightful wife as you certainly are, I would travel to Prague.

Do you really think that a man like me lives only on bread and creature comforts?

Can a man, a Czech man, a Czech composer, just sit by the oven? Shouldn't we have such cultural brilliance, such artistic richness, so that although small in the world we are still the first? You, good soul, do not understand it. When you are happy in your family, that's quite

1 He was getting towards the end of composing the second part of *The Excursions of Mr Brouček*, completed in December that year.

enough for you. Even if I had been happy, I would nevertheless have never stopped longing for spiritual nourishment – and I would certainly have 'infected' you also in this respect: even you would long for that busy artistic life. [...]

And the next meeting took place a week later in Přerov on 6 January. Zdenka did not come and, with inconvenient train times (Brno to Přerov took between two and three hours), Janáček had a long day of it:

37   Brno, 7 January 1918

So in the company of your family I had another sunny day, dear, pleasant, quiet and warm. In that way one feels just like a human being [again]. I was glad to come to see you despite the early rising and late getting back. I waited in the train for another whole hour; I got in to Brno at 12 sharp. [The train] was heated and it wasn't crowded; so you mustn't fear the journey, it isn't so bad.

So, first of all, thank you for your hospitality. But I cannot accept any more now if you don't want to come in return.

Two books are waiting for your messenger; when you've read them you'll get others. Whether, according to your wishes, they're only about 'passionate love' I don't know; but one can read about other things too. [...]

Janáček's attempt to get Stösslová to follow his earlier injunction to 'read prudently' (5) seems to have failed; there is no more mention of his attending to her reading needs until the last year and a half of his life. From this letter it is also clear that Stösslová was unwilling to visit the Janáčeks in Brno. But his next invitation was too prestigious to turn down: to see the German-language première of *Jenůfa* staged in the imperial capital of Vienna.

38   Brno, 22 January 1918

Do please decide on that journey to Vienna.

You have an evening dress, you don't need a new one.

It's meant to be about 2 February.

You would give me pleasure; Zdenka would have someone to lean on for there won't be much talk with me that evening. [...]

The event, which took place rather later, on 16 February, was a grand occasion which surmounted local political difficulties only through the direct intervention of the young Emperor Karl. The imperial couple were in fact due to attend (Janáček made notes on what he would say to the Emperor in his diary),[1] but, in the end, were not able to be present because of Empress Zita's pregnancy. It was difficult for Janáček to obtain seats for all his guests (*40: 5 February 1918), but the Stössels had a high priority and duly attended. When they all got back, Janáček was clearly put out when Kamila did not hasten to thank him, and show the regard that he might have imagined was his due:

43   Brno, 16 March 1918

A mistake! I waited for your first response after returning from Vienna and nothing, absolutely nothing from you. [...]

Jenůfa has already been given six times in Vienna. Now Mrs Weidt [the Viennese Kostelnička] has fallen ill and has gone off to Switzerland until the [?Easter] holidays. So there's now a break with *Jenůfa*.

But believe me I have had enough of this theatrical rushing around. Four weeks just of printed reviews. One was fed just on fragrance – and that's not enough, is it? [...]

Kamila Stösslová to Leoš Janáček, Přerov, 18 March 1918

Dear Maestro

I received your letter. You don't write about my letter which I wrote to you when I got back from Vienna. [...] I was very pleased that I enjoyed myself so much. Here I was to get first prize for my dress, but I was sure I would be overshadowed in Vienna, but I saw that I was equal to those ladies also. But what's in it for me? You need rest and this you will find not only in our company. As for the reviews I say it's all very fine and you should be satisfied since I paid the most in Vienna and from the proceeds you can easily buy an estate for yourself. [...]

This is as good an example as any of Kamila Stösslová's writing style. In the Czech its non-sequiturs are compounded by numerous slips in spelling and grammar. To give her her due, she had in fact written a few days after the Vienna première (23 February 1918) but her brief reference to the opera, buried in the middle of more mundane concerns, was easily missed. After this isolated artistic venture, the rather humdrum nature of the correspondence resumed with Janáček's repeated requests for flour (*43 and *44: 16 and 20 March 1918) and other provisions.

1 BmJA, Z 48 (see Janáček 1990, 29, fn.).

45   Brno, 21 March 1918

Well there was jumping for joy in the kitchen! For the butter, the fresh eggs.

So please sit down at once and write to me what it costs – the cakes for free, I enjoyed them – but the eggs and the butter how much? Answer immediately or I will send you myself the amount they cost in Brno. [...]

In his next letter (*46: 26 March 1918), Janáček sent K 35 and repeated his request for flour.

Occasionally Kamila sent photographs. One picture seems to have stirred rather more personal thoughts and desires.

48   Brno, 14 April 1918

They've caught you nicely and always[1] with that little tree. That was a good idea of yours. But who will take care of the tree when you're not in Přerov any more?

You look well; it's clear that you lack for nothing. You have no idea what a heavy mind I have.

To live *in this way*, so isolated, shut in on myself, without any inclination whatsoever for the world and its trappings – I won't survive for long.

Despite all that glory and great success I see myself as one of the most unhappy people, as [fate's] laughing-stock.

You at home have a little warm nest, a good husband, children for a little trouble, but more for joy – and what do I have in comparison?

I drug and deaden myself only through work; I throw myself into difficult tasks to forget the *man* who is also in me, and who cannot be as warm-hearted as he would like.

Such is my fate.

You can imagine now how glad I was that I could forget about it all last year in Luhačovice! I do so like happy people. [...]

One of the more dramatic incidents in this early correspondence concerns the wife of the caretaker at the Organ School who, in her husband's absence, had taken on his duties:

1 The 'always' suggests a series of photographs which include Stösslová's tree. One is shown on Plate 6.

51 Brno, 4 May 1918

I have spent a terrible night and I shiver at the memory of it.

In the night between Wednesday and Thursday[1] I was treacherously attacked by the caretaker's wife.

You know, once she murdered her sick child;[2] during the attack and her shrieking the possibility came to my mind that she also wanted to do away with me; the struggle was short but terrible! I managed to get rid of her and fled. Now she has come to apologize, asking me to beat her, to beat her to death! Before me I saw a brutalized, sick-minded woman and I'm waiting only for her husband to take her from the school.

Now she writes to me the whole time,[3] and *how* she writes about my servant and my wife! In such a way that I didn't even go to Vienna in case something happened at home. Such a terrible incident. Believe me, I go about not feeling myself.

In her memoirs,[4] the Janáčeks' servant Marie Stejskalová provides more details. The caretaker, Mr Simandl, was away at the front leaving his wife to take over his job. She in fact did little and left everything to her brother. On one occasion she needed a reference from the Organ School but was refused and took out her anger on Janáček by attacking him one evening as he went up to sleep in the Organ School. She was dismissed and Simandl was recalled. On 13 May 1918 (*53) Janáček reported that the caretaker had returned from the front and had moved out with his wife.

58 Brno, 27 May 1918

Sometimes events persecute a fellow.

I left Prague tired and in a disgruntled mood.[5]

I fell asleep and woke up in Brno too late – when the train was already on its way to Vienna! They took me as far as Kounice–Ivančice.[6] From there I got to Brno at about 8 o'clock with a workers' train instead of at 2 in the night!

Whose fault was this? The conductor didn't announce 'next station

1 i.e. 1 May; however Janáček appears to have misremembered the date since he wrote to his lawyer, Dr Jaroslav Lecian, straight after the incident on 29 April (BmJA, B 1597).
2 Nothing is known about this.
3 No letters from Simandlová to Janáček survive.
4 Trkanová 2/1964, 88.
5 Janáček's negotiations over the forthcoming production of *The Excursions of Mr Brouček* were not going well: 'That they reached out pantingly for my new opera is not something I can say' (*57: 25 May 1918).
6 Today the station of Moravská Bránice, 23 km from Brno.

Brno!' – as he always does; that was his fault. I ought not to have fallen asleep before Brno – my fault. At home I then found a court summons against the caretaker's wife straight away for 10 o'clock.

I got in at 8, I taught from 8.30 until 10.30 and then went hurriedly to the trial. The action there lasted until 12.30. Zdenka was called, also the servant. When I'd got home, the caretaker informed me that your husband had been here and *couldn't* wait.

I ran to the tramline, so as to catch him up by 1 o'clock.

I stood on the steps of a tram and I won't tell you what happened next. It would give your husband a conscience.[1] [...]

59   Brno, 29 May 1918

[...]

Yesterday the caretaker attacked Máŕa.[2] I reported it all to the police; the caretaker and his wife were arrested even before nightfall and taken off. With Zdenka there was serious argument, discussion and reproof. The servant Máŕa herself gave notice; perhaps the air will clear. It was chokingly thick.

After their voluntary agreement why on earth couldn't two people live peaceably side by side![3]

I don't know how the police will deal with those they've arrested.

If they release them then we'd go away until the caretaker's flat is vacated, I perhaps to Bohdaneč, Zdenka to Hukvaldy, and the servant to her home; the flat has to be vacated by 15 June. [...]

In fact it went a little differently in the end. Stejskalová reported that when he had attacked her in the laundry, Simandl and his wife were then jailed after Janáček had reported the matter. 'Later they tearfully begged forgiveness and the Master was mollified; Simandl went off again to the front and his wife remained at the Organ School until the end of the war.'[4]

Provisions continued to play a part in Janáček's correspondence with Kamila Stösslová. While making arrangements for a meeting that summer in

1 If the reminiscences of František Svoboda (BmJA, D 289 LJ) refer to the same incident, then what happened next was that Janáček fell from the steps of the crowded tram and was dragged from the tracks out of its path only in the nick of time. However Svoboda dated the incident to 1928; he also mentioned that there was snow and ice around (unlikely in late May) and that the tram was leaving the station, not entering it.
2 It is not clear why this happened, or what Zdenka's part in the incident may have been. Mrs Janáčková does not mention the incident in her memoirs, and Stejskalová's version is suspiciously brief.
3 A reference to the separation agreement between Janáček and his wife (see Glossary: 'Janáčková, Zdenka' and Appendix 2.)
4 Trkanová 2/1964, 88.

Luhačovice and giving a brief report about his negotiations over *The Excursions of Mr Brouček* in Prague (it was almost two years before the opera reached the stage there), Janáček asked for sugar (*63: 9 June 1918), repeating the request on 14, 16 and 21 June (*66, *67 and *69). It arrived, but only in the nick of time:

70 Brno, 26 June 1918

Dear Auntie

Today, 26 June, Tuesday. Storm clouds in the sky early morning so that the sun wasn't visible. The rain could come down at any moment. So what; even without sugar the cherries had to be picked.

At the height of the work, it was 10.30 in the morning, in comes the messenger with the sugar. Pure jubilation!

So I'm letting you know about it with my thanks.

Now, 3 o'clock in the afternoon, you already have your own five kilos of cherries nicely preserved in bottles. Five kilos of apricots and three kilos of apricot jam are also waiting for you. That's Zdenka's message to you. [...]

As the summer and the anniversary of their first meeting approached, Janáček began to wonder whether there was a possibility of meeting up again in Luhačovice. The Stössels indeed returned to Luhačovice, but earlier than in the previous year, and inconveniently early for Janáček (the academic year at the Organ School ended on 6 July 1918). In his letter of 4 June 1918 (*62) he announced his surprise at her being there already ('Was it necessary to go there so soon?'), and suggested that she should get a doctor to tell her to stay longer: her anaemia would need more than four weeks to cure. In his next letter (*63: 9 June 1918) he announced that he would come on 8 July if she remained longer, though he was having trouble in getting a room, having turned down as too expensive the room at the Pospíšils (where he stayed in the summers of 1914–17).[1] On 20 June 1918 (*68) he mentioned that he was writing to the Augustinians to see whether they had something vacant. They did, and for the remaining ten years of his life Janáček stayed in the Augustiniánský dům (see Glossary). On 5 July 1918 (*72) he wrote that he was arriving the following Monday (8 July) by the 1 o'clock train from Brno: 'I'd like to have a bit of a rest, but I've got piled-up proof corrections of *Jenůfa*[2] and after that corrections to the copies of *Brouček*.'[3]

1 Štědroň 1939, 23.
2 Janáček was in the final stages of correcting the proofs of the full score of *Jenůfa* (published on 9 September 1918).
3 i.e. corrections to the manuscript vocal score of *The Excursion of Mr Brouček to the Fifteenth Century*. Roman Veselý had been working on the piano reduction since June; Janáček wrote to him on 6 July urging him to be ready with the final part by the end of the month.

Things, however, did not go smoothly. Kamila seems to have departed abruptly in the middle of her stay ('What took you away from the spa? Now just return soon and bring your husband with you!'; *73: Luhačovice, 15 July 1918), and on her return some sort of public incident occurred between them:

74 Luhačovice, 29 [*recte* 27] July 1918

I wanted to take my leave of you; however you humiliated me in front of the servants. After all I have never so insulted you.

This was not, however, the way Stösslová saw it. In a couple of letters she wrote to Zdenka,[1] she complained that Janáček had shouted at her on a public path (perhaps because she was ignoring him?) and she could not get the sound of his 'rough voice' out of her ears. The contretemps is not explained in the letters (Kamila promised to tell Zdenka about it when she next saw her), but something of its background emerges from Janáček's next letter when, after pleasantries about his forthcoming trip to Hukvaldy and about handing over supplies, Janáček moved on to more serious things:

75 Brno, 28 July 1918

[...] Today I've sent that niece of mine a letter she should keep.[2]
    She said that you go walking with her –
    that you've wept over Zdenka's fate –
    that you've boasted to her how you've been able to keep me away from your body – to which she added that, there again, I've got a relationship with Bogucká.
    One thing is sure that I'll never let this slander come up again.
    I was 'on show' in Luhačovice; but I think that I didn't do anything dishonourable.
    And if I am more passionate than other people, that is just my pain, my suffering. Forgive me if I was in the way. I believed that I had sincere friends in you and your husband; that's why I sought your company.

Marja Bogucká (1885–1957), a leading soprano at the Prague National Theatre, makes so few appearances in Janáček's correspondence that the allegation is unlikely. As it was, Janáček's niece Věra Janáčková (1891–1967, the daughter of Janáček's cousin Augustin Janáček) seems to have been

1 BmJA, E 1037 (Přerov, 2 August 1918) and E 1044 (?Přerov, 12 September 1918).
2 Janáček's curt letter to Věra was written the next day: 'Věra, You're growing into a real gossip as your mother's letter proves. I suspected it, so I left Luhačovice. Leoš Janáček' (BmJA, B 2336). Presumably the accusations that Janáček then lists in his letter to Stösslová were those reported to the Janáčeks by Věra's mother Josefa Janáčková.

something of a trouble-maker, and from a better documented incident ten years later (see 571) it is evident that her motive was principally to keep her uncle (and possibly his wealth) away from Kamila Stösslová. Both times her intervention seems to have momentarily deterred Stösslová, but not Janáček. In his next letter (*76: 30 July 1918), exceptionally addressed to 'Dear Mrs Kamila', there is no further mention of any unpleasantness. Instead there are the usual suggestions about how to hand over supplies of goods. His next three communications, all about Hukvaldy, include two letters which were longer and more lyrical than anything he had so far written to Stösslová.

77 Hukvaldy, 5 August 1918

We arrived at 7.30 in the evening and had left Brno at 6 in the morning. So that was quite enough [travelling].

In the night between Sunday and today a terrible storm descended and today, Monday, it rains 'nicely' [i.e. heavily]. But it is so beautiful here that I go walking even in the rain; the paths are good, without mud.

You can see for yourself on the postcard that it's more beautiful here than in Luhačovice. It's possible to relax here. Close to the castle there's a game park and in it herds of fallow deer. You can go up to within a few steps of them. They have antlers like shovels. In this park there is also a stud farm with a herd of sixty Andalusian horses which graze here freely. The footpaths go on for hours, are well maintained, provided with benches. In the second picture you can immediately see the village; Zdenka lives near the church, I a bit lower down with the forester.[1] I'm thinking of you; here you'd have a health-cure like nowhere else. If not this summer, think of it for next year. Admittedly it's difficult to get by here, but it's possible. Together with my sister[2] we have five litres of milk daily; a litre for 90 hellers. From part of this we make butter. New potatoes are K 1 a kilo; for a roasting chicken I pay K 10 each. Mushrooms are growing again. For meat I have to fend for myself from the nearby town of Místek. Perhaps I'll still manage to get some 'real' ale from the brewery, it's the oldest brewery in Moravia.[3]

Walks to the 'old castle', sitting on the peak (not high) is magnificent. The sun, when it comes out, gives warmth here as if quite near. And the air! It smells of resin. If I had power over you, I'd bring you

1 Janáček lived in the house of the Hukvaldy forester Vincenc Sládek (1865–1944).
2 See Glossary: 'Dohnalová, Josefa (Adolfína)'.
3 It was founded by Bishop Vilém Prusinkovský in 1567 (Procházka 1948, 130). Moravia's brewing industry was much later and less developed than that of Bohemia.

here at once for your health. The water is from a spring; they call it 'the holy [spring]'.

Down below the castle flows the mountain stream, the Ondřejnica [Ondřejnice]; perhaps I'll get acquainted with the trout which gambol in it. There'll be lots of fruit here; they still have corn in the fields and it's getting rained on.

Today my forester brought in a head of cabbage from the field; cleaned, it weighed seven kilos. Zdenka sends you a message that she'll be writing to you soon. Certainly not as much as I have. I know that I won't get a card from you; I've got no option but to wait until you forget 'my rude words'. I didn't want to say them, but they hurt me more than you. [...]

Four days later Janáček sent off a card to Stösslová (*78: Hukvaldy, 9 August 1918) and the next day another long letter, from which it emerges that Kamila has written to Zdenka; Janáček has read the letter and advises against Kamila's proposed visit to Trieste, based on his own experience there in 1912.[1] Much of the letter repeats his account of his daily life in Hukvaldy (77), but there are a few new thoughts:

79 Hukvaldy, 10 August 1918

[...] I don't praise it [Hukvaldy] to you because I am an honorary citizen[2] here, and because I was born here – but I praise it because there's no purer, healthier and stronger air anywhere else and during the summer days no hotter sun.

I have also found peace here. I work from time to time and in the evening I sit beneath my lime tree and gaze into the forest until the night envelops it. Silence goes to sleep under every tree. The cock wakes me in the morning. He 'sings' such a strange melody that I haven't yet been able to notate it. [...]

Despite the friendly relations that Kamila retained with Zdenka, and despite the beautiful letters that Janáček wrote to her, Kamila did not reply, as is clear from his first letter on his return to Brno (*81: 20 August 1918): 'Have you gone silent for ever? The forest solitude and beauty have cured me for a while.' A fortnight later, he tried again. The reason he gives for not finishing *The Diary of One who Disappeared* is sheer whimsy, but there is no mistaking the hurt that Kamila's silence caused:

1 Janáček mentioned visiting Trieste and its 'osterie' in his autobiography (Janáček 1924, 71).
2 Janáček had been made an honorary citizen of Hukvaldy in 1916.

82   Brno, 2 September 1918

[...] It's too bad my Gypsy girl can't be called something like Kamilka. That's why I also don't want to go on with the piece.

I can't explain why you don't write to me.

I haven't done anything to you, I haven't wanted anything from you. I really don't know. That I nevertheless write to you is because of memories of the most beautiful [time of all in] Luhačovice, that of the year 1917.

I have nothing more than memories — well then, so I live in them. [...]

85   Pardubice, 9 September 1918

I'm writing to you because I don't have anyone to send these lines so they'll be read, and yet unread because unanswered. So it's like a stone falling into the water. It's like talking to myself, feeling sorry for myself, cheering myself up.

The time for which I longed a whole year, not just this year, but the whole of my life: the time where I lived for my own free feeling, where I forgot about everything that oppressed me, when I met new people, ignored them, or fell in love with them, where my eyes saw only whatever wanted itself to be seen, my holiday time has run out. I have said farewell to local friends and with sad thoughts I'm wandering here in the evening about the park.

If I kept myself apart in Luhačovice, sought solitude in Hukvaldy, here even more I have sat for whole hours on the high walls of dried-up fish ponds. Had a water goblin, driven out of the ponds, appeared to me, it would hardly have frightened me; the single reason for my [low] spirits was a single regret. I couldn't take it any longer. I know myself; I know that I can't take what's evil, ugly, whether in body or soul. And is it strange that I like what's beautiful, good?

My thoughts dwell on you. That I said to you that one thing, that you are beautiful. After all it wasn't just your outer appearance that moved me to do so, but rather your character, that good, open nature of yours.

I examine myself and look into myself for a serious wrong done against you — but I don't find anything. I'm just sorry that it's you who disparages me. It's about nothing other than to tell you that you've spoilt my holidays. But let it drop — like that stone into the water — unread, unanswered.

Seven weeks later she still had not written, and Janáček mentions discussing her silence with Zdenka (*87: Brno, 22 October 1918). The ostensible reason for his writing now was disturbances in Písek,[1] where Stösslová had taken the children and was living at her parents' home. The disturbances, provoked by the general strike organized in the Czech lands, were connected with the approaching end of the war and the establishment of an independent Czechoslovakia. This seems to have helped Kamila break her long silence: she signed off her brief postcard 'Au revoir in this Czech state' (undated; after 28 October 1918). Janáček of course wrote back immediately (*88: Brno, 1 November 1918). Soon there was another visit to Brno, urged through a series of postcards of which the last (*93: postmarked Brno, 24 November 1918) provided the date of the visit, Saturday 30 November. The letters that both wrote after the visits are revealing. Janáček did not disguise the gap that separated them; Stösslová herself seems to have felt happier thinking of herself as Janáček's daughter, the Olga who had died in 1904 and who would have been nine years older than her.

94   Brno, 2 December 1918

It's as quiet as the grave here again. The black-haired chatterbox is missing here.

We are so far from one another in the field of our interests and activity – but that's the very reason why I like listening to you. [...]

Stössel family to Leoš Janáček and Zdenka Janáčková, Přerov, 3 December 1918

Dear Friends

We got home happily, apart from being cold the journey was quite pleasant.

We thank you once again for your kind hospitality it was all very good and the food tasted so nice that I just can't write anything to you. The nicest thing for us your contented faces I am so happy that the sun's rays shine again at least a little more strongly in your home than when I was with you last.[2]

It was only this time that I felt in your company as if I were your daughter. [...]

---

1 Reported in that day's *Lidové noviny* (see Janáček 1990, 51, fn.).
2 With her words 'in your home' Stösslová can only be referring to the family trip to Brno 4–7 August 1917 (see Diary of Meetings), when she had to put up with Janáček complaining about Zdenka, and Zdenka complaining about Janáček.

Relations, however, were somewhat cooler. In the first year of their acquaintance Janáček wrote seventy-three surviving letters or notes to Kamila; the next year this had slackened by a third and the rate continued to slow until the final years of Janáček's life. Meetings were also less frequent. A reciprocal visit to the Stössels was discussed during February 1919, but various things got in the way and so it took place only at the third attempt, as can be deduced from the rather perfunctory thank-you note that Janáček wrote on 18 February 1919 (*108). Once the Stössels moved to Písek in April 1919 meetings virtually ceased for four years.

In the first year and a half the friendship had been kept alive by contacts over provisions but this pretext no longer served as the situation improved after the war. New topics emerged. Janáček was enlisted into collecting Kamila's debts in Brno (he sent the maid, who always failed to find Kamila's debtors at home: *97, *98, *100: 19 and 22 December 1918, 12 January 1919). There are occasional news flashes about his works: revising *Šárka* (*100: 12 January 1919); finishing *The Diary of One who Disappeared* (*111: Brno, 11 March 1919); and various bulletins about how the Prague theatre was dragging its feet over *Brouček*. By the next anniversary of Luhačovice there was no question of meeting up there: instead Janáček had to send more than one note wondering why Stösslová was not writing to him (*123: Luhačovice, postmarked July 1919; *124 and *125: 7 and 12 July). As in the previous year, Janáček's summer trip to Hukvaldy, with more time on his hands, produced his longest letter. The minor disaster he described in it did at least elicit Kamila's response. The letter is also important in marking the beginnings of Janáček's desire to own property in his home village.

127 Hukvaldy, 11 August 1919

Total misfortune! Thus it is when a fellow gets in exchange for his solid, gold, pretty little ring, an inferior ring, damaged, twisted. So that one has to have it fixed all the time! But it's gone!

I looked at my hand the second day after arriving and saw on my finger just an indentation and no ring. I suppose it got broken when, repeatedly getting in and out of the train, I was getting my heavy case ready. Now somebody else is wearing my 'luck'! But to business. I think that your conscience and pity will answer to my misfortune and that you'll get me a new little ring for 'luck'. A better one, more solid, altogether worthier of me and you. At the same time I'll give you my promise that I'll bequeath it to you. So you'll not lose on it anything other than the interest – I'm thinking of at least ten to twenty years!

But believe me this accident annoys me.

Here it also rains frequently, but it has warmed up. So I can go and sit out with a book. But there's nothing to buy. Just think, I managed to buy four chickens, small, miserable ones. And with that I shall have to make do for a fortnight! No-one wants to sell me anything. A litre of milk, which I have daily, has to suffice for me.

But still I'm at home here. All these places speak more warmly to one who's born here. I don't feel I'm in foreign parts.

I'd like only to have my own home here. A pig in the sty, poultry in the hen-house, a cat, a dog, a goat – to have someone to talk to. [...]

Kamila Stösslová to Leoš Janáček, Písek, before 20 August 1919

I'm sending you here a little ring with my name you'll like it and the main thing is that [the man] from whom this ring [comes] had great luck I've had it now for ten years and I've had luck too except that it got caught in my hair a lot. So I wish that for the next ten—twenty—thirty years that you wish the ring will bring you the same luck for yourself that I've had so far myself. [...]

131   Hukvaldy, 20 August 1919

You can't imagine what joy you've given me with that ring for luck.

I'll certainly not lose it or break it.

So you'll have an inheritance with me.

I want to buy a house here from my sister-in-law; she's selling it but wants to keep a room in it. No-one would buy it like that.[1] It doesn't matter to me. I'm leaving here tomorrow. [...]

Janáček's 'wedding' ring from Kamila – for that indeed seems to be the unspoken fantasy behind his request – makes a number of appearances in the correspondence and was still in evidence six years later (329) when Janáček reported: 'day after day I take off your ring and put it on – and think of you all the while'.

Janáček was now sixty-five. Since the acceptance of *Jenůfa* by the Prague National Theatre in late 1915 he had spent his time mostly clearing his desk of early unfinished projects such as *Brouček* and revising his first opera *Šárka*. *Brouček*, problematic in composition, was equally problematic in its passage to the stage. Negotiations with the National Theatre went on for

---

1 The house had been acquired by Janáček's brother František on his return from St Petersburg in 1905 and left to his widow Marie at his death in 1908. After the war Marie had gone to live with her sister in Gleiwitz, Prussian Silesia (now Gliwice, Poland), and thought of disposing of the property; this did not take place until the death of the sitting tenant two years later. The sale was completed on 31 December 1921, with a stipulation that Marie Janáčková had the right of abode there until her death, a right she never exercised (Janáčková 1939, 156–7; Procházka 1948, 147–8).

years and it was only on 18 December 1919 (*148), eleven years after he began composing the piece, that he announced to Stösslová that it was in rehearsal and would be given at the end of January. A month later the première had been postponed until the beginning of March (*152: 21 January 1920).

153 Brno, 24 January 1920

[...] There are already orchestral rehearsals in the theatre. This is a sign of the approaching première. I've already had a meeting about the sets. On the moon everything will be pale blue with silver. From all accounts it will be nicely designed. Let's hope that my music will be liked too.
[...]
NB the première of *Brouček* will be between 1 and 15 March.

160a[1] Brno, 23 February 1920

[...] I had to go to Prague on Wednesday and the director[2] there fell ill. But I heard at least some rehearsals and these have reassured me. No matter if it comes in the middle of March. It will at least be warmer. [...]

163 Brno, 12 March 1920

So *Brouček* will be in Prague between 6 and 10 April; i.e. immediately after the [Easter] holidays.[3]
    After 21 March I'll go to Prague for another few days then I'll remain there after 6 April. So make your plans accordingly.
    [...]
So do you know what that Brouček is?
A quite ordinary fellow; he gripes at the whole world, and drowns his whole life in a glass of beer. He's not up to anything good on earth.
    You ask: 'So why did you choose such a person for an opera?'
    Because I wanted everyone to be disgusted by him, for him to be a laughing stock, a warning!
    The Russians also have such a 'spineless' man; he's called

1 The continuation of this letter appears on p.30.
2 Gustav Schmoranz (1858–1930), administrative director of the Prague National Theatre and the stage producer of *The Excursions of Mr Brouček*.
3 That year Easter Day was on 4 April. The première took place eventually on 23 April.

Oblomov.[1] Really every second Russian was an Oblomov – and where did that lead them! A terrible revolution is cleansing it now with rivers of blood.[2]

That's why I expose Brouček – as a warning. There are also many, many *Broučeks* on all sides in our nation!

The stomach alone is everything to them.

So my dear *Brouček* gets drunk again, somewhere on Hradčany he falls asleep and has a dream: He's flying to the moon!

There he lands. Oh, horrors! The people there feed only on the scent of flowers. They give Brouček only flowers to smell. And now a female Moon-being falls in love with him there! Bloodless, a body like gauze.

Well, more about it next time.[3] [...]

164   Brno, 23 March 1920

[...] Zdenka is afraid that next to you she'll appear like Cinderella. I told her to pass herself off as your mother, who has given everything nice to her daughter. Where she will stay is not yet decided. You know I have a sister-in-law in Prague;[4] but to stay with her would mean tying oneself down. When it's decided please let your husband organize a room for us too in the Imperial [hotel] in good time. [...]

However, neither Kamila, nor her husband, nor Zdenka attended the première of *The Excursions of Mr Brouček* on 23 April. It was a fortnight later before Janáček could bring himself to write to Kamila about it:

165   Brno, 6 May 1920

[...] I was calm; during the preparations I saw only eyes that wished me no good. I didn't hear even a single warm word. I feared the performance, especially when during the last rehearsal the theatre was filled to the last place and heard the whole work in icy coldness. What sort of people were they there? And yet it is my best work, and certainly it will be liked more and more as it goes on.

In all things now this is my lot that I win through only after a battle. [...]

1 The chronically apathetic anti-hero of the novel (1859) by Goncharov.
2 Janáček had already expressed the main point of this paragraph in his article on the opera published in *Lidové noviny* (23 December 1917).
3 Sadly, Janáček never did complete his exposition of *Brouček* to Stösslová.
4 Josefa Janáčková (1865–1937), widow of Janáček's cousin Augustin and the mother of Věra Janáčková mentioned above (p.20).

I have never witnessed the success of a work of mine with such indifference as this time. I wanted to leave the theatre before the performance.

The more it continued, the more the piece was liked until the audience burst into a storm of applause.

In the papers they called me the foremost [Czech] opera composer – but how reluctantly! I was in Prague for a fortnight, but believe me it was like a foreign town; noticed by no-one anywhere.

[Even] in that confounded Vienna what a lot was written in the newspapers for a whole month before the day of the performance of *Jenůfa* arrived! And here? Not a word in the periodicals! Couldn't they have reminded [the public] in some way what would be on in the theatre! They kept stubbornly silent. And believe me, I also grew hard and cold against *that* [wretched] Prague! [...]

It is extraordinary that the time of *Brouček*'s bumpy progress to the National Theatre stage provided the background to the birth of Janáček's most tender opera, *Káťa Kabanová*, the first of the four great operas of his old age and the first to be inspired by Kamila Stösslová. 'If only I could throw myself into some composition and forget about myself,' Janáček had written to Stösslová in a letter of 10 November 1919 (*138) when, with just one more year running the Brno Conservatory, he felt himself to be 'at the crossroads'. By the time he wrote this letter Janáček had already made preliminary soundings about the text which served as his libretto for *Káťa Kabanová*.[1] A catalyst in the process which led to his choice of subject matter was his attendance at a performance of Puccini's *Madama Butterfly* (or 'Batrflay', as he chose to transcribe it):

145   Brno, 5 December 1919

[...] I've just come from the theatre. They gave *Batrflay*, one of the most beautiful and saddest of operas. I had you constantly before my eyes. Batrflay is also small, with black hair. You could never be as unhappy as her. [...]

I'm so disturbed by the opera. When it was new, I went to see it in Prague.[2] Even now many places move me deeply. [...]

A few weeks later Stösslová and Janáček (and their respective spouses) finally met up again, at a performance of *Jenůfa* at the National Theatre on 28 December 1919.

1 See Tyrrell 1992, KK2–5.
2 Janáček saw it at the Prague Vinohrady Theatre on 16 February 1908. The production he attended in 1919 in Brno was an old one, which had opened in 1914.

[29]

149 Brno, 2 January 1919 [*recte* 1920]

I arrived back happily and you, under the protection of the most exemplary impresario [i.e. David Stössel], have certainly got back safely.

First of all thank you for coming. Those two days I was so happy in the world. And the presents! Zdenka had great pleasure, and I? [...]

The present that Janáček received was a silver writing-set. A few days later, on 5 January, according to an entry in Marie Stejskalová's diary,[1] he began composing *Káťa Kabanová*.

150 Brno, 9 January 1920

[...] Your present, decorated with ribbons, is on my writing-desk.

I, who work by the pen, take great pleasure in it. I drag everyone to have a look at it. But with this silver pen I won't write anything ordinary; when I take it in my hand, it will be something special that I write. [...]

I've begun writing a new opera. The chief character in it is a woman, gentle by nature. She shrinks at the mere thought [of hurting, of evil]; a breeze would carry her away – let alone the storm that gathers over her. [...]

160b[2] Brno, 23 February 1920

[...] I'm working happily and industriously on my new opera.

I tell myself all the time that the main character, a young woman, is of such a gentle nature that I'm frightened that if the sun shone fully on her, she would melt, yes even dissolve.

You know, such a gentle, good nature.

The words with which he described his new heroine are suggestively similar to those with which he had described Kamila Stösslová at this time: 'You're still a tender child who wants to be [kept] in cotton wool all the time; always stroked, pampered' (*155: Brno, 2 February 1920). A few weeks later Janáček attempted another description of her:

---

1 Smetana 1948, 113.
2 An earlier part of this letter appears on p.27.

161   Brno, 29 February 1920

[...] You're such a practical, prudent little person, sparks almost fly from you; your gait and the way you hold your body are full of freshness and energy. You, who know how to speak to three people at the same time and all the while don't forget about yourself – how can you wail like a sickly child and whimper for your husband when life takes him into the world. Let him be! He won't run away from you. [...]

Once again there was no meeting in Luhačovice that summer, and the contacts between the Janáčeks and the Stössels became even more infrequent. This year, 1920, Janáček sent a postcard from Hukvaldy (*166: 23 August 1920), and unless other letters have been lost, the next communication was not until the autumn, when on 15 October 1920 (*167) Janáček mentioned that his official appointment (as professor at the master school) at the Prague Conservatory had come through. This was virtually a sinecure and since at the same time he was relieved of his heavy administrative post as director of the Brno Conservatory, he was able to devote himself wholly to composition. The state, too, had been generous in allowing Janáček and his wife continued use of their house in the grounds of the Conservatory until their deaths.

It was Zdenka who provoked Janáček's next substantial letter to Stösslová. After the death of her mother Anna Schulzová in Vienna (18 December 1918) Zdenka brought back her father Emilian Schulz to live in Brno. Janáček and Schulz did not get on, so Zdenka found rented accommodation for him, where he lived until his death on 28 July 1923. It seems that as her father's health began to fail, she thought of enlisting Kamila's help in getting Janáček to change his mind about having him in the house. This produced a more revealing and personal letter than Janáček had written for a long time.

170   Brno, 14 February 1921

How to write to you?

I can't believe that Zdenka could have written something like that to you.

After all, she knows more than anyone else that both she and Máŕa are frightened to enter my room while I'm working.

When I'm at work, I have to stop immediately at the entrance of any person whomsoever, at any incident whatsoever.

If a bothersome fly were perhaps to buzz about in the room, I wouldn't put up with it.

If unknown steps or a rustling were heard nearby in the next room, it would disturb me. Disturb me?! I'd explode, incensed, I'd be angry, unbearable. This is how it is in creative work – I tell you frankly – just as if a mother had to give birth and someone were to make it impossible, to prevent her in the natural act.

Just as you have to breathe and someone were to stop up your mouth. Just as you need the earth and someone were to take it away from under your feet. I know that Zdenka suffers because of this. But I warned her against this step. Thoughtlessly she brought her father to Brno; a father who's got a son, certainly nearer.[1] I too had a mother, a poor wretched mother – and she couldn't live with me: but not on my account![2]

Here it's nothing to do with her father; it's about me, about my whole existence, about my whole working life, about all my work, about all my modest happiness such as it is, the hard-won domestic peace and quiet, not about creature comforts – it's about the whole of my spiritual balance.

I'm not preventing Zdenka from looking after her father – although she rather needs looking after herself. She's certainly taking upon herself the duty which belongs to a son. [...]

In his next letter (*171: Brno, 6 March 1921),[3] Janáček announced that 'after unusually hard work' he had finished *Káťa Kabanová*. He celebrated the news by dragging Zdenka out on a four-and-a-half-hour walk on what was, he said, 'a wonderfully fine day'. News of *Káťa Kabanová* dominated the letters of the next few months, as did that of *The Diary of One who Disappeared*, which received its première on 18 April:

172   Brno, 30 April 1921

[...] In Brno they gave my *The Diary of One who Disappeared*. It was much liked. Dr Brod came to listen. He wrote in both the Prague and the Berlin papers a song of praise about me which has raised a great stir everywhere![4] Once I wanted to have your head with your hair let down as the [cover] picture for this *Diary*. [...]

1 After his mother's death, Leo Schulz (1880–1944) married and remained living in Vienna.
2 After the death of her husband in 1866 Amálie Janáčková (1819–84) was forced to live with relatives; from 1877 she was in Brno with her son Leoš. After his marriage to Zdenka in 1881 she moved to Švábenice to live with her eldest daughter Eleonora but hoped soon to return to Brno. Zdenka's unwillingness to have her husband's mother (socially much inferior) in the house was one of the factors that led to the early breakdown of the marriage. Though Leoš regularly sent her money he was unable to do much more for her.
3 Tyrrell 1992, KK15.
4 Brod wrote about the *Diary* in the *Prager Abendblatt* (21 April 1921) and in the *Berliner Börsen-Courier* (24 April 1921). Janáček was probably reacting to a news item in *Lidové noviny* (29 April 1921) which reported Brod's promotional efforts.

The next month Janáček reported that *The Diary* (with an 'imaginary' version of Stösslová's head) and several choruses and folksong arrangements had been accepted for printing (by the Czech firm Hudební matice), and that the Brno theatre had made a bid to present the première of *Káťa Kabanová*:

173   Brno, 23 May 1921

[...] *Káťa Kabanová*, that latest opera of mine, is to be given in Brno and perhaps even in Prague. But I don't have much stomach for the Prague theatre. [...]

What can I say about myself? You know I dream up a world for myself, I let my own dear people live in my compositions just as I would wish. All purely invented happiness.

On you real joy, real happiness, smiles at least sometimes. But on me? When I finish a work – even this dear *Káťa Kabanová* – I'm sad about it. As if I were parting with someone dear to me. [...]

Various meetings were proposed – a visit by Janáček to Písek in June and by Stösslová to Brno – though none seemed to work:

177   Brno, 11 August 1921

Every moment a different decision with you!

And those telegrams!

The night train arrives from Luhačovice at 9.25 p.m. On receiving the telegram we went to the station. Who didn't arrive? Mrs Stösslová. Well, we turned round and went home – and not for the first time. A week today I leave for Hukvaldy u Příbora.

I don't know how long I'll survive there. When appetite for work takes hold of me again then that will be the end of loafing in the world. [...]

In her guilt, perhaps, Stösslová renewed her invitation to Janáček to visit her new abode in Písek, where she had moved in April 1919, and which he had not yet seen. He answered enthusiastically ('You can be sure that I'd like to see Písek, that kingdom of yours' (*179: Brno, 18 August 1921)), but was already committed to Hukvaldy. It was not until 1924 that he visited her in Písek. Communications then fell off again. On 27 September 1921 (*184) Janáček complained that he had had no word from Stösslová for a month, and when he suggested (*185: Brno, 15 October 1921) that she might like to attend the Prague première of *The Diary* with her mother or father, he received a forthright refusal in which she made her position abundantly clear: she did not wish to be alone with Janáček.

Kamila Stösslová to Leoš Janáček, Písek, 17 October 1921

[...] It's not possible for me to come to Prague for my husband has not arrived back. [...] If you bring your wife with you then I might come without my husband but in this way it's impossible. [...]

186   Brno, 24 [*recte* 23] October 1921

In vain I waited for you in Prague. I had great success with *The Diary of One who Disappeared*.

[...]

On 6 November they'll perform my work *Taras Bulba* in Prague.[1]

I'll go to Prague for it. I'll no longer invite you: 'because in this way it's impossible!'.

The première of *Káťa Kabanová* will probably be in Brno on 10 November. Perhaps Zdenka will invite you to it if you set no store by my invitations.

And now something in the business line.

What do you say to this: I have bought a nice little house with four rooms, a garden, stables, and a field.[2] It belonged to my sister-in-law [see 131]. I wasn't keen to see that family property in my birthplace passing into foreign hands.

It's in beautiful Hukvaldy. One always likes going somewhere for the summer. In that village they are now asking Kč 200 monthly for a little room. I think that in this way I've spent Kč 40,000 well.

Zdenka of course doesn't think much of it, but that's probably for different reasons.

When you see it some time, you'll certainly like it. [...]

187   Brno, 29 October 1921

[...] Come to the Brno première: everything promises that it will be beautiful.

And you know, when I became acquainted with you in Luhačovice during the war and saw for the first time how a woman can love her husband – I remember those tears of yours – that was the reason why I took up *Káťa Kabanová* and composed it.

I invite you, then, now that the work is finished.

---

1 In fact the Prague première took place only on 9 November 1924; it had recently had its première in Brno (9 October 1921), though this went unmentioned in Janáček's letters to Stösslová.

2 For a description of the house see Glossary: 'Hukvaldy'.

Zdenka has already thanked you for the present. From the nut harvest you will always get something to nibble at. [...]

But even Janáček's personal invitation to *Káťa* was to no avail. That he was hurt is evident from the long gap of a month and a half before his next letter (*188: Brno, 14 December 1921), when he reported briefly on the success of the two pieces that Stösslová had inspired: *Káťa Kabanová* and *The Diary of One who Disappeared*. And with these creative successes behind him he was off, as he said, to his 'estate' for the holidays: 'to plant trees, do up the stables, prop up the sheds, and walk lots and lots'. But the isolation there stirred earlier memories:

189   Hukvaldy, 28 December 1921

So I'm in the mountains, in winter. Ah how sad when I wander all alone. I would like at least to come across you unexpectedly as in Luhačovice.

I sit in 'my own house' — but for warm happiness it's nevertheless still not enough.

I flee from people. That's not good. Who to talk to anyway?

There'd be one talk which I'd long for, which doesn't need words. There I'd find relaxation, there I'd recover my powers.

I fled here and think that I'd rather flee from here. You really don't want to come to Luhačovice this [next] year?

[...] When I passed through Přerov — it seemed to me that I still heard your bell-like laughter, which you left behind there.

190   Hukvaldy, 29 December 1921

Yesterday I wrote to you so plaintively — that tears could have flowed! It's already different today.

What a bit of rest does after exhausting work!

Here it's as if spring. Dry paths and not a living soul anywhere. That's right for me. What long walks I go for!

On Saturday on New Year's Eve I'll be going off to sign the contract.

Do you know what my estate looks like?

I'll draw it for you as well as I can. I can't do everything.

In front of the house, over the road a large deer park with an old castle. Beyond the stream, great forests: Babí hůra [Granny Hill]. Beautiful paths everywhere, dry.

Isn't that pretty?

[*cesta*, road; *stáje*, stables; *kůlny*, sheds; *záhonek*, flower-bed/vegetable patch; *pole*, field; *potok*, stream]

I hope you'll come sometime to take a look!

I'm surprised myself how beautifully I've drawn it. Your Rudi would have done it better.

Kamila Stösslová to Leoš Janáček, Písek, 2 January 1922

Dear Maestro

I got both letters. One sad and the other full of drawings. So holidays over? You'll yet turn out to be a professional painter! [...] I've had lots of work since I put on a tea party for twenty children [giving everyone] a bit of Christmas cake and a little present[1] I had the entire poorhouse here. I had my husband home he brought me a gramophone so I shouldn't be lonely. You felt sad so why didn't you come to us? You would have had a good time here. [...] So now you're a home-owner but repairs cost a lot of money. You write that I'll come and see [Hukvaldy] some time. Why did you buy something so far away? My husband left today for a longish period I don't know how this new year will begin for us. The main thing is that we should all be well. [...] I never thought that we'd be writing to each other for such a long time and be such good friends. [...]

Janáček responded enthusiastically. 'I read [your letter] frequently: I'm glad I have a girlfriend. That one can have a girlfriend without the world wagging its finger at it' (*191: Brno, 9 January 1922). Even so, he kept the letter hidden from Zdenka, as 'she also wouldn't understand the friendship'. In his next letter he responded to the news of Kamila's gramophone:

1 *koleda*, usually a present (something to eat or a little money) given to carol-singers.

[...] You know, I never took pleasure in dancing, I never longed for it, I never sought it out. I never danced.

[...]

So you have a gramophone! If you'd listened to my advice long ago and learnt to play the piano you could have played decently by now and cheered up your moments of boredom.

You'll soon get tired of a gramophone: it always grinds on in the same way: [playing] laughter when you cry, crying when you laugh. It's a heartless puppet, unsightly. [...]

So, dear friend, I've told you all that oppresses me; thus half of it has fallen from me.

193   Brno, 10 February 1922

[...] I have begun writing *The Cunning Little Vixen*.[1] A merry thing with a sad end: and I'm taking up a place at that sad end myself. [...]

And I so belong there!

In the light of this remark about Janáček's place at the 'sad end' it is tempting to see some connection between the composition of *The Cunning Little Vixen* and the acquisition of his country cottage, which he began to regard as something of a retirement home.[2] The subject of the opera had been with him since the serial publication in *Lidové noviny* of Těsnohlídek's novel *Liška Bystrouška* in the spring of 1920; the first indication of his interest in acquiring property in his birthplace came just a few months later (131). By the time Janáček had finalized the purchase of the cottage in October 1921 (see 186) he had indicated in the press that *Liška Bystrouška* would be the subject of his next opera.[3]

Janáček also mentioned in 193 that the vocal score of *Káťa Kabanová* was about to come out (Universal Edition sent off the first copies to him ten days later, on 20 February)[4] and that he would be sending Stösslová a score of it: 'after all I had you much in mind during *Káťa Kabanová*'. Two weeks later he redeemed this promise:

1 He had begun almost three weeks earlier (see Tyrrell 1992, LB15+).
2 In an interview given to Adolf Veselý in May 1928 Janáček referred briefly to his plans to retire to Hukvaldy, an intention confirmed by Otilie Krsková, who helped out in his house during his stays in Hukvaldy (Procházka 1948, 147).
3 Tyrrell 1992, LB7–8.
4 Tyrrell 1992, KK26.

195 Brno, 25 February 1922

[...] So you have *Káťa Kabanová*. During the writing of the opera I needed to know a great measureless love. Tears ran down your cheeks when you remembered your husband in those beautiful days in Luhačovice. It touched me. And I always placed your image on Káťa Kabanová when I was writing the opera.

Her love went a different way, but nevertheless it was a great, beautiful love!

Much to his hurt, Stösslová needed a reminder (*196: a postcard from Prague, 14 March 1922) before she got round to thanking him for the score, though this was not enough to upset work on *The Cunning Little Vixen*. Stösslová, who had offered general malaise as an excuse for her late reply (16 March 1922),[1] was recommended 'serious work' as a remedy.

197 Brno, 18 March 1922

[...] I'm now out of that bad-tempered, in fact tiring, mood. I have been working on the girl's novel *Liška Bystrouška*. So I don't have a moment now to think about *myself*.

If you too were to have more serious work which would occupy you entirely, you'd also perhaps shake off that bad-tempered mood. I'd like to see you. I don't know whether I'll manage it over Easter [23 April]. They've chosen me as a judge in singing competitions which will take place in Prague 16, 17 and 18 April.[2] If I go there I'll tell you in good time. [...]

The advice did not go down well: by the time of his Hukvaldy holiday (*200: Hukvaldy, 21 August 1922), he had again to ask why she was not writing. This opened up the old wound. If we are to accept her account, the long refusal of Stösslová to see Janáček in Brno was based largely on her assumption that it would upset Zdenka:

Kamila Stösslová to Leoš Janáček, Písek, 25 August 1922

[...] You know very well why I don't want to stay at your place. For I still haven't forgotten about the last time. Why cause pain to another

1 in Tyrrell 1982, 103.
2 The Czechoslovak Singing Society [Pěvecká obec československá] organized the first national singing competition to take place at Easter and in a letter of 15 February 1922 invited Janáček to be a judge. He seems not to have taken up the invitation.

person unnecessarily. I had thought I wouldn't write to you again. But, as the old saying goes 'Old love never dies'. Even if between us there's no love just innocent friendship. My husband's away all the time he's always got things to do. [...]

201   Hukvaldy, 27 August 1922

So you can be angry such a long time? Believe me, you've made my holidays sad by it. It doesn't matter about the holidays! But believe me that I need your twittering and your scrawling as the dry weather needs the rain, the dawn needs the sun, the sky needs the stars. Yes, that last comparison is the best. What's the sky without that little star?!

You're the star that I look for in the evening. Out of love? Out of sincere friendship. That's why I was so sad when you didn't write.

You know, don't you, that otherwise I'm indifferent to the world. And Luhačovice [this year] was the saddest of all years. [...]

Don't wrong Zdenka. We were always glad to see you. Don't wonder that she was a little unnecessarily jealous. She knows that I've got you in my mind all the time. Write to her about all the places you've been.

So, dear Mrs Kamila, make up now for what you've not done!

During his stay in Hukvaldy Janáček clearly went on brooding about his relationship with Stösslová, and after his return to Brno wrote again with one of his clearest statements so far about what this friendship and correspondence meant to him:

204   Brno, 30 September 1922

[...] I'm glad that I've escaped from my Hukvaldy seclusion. I left pears, apples and plums on the tree.

But nevertheless I cooked up ten kilos of damson-cheese and I've pressed twenty-five litres of apple wine!

I'm so glad that we've said openly to one another that we're friends. It's an ideal friendship, and I'm so glad that it's so pure and elevated above everything bad.

To entrust myself [to you] with my thoughts, my longings, to reveal my internal life – and to know that it's as safe in your mind as if it were hidden in mine.

You don't know how sad it would be for me without you – although sometimes I don't see you for years! [...]

Kamila Stösslová to Leoš Janáček, Písek, 12 October 1922

[...] I must tell you that this week I came across your first letter. What a long time it is that we've known one another and yet how little we see one another (and get cross with one another). We're just so far from one another now. [...]

The Prague première of *Káťa Kabanová* was fast approaching and Janáček clearly hoped that this time he might tempt Kamila to come and see the work she had inspired. Remembering that she had refused to attend the première of *The Diary of One who Disappeared* without Zdenka's being there, he suggested that she write to Zdenka to say how much she was looking forward to it (*206: Brno, 12 October 1922). A second invitation made clear that he expected her husband to come as well (*208: Brno, 2 November 1922). By this time the production had already been postponed once. After a further postponement – the sets had not arrived from the Viennese firm that supplied them – the Prague première finally took place on 30 November, without the Stössels, and without even Zdenka (who apparently had nothing suitable to wear; *210: 22 November 1922). Janáček reported on the press reactions (generally favourable; *212: Brno, 14 December 1922) and then quietly dropped the subject. By Christmas the first seed of his next opera but one had been planted. It is interesting that although Janáček saw Čapek's new play at the Prague Vinohrady Theatre on 10 December 1922, soon after it opened, it was only now, three letters and two and a half weeks later, that he mentioned it. It had clearly gone on resonating in his mind.

214 Hukvaldy, [28 December 1922][1]

So I'm away for a week in a grey winter countryside. So grey that the deer get grey coats from it.

The paths up the hills are passable, along the level just mud. So I walk up and down the hills. But I'm getting away from notes. I already had notes spinning in my head all night long.

And what spins in your head? No worries – but don't you get bored from that?

They've now been giving *Makropulos* in Prague. A woman 337 years old, but at the same time still young and beautiful. Would you like to be like that too?

And you know, she was unhappy? We are happy because we know that our life isn't long. So it's necessary to make use of every moment, to use it properly. It's all hurry in our life – and longing.

1 Janáček dated this letter merely 'Ukvaldy u Příbora, Thursday, before New Year'.

The latter is my lot. That woman – the 337-year-old beauty [–] didn't have a heart any more.

That's bad. [...]

Soon after, Stösslová wrote one of her most revealing letters, making clear how lonely she was during her husband's long absences on business trips (in a later letter, 18 January 1923, she complained that sometimes she did not get out of the house for four to six weeks at a time and that her husband was interested only in business). Her letter also shows how the friendly relations between her and Zdenka seem to have broken down to the extent that Zdenka was not responding even to seasonal courtesies:

Kamila Stösslová to Leoš Janáček, Písek, 11 January 1923

Dear Maestro

So you're home again now. You spent the holidays on your own. This wasn't really a proper Christmas not a trace of snow. I got a nice coat but it doesn't give me much pleasure this year I'm at home all the time so I don't even need it. My husband went off on New Year's Day and I don't know when he'll get back. This is such a dreary life that I just can't write about it to you. If I didn't have the children I'd have to escape they're doing well at school so they give me joy.

I wrote to your wife for the holidays [i.e. for Christmas or New Year] but she didn't even write back to me didn't even write to me for the holidays. Perhaps she's right not to write because I write so seldom myself. I really have nothing to write about. Nothing at all after my last visit to you. For with me what's on my heart is on my tongue.[1] However I don't know how to lie. Or for somebody to take me for something other than what I am that pains me very much. You don't have to tell me why she didn't write to me. For I don't like anything forced. It doesn't come from the heart I know that best myself. Perhaps she's in the right possibly it annoys her that you write to me. [...]

215 Brno, 12 January 1923

The fact that we correspond would upset a certain person? Zdenka didn't tell me that she got a letter from you. Since you didn't write for so long she'll similarly leave you waiting for an answer.

1 i.e. she didn't hold anything back.

[That's the result of] writing only when one wants to.

It would really be sad if I couldn't write to someone from the heart.
[...]

Despite, or perhaps because of, this frankness, there seems to have been something of a hiccup in correspondence. It is also possible that some letters have gone astray. The reference in 217 to a 'long letter' can only be to 215, i.e. three months earlier (less than a quarter of it is given above), or to a lost letter written in between. Only one of the 'two cards' Janáček mentions survives.

217   Brno, 3 April 1923

As if I wouldn't have written to you in Vienna! You didn't get my long letter! I was in Prague and wrote you two cards to Písek from there too. I was in Bratislava for the première of *Káťa Kabanová*; but there was no time to remember [you with a card] from there. They performed that work of mine most beautifully of all there. More beautifully than in Brno, more beautifully than in Prague.

I was taken with Bratislava. In Brno they hate me, in Prague they envy me, but in Bratislava they really like me.

A beautiful old town, the fast-flowing Danube. In the holidays I've a mind to cruise down the Danube until it opens into the sea – or at least until Belgrade.

You wouldn't like to come on board, would you?

[...] I didn't go anywhere for the [Easter] holidays; I'm up to my neck in work with copying out *Bystrouška*.[1]

I'm doing *Bystrouška* like a devil catching flies – when he's got nothing else [to catch].[2]

I caught Bystrouška for the forest and for the sadness of the late years.

Are you still as pretty as in Luhačovice? I think prettier.

In his correspondence Janáček said less about composing *The Cunning Little Vixen* than any of the other later operas. It seems to have been the easiest to write and thus the least necessary to write about, though another reason may be that this was a lean period in Janáček's correspondence with Stösslová, when fewer letters were exchanged or at least survive. The trip to Bratislava

1 In *The Cunning Little Vixen* Janáček worked closely with his copyists, using them more as amanuenses. Kulhánek's copy of Act 1 had been completed just a few days earlier, on 29 March 1923; Act 2 was completed in this way on 20 July 1923.
2 See 531: 'It's said that if a devil's hungry he even catches flies.'

was memorable not only for the first production of *Káťa Kabanová* that Janáček really warmed to, but also for the first seed of his *Danube* symphony. In a letter two months later (*220: 9 June 1923) Janáček was still looking for a companion for his proposed (and ultimately unrealized) Danube trip. The symphony, too, though sketched, was never completed, being overtaken by a new creative plan that Janáček had formulated over the summer: 'I will compose [an opera] about a certain beauty by now 300 years old – and she doesn't want anyone' (*224: Prague, 13 October 1923). Janáček had finished revising *The Cunning Little Vixen* just three days earlier. Within a month he was hard at work on *The Makropulos Affair*, his new opera:

226   Brno, 11 November 1923

[...] I've begun a new work and so I'm no longer bored. A 300-year-old beauty – and eternally young – but only burnt-out feeling! Brrr! Cold as ice! About such a woman I shall write an opera. You write about yourself that you're putting on weight. Even that would certainly suit you. In my eyes you're always just like then in Luhačovice. [...]

Kamila Stösslová to Leoš Janáček, Písek, 22 November 1923

[...] I've got a good stove that's not 300 years old at which I sit for days on end. It's not so burnt-out as your new opera. [...] You always choose operas which make one's blood run cold. [...]

227   Brno, 4 December 1923

[...] I'm now doing that brrr! But I'll warm her up, so that people sympathize with her. I might fall in love with her.
   [...]
And do you know that my Kamila has now twice scratched my nose?
   That cheap little ring of yours, when I was washing myself in cold water, turned round on my finger and I scratched my nose with its lettering! There was a little stream of blood. When we meet up sometime you must give me a rounder Kamila.

In 1924 Janáček turned seventy. Most of the celebrations came later in the year, after his birthday (3 July), but Brno got in early with a concert which also marked the year of Josef Suk's fiftieth birthday. The concert by the Brno National Theatre orchestra on 13 January included Suk's symphonic poem

Ripening and Janáček's *Taras Bulba*. But of more interest to Janáček was an invitation from Mrs Stösslová to visit her in Písek. They had not met since 1921.

229 Brno, 31 January 1924

[...] You can imagine that I'd like to see you once again after so many years [...] Too bad that you're no longer in Přerov, then we could have seen each other frequently!

[...]

That was a bit of fun in Brno, you know! They did a sort of celebration of me and the composer Suk. I couldn't even buy tickets – so I didn't go there. They called out and kept on calling out for me – and I was somewhere beyond Brno in the snow-covered fields!

So tell me how I should imagine you. In the morning? – I have you in my mind's eye just as you went out barefoot on to the 'balcony' in Luhačovice with your black hair undone.

At noon? I have you in my mind's eye just as you were with the wooden spoon in that kitchen at the concierge's.

In the afternoon? Just as you were on that bench in the garden behind the house in Luhačovice.

And now it's all different! Write to me how it is now.

Well now, and how are you getting on business-wise? Your husband's certainly not running round the world for nothing. When will he have enough? And what about your brothers?[1] Children?

In Moravská Ostrava I was taken to the biggest power station. They had an x-ray apparatus there. They shone it through my right hand. I saw my bones and on the little finger was your black ring! It went right through!

The première of *Jenůfa* under Erich Kleiber in Berlin also took place in 1924. It was much more effective in launching the work on the German stage than the German-language première in Vienna six years earlier:

---

1 Mrs Stösslová had two brothers, Emil Neumann (1896–1980), who figures quite frequently in the complete correspondence (e.g. 306), and a younger brother Karel Neumann (1898–c1944).

231   Brno, 10 March 1924

[...] On Saturday [15 March] I leave for Berlin; the Staatsoper is giving *Jenůfa* that day. I'll still be there on Sunday, on Monday I return to Prague – to have a look at the World Fair.[1] I'll be staying there on 18 March. Can you come, according to your promise? Let me know at the Karel IV. [Hotel], Smíchov.

It seems to me that you're a star which has its course in the heavens and I another one; I run along my own course, I think that I'll soon catch up with that first little star, I run and I run – but not a bit of it! Our courses never meet. They smile at each other – that's all.

I think that the doctor will send me to Mariánské Lázně[2] this year. Then our paths would cross!

And they are also going to give *Jenůfa* in New York at the Metropolitan Opera.[3] That's the highest thing that I could achieve. I achieve this – but happiness in life – not that.

And I would have liked so much to be cheerful and I would have liked so much to have taken good care, nothing less, of the one I love.

[...] And you know that it was nicest when each of us told the other from the heart our worries and desires – there in Luhačovice on that path, on that bench, when you split off a branch of a shrub. It was close above the villa of Dr Glücksmann.[4]

Because of those memories I so like to go to Luhačovice.

So keep well. [Any more and] I'd grow sad and perhaps even burst into tears.

233   Brno, 3 April 1924

[...] And Berlin? That was so much glory and victory! But I caught flu there. Straight after the première I left in haste for Prague. By chance I noticed your card on the table there. Straight to the doctor. He didn't give me much cheer. In Brno the flu got worse and it was only really after a fortnight that I got free of it. This is the second day that I've gone out a little. I knew that you wouldn't be writing for some time. An outside person could get the wrong impression from our letters.

And who is to blame that you are, my dear Mrs Kamila, everything

---

1 Soon after the creation of Czechoslovakia world fairs were organized on a regular basis at the former site of the 1891 Provincial Jubilee Exhibition.
2 The famous spa town (Marienbad) in western Bohemia, nearer Písek than Janáček's usual Luhačovice in Moravia.
3 Janáček learnt about the Metropolitan Opera's interest in *Jenůfa* in a letter from Universal Edition dated 4 March 1924 (BmJA, D 1007).
4 See Glossary.

in the world to me, my one and only quiet joy, that I know of no other desire than to think about you, to get drunk on your dear cheerful presence? You're so far away – and I'm here with my feelings and it seems to me as if you were here beside me. [...]

The visit to Písek discussed in January continued to recede and letters were still infrequent. The gap of two and a half months before Janáček's next surviving letter is bridged only by a card from Hukvaldy (*234: 24 April 1924). The Stössels seem to have visited Brno in June, though judging from the absence of further comment in Janáček's letter (235) they may only have passed through on the train.

235 Brno, 20 June 1924

You know the saying 'bad luck doesn't walk along the mountains but among people'? The same day that you left Brno, at the same time perhaps, a glass panel above the door fell on Zdenka. She could have been killed, she could have lost her eyes. Luckily she has only a cut nose, her skin grazed on the right temple. The flow of blood was terrible. Fate.

I won't go to Mariánské Lázně, it's not necessary.

On Wednesday 25 June I go to Prague. I've got rehearsals there 25 and 26 June.[1] I'd return on Friday or Saturday and would like to go to Písek. To look at the town and perhaps at Zvíkov?[2] Please write to me at the Karel IV., Smíchov, how to get by rail to Písek. From Wilson Station?[3] In the morning, when?

Would you please book me into some Písek hotel for one night.

Don't let your husband go off, otherwise I'll [seem to be] carrying you off from him by car!

I'll let you know by telegram from Prague whether it will be Friday or Saturday.

In fact he let her know with a brief note (*236: Prague, 25 June 1924) that he would be coming on the Friday. This was Janáček's first trip to the Stössels' house in Písek and it was evidently a success. For one thing it was longer than intended. In 235 Janáček asked for a hotel bed for a single night (there is confirmation in 429 that this happened) but it is clear from his reference to

1 These were for concerts of student compositions by his graduates from the master school in composition at the Prague Conservatory.
2 An historic town near Písek with important architectural remains dating back to the thirteenth century.
3 Now Prague Main Station.

'three beautiful days' (237) that he spent two nights in the town. From 238 one can infer that the second night was on an improvised bed in the Stössel household. His letters suddenly became more frequent and warm-hearted than they had been for years:

237 [undated, postmarked Brno, 30 June 1924]

Dear Mrs Kamila

The first word that I write belongs to you. I thank you warmly for the happy and light-hearted days, for your continual smile and wicked high spirits, for your kindness and care of me.

Those were three beautiful days without a shadow.

I'm glad that your picture came alive in my mind, always just as engaging as that Luhačovice one was. You know that I wouldn't harm you, and I know that you'll see that I don't get hurt. You wait for my letters and I pant for yours; neither the ones nor the others are learned; but friendship breathes from them both.

I thank you for your hospitality, and your good mother, as well as your father and your husband, for my friendly reception. I went on about it at home and I'd like to pay you back.

A few tears moistened my eyes in the railway carriage! What can I do when time runs on so relentlessly?

So arrange your visit to Luhačovice for the second half of August.

And now a merry note!

I would like to — but a sorrowful note forces its way into my pen — because I can't always be around you! [...]

238 Brno, 1 July 1924

Dear Mrs Kamila

I'm enclosing a cutting. I wanted to escape from every sort of celebration of those damned seventy years but it just can't be done. It wasn't too bad when a German newspaper called me a 'Greis-Jüngling'.[1] If the second epithet were true I'd carry you off even if you were behind seventy-five locks! But I know that you wouldn't let me. For you have not only the power of eloquence, but also the strength to break bones. But nevertheless I'd overpower you!

So you're glad now that you have a little quiet in the house. We laughed enough [to last us] for months, didn't we!

And why was it that we could laugh, always laugh?

1 old man/youth.

[47]

I still remember now the sorrel and your indecent frogs! And your even more indecent peas, and still we didn't get spoilt. And that last night on a bed made up for a king! I thought that my blood would run from my nose because of the heat. I was frightened that the pillow-cases would be red the next morning – but there was nothing like that, they stayed so beautifully white.

And do you know what else makes me glad? That once again I saw your raven-black hair, all loose, your bare foot: and you are beautiful, wonderfully beautiful – and what else I caught sight of ... And your eye has a strange depth, it's so deep that it doesn't shine. But it's more attractive: as if it wanted to embrace. But enough now of these ramblings of mine.

And now my care for you: every day before you go to bed, drink a small glass of fresh water.

That's not a difficult prescription, is it now? And it will keep you in freshness and in health.

Kamila, if it weren't for you, I wouldn't want to live. It's just an alliance of our souls which binds us; but if you were to fall ill, I'd suffer more than you. No, now you overflow with health, no bad thoughts.

If I were a painter, I'd be able to paint you from memory: with those blue slippers! Write me a long, long letter. [Without it] the day wouldn't have a good ending for me.

Yours completely devotedly
Leoš Janáček

I've already got a room booked in Luhačovice from 15 August.

This letter is striking in the involuntary use of Mrs Stösslová's first name without the usual 'Mrs'. It is also memorable in the way it foreshadows the manner of much of the later correspondence: memories of the visit continuing to surface in the letters following his return; concern for Mrs Stösslová's health (with fussy prescriptions on how to improve it); and a free and passionate celebration of her beauty. On 3 July, the day of his seventieth birthday, he slipped off to Hukvaldy, pursued by letters and telegrams from his well-wishers (though not from Mrs Stösslová, who got round to it only the next day). From Hukvaldy he wrote more and more frequently.

239   Hukvaldy, 4 July 1924

I thought that at least a little line from you would be waiting here for me in the quiet and shade of the forest, and nothing.

So I for one am sending an article for you to read.[1] I walk here alone with an image of you no-one else can see.[2] You're here in wicked red, in twittering blue. Another time your little eyes peer out in a ladylike fashion from beneath your wide-spreading hat, here again beside me a young and tender apparition in a white dress and blue slippers. It's full of laughter and no-one hears it, full of conversation and no-one understands it: it's the pleasant mystery of two souls.

Several telegrams and letters flew here – even from the President of the National Assembly, Mr Tomášek[3] – and soon that will be the end to this comedy.

What do I get out of it when they're always telling me that I appear young?

They should rather ask for whom my heart aches and give me a cure. I'd drink it by the spoonful not only three times daily but all the time.

You don't understand this, and that's good.

240 [undated, postmarked Hukvaldy, 8 July 1924]

How much I'd been waiting for your letter![4] And it came – whimsical, merry, just like you yourself! What if I had an aeroplane here! That would fly from here hither and thither all the time, Písek–Hukvaldy–Písek–Hukvaldy – until I at last caught you, spun you round and stayed with you in the skies! That would be lovely, wouldn't it? And what if I forgot to fly the plane and it hurtled headlong to earth? Then I'd put my arms round you – and we'd land more gently, for you're just like smiling butter.[5]

[...] Oh you know Kamila, I'm so unutterably fond of you. I'd call out Kamila all the time! And sometimes, ah, I fear to say it ... because it's something not to be uttered. Not for this passion, for something higher... They say of me that I'll live for ever; that's metaphorical. But it's possible to live for ever in other ways. Eternal life springs from

1 Presumably one of the many articles that came out for Janáček's seventieth birthday.
2 Janáček develops the 'invisible presence' motif most strikingly in 658.
3 František Tomášek (1871–1938).
4 An undated letter, postmarked 4 July 1924 (BmJA, E 1219): 'I also wish you much health, at least up to a hundred. If you'd said something then we could have celebrated your birthday here. It wouldn't have mattered whether it was three days earlier or later, the main thing is simply that you were born.' It is clear that Janáček had kept quiet about his birthday during his visit to Písek at the end of June.
5 Janáček's later references to Kamila's increasing corpulence, always made approvingly (see e.g. 640), began to take on a different meaning as he fantasized about her being pregnant with his child (see Glossary: 'Kamila's baby').

you, from that dear Kamila. Oh, I'd write things like that without stopping!

You know that our President[1] has asked for my *Jenůfa* on Wednesday 9 July at the Vinohrady Theatre; the Brno opera will sing there. They invited me to go. It's a world away, but I'll go. On Wednesday towards 3.30 I'll be in Prague. Again at Karel IV., Smíchov. If only you could come there! In that case I wouldn't regret the journey. At least send a letter to me there, but preferably yourself. [...]

Kamila Stösslová to Leoš Janáček, Písek, 9 July 1924

Dear Maestro

I hope you've got my letter already. I'm by the water[2] the whole time, I'm already so black that I can't even tell you. I was suddenly so sad that I didn't want to write immediately, not until I'd calmed down again a bit. I was glad that you liked it at our place and that you were satisfied. [...] I also enjoy talking with you because I know that it's innocent friendship. You write about my beauty there you're terribly wrong. For you have the chance to see beautiful women perhaps you don't notice them. But in my case there may have been something [but] what it is I can't say myself. If perhaps you told it to someone it's possible he'd think quite differently. For I'm really quite an ordinary woman of which there are thousands. [...] Your heart would stop aching if you were with me more.

It's good that I don't understand that little spoonful of medicine.[3] I'm happy so long as I don't understand. Then it would be the end of my high spirits and my whole life. It would seem to me as if you'd torn the head off a flower and it still stands up but how?

I couldn't survive that because I love my husband so much that I'd perhaps want to lay down my own head for his life. Perhaps he doesn't even know himself how I long for him perhaps just as you for me.

I write a bit sadly but I've read your letters and so I sense that love of yours for me.

Where I'm sorry is if someone is suffering. It would have cost me my life. So be terribly cheerful because that's what I wish. For it's beautiful that you have these memories of me that's enough for you and the main thing is [that they are] so innocent. I never thought I'd

---

1 T.G. Masaryk (1850–1937).
2 See Glossary: 'rocks'.
3 A reference to the end of Janáček's letter 239.

correspond with some man and I resisted even you I didn't want to talk to you. But fate wanted otherwise so we'll now leave everything to fate. It's better that you're so old now if you were young my husband would never permit this [correspondence]. [...]

This is an important letter, one of Kamila's most frank and thoughtful. She seems to have accepted Janáček's idealization of her, but also makes it clear that she still loves her husband. Most withering of all is the final sentence. Janáček's dignified response (243) was written after he had returned from the brief trip to Prague for the gala performance of *Jenůfa* in his honour.

242 Prague, 10 July 1924

I left Hukvaldy on 9 July at 3 o'clock in the morning (you've probably never ever got up so early); halfway through the journey I remembered that I'd forgotten my identity card;[1] that was Kč 100 thrown away unnecessarily on the railways. [...]

I passed through Brno, on the way I caught my black suit thrown in [through the window of the railway carriage][2] and I got to Prague at 2.30 in the afternoon. On the way I learnt that President Dr Masaryk had fallen ill and couldn't come to the theatre! [...]

They were pleased when they saw me in the theatre. Endless curtain calls, introductions, a session with Minister Dr Beneš[3] etc.

In the night my heart began to pound because of all this. I learnt that all the Prague newspapers wrote about me, and had pictures. Only nothing in *Národní listy*![4]

I learnt about the Ministry's present – apparently something in a little case? – What will it be? I still don't have it.

I went into one bookshop thinking they wouldn't know me. I bought a copy for myself of Dr Brod's book about me;[5] and all the

1 Janáček, like other state employees and ex-employees, had a card that allowed him to travel on the state railways at a reduced fare.
2 Janáček had written to his wife from Hukvaldy on 5 July 1924 (BmJA, D 1223) asking for his dinner jacket, trousers and shoes to be packed in a case and brought to the station at the time of his arrival in Brno at 10 a.m. His train went on to Prague at 10.30. Presumably the case was handed to him through the window of his train.
3 Edvard Beneš (1884–1948), then Minister of Foreign Affairs; he replaced Masaryk as President in 1935.
4 The long-term music critic (1910–41) of *Národní listy*, Dr Antonín Šilhan, was not necessarily hostile towards Janáček, having helped promote the Prague and Vienna premières of *Jenůfa* (see Tyrrell 1992, 85 and 98), but he was unenthusiastic about his most recent opera, *Káťa Kabanová* (see Tyrrell 1992, 269).
5 Max Brod: *Leoš Janáček: život a dílo* [Leoš Janáček: life and works] (Prague: Hudební matice Umělecké besedy, 1924).

while they recognized me! So even in Prague it's not possible to hide myself. Only in those newspaper offices in Písek could I call myself whatever I wanted. It was all the same to them, not so?

That was fun.

I wrote to you that I was sad in Hukvaldy this year. I have my eighty-five-year-old sister[1] there in my house; she cooked for me and kept house – and now she has suddenly begun fading away and complaining [of poor health]! That's how it is in life.

So how is my regal room at your house, is it deserted? Or do you sleep in it? [...]

243   Hukvaldy, 15 July 1924

You know that I opened your last letter with misgivings? And I had reason to.

How can one not want you, when one loves you?

But I know, don't I, that I'll never have you. Would I pluck that flower, that family happiness of yours, would I make free with my respect for you, whom I honour like no other woman on earth? Could I look your children in the eye, your husband and parents? Could I walk into your home?

You know, we dream about paradise, about heaven and we never get to it.

So I dream about you and I know that you're the unattainable sky.

But not to want you, though that's an impossibility – I can't do that. You are entire in my soul; so it's enough for me to want you always. And to forget you, that would be sad for me and it's impossible. So I'll be merry according to your order.

I walk here isolated; the weather's chilly. Luckily I brought work[2] with me.

[...]

Do you have somewhere to stay in Luhačovice yet?

---

1 See Glossary: 'Dohnalová, Josefa Adolfína'; in 1924 Janáček's sister was eighty-two, not eighty-five.
2 He could perhaps have brought *The Makropulos Affair* (he had begun his draft of Act 2 on 19 March 1924), but more likely he was working on *Mládí* [Youth], which he reports finishing nine days later (245).

245 Hukvaldy, 24 July 1924

[...] Well, when I come to you for the second time – it will be soon: they're giving *Káťa Kabanová* in Plzeň[1] – so when I come to you again, we'll make those further visits.[2] And I'd come to you gladly because I cannot look at you enough.

And Káťa, you know, that was you beside me. And that black Gypsy girl in my *Diary of One who Disappeared* – that was especially you even more. That's why there's such emotional heat in these works. So much heat that if it caught both of us, there'd be just ashes left of us. Luckily it's just I who burn – and you who are saved.

And Luhačovice? Don't promise anything – and come. I'd be your shadow. I leave here on Saturday. And on 1 August I should be in Štrbské pleso.[3]

[...]

I've composed here a sort of memoir of youth.[4]

Do read that book by Dr Max Brod.[5] Anything you don't understand – just skip. He writes beautifully about me – and you'll understand all sorts of things better.

Kamila Stösslová to Leoš Janáček, Písek, 25 July 1924

[...] I had a dream about you last night that when I woke up I couldn't even believe it, that I could dream I was your wife what do you say to it. Such silly things where do we get them from? Mummy laughed when I told her about it. She said that my head's full of nonsense, and I had to admit she was right. [...] Please burn the silly things that I write to you. Someone would think that I am sixteen, that I have no sense. [...]

1 Plzeň was relatively near Písek, so presumably Janáček had in mind to take in a trip to Písek at the same time. However the Plzeň première of *Káťa Kabanová* did not take place until 13 February 1925.
2 From Kamila Stösslová's letter of 22 July 1924 Janáček had learnt of Alois Kodl's complaint about the number of people who had wished to meet Janáček during his trip.
3 A mountain resort in Slovakia where Janáček had gone the previous summer with his wife and where he had taken the decision to compose *The Makropulos Affair* (see Tyrrell 1992, 307).
4 The earliest reference to the composition of the wind sextet *Mládí* [Youth].
5 See p.51, fn.5. Janáček wrote on 7 August 1924 (*249) that he had asked the publishers to send her a copy of the book.

[...] Well you must have dreamt, dreamt at least, that you were my wife, when I dreamt, perhaps the same day, but also only dreamt, that you were standing close to me in some room in Brno, in a salon, so close that I was unutterably hot; then I didn't know, did I embrace you, or did I only want to embrace you? The people here and there, waiters perhaps, looked at us. But so what? You elegantly dressed – and so that heady dream lasted a moment and faded again. But I always want to dream about you. It's said one can't help one's dreams, whatever they are. But it was so lifelike that I wished that the beautiful, intoxicating dream wouldn't stop. And afterwards during the day? One sobers up! [...]

When you came in the morning, and also towards evening, during the hot weather, with that black hair of yours loose – it was like a storm cloud and it was a wonder that lightning didn't flash from it; and when you bent down, I saw, but rather I didn't see, I suspected – but I say to you, after all it was just a dream [–] it was the curve of your surely beautiful breasts! Surely, surely beautiful.

Dream or reality?

So enough of these words; there'd be no end of them. On 2 August I go with Zdenka to Štrbské pleso, then to Sliač,[1] and via Bratislava to Brno.

On the 15th I set off for Luhačovice, for that healthy water. I don't wonder that you find it difficult leaving Písek. You're healthy, you don't need spas yet. But I'd be glad to find you there!

Of course I'm writing off only now for accommodation in Štrbské pleso and in Luhačovice. Everywhere is said to be overfull this year.

Do remember me a little; and I'll imagine your dreams for myself.

My wife! See, how easily it comes! The dear Lord cares for us, and is good! What can't be in any other way he gives at least as a dream.

Dear, dark Mrs Kamila, [heart-]warming sight, keep well!

247 Brno, 2 August 1924

I read today in *Lidové noviny* that between Choceň and Pardubice a case was stolen from Mr David Stössel with pictures to the value of Kč 10,000. Is he so careless? Here in Brno he also left his case behind then! I'm sitting in Brno, I didn't get a room in Štrbské pleso!

I still haven't had an answer from Luhačovice.[2]

1 A spa resort in Slovakia.
2 He heard the next day that he had a room from 15 August (*248: 3 August 1924).

This year it's as if there's a spell put on it.

I enclose a picture for you. *Ex libris* is a sign which is pasted into books or music.[1]

Am I listening to a woman or a tree? I think it's a woman, like Mrs Kamila.

The performance in Prague[2] brought me Kč 3000. I'll buy a rug from you.

On 15 August Janáček took up his booked accommodation in Luhačovice. He wrote the next day to Stösslová (*250), mentioning the warm weather and also complaining that he had not heard from her. This lament was renewed a few days later in a letter which describes more clearly than ever Stösslová's directness and simplicity as well as his own unhappiness which he felt to be the mainspring of his art:

251   Luhačovice, 20 August 1924

You're economical with words and lines. The solitude of the forests, through which I wander here, is restoring me. I feel that I'm coming to myself again; after all, there was never a more disturbed year in my life than 1924.

And believe me, Kamila, there were no more beautiful days for me in my life than those few spent in your company. I felt a pure friendship, it showed itself simply and warmly. You were like an open window: one could see through it all just as it was. I had nothing to hide, it was peaceful and so pleasant in my soul. I saw you in your household, always natural in your behaviour, not artificial, with slippers and even bare feet; some sort of secret flame always shone and one warmed oneself up with it. Not with starchiness, affectation. No-one looked for a speck of dust on the furniture.

You came out of the house like a housewife, but also like a lady, and at home you were the prudent wife and untiring hostess.

This is the way everything strikes me now and I can't praise you enough. And that's why in your company, and between us, there was a laugh on the lips and on the face. I was among good people and that's why I so like to remember it and why I so like you.

My life is sadder, more disordered, which is why I bind it with this 'art' of mine, I glue it together, I re-create it in my imagination more tolerably for myself. Who knows, if fate had united us closely,

1 Janáček sent the bookplate which Eduard Milén (1891–1976), the stage-designer of the Brno *Cunning Little Vixen*, had made for him (see Plate 33).
2 Presumably the gala performance of *Jenůfa* on 9 July described in 242.

whether I would have needed this art, whether it would ever have made itself felt within me at all?

Whether in your eyes which look on so sincerely there wouldn't have been the whole world for me? [...]

Janáček returned from Luhačovice on 30 August having had a thoroughly 'miserable' time, as he put in his note of 12 September 1924 (*256), written just before he went off to Hukvaldy with Zdenka to pick fruit. From Hukvaldy he sent only a couple of cards. On his return he learnt that Stösslová would be passing through Brno on her way to her husband's family home of Strážnice.

259 Brno, 29 September 1924

I arrived in Brno on Saturday evening [27 September] and found your card.

I read and read, with pleasure. On Sunday I ran off to the station towards 4 o'clock; in my arms a little package of nuts freshly shaken [from Janáček's tree] and I waited and waited. Eventually I asked an official if a train was coming on this line, the fast train from Jihlava?

It's not coming he said, but *is leaving* from Brno here at 4.20!

It kept worrying me that it was rather a long journey from Písek by fast train from morning until 4 p.m.!

But on Sunday morning I had so much work that there was no time to think about it, and I believed your 4.50!

So you passed through Brno and I returned home sadly from the station with the little package of nuts. To make up for it, stay longer when you return and I'll make really sure this time what the trains are up to.

[...] During those fourteen days in Hukvaldy the weather was magnificent. The sun nearly burnt, so much that I got sunstroke on the last day. I couldn't get enough of the sun. That sun in Písek, that's the real one; it warms and smiles and one gets warm even in the heart.

So keep well now and write lots to me to make up for giving me the slip in Brno.

As proof I enclose a platform ticket.

I wish those days in Písek would come again.

In October there were further concerts in Prague in celebration of Janáček's jubilee, on the 17th (arranged by the Society for Modern Music) and on the 20th (by the Czech Society for Chamber Music). Both included the Violin Sonata and the first performances of the String Quartet no.1, *The Kreutzer*

Sonata, by its dedicatees, the Czech Quartet. In his letters Janáček provided Mrs Stösslová with exact details of his movements, in the hope that she would see him in Prague, but all he got from her was a brief letter of congratulation (*16 October 1924).

263   Prague, 14 October 1924

You neither answered with a note, nor did you come. [...]

Tomorrow I've got rehearsals here and on Thursday morning [16 October] I return to Brno.

On Monday [20 October] I'm here again. They're giving my works in the Chamber Society.

So I feel myself deserted here.

You see, we could have merrily run around Prague. On Monday I'll arrive here towards 3 o'clock in the afternoon. Don't you want to hop over here for a moment?

264   Prague, 14 [*recte* 15] October 1924[1]

I've not yet heard anything so magnificent as the way the *Czech Quartet* played my work.

[...]

I myself am excited and it's already a year since I composed it. I had in mind a poor woman, tormented, beaten, battered to death, as the Russian writer Tolstoy wrote in his work *The Kreutzer Sonata*.[2] They're playing it on Friday [17 October] and again on Monday – and they'll play it throughout the whole world perhaps.

266   Brno, 2–3 November 1924

I wrote to you from Brno, and two cards from Prague – and you as if dumb?

I thought that I'd see you at that Prague chamber concert, in fact I didn't really think so.

It wasn't even so particularly necessary for me to be there. It's said

---

1 This letter was clearly written after the rehearsal with the Czech Quartet on 15 October, hence the corrected date.

2 Tolstoy's novella *The Kreutzer Sonata* (1889) served as the programmatic basis for Janáček's Piano Trio (1908–9), later rewritten as his First String Quartet. Pozdnyshev does not in fact batter his wife to death; his attack on her, discovering her one night with her violinist lover, is with a 'curved Damascus dagger'. Any previous battering was seemingly mental (this is a first-person narrative): frequent arguments between married partners who had fallen out of love during their honeymoon.

to be the most strait-laced audience. They clapped – when every fool would clap; and when they didn't clap – that's when there came through the air something one doesn't hear every day.

On Thursday in Brno I have the première of *The Cunning Little Vixen*.

I won't invite you for that day; all sorts of curious people are coming here and I'll be tormented.

I've been going to the rehearsals all the time; I think there'll be something to hear and see and also think about. Come when there's a repeat performance and when I'll be able to devote myself to you. I haven't paid you back yet for the summer.

It's now three days since I went for the post.[1] Perhaps there'll be a letter from you there. And from Prague too. The Czech Philharmonic, apparently, is giving my big piece for orchestra, *Taras Bulba*, on 9 November.[2] I'm waiting for an invitation to the rehearsal. A second book is coming out here about me.[3] In it I write about everywhere I've roamed throughout the world. I write about Písek, about the flowery clothes of my lady-friend who darted through the square. About the visit to Ševčík.[4]

Even your words will be there: 'why don't they celebrate you for simply being born?'[5]

And what if tomorrow there was nothing from you? What could have happened to you?

I'll finish this letter only tomorrow.

---

1 See Glossary.
2 The concert did indeed take place on 9 November 1924, conducted by Václav Talich.
3 Janáček's 'autobiography': *Leoš Janáček: pohled do života a díla* [Leoš Janáček: a view of the life and works], ed. Adolf Veselý (Fr. Borový: Prague, 1924). The passage he refers to (p.39) is as follows:
    Písek. Why does the gold-bearing Otava hurry so? It is looking for its lost gold.
    Shady forests, clearings through them like little streets.
    The old stone bridge. The floral dress of my lady-friend twinkled in the market.
    In a corner house in the new quarter the violins of the community of Otakar Ševčík chatter like swallows.
4 The violin teacher Otakar Ševčík (1852–1934), after a distinguished career at the Imperial music school in Kharkov (1875–92) and at Prague Conservatory (1892–1906), retired in 1906 to Písek, where he attracted an international colony of outstanding young violinists. Janáček failed to lure him to teach at the Brno Conservatory in 1919 (see Janáček 1990, 60, fn.). Though it is not otherwise mentioned in the correspondence, Janáček must have visited Ševčík during his trip to Písek in June 1924. Another meeting (8 September 1927) is recorded in a group photograph including Ševčík's American pupil Arthur Bennett Lipkin (see Plate 23).
5 An inexact rendition of Kamila Stösslová's letter for his seventieth birthday, see p.49, fn.4.

I mustn't keep back that they've honoured me again with a state prize of Kč 5000.[1]

[...]

Up to here on 2 November.

And 3 November nothing at the post office.

The performance of *Taras Bulba* in Prague provided Janáček with yet another opportunity to invite Stösslová to meet him there: 'Wouldn't you both like to fly off to Prague? I go there on Friday evening [7 November]. On Saturday at 9 I've got a rehearsal in the Obecní dům [Municipal House; see Glossary]; then I'll be free the whole day. Should you come, I'd remain there for the concert as well; otherwise I'd go back to Brno on Sunday morning' (*267: Brno, 5 November 1924). But there was no answer, as is clear from the note that he dropped her from Prague the day after the première of *The Cunning Little Vixen* in Brno.

268   Prague, 7 November 1924

What's happened to you? It seems to me like the mysterious night above the countryside.

You cannot be so silent without a reason.

The celebratory concerts in Prague of Janáček's compositions continued: on 23 November a solo piano, chamber and vocal concert arranged by Janáček's Czech publisher Hudební matice; on 27 November a chamber concert at the Prague Conservatory; and on 8 December a second concert arranged by Hudební matice, this time a large-scale choral and orchestral concert[2] which President Masaryk would attend. It was only with this last concert that Janáček managed to persuade Stösslová to go to Prague.

274   Brno, 4 December 1924

It's nice that you're coming as early as Saturday [6 December].

If only you'd written when the fast train from Písek arrives in Prague! I've got a 9 o'clock rehearsal in the morning in the Obecní dům. I don't know how long it will last.

In any event we'll meet for lunch after 12 at the Obecní dům.

I'm free by the afternoon. I'll arrive in Prague tomorrow, Friday

1 for *Taras Bulba*. State prizes, generally of Kč 5000, were awarded annually on the anniversary of the founding of Czechoslovakia (on 28 October) for specified works or in recognition of artistic services by the Ministry of Education.

2 The full programmes, giving a comprehensive survey of Janáček's non-operatic works, are listed in Janáček 1990, 132–3, fns.

evening at 10. I'll stay at the Karel IV. in Smíchov.

If you want to get a message to me – particularly about where you'll be staying – then write there. [...]

275 Brno, 10 December 1924

So it's all over already! We had a good time, we enjoyed seeing one another. The 'buchta'[1] is taste itself; I'll enjoy it the whole week.

When eating it I'll feel as if I was taking a bite of you.

[...]

I imagine that you've got home safely,[2] that you've already gone on about it all at home.

I'm glad that I could show you off in Prague; you my good Negress.[3]

You've suffered a lot, but nothing will scar a pure soul.

Kamila Stösslová to Leoš Janáček, Písek, 13 December 1924

So here I am back on my old track from which you derailed me for a few beautiful hours. [The concert] was a collision of people minus the train, where so far you've vanquished your enemies. You were standing like the victorious Napoleon. Just take care that they don't take you off to the island of St K[amila]! That would be fun – wouldn't it? [...] Once again I must write to you how beautiful it was. I thank you for that beautiful spiritual experience, except for one thing – that you shouldn't have spoken – but it's happened now. [...]

276 Brno, 15 December 1924

I don't even recognize you from the last letter! So it had such an effect on you in that magnificent hall, in that light, brilliance and sound?

Don't think that it so dazzled me that I would have lost cool common sense. I'd like to go to the Island of St Kamila. What would it look like there? Would there be loose, hot sand?

But I wouldn't want Saint Kamila there, but this chattery one, needled by all the little devils. And faraway, on the sly, I'd gaze at

1 See Glossary.
2 The plural form *dojeli* implies that Stösslová was not alone; presumably David Stössel also went to Prague, a fact corroborated by Janáček's remark (276) that he was not able to speak to Stösslová on her own.
3 See Glossary.

that Kamila, as she was in the Hofman exhibition,[1] but alive, full of blood and high spirits.

I need a heart beat and the gush of blood. Oh how could I compose when I'm dejected. I imagine that your blood certainly boils.

You won't read this again?

Now I'm coming to myself after these two and a half months.

On Saturday 27 December I set off for Hukvaldy; I'll stay there for a week. I'll rid myself of all these visits here.

Write to me in Brno still; don't forget that the post office is shut over the holidays (25, 26 December).

But in fact I didn't even speak alone with you in Prague. [...]

280   Hukvaldy, 2 January 1925

What's happened to you? You've become as silent as a Christmas fish.[2] I don't want to think that the reason for it could be illness. I sit here deserted in the quietness. My sister must think it strange that I gaze out somewhere and keep silent!

In the morning I work, at ten I go for a walk. In the wood I don't meet a living soul. A little snow has fallen; I gaze at animal tracks in the snow. A roebuck trails its legs and its track is as if a toboggan had gone by. The hare is easy to distinguish. But the fox! As if it always kept its paws clenched, a sort of deep hollow in the snow.

In the afternoon I work until four, and then again into the forest. I'm usually overtaken by darkness, and that's when it's very sad in the forest.

I am sad altogether.

In Dresden they will give my *Vixen*[3] and in Venice (Italy), my quartet.[4] It's as if it doesn't affect me. Tomorrow I leave for Brno. I don't even know why I'm becoming so sad, whether because I'm going to Brno or because I'm leaving here.

You ought to have written!

1 An exhibition by the painter and architect Vlastislav Hofman (1884–1964). Hofman was also a stage-designer, at the Vinohrady Theatre and National Theatre in Prague; a year later he designed the sets for the Brno première of *Šárka*.
2 It is Christmas Eve which is the chief Christmas holiday in the Czech lands, and since this is a fast day, fish (traditionally carp) is served.
3 This production did not come off. The German première of *The Cunning Little Vixen* was in Mainz, 1927.
4 At the Third ISCM Festival, September 1925 (see 78).

281   Brno, 7 January 1925

You'll be surprised at the way I'm signing my name today. I was coming from Hukvaldy – where you left me high and dry – and here at some station they were calling out '*Lidové noviny*!'. I bought a copy; I read and it almost fell from my hand! 'The Minister of Education etc has confirmed the choice of Leoš Janáček by the Philosophy Faculty of Masaryk University ...'[1]

The rest you'll see at the end.

My head's full of it.

I'll invite you to the celebrations connected with it; they'll be in Brno between 27 and 30 January.

It's a very pleasant recognition.

I don't write only music, but I also write all sorts of things, really; so something of this they considered valuable.

[...]

What sort of holidays did you have? Evidently a head full of something else since no thought was left over for me there.

[...]

Your wholly devoted   Drph. Leoš Janáček

I sign myself like this for the first time since I know that no-one will see it.

283   Brno, 12 January 1925

What a poetical vein has appeared in you! You've no idea how you've improved; when I look at your first letters and this last one, I don't believe my eyes and ears.

Now even more so when you've got a doctor of philosophy as your teacher, what further might become of you! All the instruction is free to you – except perhaps I'll take a *buchta* or two in return.

[...]

The Vixen will be in Prague on 18 May; I'm sure you'll come to it.

[...]

I'll sign myself as before. I'd rather contract than expand my name.

Keep well, dear merry soul!

Your wholly devoted

Leoš Janáček

1 The Masaryk University of Brno (founded 1919); 'philosophy faculty' is the equivalent of 'arts faculty' in English-speaking countries.

Despite Janáček's confidence, Stösslová did not attend the Prague première of *The Cunning Little Vixen*, a fact that caused the composer evident pain (see 317). Nor did the Stössels attend Janáček's graduation, which took place in the great hall of Brno's Masaryk University on 28 January 1925:

Kamila Stösslová to Leoš Janáček, Písek, 20 January 1925

[...] As for your celebrations in Brno, we won't come since we don't want to disturb your wife's peace.

We'll leave [celebrating] until [you're] here in Písek. As far as your signature's concerned sign as you like.

For me, you'll always remain that old friend from Luhačovice. I have to smile to myself when I remember it all; how I didn't want to speak to you. I don't know whether another man would have had your patience. It's long ago now, everything will slip by for us, and there'll be nothing for us except the bare memory. [...]

285   Brno, 28 January 1925

I have to say thank you for all the telegrams; I'm writing my first thank you for yours.

I was pleased that you remembered [to write] at the right time.

[The ceremony] was dignified and festive beyond imagining.

In those robes and gowns, what a splendid audience, what warm-heartedness.

At some moments it was like being in church.

The speeches about me[1] were so flattering that I don't want to believe them. But they were delivered with such sincerity that they were believed.

I replied as my understanding and heart dictated; many an eye became moist. So the solemn ceremony's all over.

There are only a few doctors of philosophy among composers; there are perhaps only two of us living in the world.[2]

---

1 Janáček was introduced to the faculty and the academic senate in a speech by the dean, Arne Novák (1880–1939). The whole ceremony, including Janáček's spirited response, is transcribed in Janáček 1925.

2 Although Dvořák received doctorates from both Prague and Cambridge, Czech universities were not in the habit of honouring their composers in this way, and Janáček was probably not aware of the proliferation of the custom in Germany and the English-speaking world. So it is not surprising that he may have overlooked the claims of six of the following composers then living: Elgar (Cambridge and Yale), Glazunov (Oxford and Cambridge), Paderewski (Lwów, Yale and Cambridge), Alexander Mackenzie (Edinburgh and Oxford), Sibelius (Yale), Strauss (Heidelberg and Oxford) and Vaughan Williams (Oxford).

I can hold this degree in high esteem but even when I sign myself with it we'll remain together those old friends from Luhačovice. Nothing will change between us. [...]

Your wholly devoted

Drph. Leoš Janáček

And from then on until March 1927, Janáček continued to sign himself with his new title. As Mrs Janáčková reported in her memoirs (p.159), Janáček was suffering from a continual dry cough from the day before the graduation ceremony. It was a week before he fully recovered and got down both to Act 3 of *The Makropulos Affair* and to writing again to Stösslová.

286   Brno, 5 February 1925

I recover quickly. I'm now a merry fellow again and hard at work. I'm already near the end of that 300-year-old beauty.

She's already freezing with horror – and doesn't want to live any longer when she sees how happy we are, we who have such a short life. We look forward to everything, we want to make use of everything – our life's so short.

That part of my opera is moving. I think that I'll be finished with it by Easter.

Is everything turned upside down at your place, then? If you have so much work – you know I'd help you. In fact I'd do everything for you. I peep into the pots when they're cooking, I lay the table when I'm hungry. And you know that I helped you shop – when you paid! [...] I'm buying a part of the forest again. What are those farmers doing selling it? They're probably not doing well. It's an adjoining piece [of land]. [...]

289   Brno, 19 February 1925

[...] I'm in such a depressed mood today. I was present at a rehearsal in the theatre and saw how the conductor there was burrowing like a gimlet into the score – and didn't see the players. That's bad! It sends [the listeners] to sleep.

They wrote from Prague to me that they'll design *The Vixen* in *their* way.[1] The Brno designer got Kč 10,000 for it. So let someone else also help himself.

1 Janáček had been so enthusiastic about Eduard Milén's sets for the Brno production of *The Cunning Little Vixen* that he suggested they be used for the Prague production, but this idea was rejected (see Tyrrell 1992, LB44–5).

I've already booked a room in Luhačovice for the beginning of June.

What will you do in the summer? You aren't thinking of it yet.

When in the next few days I finish my 300-year-old beauty, I fear that I shall – be sad.

The 'finishing' of *The Makropulos Affair*, which Janáček reported in his next letter (*290: Brno, 23 February 1925), was in fact only of a preliminary version; Janáček continued to revise it until the end of the year.[1] In the next few months he was also kept busy in various towns with concerts continuing to celebrate his seventieth birthday, though in the midst of all this he did manage a day trip to Písek on 25 March (*296: Brno, 22 March 1926) before looking in on rehearsals in Prague for *The Cunning Little Vixen*:

297 Prague, 26 March 1925

After six months a contented mind, even if only for a few hours!

My first lines are for you as a memento. I sincerely thank you for your smiles, your friendly words and all the rich hospitality.

If only I could repay you as I'd like!

Greet your mother and your sister-in-law.[2] Did you buy much at the market?

The journey was fine – all the time as if I was in Písek with you!

298 Brno, 29 March 1925

So you're now perhaps in a whirling dance at the ball.

And I again among a stack of written-on paper.

I got on well in Prague; they already know *The Vixen* well.

The designs of the painter Mr Josef Čapek[3] will be very effective. I'd like us to be merry in Prague.

I've already booked a box for you.

I leave Brno for Hukvaldy at 5 in the morning on Tuesday 14 April. [...]

It would certainly please my wife if you'd personally invite her to the concert in Písek.

So write back to me still. Are you well?

I'm frightened that with your cold you didn't even go. [...]

1 See Tyrrell 1992, VM19–25.
2 Emma Neumannová (1896–1940s), wife of Kamila's brother Karel (see p.44, fn.1.).
3 Josef Čapek (1887–1945), painter and stage-designer, brother of the writer Karel Čapek. Josef Čapek also designed the Prague production of *The Makropulos Affair* (1928) and the Brno production of *The Excursion of Mr Brouček to the Moon* (1926).

Thus Janáček began making plans for future meetings with Mrs Stösslová. He took for granted that she would go to Prague for the première there of *The Cunning Little Vixen* in May. Before that there would be the regional celebratory concert that concerned him most – in Stösslová's home town of Písek, which took place after many delays on 2 May 1925. The Hukvaldy trip was cut short because of 'the continual rain' but did at least give Janáček the chance to compose his Concertino for piano and chamber instruments: 'I've composed a piano concerto – "Spring".[1] There's a cricket, midges, a roebuck – a sharp torrent – yes, and man,'[2] as he reported in a brief card (*302: Hukvaldy, 23 April 1925). By late April, however, Mrs Janáčková had changed her mind about going to Písek:

303   Brno, 27 April 1925

First and foremost I thank you respectfully on behalf of myself and my wife for the invitation.

It's too bad that it's not a week later, then Zdenka would come with me and go immediately to Prague.

The ways things are there's still a big time gap, which would cost a lot of money for two people.

I'll go from Písek straight to Prague to the stage rehearsals for *The Vixen* and still return – whether it's good or bad there – from Prague to Brno.

You have a box reserved for the première, which is on 18 May. After that we'll return via Písek to Brno. I hope it will already be sunny weather!

And now about Písek.

It's difficult for me to come if I don't have an invitation from the organizers. I don't need a concert to come on *your* invitation.

If I stop in Písek it's because of you.

To hear the rehearsal will be enough for me; and were I to remain for the concert *let it be a simple concert without any celebration of me personally*. I earnestly ask for that and you'll surely carry that through with the organizers.

I'm going to be a trouble again; but you know what I like eating most?

A bit of beef
with sauce.

1 A trial title written in pencil on the verso of p.2 of the fourth movement of Janáček's autograph begins 'Spring/Suite/for piano (concerto)/' but both 'Spring' and 'Suite' were discarded on the final title page (Štědroň 1973, 334).
2 Two years later, when he wrote a whimsical introduction for the German periodical *Pult und Taktstock*, the selection of animals had changed.

So that, and don't do anything else – perhaps a little bit of sweet with it.

In return we'll eat together in Prague on 18 May.

I'll arrive at 3 o'clock by the slow train on Friday (1 May). I think that the rehearsal will be that day. You didn't write about it. So au revoir!

The Písek concert duly took place on Saturday 2 May in the local *Sokol* hall with the composer present. The programme included Janáček's Violin Sonata, *The Diary of One who Disappeared* and the *Lachian Dances* conducted by a local musician, Cyril Vymetal (see Glossary). Janáček thanked his hostess with two brief notes from Prague (*304–5: 4–5 May 1925), where he stayed for rehearsals of *The Cunning Little Vixen*.

306 Prague, 6 May 1925

I had lots of work again yesterday in the theatre! From 9 in the morning to 4 in the afternoon. But it will be nice; and also something to laugh at.

However, my doctor has now most firmly ordered me to unharness myself from work if I don't want to get seriously ill!

I gave him my promise. However he's sending me to Mariánské Lázně.

So I'm going there, although that German-speaking region is not congenial to me.

Your brother[1] will probably know the town. Could he inquire there about decent lodgings for me?

I'd be there for about three weeks from 4 June. Today I go to Brno and on Monday [11 May] I'll again be in Prague.

Then I'll write in more detail to you so that we can see each other at the première.

307 Brno, 7 May 1925

I'll soon be writing to you almost every day!

The Cunning Little Vixen grows remarkably at the Prague National Theatre. In a week her fur-coat will already be like red gold.

It will be something to laugh at. They perform it excellently.

But I had to get away from Prague: those rehearsals within the

1 Emil Neumann, see p.44, fn.1, whom Janáček had first met in Brno in February 1920 (*160: 23 February 1920).

[67]

gloomy walls of the theatre from morning to late afternoon, day after day, would have killed me as I'm exhausted already. And outside the sun shone and the warmth spread around. [...]

308   Brno, 9 May 1925

[...] On Monday [11 May] I'll already be in Prague. It will be fine. On Sunday 17 May perhaps we'll make an expedition to *Karlův Týn* [i.e. the castle of Karlštejn].[1] It's on the railway line from you.

Wouldn't both of you also like to be there then? If the weather's fine.

The première's on Monday 18 May. We'll lunch together at the Obecní dům, then to the theatre and after the theatre there'll be a merry company.

So write to me at the *hotel-pension*
        Karel IV., Smíchov.

Did you write to your brother to look out for somewhere for me to stay in Mariánské Lázně? Last year I couldn't get a room there.

On Monday 11 May 1925 Janáček arrived in Prague and from there issued a series of insistent notes about his plans for the Stössels in the city and demanding immediate answers, but five days later he still had not heard from her:

312   Prague, 16 May 1925

Why are you doing this to me? Have I done something to you?

Or has Zdenka? Or are you afraid we'd come on to you after Prague? What sort of reason can it be that you don't write openly? I can't understand it. For we'd love to see you here. And believe me, I'd know whom I should respect.

I'll wait for you and your husband on Monday [18 May]. Or write the truth to me as befits friends.

Janáček duly waited for the Stössels on Monday morning at the station (317); only David Stössel turned up with a message to say that his wife was ill (*315: Brno, 24 May 1925). Janáček wrote a measured letter of regret (*313; Prague, 18 May 1925), which Zdenka signed as well, confining his disappointment to the single comment that 'the professor here would have cured you in a moment'. But in the letters that followed, describing the

---

1 See Glossary.

première, he found it difficult to contain his bitterness, even declining an invitation to visit Stösslová in Písek:

314   Brno, 21 May 1925

I now see that you're the sort of domestic cat that one has to take away somewhere in a sack – and still it runs home. That very Monday was the sort of day where we could have had a good lunch, walked a bit, gone to hear *The Vixen* and sat around in the evening.

Of course the other days were [sheer] Babel; no-one went home before dawn; foreign people from the ends of the earth always around;[1] tortured by music, baked by the sun – so that in the afternoon one collapsed on to a couch like a wooden log.

They would have been unbearable for you. In addition to all that, [I got] nerve-, or the devil knows what sort of, pains in my back – so that I'm just waiting for 3 June when I leave for Luhačovice. They say that when someone doesn't want to go it won't help him; that would have been the case with Mariánské Lázně. [...]

They performed my *Vixen* but not as I wished.

The whole foreign company – up to 200 people – went by boat from Prague to Závist.[2] That was fun.

[...]

So I think that you're well now; I know it wasn't that bad...

But your husband could at least have taken a look inside the theatre. I invited him, but he didn't want to.

I was looking forward to it for months – and it didn't turn out as I'd imagined it. One thing is certain; you *won't convince* anyone through art. It's like punching an eiderdown: it moves aside. People clap everything. But surely there's just one truth in music and not everyone has it; everyone wants to have 'his own' truth. [...]

Instead of going to Prague for Janáček's première, Stösslová invited the Janáčeks to Písek. Janáček emphatically declined the invitation (*315: Brno, 24 May 1925), listing his reasons, though it is clear from his next letter that the chief, unstated, reason was sheer pique. The letter, too, provides a clear indication of the reason for all of Janáček's invitations to Stösslová to participate in premières: not just to see her, but for her to see that the world valued him.

1 *The Cunning Little Vixen* was given in Prague during the Third ISCM Festival.
2 This memorable occasion captured the few surviving seconds of Janáček on moving film (greeting one of his guests, Mrs Marie Calma-Veselá).

[69]

I go for post daily, always with the thought: 'will there be a letter from you?' And in vain.

And why are you angry with me? I told you that if you won't come to Prague I won't go to Písek. Why should I leave it only to you to play host continually, to give you work and anxiety in the whole house – and not be able to pay you back at least a little?

I wanted to get up a joyful banquet for you in the Obecní dům. It should also have been an expression of all the pleasures which I've experienced in Prague. Those Prague days were, after all, the peak of recognition of all my life's work! And I wanted you to be present. You who for almost ten years[1] have been my comfort in the most painful moments of life. That's how I imagined it and that's how it was all organized. I had two boxes in the theatre, nos.6 and 7 on the left – and then I had to put unknown people there! I run off to the station; your husband gets out and I look for you – and you weren't there. Your husband must have seen the disappointment on my face and also in my voice.

I'm just sorry that I didn't at least make him come to the theatre. Didn't he have a dark suit packed in the case? I should perhaps have put more pressure on him. I regret it now. Were you really ill? Zdenka really got a rash on both legs; a rash which they've been treating in Brno with radium for months now. She couldn't travel;[2] just home, home. As for me, I've already written to you that I was half dead with tiredness. In Brno my nerve pains increased – until today, when they were unbearable and I ran off to the doctor. According to him I'm healthy for a thousand years! So he returned me my appetite for work and joy in life. I'll leave then on Wednesday 3 June for Luhačovice. And if I don't get a letter from you, I'll set off some day and bang on your door at night so much that you'll get a fright.

But rather come to Luhačovice to drink the healthy water and acidify the blood. We'll celebrate ten years.

I'll certainly be there only with you; in my thoughts I'll lead you, I'll sit beside you and call out words which I say so many times when I see you.

So answer me now and don't make me sad. It shortens life and you'd have that on your conscience.

---

1 Janáček had in fact known Mrs Stösslová for almost eight years by the time of writing (he invariably got the number wrong).
2 At least not to Písek; she got to Prague for the première.

Kamila Stösslová to Leoš Janáček, Písek, 1 June 1925

I've received your letters where I was really cross with you until today, because I definitely expected you and your wife. [...] There was nothing for it but to eat all the food myself. [...] The photographs have come out very well, you look like King Herod there, lacking only a crown but you must have had it in your pocket. [...]

318   Luhačovice, 3 June 1925

Your letter greeted me here. That's a good sign.

But you know how to be angry for a long while; I can't manage that.

At least you're convinced that it couldn't have been otherwise.

I'll write to Zdenka about all that you prepared.

But you were at fault; I'd have made you well in Prague in a trice.

These will be my sacred walks, there where we used to sit.

God, nine years ago![1]

Is it true? Why didn't time stand still. I'd chain it up.

Oh dear Mrs Kamila, those were beautiful times.

And when at Kunovice you went off by the right path, and I the left![2] But you should have stayed in Přerov, it wouldn't have been so far to you. I want to rest here now. To forget about everything except you.

Zdenka and I have made up after nine years.[3]

That's why she's a different person now, not looking gloomily at everything.

She remembered how you took down off the wall the photograph of that old witch from Prague.[4]

She [i.e. Horvátová] was all over me again in Prague at the theatre; it's said that she's divorced.

I've signed a contract with Brno [Theatre] for a year; they'll give my *Šárka* and *The Excursion of Mr Brouček to the Moon*.[5] So I thank you for your letter and please write back at once.

1 Now in Luhačovice, Janáček recalls his first meeting with Mrs Stösslová, eight (not nine) years ago.
2 At Kunovice Mrs Stösslová would have picked up the train to Přerov; Janáček's left path would have taken him back to Brno.
3 In 1917 the Janáčeks were 'divorced' though they continued to live together (see Appendix 2). The reconciliation with Zdenka took place, according to her memoirs, during their stay in Prague for *The Cunning Little Vixen*.
4 A reference to the incident described in Zdenka's memoirs (see above, p.8).
5 *Šárka* was given in Brno on 11 November 1925; *The Excursion of Mr Brouček to the Moon* on 15 June 1926.

320 Luhačovice, 6 June 1925

So I went above the 'búda'[1] where, like an exhausted bird who doesn't yet know how to fly, you sat down on the grass.

I addressed you: 'You must be a Jewess!' You replied: 'How do you know?'

And the little fir trees were [then] so low: and today what trees they are now! It's a forest already and then they were little Christmas trees. So this is how everything around us is changing and will change: and I felt so sad about it.

I went to the 'búda' for supper; alone at the table. I waited until the moon came out: [I thought] you'll surely see it too. My gazing at it, and perhaps yours: what a gigantic bridge and two people build it through the moon!

As you see: I'm pining. If I hadn't taken urgent work with me,[2] I wouldn't have lasted out here, like last year. [...]

324 Luhačovice, 11 June 1925

You think that I didn't suffer? By what chance I don't know she [Zdenka] read one of your letters.[3] You wrote in it that you know how I suffer but that you'll always remain a proper, honourable wife to your husband.

She didn't suspect you, but it probably upset her that you're spiritually nearer to me than she is.

And I wanted and needed to talk well and gladly about you, and talk often. For you deserve it!

That's the reason why we came to an eventual reconciliation in Prague! For in reality we were divorced.[4] Our friendship, mine towards you, as you well know, is deep. I have need of it to live contentedly, to live happily. That's why we'll all understand one another [eventually]. I sent your letter to Zdenka in Hukvaldy. It's a nice expression of you. [...]

1 The Slovácká búda [Moravian Slovak Den], a wine bar built in 1906 after the design by Dušan Jurkovič in imitation of local models and often used for the singing of Moravian and Slovak folksongs.
2 Probably the revision of Act 2 of *The Makropulos Affair*.
3 Perhaps that of 9 July 1924.
4 See p.71, fn.3.

Some well-known lady sent the painter Mr Kopřiva[1] to me here to paint me. Just imagine here, in the spa, it's already the fourth day I'm sitting for him from 2 to 4.30!

A communicative man, he tells me his life history: nothing but hunger, need, sickness, suffering! Better to tell you all the rest than to write.

My likeness is very good; but the main thing is my right hand with your ring for luck! When I noticed it it made me feel better towards him.

And some months he doesn't make a penny!

I'm merrier now; I leave in a week. But I've also recuperated.

In Prague I was already just dragging myself along.

From my experience, I don't believe I'll see you here.

Thank your brother for me.[2] Perhaps in a year's time I'll ask him again.

Here everyone knows me – and it's boring; what would it be like [i.e. in Mariánské Lázně], where there's not even a familiar face!

Is your Ota alright again?

I think that tomorrow at least a card will come from you.

And I remember when I lived opposite you in Žofín,[3] how I watched until you came out barefoot on the balcony with your hair undone like a black mane.

And in the evening when the lights went out in your house. And I watched until you eventually emerged from the house; to the gardener for cucumbers and further on the right side of the river right up to the market – for meat. And you bought pears and we ate them sitting there on the bench. Oh, how many trivial things like this there were. But it wasn't boring! Everything pleased one – and now nothing. Just like in the theatre when the curtain's down.

Keep well!

329   Brno, 7–9 [recte 7–8] July 1925

You must have very special and dear guests when you cannot get round to answering my letters.

---

1 In her letter to Janáček of 8 June 1925 (BmJA, B 1050) Zdeňka Blatná of Náměště recommended the painter Emil Stanislav Kopřiva (1885–1938). His large oil painting of Janáček is now owned by BmJA.
2 See 306 and 308.
3 The *pension* in Luhačovice in which the Stössels stayed in 1917.

I'm writing, but really for myself, to relieve the pressure on my mind.

I'm leaving again. But with pleasure? God forbid. I saw a fallow deer in the forest, in the game park. He was left from the whole herd which they brought here from somewhere or other. He also wandered, he didn't touch the grass. In the densest bush, the most inaccessible, there he pushed through. He was sad, he ran and ran – until his end. It's a little bit similar to my life. I run from place to place because I can't be where it would be nice for me.

Luhačovice, Hukvaldy. To Venice, along the Danube; but with me everywhere will simply be mourning.

Day after day I take off your ring and put it on – and think of you all the while.

A word or two, you near me; what is it that comes with you, what glows from you so that all this sadness falls from me?

Why is the mere sight of you enough for me not to look elsewhere for contentment?

You ought to have come to Prague then.

I left Luhačovice as I came – and I think for the last time. Nothing there interested me. I'm waiting for your letter. Perhaps it will distract me, perhaps raise a contented smile. I won't send off this letter – until yours comes.

7 July 1925

So some have the power to attract, and others, involuntarily, the power to repel.

Tomorrow I go to Hukvaldy u Příbora.

9 [*recte* 8] July 1925

330 Brno, 9 July 1925, evening

And you know why for fourteen days I floundered around at home like a butterfly with a broken wing?

This evening I remarked that you aren't writing and who knows whether anything will come of the Turkish carpets.[1] And then Zdenka said that you had written to her, and that she had already written back to you.

And at once I was cheerful. And I'll go off to Hukvaldy more cheerfully.

I'll wait there working [to see] whether my supposed muscle pains

---

1 See Glossary: 'carpets'.

stop. If not, I'll still look out either for Mariánské Lázně or Jáchymov.

And I'll give Venice a miss. That would have probably been in the middle of August.[1]

At the beginning of September I'll be needed in Brno. I have the première here of my first opera *Šárka*.

But I'd see you from Mariánské Lázně or Jáchymov! So now don't pamper your guests so much, and if you'll be making the journey to Přerov, hop over still further to Hukvaldy.

I'll put a room at your disposal.

[...]

At Hukvaldy I want to 'clean up' Act 2 of that cold one.[2]

I've written a small concerto for piano;[3] perhaps it will be played often.

You see, this is now a more cheerful letter than yesterday's one.

331   Hukvaldy, 12 July 1925

[...] Your letter cheered me.

I'm sorry that you're sickly so often. But you can't be in a more healthy little nest than you are!

With the fatty foods [you eat] you must wash out your body once a year.

You're as round as a little apple ripe for biting into, but fat prevents the blood from flowing and the creation of blood. That's why your feet ache.

If I were at your place I'd order 'comfortable shoes on, into the forests, physical exercise, bathing, massage!'

And so dear Mrs Kamilka simply sticks by the oven!

I'll stay here perhaps a month. I work easily here; as I've already written to you, I want to have Act 2 of 'that cold one' cleaned up, so as not to have do it in Brno.

[...]

Zdenka will have her sixtieth birthday on the 30th of this month.[4]

And on the 18th of this month you have the 'feast' [i.e. name-day] of Kamila. I wish you as merry that day as I'd wish to be myself. [...]

1 Janáček got the month wrong: in the end he did attend the ISCM Festival in Venice, in early September.
2 i.e. of *The Makropulos Affair*.
3 See p.66, fn.1.
4 Janáček sent her Kč 1000.

[75]

[...] Today was the first beautiful day here. I went out into the forest; we've put a bench at the very top of the hill. The view from there is indescribable! The sun walks round my cottage during the day. It goes down over the copse. Today it was red and the forest seemed as if it were on fire. One day you must see it here!

Zdenka wrote to me that you've invited her. She'll surely invite you also and then we'll [all] come here.

In the second half of August I'm going off to the quartet[1] which is to play my work in Venice. They are near you there in their summer lodgings. Then we'd hop over to you.

I work in the morning; at noon I wait for the post and in the afternoon I defend my forest. I planted it with young saplings and – a gang of ruffians drives goats on to it to graze there. That makes me angry!

We're rearing a delightful little pig here. He has it good here, he gets milk, vegetable dumplings. He's already like a chubby white cherub.

So I have at least a diversion here. In Brno I was almost at my wits' end.

Write soon.

It was another twelve days before Janáček eventually heard from Stösslová. By that time he had finished his revision of Act 2 of *The Makropulos Affair* (*336: Hukvaldy, 27 July 1927) and was still debating whether to go to Venice to hear his First Quartet played at the ISCM Festival there. Three days later he had unexpectedly begun composing his *Nursery Rhymes* ('something for laughter'), and quoted the text of what was to become no.17 ('Vašek, pašek'): 'Don't you know any texts like that?' (*337: Hukvaldy, 30 July 1925). By early August he was ready to leave:

339 Hukvaldy, 5 August 1925

I'm packing now. I throw one thing after the other into the basket. However they won't bite one another. Have I had a rest or not? I don't even know. One thing's certain, that I was a recluse here.

I was wandering through my forest until evening. It gets dark; I go along the path, lost in thought. Then suddenly, as if someone cut into living bone. Then again, again. I stopped and held my breath. Trespassing in the forest. Someone's stealing a tree. I, [armed] only with a

1 Zik Quartet.

little stick. How can I dare to go after thieves with axes! I bided my time on the edge of the forest. After a while two men emerge from the forest. One carried a saw. I say: what are you doing with a saw in the forest? The older one: We're going from Sobotík[1] to Rychaltice. I reply: is this the shortest way?

They were taken aback and shrank away from me. I stared after them until they disappeared.

The incident has kept me awake.

Today, 5 August, I was already in the forest at six in the morning. I looked for the spruce which they'd chosen. Which one? I found pine and fir loppings. A freshly cut down tree nowhere. They know how to smear the trunk with earth so that it wouldn't strike the eyes.

So you see my work!

But I've also looked through the symphony *The Danube* here. In it there'll be the interesting incident of Lola. At first – and then she trembles with cold and hunger before she jumps into the Danube.[2]

[...]

NB my little pig grows happily. When I say 'lie down' to him, he immediately lies down. He wants me to scratch him. He closes his eyes with pleasure and snorts

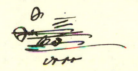

Sadly Janáček's examination of *The Danube* came to nothing. Even a request from the Prague conductor Otakar Ostrčil a year later (16 August 1926) did not give him sufficient impetus to complete the work and it remained one of the pieces of unfinished business on his desk at the end of his life. Instead he began looking more favourably at the trip to Venice. Part of the attraction was his thought that the Stössels might want to come too, and his next letter was taken up commenting on an application form for concerts and accommodation that he enclosed (*340: Brno, 10 August 1925). As usual Stösslová did not answer, and as usual Janáček bombarded her with demands for a reply. By 26 August 1925 he had resolved to go, having devised a route that would take in an overnight stop at Písek on the way on 31 August (*342: Brno, 26 August 1925). Three days later the trip was off – the Ministry was not prepared to pay:

1 Jan Sobotík, mayor of Hukvaldy.
2 One of the many sources of inspiration for *The Danube* was Alexander Insarov's poem *Lola*, about a prostitute fallen on hard times. It was Janáček's idea that Lola ended her life by jumping into the Danube.

I was looking forward not to Venice, not to that concert, but to seeing you before it.

Then this morning they [the other members of the Czech contingent to the ISCM Festival] inform me by express post that they're travelling from Prague already on Monday 31 August.

For a whole year now, it was 'I'm going, I'm not going' the whole time and at the last moment my happiness is spoilt.

So I won't go to Venice. Regardless of the fact the others are having their journey paid, although they really have nothing to do there. After all, it's my work that's being played, I perhaps am carrying the honour of the Czech name there into foreign parts (or perhaps I'm not), the Government has not seen fit to sweeten it for me as for the others – I don't want to name names. [...]

Later that day, Janáček had changed his mind again and wrote (*344) saying that he could not get out of it, and confirmed his original arrangements (he ended up travelling separately from the rest of the Czech delegation). Since Zdenka was accompanying her husband to Venice, she also had to stay in Písek with the Stössels, a visit recorded in a group photograph of the two couples, Kamila earnest and elegant in her fox-fur stole, and Zdenka looking distinctly awkward in her travelling suit and clutching her handbag and umbrella (see Plate 24). Cards signed by both the Janáčeks were sent to Písek along the way from Trieste (*345: 3 September 1925) and from Venice (*346: 4 September 1925) and Janáček added one of his own, writing from a picture gallery where he was admiring 'originals of Bellini, Veronese, Titian' and reported the success of his string quartet: 'My quartet will go from here to Rome, Paris, London. I won!' (*347: Venice, 7 September 1925). A more detailed report had to wait until his return to Brno:

348 [undated, postmarked Brno, 15 September 1925]

It's not possible to describe this journey of ours all at once.

Just think, we couldn't find accommodation at night in Trieste! If some servant hadn't taken pity on us and offered us her room then [there would have been] nothing for it but to spend the night on the street. She knew Czech; she had learnt it many years ago from our soldiers when they were still there.

In Venice we had a room already booked; again no-one came [to take] us to the concert, and to make one's way at night in that town when hungry is out of the question. So we sat in the room and the next day were without food. Had it not been for your *buchta*! And I remembered your smoked meat!

The next day all was explained, with map in hand I found my way in the town, which instead of pavements has only the deep blue sea. Little streets [so narrow] that if you put your arms out you'll touch the houses on both sides. Just high bridges, only gondolas and boats.

We made ourselves understood only through sign language and ordered meals for the whole day. Italian food! You'll eat anything out of hunger.

Satisfied at last, we looked on the beauty of the town. The most beautiful on earth. Just palaces, white marble, pictures of the old masters, St Mark's Square, St Mark's Cathedral, the Doge's Palace.

One has to see it, it's no good talking about it!

Then we were ferried about or walked criss-cross through the town and came to like it there. Good, willing people these Italians. The journey home was the most direct and not such a zigzag and unnecessarily long. That's enough for today.

Abroad fit as a fiddle, the very first day home I catch a chill and irritate my kidneys.

On Monday of next week [21 September] we go to Hukvaldy for fruit. We'll stay there a week.

And then quietly sit at home for a while.

Nothing for myself but there's a present waiting at my place for you and your boys. You won't be able to carry yours; the boys can stick theirs into their pockets.

I'd like to be well again already.

I greet you and thank you kindly for your hospitality. [...]

Janáček's illness, his most serious at this time, turned out to be shingles and plagued him for many weeks. Recovery was slow:

352 Brno, 22 October 1925

Six weeks now of this burning pain! The wounds are healed, but towards evening it's as if I were being stabbed with pins. And on 11 November they're giving my opera *Šárka* here and in the town theatre unveiling a bronze bust of me by Štursa![1]

I'm not keen to be present; this is usually done when someone's dead.

1 Jan Štursa (1880–1925), a prominent Czech sculptor. Janáček's bust was unveiled on 24 January 1926 (see 365); a copy presides on the balcony of the former Organ School, now the Music History Department of the Moravian Regional Museum.

[...]

I'm indescribably out of sorts. I can't bear sitting, walking even less so, and in bed I keep turning like a sheep on a spit.

353 Prague, 28 October 1925

The pains were no longer bearable! I got on to a train and went to Prague. Dr Libenský himself declared that they're cruel – and gave me relief from them and advice so that there'll soon be an end to them. To take a car now and drive to you – my health would be wholly restored at once. But I've got rehearsals now in Brno for *Šárka* and the Piano Concertino. I'm waiting for you to knock on our door on 11 November.[1]

354 Brno, 6 November 1925

[...] My health has begun to improve. But to suffer for eight weeks! Recognition has poured on to me: the state's first prize of Kč 10,000,[2] receipts for compositions Kč 6000 and many other sources of income! And some time ago I broke an ear off a silver [cup?], to have something to spend!

So on Wednesday there's the première of *Šárka*. It will be nice. Will you knock on our door?

You could both sleep in the office,[3] or we could go there, and you in the house.

And wrap yourselves into those long-awaited carpets, so you don't get cold on the journey. That little animal which I prepared for you from Venice has already produced young and the souvenirs for your children are getting rusty.[4]

If you've got a pain in your ear, that can't be an inflammation of the middle ear. That would be unbearable. You've got it from having the window and the door opposite always open in the kitchen!

Heat up a little piece of walnut over a candle, wrap it in cotton wool and put into your ear. It will give you relief.

[...]

1 i.e. Janáček was hoping that the Stössels would come to the première of *Šárka*.
2 for *The Cunning Little Vixen* (see also p.59, fn.1).
3 See p.7, fn.2.
4 See 348. Janáček ended up sending the presents on 5 December (357), from which it is clear that the Stössel boys both got penknives; Stösslová seems to have got some rather heavy ornament featuring an animal and its young.

And I ask you, go to that photographer and get him to send, with his bill, all the photographs, especially that one where we're together!

Don't forget![1]

On 9 November 1925 (*355) Janáček and his wife sent a Venetian postcard of a gondola – a little boat to bring the Stössels to the première of *Šárka* on 11 November or, if not, then to the repeat performance on Sunday 15 November. As usual he was disappointed:

356   Brno, 23 November 1925

I sent a little boat for you to come here – but all in vain.

It went off peacefully; good work of forty years ago! [...]

357   Brno, 5 December 1925

I can't explain to myself why you don't let me have news of yourself?

I wait daily – and daily in vain!

I know now that Brno is a long trip for you. You wouldn't wait for the souvenirs from Venice; so we'll send them to you on Monday by post.

The little animals are yours; give the little knives as presents to each of your boys. Make sure they don't cut themselves when they sharpen pencils. Let 'Santa Claus' give a bit more to them [this year].

I wish you a bountiful Christmas. After Boxing Day I'll probably go to Hukvaldy. I'm finished with *The Makropulos Affair*. Poor 300-year-old beauty! People thought she was a thief, a liar, an unfeeling animal. 'Beast', 'canaille' they called her, they wanted to strangle her – and her fault? That she had to live too long.

I was sorry for her. Three years of work at an end. What now?

The end of Janáček's work on *The Makropulos Affair* brought to a close the trio of operas that he had been engaged on virtually continuously since January 1920, and it was to be more than a year before he embarked on his last opera, *From the House of the Dead*. But 'What now?' was answered in a most resounding fashion during 1926 with the composition of the

1 Janáček is referring to the photographs taken during his trip with Zdenka to Písek on the way to Venice (see p.78).

[81]

Sinfonietta, the Glagolitic Mass and the Piano Capriccio, and a trip to England. He also continued to be concerned about the fate of his first opera, *Šárka*.

358   Brno, 15 December 1925

[...] *Šárka* will now be printed. At least it can't be silenced. They came here from the Prague National Theatre to listen to it, but say nothing about it! They silence all my things there: *Jenůfa, Káťa Kabanová, The Vixen*!

I no longer have any stomach for them to play something of mine there.

I'll be in Prague perhaps in February; my Piano Concertino should be played there. [...]

The Concertino was indeed played in Prague on 20 February, four days after its highly successful première in Brno, but Janáček's optimism over *Šárka* was not justified – after his death, plans for the long-delayed printing of the vocal score were quietly shelved by Universal Edition. Following the new warmth between the Janáčeks, Zdenka Janáčková frequently added her signature to cards which Janáček sent the Stössels:

359   Brno, 24 December 1925

We think that you've got a tree in 'my' room, underneath it so many gifts that one can't walk on the carpets – so that they become unnecessary. A table with so much food that one forgets to eat but at the same time doesn't remember those who are far away! A happy new year from us to you all.

  Drph. Leoš Janáček
  Zdenka Janáčková

Straight after Christmas Janáček went off to Hukvaldy as announced. And once again the theme of how Kamila Stösslová would one day visit Hukvaldy was elaborated in Janáček's letter to her from there:

360   Hukvaldy, 29 December 1925

So I'm here again in this beautiful countryside.

  We'd go through the game park, fallow deer to left and right – beautiful level paths for two hours!

  And we'd go along the little path to the bathing place and to the

[82]

river Ondřejnice; a soft, gritted path and water splashing, and in it rare fish.

And we'd go along the white road to Měrkovice, and the three pretty peaks of Ondřejník, twice as high as the Písek hills, would be surprised to see us. And we'd go into my forest; and from the summit, the view of half the world of Valašsko and Lašsko!

And I have a little bench there; we'd sit on it and laugh merrily as only you know how, and as I well understand! Well, I know that one day that walk will still come true!

I've repaired my cottage; it had 'dropsy'. It cost Kč 650, but I've got dry cellars.[1]

The rooms would be in good shape if I had those promised carpets.

But Mrs Kamila is as silent as the grave! If at least she said, I haven't got them, don't wait. But it's neither one thing nor the other.

I'll stay here until Tuesday (4 [*recte* 5] January 1926). I'm waiting for lots of news; it could be good.

And if Mrs Kamila would sit down

immediately

and *immediately*

write back, then I'll have the nicest news of all! [...]

A new production of *Jenůfa* at the National Theatre in Prague under Ostrčil opened on 12 January. This provided another opportunity for a meeting, and although Stösslová still had not written, Janáček wrote to her twice from Prague (*361–2: 8–9 January 1926), the first telling her a box was reserved for her, the second giving her more details and declaring that since she could not trouble even to reply he would not come to Písek as he had planned. Anger at her lack of response, and anger at the news that the National Theatre would not be performing *Šárka* contrived to send Janáček back to Brno in a huff, deliberately not staying for the première of the new production and thus permanently straining his hitherto excellent relationship with the head of opera in Prague, Otakar Ostrčil.

363   Brno, 12 January 1926

I was waiting in Hukvaldy for a card from you, also in Brno, also in Prague – well, in vain.

Influenced by this saddened state, I acted harshly in Prague.

1 The project for eliminating damp from Janáček's cellars was undertaken by workmen from Hukvaldy under the direction of engineer František Navrátil (see Janáček 1990, 170).

On Friday [8 January] the meeting there was from 9 in the morning to 5.30 in the afternoon; I was chairman, so I had more than enough of it.[1]

On Saturday I learnt that I'll probably not be represented at the musical festivities in Zürich (Switzerland).[2] It didn't upset me much, and I looked forward to the fact that you'd be coming to the theatre at my invitation – they're giving my *Jenůfa* there – they invited me to it specially. No news from you. I go into the theatre.

I learn there that they've refused to give my *Šárka*.[3]

And so I turned round – and back to Brno! I wrote to you that box no.3 was prepared for you. Well, I know that you'll certainly not be there today.

In addition I sent my niece there so it wouldn't be empty.

I wanted to go home via Písek – by car to Písek; the man was asking Kč 800 [for the journey]. And when you didn't reply, I got into a train and went to Brno. Today Zdenka showed me your letter about those carpets. Thank you, I'll enjoy walking over those on which you've trotted.

[...]

Forgive me that I wrote so irritably in that last card, and come to us soon. Zdenka has already invited you.

365   Brno, 29 January 1926

[...] They've erected my metal bust[4] in the town theatre.

I addressed myself; except that a bust like that suggests that it's done for the future – when the living one will be no more. It saddened me.

How wrong can one be about someone! I about Mr Ostrčil, whom you once sat next to. I considered him one of the most decent of men – and now! It's unpleasant to be caught lying.

In February about the 19th to the 21st they'll be giving some things

1 The meeting would appear to be that of the Institute for Folksong in Czechoslovakia (see Glossary: 'Moravian Love Songs').
2 The Fourth ISCM Festival, 18–23 June 1926.
3 'Decided not to apply to stage it' would be a more accurate way of describing this action: the opera was never formally submitted to Prague, and so was never formally 'refused', as Otakar Ostrčil wrote in his long letter to Janáček on the subject (see Tyrrell 1992, SR37–41).
4 See p.79, fn.1.

of mine in Prague: the Czech Philharmonic my *Lachian Dances*,[1] Ilona Kurzová my Piano Concertino.[2]

So get ready for it. [...]

371   Brno, 24 February 1926

We got back dead tired, but content.

I've never experienced so much honour (although it will always be just straw) in Prague. But among the audience there was also sincere pleasure from my dances. Some of the pieces were played at that time in Písek;[3] of course here in Prague it was an outstanding orchestra.

People waved scarves, kept on calling for an encore – until the last dance had to be encored. And that's unheard of in Philharmonic concerts!

Well, it's over and now I must relax a bit to be at full strength for this trip to London.[4] Just as I got up my strength for Saturday and Sunday by hopping over to you in Písek.[5]

[...]

On Tuesday we waited for your 'lord and master'.[6] Silver, glass, porcelain on the table.

Soup, beef as soft as gingerbread, tomato sauce, mushrooms, beetroot, gherkins, and a dessert with peaches, black coffee – and no-one came from Písek!

And not again today. [...]

1 The Brno theatre conductor František Neumann (1874–1929) conducted the Czech Philharmonic on 21 February in a concert including Janáček's early *Lachian Dances* (c1893), and works by Neumann, Jaroslav Kvapil and Janáček's pupil Osvald Chlubna.
2 Ilona Štěpánová-Kurzová (1899–1975) played the Piano Concertino in Prague on 20 February 1926; the programme was completed with chamber pieces by Miroslav Krejčí and Jaroslav Řídký.
3 The *Lachian Dances* were played at the Písek concert of Janáček's works on 2 May 1925.
4 See 378ff.
5 This casual reference is to a brief trip to Písek proposed on 14 February 1926 (*368) for 'Thursday' if there were no rehearsals in Prague that day. In fact both Janáčeks arrived in Prague on Thursday 18 February from where they sent a card (*369) to Písek saying that Mrs Stösslová should 'look out of the window' for their arrival at 12. This must mean on Friday 19 February since the Janáčeks attended concerts in Prague on 20 and 21 February.
6 The expected, and unrealized, visit of David Stössel was another incident in the long-running carpet saga (see Glossary: 'carpets') – according to Janáček's letter of 21 February 1926 (*370) he was due to have brought the carpets with him.

373   Brno, 29 March 1926

[...] You have no idea how many things I'm finishing now!

1. Suite for Strings
2. The chorus 'Our Flag'
3. *The Makropulos Affair*, an opera
4. Work: Folksongs
5. 'Take your Rest', a funeral chorus.

It's for those poor people leaving this beautiful world – reluctantly. That's enough for me to lay down my pen – once I've finished a beautiful little Sinfonietta with fanfares!

I remember those fanfares in Písek! That was nice then. [...]

'Finishing' covered a wide range of activity. Janáček had completed his autograph of *The Makropulos Affair* at the end of 1925, and had been checking over the copy made by Jaroslav Kulhánek. The Suite for Strings (1877) and *Take your Rest* (1894) for male voices were both early compositions now being prepared for publication that year, while no.4, his edition of *Moravian Love Songs*, continued to occupy Janáček until shortly before his death (see Glossary). Of the five items, *Our Flag* was the most recent (December 1925–January 1926), a *pièce d'occasion* written for the Choral Society of Moravian Teachers in gratitude for their performance of Janáček's chorus *The Seventy Thousand* in France, 1925. The chief interest of this letter, however, is the announcement of the composition of what was to be one of his most successful and popular orchestral pieces, the Sinfonietta. Janáček's linking of it with 'those fanfares in Písek' suggests that the idea for it came during one of Janáček's four visits to Písek to date, a fact corroborated by Cyril Vymetal, who accompanied them. In Vymetal's account (1958, 35) the event took place in September 1925, but Janáček did not visit Písek then. The most likely date for his hearing the fanfares would have been May 1925, during his visit for the concert of his works in Písek.

Letters and cards to Stösslová in early April recorded a visit over Easter to Štrbské pleso and a small ear operation (*377: Brno, 14 April 1926), but by his next substantial letter he was chiefly preoccupied with his impending trip to London, arranged by Rosa Newmarch.[1]

378   Brno, 24 April 1926

I still don't hear in my left ear, but there's no pain, it's improving, so on Tuesday [27 April] I leave for Prague and on Wednesday at noon I start my journey to London.

1 The full correspondence between the English critic and writer on music Rosa Newmarch (1857–1940) is published by Zdenka E. Fischmann in Janáček 1986, together with many other documents relating to Janáček's trip to England.

They're inviting me there very insistently. I've taken a 'secretary' with me, a Mr Mikota from Prague.[1]

I'll stay abroad about a fortnight. I'll be thinking of you.

Here it's like being in a hive. In Brno they're now rehearsing my *Mr Brouček* in the theatre. My Military Sinfonietta[2] with the fanfares will be played at the *Sokol* rally. Do you remember the Písek fanfares?

Would you also come for the rally? In Hukvaldy in July they'll unveil a memorial plaque to me on the house where I was born; there'll be a whole national celebration there.

And yesterday I submitted my 300-year-old [*The Makropulos Affair*] to the theatre.

So you see, there's not an empty moment.

I'd be glad to be home again after the journey, and well.

All the things one needs for such a long and distant journey!

If at sea a shark should hold me in his jaw, then my last thought will be Mrs Kamila – and the carpets I didn't get![3]

Keep well. Greetings to all of yours – except to your husband, who doesn't keep his word.

381 London, 30 April 1926

How a distant world divides us – and nevertheless doesn't separate us! I've arrived here happily – without being seasick. My eyes are being opened here. Greetings to everyone.

382 London, 1 May 1926

There's such a sea of houses here and eight million people in one heap that one can only travel by car. I've not yet gone on foot.

It's the first of May, they're busily working and travelling here.

---

1 Jan Mikota (1903–78), secretary of Janáček's Czech publisher, Hudební matice. Janáček got to know Mikota during his trip to Venice the previous autumn and at the composer's request accompanied him as interpreter and general assistant to London and in 1927 to Frankfurt. The arrangements for the London trip were discussed in a letter from Janáček to Mikota (19 March 1926; see Janáček 1990, 177).

2 Janáček's title is a reminder of the military band whose fanfares had inspired the opening movement. This title was used only at the first Brno performance on 4 April 1927. (The première in Prague at the time of the 1926 rally of the *Sokol* movement was billed as Janáček's 'Rally Sinfonietta' by the organizers of the rally.) At foreign performances (e.g. under Klemperer in New York and Berlin) the work was known simply as Janáček's 'Sinfonietta', a title that became standardized with the work's publication in this form.

3 See Glossary.

The celebration of work is in work, not in idleness.[1]

What they're playing of mine is nice music; just made for these calm Englishmen. They eat a lot here!

By the time he left, Janáček's assessment of the 'calm' English had become rather more jaundiced: he was not at all taken by Fanny Davies (1861–1934), due to play the piano in his Concertino (*383: 3 May 1926), and the piece was dropped. The concert at the Wigmore Hall on 6 May 1926 thus consisted only of *Mládí* and the First String Quartet, and two earlier pieces: the Violin Sonata, and the *Fairy Tale* for cello and piano. It was something of a wonder that the concert took place at all. The General Strike began on 3 May: there was neither transport nor publicity, and the audience was confined to those (like the players) who got there on foot or by private transport; there were no reviews.

384   London, 5 May 1926

If I lived the whole time as I do here I wouldn't last a month.

Nothing but visits, food and rolling round in a car the whole day long. There's a strike here. Today in London they hardly got milk. All has rapidly been getting more expensive. A bad atmosphere for a concert. But I've handled my mission well. I've made contacts – and gained a patroness who will push through a performance of *Jenůfa* in a year's time. So to travel home and as soon as possible – or I'll never get away from here!

Janáček was too sanguine about the 'patroness'[2] since it was a quarter of a century before any Janáček operas were performed in Britain. He was, however, more successful with other contacts, for instance his visit to Sir Henry Wood, who became an enthusiastic advocate of his music, giving the English premières of *Taras Bulba*, the Sinfonietta and the Glagolitic Mass.

386   [undated, postmarked London, 6 May 1926]

I've just got your letter where you're concerned about me. I already hear well again; but you'd go rigid if you knew all I've been through here. The concert's taken place, but with such disruption! The strike

1 Janáček clearly approved of the English habit at the time of not making a public holiday of May Day.
2 Mrs Elizabeth Courtauld, then on the Board of Covent Garden. With her husband Samuel she sub-leased the opera house in the years 1925–7, subsidizing it considerably during this time (Janáček 1986, 140–2).

provoked by the Russian Bolsheviks and Germans has caused billions of damage. No transport, the railways aren't running and it's impossible to go around London on foot. It's like having to walk from Písek to Prague. I must get part of the way from here to Paris and then to Holland and to Prague. I don't know when I'll get there. From there I'd most wish to come to you if it's possible. Zdenka of course is also concerned about me. If I arrive in the evening then I'll hop over to Písek the next morning.

There's much to tell. A quite different world. I was *invited* into [the homes of] the foremost families; without an invitation you can't get anywhere.

Among the workers things are boiling. Today they shot a driver on the street, for no reason at all. [...]

It would be interesting to speculate what was the source of Janáček's information about the General Strike. Most of the people with whom he came in contact would have been unsympathetic towards it; Mrs Newmarch in particular (an expert on Russian music, with many pre-revolutionary contacts there), had no reason to be sympathetic to the young Soviet regime, and, as Janáček's chief minder during the trip, may well have passed on her views. Janáček's mention of the death of a driver is significant. As soon as he returned to Brno Janáček began writing a violin concerto ('Pilgrimage of a Soul'). Although this work ended up, in a final revision, as the overture to *From the House of the Dead*, its inspiration is sometimes linked with this incident. He eventually left London for Folkestone on a train manned by volunteers, and then sailed to Flushing, Holland. It was from Holland that he reported his arrival with two postcards (*387–8: 9–10 May 1926). Janáček arrived in Prague in the evening of 11 May and, seemingly, that very evening, made a quick visit to Písek before returning to Brno on 14 May:

389 Prague, 13 May 1926

So I'm sitting here in Prague again and soon will be in Brno – and all will be like a past dream. What a lot of preparations there were, what expectations! And yet it's so simple: to write something which neither oppresses anyone, nor hurts. But what's worse is that in that great swarm of life it seems – *pointless*.

Whether London, really just a bit of London, heard my little works or not won't change anything in the course of events, even in the lifespan of one single individual out of those eight million inhabitants.

In short I am conscious of the insignificance of musical works. It's useless to talk much about them!

Then to some it's too important; I don't belong to those.

[89]

It's all over.

Here in the hotel they walked around on tiptoe until 10 o'clock so as not to wake me! Eventually they got up courage – perhaps, they said, I might have had a heart attack! – they went in and the cage was empty, the bed untouched! They breathed a sigh of relief when the telegram came from Písek.

I had a good laugh. [...]

390   Brno, 15 May 1926

[...] In Prague it was a long afternoon. In the evening they gave me a ceremonial welcome.[1]

Hurriedly eating pastries,
hurriedly a welcoming speech,
hurriedly I made an answer to it,
hurriedly getting the tables out of the way – and chop-chop they begin dancing shimmies, foxtrots and all those twirly things!

I extricated myself ever so quietly from them and just made for home!

This was the way they welcomed me and I felt ashamed!

The carpets are very nice; I'm not surprised that Zdenka has put them on display. Are they Kč 1600 each? So twice that is Kč 3200? Is that right? Please answer me right away, so I'm not in your debt.

Please choose me one more for Hukvaldy; it can be only up to three metres. But send it immediately direct to Hukvaldy, otherwise it will get stuck in Brno again.

The address is: Mrs Josefa Janáčková-Dohnalová
       Hukvaldy, Moravia.

They keep on inviting me to Berlin[2] and I have no wish to go there any more!

I probably won't go to the rally; they want only the 'fanfares' and I want to hear the whole Sinfonietta.[3]

1 The music section of the Umělecká beseda arranged an informal evening on 12 May 1926 in its club rooms. Janáček took part, and related his experiences in England.
2 for the première there of *Káťa Kabanová* (see 391).
3 See p.87, fn.2. As is clear from the letters to Janáček of Antonín Krejčí (see Procházka 1978, xxi–xxiii), the Rally Committee in its letter to Janáček of 5 May 1926 had indeed indicated that only the fanfares, i.e. the first movement of the Sinfonietta, would be played. This decision was soon reversed and, as Krejčí wrote on 22 May, the entire piece opened the Czech Philharmonic concert, conducted by Václav Talich, on 26 June 1926. Janáček duly attended rehearsals ('Here they're playing my Military Symphony marvellously!'; *400: 24 June 1926) and also the première. The fanfares were also played from the tower of the Týn church as the rally procession made its way through the Old Town Square on 6 July.

[...]

Today was the main rehearsal here for *The Excursion of Mr Brouček to the Moon*.[1] They're doing it really nicely here. You'd get a good laugh out of it. No comparison with that Prague production. It's clear now that they simply slaughter me in Prague.

I was glad that I could get over to you and see 'my old girl' at home.

391 Brno, 20 May 1926

I'm sending money at the same time. Everyone likes the carpets and we most of all. And now down to business.

Zdenka and I have agreed to invite you and the whole family, your husband and the boys, to Hukvaldy.

[...] You'll see beautiful countryside at our place, beautiful forests, healthy air, healthy water. You know that on 10 July they'll unveil that memorial plaque on the house where I was born.

Lots of people will gather in Hukvaldy.

I'll keep open house at home that day.

It's small and won't take everyone. But you'll be with me at home. For you to be comfortable at night, I'll arrange it so you'll be able to sleep peacefully two houses down. After that you'll be with me the whole day.

You'll see that you'll all like it, and it will also be healthy for you.

So count on setting out for Brno at the beginning of July and then go on to Hukvaldy with Zdenka. I'll write to your husband also to take a holiday for himself at that time.

So don't make any excuses in this matter and – obey!

After many entreaties I'm going to Berlin on Friday 28 May. The main rehearsal is on 29 May, the première of *Káťa Kabanová* on 31 May.[2] On 1 June I travel back and on 4 June I'll already be in Hukvaldy. Zdenka is also travelling with me to Berlin and looking forward to the amber stones.[3] I'll still write often, but as far as Hukvaldy's concerned it's now settled.

1 *The Excursion of Mr Brouček to the Moon* (i.e. the first part of *The Excursions of Mr Brouček*) was given its Brno première under František Neumann on 15 June 1926, produced by Ota Zítek, with designs by Josef Čapek.
2 For all Janáček's reluctance, the Berlin première of *Káťa Kabanová* was a huge success, as Janáček reported from Berlin on 1 June 1926 (*393): 'You can have no idea what a tremendous theatre it is and when the thousands of people began stormy applause in it! One's hearing and sight fails one.'
3 Stösslová had found two amber stones from which Zdenka was to choose; Janáček wrote that she should send them both to make the choice easier (*390; Prague, 13 [*recte* 12] May 1926).

Janáček had suggested several times that Stösslová should come to Hukvaldy, but the plan for her to come for the unveiling of his memorial plaque was by far the most emphatic and caused by far the most pain when, like the all the others, it was not taken up.

396   Hukvaldy, 15 June 1926

So why don't you answer?

I'm preparing everything for you here, I've come to a nice arrangement with St Peter about the weather, I'm stopping the fish in the stream, I'm looking out for roe deer in the woods – and nothing from you!

Come without argument. For as long as you want to stay. When we've seen everything, when we've grown weary of everything – we'll run away.

Zdenka writes that you mustn't forget your famous *bábovka*.[1]

We'll cut off a pig's leg and make ham.

We'll make supper ourselves, we'll have lunches prepared for us.

However it's raining here now. A sculptor[2] is sculpting me, the painter Ondrúšek[3] is painting: and I sit for them at home!

When will they leave me in peace!

I'm waiting for an invitation from Prague. Then we'll agree on the day of departure from Brno. [...]

Kamila Stösslová to Leoš Janáček, after 16 June 1926

Dear Maestro

So now, have you come to terms with the thought that we're not coming? Believe me that it's an impossibility now, perhaps later.

For I need peace and I have that only at home. So don't be cross any more and just come to us. I'm glad that your wife likes the amber stones and is pleased.

Don't stop the fish in the stream just let them go on swimming, don't look out for roe deer, let everything live joyfully as we do ourselves. Why should everything stop swimming and running because of me?

In any case I'll send you a *bábovka*. [...] So you're now sculpted and painted. [...]

1 A large sponge cake usually baked in a fluted mould.
2 Julius Pelikán (1887–1969) prepared in a mere six weeks a memorial plaque which was unveiled in Hukvaldy in July.
3 František Ondrúšek (1861–1932; see Glossary) completed a pastel portrait of Janáček at Hukvaldy on 16 June 1926 (Plate 32).

397 Hukvaldy, 17 June 1926

[...] And now about this excursion here. First and foremost don't imagine that it's so extraordinary.

To Brno it's not a long journey. We'll make preparations there and with Zdenka we'd travel here to Hukvaldy. Transport would be ready waiting and after a nice journey we'd be here in an hour.[1]

Here I've already got everything organized for you to have a pleasant time. There's even a doctor here. Tell that one of yours in Písek not to give you silly ideas!

On Saturday 10 July we'll take a trip to Kopřivnice nearby – ten minutes. There's a short concert there.

On Sunday they're unveiling that plaque and in the afternoon we'd go to the deer park to the military concert.

In this way we'll be rid of all the other, local people and can move around as we want ourselves.

I've a car at my disposal.

One day we'd take a trip to the most beautiful place in the Republic: Štramberk. The second day by car to Radhošť, the third day to Rožnov and the fourth perhaps to Moravská Ostrava. That's all, and without strain. I know your husband has this sort of thing up to his eyes. But he himself said that he had work in Moravská Ostrava – and then, if you're alone in Písek, you could also be alone with us here for a couple of days!

I wanted to go to you after the 26th to pack you up and bring you to Brno. I wouldn't even go to you otherwise.

So do make me happy; Zdenka, too, will be glad to have you here.

The weather won't be like it is now the whole time!

On Monday the 21st I leave here for Brno.

[...]

We'll wait for your answer in Brno: 'I'm coming to Hukvaldy'! [...]

398 Hukvaldy, 19 June 1926

Zdenka writes to me today that she has those beautiful 'amber stones' – and also the *real reason* why you don't want to come![2]

You don't have to go to the concert, and here in Hukvaldy we're on

---

1 Exceptionally, Janáček had a car waiting (see below); otherwise the journey from the station usually took three hours (see Glossary: 'Hukvaldy').

2 In her letter to Zdenka of 16 June 1926 (BmJA, E 1110) Kamila mentioned that her husband had lots of work in the shop and that it was a long journey to Hukvaldy: she had earache and the doctor said she ought not to go anywhere.

our own, where one meets another soul only once in a blue moon.

Now then – a pure conscience knows how to look people in the eye!

So no fears. It's raining here, just pouring down. But it will stop. I'll already be in Brno on 21 June.

From Prague, where he went to hear rehearsals for the première of his Sinfonietta (given by Talich with the Czech Philharmonic on 26 June), Janáček wrote twice more, wondering how she had decided (*399–400: both 24 June). He also wrote twice more from Brno (*401–2: 30 June and 7 July). But the unveiling ceremony took place without her.

403   [undated, postmarked Hukvaldy, 12 July 1926]

The memorial plaque was unveiled in the pouring rain. But there were many people there who weren't afraid! In the afternoon the sun came out joyfully. I'm glad that it's all over now; but I calmly put up with all that talking. The whole district took part – for Prague of course I'm too far.

The room is still prepared for you.

Zdenka sends her greeting.
All the best for your name-day!

404   Hukvaldy, 26 July 1926

You should have been here, in our company, you wouldn't then have had five guests.

Good advice is lost on you.

Zdenka has recovered, I'm a bit better – and your ear[ache] and work remain.

We had the fish, eight chickens, two geese, also venison – without you.

With the car we travelled criss-cross – and without you.

It's all over and we leave here on the 30th. Naturally your room remained unused.

Preparations are already under way with me for the autumn and the winter. On 8 August there's a concert in London,[1] on 8 December in Berlin.[2]

1 It is not clear what Janáček had in mind (see Janáček 1990, 188).
2 A chamber concert took place in Berlin on 8 December 1926 with the First String Quartet, Violin Sonata, *Mládí* and the Concertino.

I'll strengthen myself for work with Luhačovice water [before I return].

I've got six chairs here, in 1830s style. I need material for a new covering, material which would be right for that period. Two metres of double width. Do advise me. [...]

The rain continued in Luhačovice and instead of 'strengthening himself for work' there, Janáček worked very solidly. In just over two weeks, from 2 to 17 August, he wrote a complete first draft of the Glagolitic Mass. Such activity goes unmentioned in his correspondence with Stösslová at the time which instead harks back to the usual theme of his loneliness at Luhačovice without her.

407   Luhačovice, 15 August 1926

The worries about my health have nearly faded. I had fears about what would happen with my throat; but perhaps I'll get well.

But this loneliness falls on me here. I think that one shouldn't return to those places where one was happy in one's youth. Now one remains here alone – to those who make friends here with a smile, with a laugh – [I'm] absolutely redundant to those people. Altogether absolutely redundant to this entire society. The isolation is embarrassing.

I know that they know me here, I observe it from their whispers when they go past; they greet me with respect – but they just talk among themselves. So I withdraw into my shell, which has no window, and in the morning take to my work again. In the afternoon from 2 to 5.30 I planned a schedule for treatment. There's no-one to talk to. At breakfast, lunch and dinner I sit alone. I throw a little food inside me – and now it's 7.30 in the evening and I'm sitting at home.

Memories – they're like a faded flower. And I'd like to smash them to pieces, at least they wouldn't hurt any more.

You see, I'm writing a bitter letter to you.

408   Luhačovice, 24 August 1926

So the Luhačovice days, which I feared, have passed.

It's had the effect on me here as when leaves fall on the countryside in the autumn. Everywhere you hear it whispering simply: it was once, it was once!

I don't understand you at all now. How can you hang around listlessly on the first floor of your house? Yes, this is no longer the

Kamila of ten years ago! Who had a will of her own and who didn't give in to everyday prattle. You would have recovered half – perhaps all [–] of your health if you'd listened to what I advised, for what I asked you! Believe me, I know now that it's useless to fight against foolishness. To see a stupid smile on a face when there ought to have been distress and concern for a dear life – it's unbearable!

It's better simply to talk about my stay here than to write.

I'm already on tenterhooks here and just want to rush home.

My nerves were terribly overwrought; it's been put right. I need to have nerves of iron. I still have things to do. On Friday 27 August I'll already be in Brno.

And I'm sad. Just as if I were simply crying into a wilderness and the echo of my own words returns coldly to me.

Keep well and do please answer!

In Brno Janáček got on with the two compositions that he had begun earlier during the summer, the Glagolitic Mass and the Capriccio for piano left hand ('I've written something for a pianist who has only a left hand.[1] Only I don't yet know how it will end. It's difficult for someone to dance with only one leg!'; *411: Brno, 29 October 1926). Stösslová still did not answer and Janáček's own letters to her became less frequent. At the end of the month he tried to persuade her to go to Prague for the German Theatre's production of *Jenůfa* under Zemlinsky (*412: Brno, 31 October 1926). More details followed on 5 November 1926 (*413) for the performance that evening which Janáček was attending with his wife. And a new première loomed: 'In Brno there are already rehearsals for that "icy one"; they will give it on 17 December.[2] "Would you care to come?" ' (*415: Brno, 23 November 1926). The studiedly polite tone and ironical quotation marks of his invitation show no great confidence of its being accepted, and when in his next substantial letter he described the rehearsals in more detail, he spelt out that he was not inviting her this time.

417 Brno, 14 December 1926

[...] These have been bad days for me now. It's the last rehearsals for that 'icy one'; I thought that the theatre wasn't up to it. Even the 'icy one' didn't want to warm herself up for this role. It was agony to listen to the scraping for a whole week. Now it's going well and the 'icy one' has warmed up.

I won't invite you; in Prague you went 'your way' and it hurt then. [...]

1 Otakar Hollmann (1894–1967), who lost his right arm in the First World War.
2 The première of *The Makropulos Affair* was one day later, 18 December 1926.

The reference to 'your way' is only slightly amplified in the letter of 23 November 1926 (*415): 'You could still have remained for that evening as well; we sat there like ones lost. That very first evening [you had free] you needn't have gone 'your' way and you could have been with us! It annoyed me.' It sounds after all as if the Janáčeks met up with Stösslová during their visit to Prague for the German Theatre production of *Jenůfa* on 5 November, and that she had not seen as much of him as he would have liked. *The Makropulos Affair*, at any rate, went off well:

418 Brno, 21 December 1926

That 'icy one' had unsuspected success! Such that she sent cold shivers down everyone's spine. They say it's my greatest work.

But it's still possible to go higher!

Have a nice Christmas!

419 Brno, 27 December 1926

For the first time I've got an empty head, i.e. I'm not working on anything. That 'cold-hot' woman is now in the world –

The 'Glagolskaja misa'[1] is now being bound –

Defiance – the Capriccio – is now being written out –

Nursery Rhymes for children I've now revised.

Now I'm coming to Prague on 4 January. I'll be there 4, 5, 6, 7 *January*.[2]

On the holiday in the afternoon I want to look up the Kretschmers[3] – if they invite me.

Then to the dentist,[4] to the 'heart' doctor.[5]

In Brno for a while and then to the snow in Hukvaldy.

In Písek they'll be giving the Suite and the Concertino.

Wouldn't you like to visit Prague? How's it going with *Vera*?[6]

You've been sparing with words. What's the matter with you

1 One of Janáček's many provisional titles for the Glagolitic Mass (for others see Wingfield 1992, 11).
2 The confidently underlined dates of his next Prague trip did not produce the response he was expecting: in his next note to Stösslová (*420: Prague, 4 January 1927) he began 'Only you are missing'.
3 See Glossary.
4 Dr Cyril Zbořil.
5 In an earlier letter (*410: Brno, 9 October 1926) Janáček had referred to the strain on his heart; a doctor in Brno diagnosed a weak heart and prescribed pills which he reported as helping him. The heart specialist was presumably Dr Václav Libenský (see Glossary).
6 'Galerie Vera', David Stössel's Prague shop (see Glossary: 'Stössel, David'). In a further postcard from Prague (*421: 8 January 1927) Janáček reported finding it closed.

again? I've now pampered myself a little.

What did Little Jesus bring you?[1] I got an oak walking-stick and a tie-pin.

A Happy New Year to you and to all at your house.

422   Brno, 28 January 1927

[...] I think that for me you'll turn into that 'icy one'. Well now, she's liked in spite of it all, and universally. Those outfits of hers! In Act 1 a sort of greenish fur as a lining. Those pearls and long gold earrings [!] In Act 2 a white fur, a long train, in Act 3 a dress made out of gold, as if out of gold scales. What a sight! And everyone falls in love with her. Yes, it will be in Prague, in Berlin. Plzeň also wants it; I don't know if they'll be up to it.

And apparently on 6 February the director of the Paris opera is coming to see *Jenůfa* here in Brno. Well that's what they're saying here – I don't know anything. So you'll come and see that 'icy one' in Prague; perhaps you'll see your photograph.

I haven't taken a holiday yet; I'll go on 10 February to Hukvaldy, to see what snow looks like. In Brno we have only black snow.

[...]

I'm again making plans now for the summer.

Perhaps Luhačovice – the Tatras – Štrbské pleso – Bratislava – Danube; then Prague – Berlin – Paris.

Where will we say to one another: 'My respects, Mrs Kamila!' 'My respects, Maestro'?

423   Hukvaldy, 14 February 1927

Madam

You're certainly no longer among the living! I ought to write to heaven, where the angels sing and fly. But I'm writing to Písek, the one place perhaps from where they'll send [my letter] to you. Here it's magnificent; I'm sure you can see the valleys from heaven. The Ondrúšek portrait[2] is an excellent piece of work.

Greetings

Drph. Leoš Janáček

1 The Czech tradition is to give Christmas presents anonymously; thanks are rendered to 'Little Jesus'.
2 See Glossary.

See, how well you know how to be cheerful! You even manage little poems. I think that a little devil will take you, but then I won't want to go to heaven.

It's magnificent here, you know; God is a good miller; he pours out only the whitest [snow]. I've had a good rest, so that on Thursday the 24th I'll leave again. I'll stop by at the painter's, Mr Ondrúšek. I think he did well with me [i.e. with his portrait of Janáček].

In addition he'd got a picture of Vrchlický,[1] the poet. It's surely the most superb work; there's the Tábor countryside in the background. Mr Kretschmer ought to have something from Ondrúšek. It's good that you're moving from Karlín;[2] at least I won't have far for visits and you'll also drop in there more often from the railway.

My Sinfonietta went down tremendously well in New York,[3] as did *The Cunning Little Vixen* in Mainz.[4]

I don't know what work to take up. One's within reach, but every person in it is fettered.[5]

And I'd rather have smiling people.

Here I've got a tom-cat to make me laugh. He likes being petted, but immediately bares his claws.

When I petted Čipera [the family dog] before leaving – he bit me!

An animal remains an animal – but man is close to it.

In March 1927 Mrs Janáčková was having the house painted and, as she related in her memoirs (pp. 172–3), wanted her husband out of the way. She suggested that he might go off to the Stössels. At first the trip was scheduled for 4 March, after a trip to Prague to attend a reception given by President Masaryk (*425: Brno, 27 February 1927). But on 2 March 1927 (*426)

1 Jaroslav Vrchlický (1853–1912), one of the best known and most prolific Czech poets of the nineteenth century. He inspired several works by Janáček including the cantatas *Amarus* and *The Eternal Gospel*.

2 In her letter of 14 February 1927 Stösslová reported that the Stössels were moving their antique shop from the suburb of Karlín to the centre of Prague, near the Václavské náměstí [Wenceslas Square].

3 Conducted by Otto Klemperer on 4 March 1927. Olin Downes, in an enthusiastic review in the *New York Times* (5 March 1927), described it as 'charming and original'; 'J.A.H.' in *Musical America* (12 March 1927) was more equivocal and concluded that it was 'unlikely that it will ever become a best-seller'.

4 The German première of *The Cunning Little Vixen* was given at the Mainz Städtisches Theater on 13 February 1927, conducted by Paul Breisach. It was hardly the success that Janáček reported (see Tyrrell 1992, LB70–1).

5 An early reference to *From the House of the Dead*, in which the cast of prisoners wear leg chains. Janáček had in fact begun work on the opera the day before (see Tyrrell 1992, 330–1).

Janáček wrote to say that he did not know how long he would have to be at the Castle and postponed the Písek trip until the Easter holidays, though there was then a danger of Stösslová's being away in Vienna. His visit was a turning-point in his relationship with Kamila Stösslová.

428 Brno, 10 March 1927

[...] I'd leave from Brno by the afternoon train on the Easter Monday [18 April].

I'd like to remain through Tuesday, Wednesday, Thursday and even Friday.

Or must I walk round Písek and say: here she goes walking, here she used to walk – and she's gone off?

I'll have finished a certain piece of work[1] and would like to take a break; and it's pleasantest with your chattering.

And in addition: my room's going to be painted. I must flee from it. So now soften your heart and write: come, I'll remain in Písek.

But I'll book a room for myself in a hotel; I wouldn't want to cause you trouble for so long.

On the contrary I'll help you cook and also go shopping.

So I'll wait longingly for your reply.

Your devoted

Drph. Leoš Janáček

429 Brno, 25 March 1927

Dear Mrs Kamila

Thank you very much for putting off your departure because of me. I'll look forward to those few days.

I'm worn out through work and I need to tear myself away from it by force. So please book a room for me in that hotel where I once spent the night.[2]

I want only to have company and I want to have somewhere to go 'home' to; and where else but to you can I go 'home'?

I'll travel from Brno on Easter Monday in the morning either directly to Písek or, if I have some sort of meeting in Prague, then I'd come to you from Prague. I'll tell you in good time. I was already waiting for your answer. I thought to myself: will she stay, won't she

1 Perhaps Janáček was planning to complete his draft of Act 1 of *From the House of the Dead* before he saw her. He did so on 2 April (Tyrrell 1992, 332).
2 On 27 June 1924 (see pp.46–7); this time Stösslová invited Janáček to stay at their house (see 430).

stay? But it would have hurt nevertheless if you hadn't stayed —
although I know that I shouldn't give you orders or even make
requests.

But you're kind, and I thank your husband too.

We'll take a trip by car to Třeboň; it's said to be a pretty town, and
also Jindřichův Hradec.

And the sun will surely shine, won't it?

So keep well.

Your devoted

Drph. Leoš Janáček

430 Brno, 4 April 1927

Dear Mrs Kamila

I really laughed at your orders. I wash myself in the morning like a
duck; at home they have to cover everything around the washbasin,
otherwise everything would be 'swimming'. And am I to get your
carpets wet?

I get up early. If the sun's shining, at 6 I'll already be somewhere
near the swimming bath. You'll have to bear with me. But I'm
looking forward to those few days.

We'll take a trip to Třeboň and Jindřichův Hradec and possibly to
Tábor.

I'm still waiting for news from Prague. From Prague to you it's
more comfortable. From Brno the express goes only at 5 in the
afternoon.[1]

We'll see.

Just let it be fine weather! But it won't worry me even if it were to
be overcast and rainy. You do know how to conjure up laughter, and
such is your nature that you disarm everything around you.

So we'll chat to one another — well in fact we won't say anything to
one another. It'll be enough for me when I see you running around.

Today I had my gala concert[2] here; but now let's put work aside!

So I'll obey your every word — although I've not known how to up
till now.

Your devoted

Drph. Leoš Janáček

1 There was only one train a day from Brno to Písek, the 16.50 express, arriving at 22.35.
From Prague to Písek the journey was under three hours on the express, and there were
more connections.
2 František Neumann conducted the orchestra of the National Theatre at an afternoon
concert at the Town Theatre in a programme consisting of Suk's *Tale of Summer*, extracts
from Berg's *Wozzeck* and Janáček's Sinfonietta.

431 Brno, 9 April 1927

Dear Mrs Kamila

So I'm not going to Prague; therefore straight to you from Brno. And that will be *on Sunday, 17 April, by the afternoon express.* I'm sorry that I'll upset your evening and night!

Please be so kind and arrange for some transport to be waiting for me at the station – if there usually isn't any there.

Also don't do anything unnecessary for me; especially as far as food's concerned. The less there'll be on the plate, the better it'll taste to me.

Zdenka's waiting for you to praise her portrait.

And I'm looking forward to being able to praise how well you look. Looking forward to seeing you soon and greeting all your family,
Your devoted
Drph. Leoš Janáček

432 Brno, 14 April 1927

Madam – auntie

The ticket's bought – so I'll be at your place *on Sunday*

17 April

after 10

in the evening.

Let the sun out as soon as I come.
Greetings
Drph. Leoš Janáček

Leoš Janáček to Zdenka Janáčková, 21 April 1927

Dear Zdenka

Well, they're looking after me carefully here. The weather's changed to warm and fair. Yesterday morning we made a four-hour trip in the company of local artists. Yes, and another one in the afternoon through the woods and villages. The wood's already fragrant. On Friday [22 April] we will probably make a trip to Třeboň, [Jindřichův] Hradec; on Sunday I'll remain in Tábor and will leave for Brno on Monday morning. So it will be when the sun will be in the sky! Mrs Stösslová likes roses very much; she was very pleased with them. However there's lots of toiling in the kitchen. I wonder if you're now finished with the painting and are putting things in order? I forgot about music and was glad that I stopped myself on the way to the madhouse.

So keep well!

Yours

Leoš

433 Brno, 23 April 1927

Umbrella! Umbrella, where did you get left? In Písek! Please could your husband take it to Prague on Monday [25 April]? And leave it at Mr Kretschmer's? On Monday evening I'll stop by there to listen to the radio.[1] [...] I'll write to you only when I wake up from my Písek dream. On Monday I'll be in Prague.

So thank you for your kind hospitality. A letter will come straight after this card.

Greetings

Drph. Leoš Janáček

434 Prague, 25 April 1927

Dear soul

Believe me, I cannot escape from our two walks. Like a heavy, beautiful dream; in which I am bewitched.

I know that I'd be consumed in that heat which cannot catch fire. On the paths I'd plant oaks which would endure for centuries; and into their trunks I'd carve the words which I shouted into the air. I don't want them to be lost, I want them to be known.

To no-one, ever, have I spoken these words with such compulsion, so recklessly: 'You, you, Kamila! Look back! Stop!' and I read in your eyes as well that something united us in that gale-force wind and heat of the sun. Perhaps something was fated to give us both unutterable pleasure? Never in my life have I experienced such an intermingling of myself with you. We walked along not even close to one another and yet there was no gap between us. I was just your shadow, for me to be there it needed you. I'd have wished that walk to be without an end; I waited without tiring for the words which you whispered; what would I have done were you my wife? Well, I think of you as if you were my wife. It's a small thing just to think like that, and yet it's as if the rays of a hundred suns were

---

1 Janáček wanted to listen to the Brno concert (broadcast only from Brno) of the complete performance of his *Nursery Rhymes*.

[103]

overwhelming me. I think this to myself and I won't stop thinking it.

Do with this letter, this confession of mine, what you will. Burn it, or don't burn it. It brings me alive. Even thoughts become flesh.

Keep well.

Your

Having suddenly become so intimate with Kamila, Janáček nevertheless found it difficult to know how to sign himself – his previous letter, after all (and for that matter his next), gave his full name and title. So he mostly left out any name, except in postcards (*444, *455), eventually adding an initial 'L.' at the end of June (461) and 'Leoš' two months later (474). In his next letter to her he began using the Czech intimate form of *Ty* [thou].

435   Prague, 26 April 1927

Dear Kamila

I write to you as *Ty*. Surely we've said so many sincere things to one another that only *Ty* is fitting between us. Do you mind? I forgot my umbrella at your house and it was returned to me yesterday evening at the house of Kretschmer, the industrialist. I was sorry that it wasn't in my power to invite your husband to supper. I'd taken my old umbrella from Brno; in the train I put it above my head and someone stole it during the journey! A thief in the second class! And there were four of us in the coupé! I dozed off for a moment – and it was gone. I'll be more careful.

What are you doing now? When I was leaving Písek, I wept as the houses went by. But what of it? I'm not ashamed. I found in you something which is so near to me and so lovable. Just the thought of you, and laughter and joy runs across my face.

I'm panting for your letter. Burn this letter, or don't burn it, whatever you do, so it will be.

Your

436   Brno, 28 April 1927

Dear Mrs Kamila

Happiness smiles on me from every side!

A month ago the Prussian Academy of Arts in Berlin made me a member[1] –

1 On 18 February 1927 the Akademie der Künste zu Berlin informed Janáček by letter that (together with Schoenberg and Hindemith) it had made him a member (BmJA, D 1338).

Today the Belgian Ambassador gave me the 'glad tidings' that the King of the Belgians, on the advice of his Foreign Minister, has made me a Knight of the Order of Leopold![1]

What a surprise!

Well I'm writing to you about it immediately; the newspapers will be full of it, bellows full of envy. However, I'm at peace; I didn't seek it and it came. And add to it those Písek smiles, glances – well, my cup runs over!

Keep well.

Yours

Drph. Leoš Janáček

437 Brno, 30 April 1927

Dear, good Kamila

I got your letter today, Saturday. In it I read great disquiet on your part; I can do no other than implore you 'oh, do love me!' In the thought that I have you, that you're mine, lies all my joy of life. By it you give me the greatest happiness I've ever wished and which I never got and never really wanted from anyone before. I beam with pleasure, where possible I wish and do only good to others.

Because you're in me, because you've dominated me completely, I don't long for anything else. I don't have words to express my longing for you, to be close to you. Wherever I am I think to myself: you can't want anything else in life if you've got this dear, cheerful, black little 'Gypsy girl' of yours. I know that my compositions will be more passionate, more ravishing: you'll sit on every little note in them. I'll caress them; every little note will be your dark eye. Oh, your eyes, in which I wanted to gaze, in which I wanted to see that thought, as in a deep pool, that thought, that desire which governed me.

Oh, Kamila, it's hard to calm myself. But the fire that you've set alight in me is necessary. Let it burn, let it flame, the desire of having you, of having you!

I think of you in those places where we went walking so eagerly together, went running in fact!

But don't walk in the woods! Kamilka, I'd worry about you; you wouldn't be able to defend yourself against evil men. Promise me that. And then write that 'yes' and again another '*Ty*'. And be cheerful and I'm also cheerful in the thought that you're my Kamila.

1 The diploma Janáček received (BmJA, C 271) was dated 11 April 1927. The honour seems to have arisen after the great success of *Jenůfa* in Antwerp (première 9 January 1927).

I'm writing on Saturday 30 April; I'll send you the letter only on Monday.

And dear soul, let that which secretly binds us never pass away. God, let no-one dare tear it asunder. I'll guard this secret so that no-one will find it out. After all I won't harm anyone by loving you so unutterably. Haven't I now worn myself out just with work, and you were like that distant quiet little moon and in vain I turned my eyes towards it? Oh Kamila, write to me saying that you could love me! With everyone else I've stood as if behind a fence; and when standing with you I want there to be not a hair's breadth between us. You can have me whole, dear soul, and please give yourself whole to me in the same way.

Yours, wholly yours

And do you know, my soul, why it's necessary meticulously to conceal things? If we really had belonged to one another, then I know what I'd do now. But that you, I, should suffer just for that yearning, for that simple longing, not that! Would anyone believe that after eleven years there was only that longing, that yearning? No-one would believe it. Therefore, my cheerful little fire,[1] have pity on us. Burn everything now fierily, as fierily as it was felt! How unwillingly I give your dear letters to it. But it's necessary for your peace.

Keep well, my soul, Kamila.

438 Brno, 2 May 1927

My dear Kamila

I'm just blessed that I've confessed my love to you, that I've experienced confessing love to someone. This never happened before, not even with Zdenka. And in life that mutual feeling has to fight its way through! Believe me, there'd be no need for life if it couldn't bubble over with that intoxication. It's the height of existence; it's like a flower which waits for the bee to bring the pollen. The flower must surely grieve when it finishes flowering in the cold, in the frost.

Oh Kamila, it's impossible for these memories to go to sleep; it's impossible to forget about our walk. I must write lots and lots to you if only because that's what you want, because that's what you're waiting for just as I'm waiting for lines from you. You read

---

1 Janáček addresses the fire in which he is going to burn Kamila's letters (see Glossary: 'burning of letters').

them many times and I read yours greedily. Kamila, at the end of the letter write once: '*Tvoje* známá [your friend] Kamila'. Will you do that for me?

So are you black like a little devil? And should I fear you? Oh no, little soul, I don't fear you. It's true you have arms which are strong, but you also have arms which are soft, which embrace. I'd long for the latter; then you'd be defenceless; and what would I do with my Kamila? I'd forget all the world – for you'd be the most beautiful world of all. I'd pour out the deepest dark around us – until only our eyes would shine like stars. I wouldn't want to see anything, only my mouth would kiss your body, my mouth would seek that greatest happiness and would find it. You know Kamila, I imagine now that you're my wife, not a little in that word, as I imagine it: one soul, one body! Kamila, Kamila, my dear beloved Kamila! – And now I walk contented; no-one sees me pondering, thinking: all's clear to me: you're mine and I live in you. It's impossible to change anything in this. We have our world in which the sun doesn't set.

If you had at least written: '*Ty* [You] mustn't come to us, I'm afraid'. And I know that I'll seek the moment when I'll look for you on the rocks,[1] and I'll beg you, 'don't be frightened of me' – and I'll long for the moment when you won't be frightened. And much happiness has already come to me; will the greatest happiness come to me, Kamila?

Yours, for ever yours,
You know who.

And why do you fear me? Would I ever do anything to you? I'd surely never do anything bad. And what would I do to you? I know, I know! I long for it unutterably! Is that why you're frightened? My Kamila!

439 Brno, 4 May 1927

My dear Kamila

I woke at 5 o'clock this morning and my first thought? What's my Kamila doing? She, to whom I confessed my sincere love, whom I love more than myself!

Your picture which you gave me, I lie down to sleep after looking at it, I reach out for it when I get up. You have a smile on your lips, and your eyes look at me so openly. You are my joy, Kamila. That decoration from the Belgian king! Only three of my former pupils

---

1 See Glossary.

congratulated me. Wild envy everywhere else. That knighthood opens the way for me beyond the borders to all society.

You, my little soul, you know me, that I hold little store by it. Despite that, we're still together in the same way as when we got to know one another many years ago – and will remain so. I'm happy in your kitchen. One looks within another person for something other than what's draped on the surface – if one loves one another. You run along barefoot beside me like a little chicken, you lie on the divan like a cat – and I see only my own dear Kamila. You're mine and please be mine completely.

And don't forget sometimes to include that little word 'yes'!

I'd write to you daily, but I fear that someone at the post office here, or in Písek, would be too inquisitive about the daily letters!

In June I want to go to Hukvaldy – for lettuces. I ate one at your place, didn't I – and it was expensive!

There in particular the postman is inquisitive; I'll always put sealing-wax on my letters, and you'll do so too.

Now you'll be coming to us. We'll look at each other during our first meeting; and in that glance there'll be just that thought: 'we belong to each other'! And then we will be merry.

I'll be summoned once again to Prague, probably when our President returns. Then I'll hop over to you. If you aren't at the station I'll go straight to the rocks.

So be well, dear Kamila.

This is the wish from someone who loves you unutterably!

Zdenka wrote to you today; she'll tell you how the operation[1] goes. I wouldn't advise it for her; it's a gamble with life.

I'll be glad only when I see you. Here it rains every day.

Your

440 Brno, 5 May 1927

Dear, darling Kamila

Your last letter breathes sincerity. It's impossible to calm myself, I need the heat and ardour which passes from you to me. You're right to say that we'll let this thing of ours run freely; we won't put the brakes on, rather, we'll push it along.

And you, my soul, on that rock! The sun's strong, do protect your

---

1 At the time Zdenka Janáčková was considering having an operation on her thyroid gland. At first she was advised against what was then a dangerous operation, but finally went ahead with it, successfully, on 17 June 1927, when Janáček was away at Hukvaldy (Janáčková 1939, 173–6).

[108]

head from its fire. The brain can't stand hyperaemia, and sunstroke is a serious illness. So do have a scarf on your head! Will you obey?

I think that everything at our place will be finally in order at the end of the month, so we'll be expecting you.

I long for you more than for the sun; in fact I'd like a cloud in which we'd see only one another and not the others.

You'll tell me more things than ever before, and I'd want just a single answer, just one wish on earth, just a single desire, just a single certainty: will we belong to each other completely? It's good that you don't want to go into the woods. I'd be this sort of protector: I'd take you unawares. 'Hands up!', I'd cry; and then I'd hug you and kiss you. A good protector, not so? So you can't, you don't want to say *Ty* to me? And I say *Ty* to you all the time. You'll say it too one day, I know.[1] As for me, my fondness, my love for you, won't pass, and neither, you hope, will yours for me. You need strong love and I'm happy that you've kindled in me such strong and undying love.

It was ordained that we don't have secrets between ourselves, that we've found one another. *Anxiety about life – model order*[2] – that's not all that a man needs. I saw that at your place, and my whole life [before that] I've tossed and thrashed about like a fish on dry land.[3] Only now have I found equilibrium. To each other, Kamila, we give what the other lacks.

My thoughts are with you, you're fully around me, invisible, necessary as air. You're mine, dear Kamila!

You went to the post, put the letter into the postbox – without a stamp. Surcharge Kč 2! I paid it with joy! Kč 100 if needs be! I'll read the last three letters for at least several days. I'll find it hard to take my leave of them!

Your, ever yours

Just let this letter go quickly to you. Today it's hot here, so that you must protect yourself on the rocks. You're passionate, I too; two fires – what a flame that would be! Write a letter such that Zdenka could read, saying that you're looking forward to Brno. She's surprised that I'm not getting letters from you![4] And we should write in blood now!!

Yours, for ever

1 She had clearly capitulated by 27 May (see **448** and **451**).
2 A reference to Zdenka.
3 See Glossary: 'fish thrashing'.
4 Since he had received three letters from her recently, Janáček was clearly being secretive about them. Zdenka would not have known about their arrival as Janáček collected his mail from a postbox (see Glossary: 'post').

My dear Kamila

So Zdenka will write to you to come to us. She is inviting you herself, of her own free will. So write back openly and sincerely that you're coming, that you'd stay the night at our house, and that you're looking forward to it.

You'd be with Zdenka for the night in the [bed]room; I'd take your [husband] with me into my office; there's a divan there, one can sleep well on it.

It would be better still if you stayed with us until your husband returned from Vienna. That would be the nicest. And don't put off this journey; rather come before the end of May.

Write to me similarly that you're looking forward to coming and that you'll be staying. Our gaze at each other will be calm; that will always mean: we belong to one another! Nothing now can change this. *Nothing* can get in its way; it wrongs no-one, nor detracts from anyone.

It doesn't detract because they don't have what we give to one another: limitless devotion and longing.

So we'll celebrate our eleven-year friendship[1] – now it's crowned – and my knighthood – so envied.

Yesterday was boiling hot here; 25° in the shade.[2] I kept on thinking of you, hoping that the sun wouldn't burn you up!

I have your picture before me; that true dear smile of yours and inquiring eye: yes, that's you truly! I want you like that, no-one will part you from me.

I've got down to work again; I hope it's successful.

Nursery Rhymes will probably be published; a shame that there aren't any rhymes by you. What isn't now, will be.

I'm happy that I'm yours, my dear Kamila!

So, dear Kamila, Zdenka will write to you and invite you.

1. You'll come at noon by express from Písek to Brno.
2. I'll be waiting for you.
3. We'll take you straight to our house.
4. We'll have lunch right away.

---

1 The friendship had not yet lasted ten years (see also p.70 fn.1).
2 Czech thermometers of the time often included calibration in both the Réaumur and Celsius scales (on either side of the glass) making it easy to provide readings in either. Janáček was perhaps thinking on the Réaumur scale, which would have given Celsius 31.25 / Fahrenheit 88.25, certainly hot for early May; if the day's temperature of 30° mentioned at the end of the letter were Réaumur (Celsius 37.5 / Fahrenheit 99.5) the day would have been unusually hot.

1 Kamila Stösslová and her son Otto aged one (1917).

2 Kamila Stösslová and her son Otto in regional costume a year later (sent to Janáček in June 1918).

3 Janáček with Stösslová's sons Rudolf (left) and Otto (right) in c1927. It is probably this portrait which Janáček acknowledged in 569 (26 January 1928).

4 Leoš Janáček in Luhačovice. He wrote the following words to Mrs Stösslová on the back of this photograph (2: 24 July 1917): 'We used to walk together, people envied us – and yet you only talked about your family happiness – and I about my unhappiness.'

5 Kamila Stösslová in Luhačovice August 1927. Janáček sent this photograph to an unnamed person, inscribing it as follows: 'We're just about to leave. You know that it's beautiful here, but you don't know that this year it was the most beautiful. Devotedly, Drph Leoš Janáček, 27 August 1927.'

6 Kamila Stösslová with ornamental tree in her home at Přerov. Janáček commented (48: 14 April 1918): 'They've caught you nicely and always with that little tree. That was a good idea of yours. But who will take care of the tree when you're not in Přerov any more?'

7 Leoš Janáček out walking during his last summer in Luhačovice, July 1928.

SESTAVIL JAK. BALHAR, NADUČITEL
V LUHAČOVICÍCH.

8 Jacket design for the third edition of
Balhar's guide to Luhačovice (1914),
which Janáček owned.

Luhačovice in August 1927:
Kamila Stösslová in company (9, *opposite left*), with
Janáček (10, *top left*), alone (11, *top right*) and with
her husband (12, *bottom right*): 'In the picture
you're striding forward: with that step you could
already be in Brno in a little while. But I like it
when you toss your head like that' (501: 16–17
October 1927).

13 Luhačovice: main square in 1907 with a view of Janův dům (left; cf Plate 8) and the mineral baths, buildings designed or renovated by the architect Dušan Jurkovič. Jurkovič left his stamp on Luhačovice with a distinctive style deriving chiefly from Moravian folk architecture and the Czech Art Nouveau.

14 Luhačovice view: main square during a promenade concert (1927).

'It's high time to put down my pen – and walk from the Augustýnský [dům] to Alojzka' (**647**: 5 May 1928). In his visits to Luhačovice from 1918 Janáček stayed in the Augustinian House (15, *above*) in the wooded outskirts of the town. 'Alojzka' (Aloiska: 16, *right*) was one of the mineral-water springs in the town.

17 Mrs Gutová's 'dairy', the vegetarian restaurant in Luhačovice, which opened shortly before Janáček and Stösslová ate there in August 1927. The next summer Janáček lost seven kilos by pursuing a vegetarian diet there: 'I have breakfast, lunch and supper at Mrs Gutová's' (**701**: 2–3 July 1928).

18 Kamila Stösslová and David Stössel when Janáček first met them in 1917.

19 Kamila Stösslová and David Stössel, with dog, in 1926.

5. In the evening we'll go to the French restaurant.[1]
6. There we'll celebrate the knighthood and eleven years.
7. You'll sleep in the room with Zdenka.
8. Your husband will be with me in my study in the main building.
So you'll be received joyfully. Just decide soon about the journey.

Zdenka's not going to have the operation now. So, at my house, you'll obey me as I obey you at your house.

Today a heat wave of 30°.

Yours for ever

442   Brno, 7 May 1927

My dear Kamila

[...] It was only today that I burnt your last three letters; I gazed so long and with pity into the little flame. Your letters were beautiful; if only I could have displayed them and called out: look, these are from my Kamila, whom I told that I love infinitely and I think perhaps that she also loves me! For it seemed that the earth burst open[2] when I said it to her and she was silent, she ran and stood still again, I stood and ran after her again – yes, just like the birds do – who don't lie about love.

Your picture says yes to all of this; yes, that's so and it was so – and do let it go on, as ordained. And if God ordains it, God who's all love, how could it not continue other than in burning longing for you!

Just decide soon now on your day of arrival!

I'm my usual self – but occasionally I'm nevertheless lost in thought; although only in thought, you're still in my mind the whole time: through you I look into the world and through you I hear the world, and see it. Even the sun must send its rays only through your heart; this is why they warm me so.

Keep well my darling.

And I remember criss-crossing the forest and through that marshy meadow, and through the field to Topělka,[3] and those dogs on that farm, and Farka, and that woman with the trolley, the one loading the wood – but it all happened and ran past just as if in the cinema.

1 The French restaurant (owner Mr Rosenbreier), was in the 'new' Zemský dům [Regional House] built in 1924–5 on the corner of Kounicova ulice and Žerotínovo náměstí. Though just a couple of blocks down the road from Janáček's house, Janáček clearly perceived it as a superior establishment (see Plate 31) to be patronized only on special occasions. It is now a reading room in the University library. I am grateful to Dr Eva Drlíková for this information.
2 See Glossary: 'earth trembling'.
3 Topělec, a village near Písek.

Until your words [saying] that you wanted to tell me something and I asked you again and again to tell me. And you didn't look at me and could hardly put one word after another, as if they were falling like dew-drops: what would I have – done – if you were mine?

And the gates of heaven opened for me! I knew I could say that you're mine! So that happiness of mine was confirmed!

Yours, for ever yours

And that unforgettable evening when you burst into tears in your isolation[1] – and I couldn't believe that it was possible! Not to kiss you, not to take you in my arms! You know, my soul, one doesn't live through that twice! The seed from Luhačovice has grown tall; a tree has grown from it on which hangs the red of your lips; I'd like to bite into it as into an apple.

443   Brno, 8[–9] May 1927

My dear Kamila

Your letter reached me today. So, fifteen years and a little ring?[2] Do you know what sort I'd like to give you for our eleven years? A solid gold circle and in it all around eleven tiny little Czech garnets. Would that be nice? You know in those garnets there's surely the blood of stones: they've sucked it into themselves from all [other] stones. That's why stone is so cold and garnet so hot: it would certainly warm you, it wouldn't leave you in peace. What's the thing that's burning the whole time? It's in the fact that you say that you're afraid of me. And from your little finger it would go into your whole body. Oh that warmth of mine would pour over you. So, until you answer me.

My nomination [as member of the Prussian Academy of Arts][3] came in today's post and a nice diploma[4] as proof of the knighthood. You know, we'll celebrate it when you come! Now, out of common courtesy, those masses of my 'friends' could have congratulated me; but not at all. Not one, Kamilka, not one! So we'll celebrate it! But I'll also pay it back now, an eye for an eye, a tooth for a tooth!

Yesterday we were in the wood. In the afternoon towards 4 o'clock I met a goldsmith I know; he was walking along [looking] noticeably flushed, without a hat in all that heat. At 7 he suffered a stroke in the

1 See Glossary.
2 The Stössels were married on 5 May 1912.
3 See p.104, fn.
4 See p.105, fn.

[112]

train. Take care, Kamila, with that sun! Take care of your head!

You know, I've got your portrait in front of me, therefore I write as if I were speaking to you, in your kitchen, you on that divan, I at the table. You'll already be sleeping now. Little picture, go to sleep too! 8 May, evening, 9.30.

Your letter has now reached me and made me sad. I don't know if I can survive not seeing you.[1] I'll go off anywhere, however far, to be with you!

Sign yourself once: 'Tvoje [your] Kamila'!

And did you have a [second] honeymoon when you celebrated fifteen years of marriage?

Do tell.

Just think that from May until sometime in September I wouldn't see you! Do manage to come!

He, for whom you're everything in the world

I think if only I could be that rock on which you lie, that water which washes you, that sun which dries you and burns you black. And so I'm just nothing at all! [...]

446   Brno, 21 May 1927

Dear Kamila

So peace.

About the house Zdenka is a perfect model.

I wanted to have children, after the death of my two poor children – she didn't.[2]

At night I'm in my study, in the morning I come, have breakfast, read the papers – and get working.

I come from the post office, have lunch; a little bit of everyday chat.

I go again into my study, towards evening I have a walk for an hour and a half; supper, I play – with the dog!!

I go to my study for the night.

Can that be enough for me?

Is that meant to be the happiness of life?

I, a passionate person by nature, naturally look for and need a soul in which there would be warm feeling and sympathy.

1 Kamila presumably declined the Janáčeks' invitation to pay a visit (see 441).
2 In her memoirs Zdenka Janáčková has a different story. After the death of Vladimír she asked Janáček to give her another child and he refused (Janáčková 1939, 49). There is no suggestion in her memoirs that they discussed having more children after Olga's death, although the marriage was in a better state then.

You came into my path by fate – and from then I have in myself something to caress, something to get pleasure from.

Is there anything bad in it, am I a bad man because of it?

I pose these questions to myself; must I really live a life embittered every moment because of the hard nature of my wife? You won't deprive her of anything, since she doesn't have what I find in your picture. I'm happy that this love for you burst out. It had to happen like that. Only you know that and therefore know me like no-one else does.

To everyone I'm just a smiling person, and will I tell anyone how Janáček, recognized throughout the world, really lives?

Condemn me, if you will.

If I've boiled over – forgive me.

My life will go on 'smilingly' in the same way. For not every apple ripens. And my one will certainly no longer do so.

And tell me if I may go on writing Ty? I'd say yes.

You are far from me and nevertheless the nearest in my heart.

Wishing you sun and 'rocks'

Yours for ever

448 Brno, 27–8 May 1927

My only Kamila

I'm waiting eagerly for your letter. Certainly I greatly upset and disquieted you, you who aren't to blame for anything. Forgive me now that this happened at all.

I respect Zdenka for the suffering she's had and I don't want anything bad for her.

However, I need freedom of feeling; I know what you are to me, you cannot suspect yourself what a protectress you are. I've become attached to you and nothing will tear me away from you to the end of my life. I think that I'll explain it to her like this: that she'll have peace and happiness in those years that will still be granted me.

I'll write this to her from Hukvaldy, where I'm going on 6 June. From you of course I'm expecting a letter to Brno before I leave.

My address from 6 June is: Leoš Janáček

  Pod Hukvaldy, Moravia

But there's a postmaster there who taught me how to open every letter.

That's a postmaster in the right place, not so?

Therefore I beg you, *seal* every letter and tell me with what seal you've stamped the wax.

I can't bear this hiding any longer. Why and how should this longing be hid! For I live only in it – and God knows how terribly far it is from fulfilment. That single 'Tvá' simply illuminated it with quiet lightning but didn't set it alight. Only to have a letter from you now. Your card came today, I was also pleased that I saw your boy.

Keep well. You're my only thought!

Brno, 27 May 1927

I'm waiting for your letter! Perhaps you're angry with me? And those letters of mine, how glad they were perhaps when they scrawled themselves and warmed you!

Everything will be alright. It can't be otherwise.

You're in my new opera under the name *Aljeja*:[1] such a tender, dear person.

28 May 1927

Yours, eternally yours

Kamila Stösslová to Leoš Janáček, 26 May 1927

Dear Maestro

I must simply tell you that Ruda came with a bad cold. [...] He had a temperature in the morning but now he's sleeping peacefully, so I hope that it will pass. He told me that you brought him four oranges and two sweets. I just think that if you'd spoken to his teacher he'd have told you that the boy was free until five. You could surely have given him something warm, tea or coffee. But that needs a little love. Can you imagine your boy in Písek? What would Kamila have done? She'd have known how to take the place of his own mother! I don't really know why I'm writing this. I know only too well what a north wind blows at your place. I still feel it from my last visit. I was so sad I couldn't sleep. [...]

449   Brno, 28 May 1927

Dear, my only Kamila

I've sent you the books. I didn't read them myself and don't know whether you'll like them. At least you'll tell me.

You know, I neither have nor read love stories myself.

---

1 The new opera was *From the House of the Dead*. Aljeja is the young Tartar lad whom the central figure Petrovič teaches to read, and for whom he shows warm affection. Janáček cast Aljeja as a breeches role, to be sung by a mezzo-soprano.

I know from my own experience how painful love is. All my works, all my operas, all include one painful love. I've experienced it in them and also in my own life – there'll never be so much truth about it in a book. Anyway I hope at least you like them.

When the books were sent your card came – [saying] that I shouldn't send them! Why?

But also the letter – for which I'd now waited so much – how it surprised me! I got out of an important meeting – Zdenka couldn't go to the station, for Maŕa had washing in the second house – I waited for the express with the package containing what I could get together quickly.

It came; I looked out for your boy; I only just managed to give him the package; the children started walking. I asked him: 'When will you continue the journey?' Rudi answered 'Towards two o'clock'. More I couldn't ask him – the whole wave of children surged from the station. That was after 12.30.

I thought to myself: if they want to look round Brno, they won't have much time until 2. The children will be worn out.

The next day I waited in the afternoon at the station – neither sight nor sound of the expedition of the Písek children!

Believe me, there's now so much love in me that if I'd only suspected how the children were tyrannized by the teacher's lack of common sense I'd have cared for *your child*, as you yourself!

And if I'd known that they'd be in Brno until 5, I'd have searched out *your child* and fed him as richly as you do me. In all that running around I didn't even see the teacher! It would be nice if Rudi could write to me himself how the trip went. I can reassure you that I'd have had more concern about your child than you yourself; for I know that terrible danger of the ravines and gorges in the countryside and trembled with fear for the children and for *your child* most of all. How could you have written such reproaches?

For I've a head full of other worries. I don't need to worry about children as well! But I'd not have left *your child* languishing – I think that there's enough love in me here.

I know that these days are just as sad for both of us.

Thinking only of you

Your, only yours

And to get angry because of your letter – no, not that; but it hurt.

Dear Kamila

I'm reading your accusation again. I didn't go to the station [simply] 'so that it couldn't be said that you wrote and I didn't go'. What was worse was that I couldn't say that you wrote! And yet I went. In the letter there was much that wasn't for anyone other than ourselves. And now for next time. When your other boy wants to see Brno – Macocha[1] – the caves, then I'll take care of him myself. I'll show him Brno and everything else – and I'll know how to bring him back to you like a flower!

I see this in these children – who as schoolchildren wander here around Brno day after day – in the rain, the cold, ill-clad, without being looked after, hanging around. I'm sorry for them.

And I'll make it up to Rudi – and his anxious mother too. If that 'mother' had come herself – as is right and proper – it would all have turned out quite differently.

I couldn't take Rudi out from the discipline of the school. So will it be good like that and will I be pardoned for the 'two cakes and the three oranges'?

When I was a student I got a piece of bread and butter for an outing – and not even a cat cared about me. ——

News: 1. I've spoken out publicly against Dr Kramář.[2]

2. They're sculpting my likeness in stone[3] and on 1 July they'll erect it on the hill Kotouč in Štramberk. Dr Hrstka[4] is there; he's got lots of antiques; I'll invite your husband to come. To invite you, my soul, is useless.

3. I'm getting ready for Hukvaldy – with your portrait. Of course it's as similar – as coffee to chicory! The portrait and you in the flesh! The portrait at least always smiles at me – but you know how to lash a fellow even with words! I don't take it ill from you, however.

So sleep well – and I'll also go to bed contentedly.

---

1 A well-known cave (138 metres deep), in the limestone region 25 km from Brno.
2 Janáček published his protest against Dr Karel Kramář (1860–1937) in *Lidové noviny* (29 May 1927), resigning from the Czechoslovak National Democratic Party which Dr Kramář had founded. Janáček, who supported Masaryk, disagreed with Dr Kramář's opposition to Masaryk during the recent presidential elections (see Procházková 1990, 179).
3 The sculptor and painter Emil Hlavica (1887–1952) prepared Janáček's bust for the National Park in Štramberk. The bust was unveiled on 3 July 1927, when Janáček was in Frankfurt.
4 Adolf Hrstka (1864–1931), the local doctor in Štramberk, collected paintings.

And today's the last day of May[1] – and cold. And you can't go to your rocks!

Yours for ever

451   Brno, 29–30 May 1927

My dear Kamila

My letter probably made you angry!

But it will remain as before: I can't live without thinking of you. We'll be the same sort of people together as we were. You mustn't suffer; it would be with me then, come what may!

To live in the way Zdenka expects – that's a way I cannot live: it's worse than torture. And I'll not allow my freedom of thought and feeling to be taken from me. You're as necessary to me as the air. I wouldn't be what I am. None of my compositions could grow from this desert at home. I'd die like any ordinary unwanted person.

Zdenka must acknowledge this. You're my light: I live as long as it burns. I don't want to live without you. There's peace in our house; Zdenka burnt the letter. There was nothing in it apart from that <u>Tvá</u>; the <u>Tvá</u> that will make me happy to the end of my life, nothing special. I said that I forced it from you. For otherwise in that letter it was only <u>Vy</u>![2] Well, let her know that I can't live in any other way. It's better that she knows. This concealment was impossible for long.

In my life you saved me from that terrible perverted woman Horvátová,[3] you save me again and again: and I'm the one who pressures you with my passion – and nevertheless don't succeed. I adore you for your tenderness, for your pure womanhood, because you suffer for me. One day Zdenka will see that you protect me and that she was unable to do so. So write again soon, let me know that you're not suffering.

And my letters? If you need them as proof that I alone am guilty, that with my unbridled passion for you I misled you into [writing] certain words, then keep them. If you want to be of one mind with me, then burn them.

That's what I'll do now – so that I can protect you from everything.

Yours, for ever yours

1 An aberration of Janáček's; according to the postmark it was sent off on 30 May 1927.
2 See Glossary: 'Ty'; Stösslová mostly addressed Janáček with the formal *Vy*, occasionally complying with his wishes by signing off with the intimate *Tvá*.
3 See Glossary.

Monday 30 May. Zdenka's not taking it tragically; there's also no reason to do so. I'll convince her that what you are to me is for her own good. I'll not give you up while I live!

452 Brno, 31 May 1927

My dear Kamila

You're angry? And there's no reason for it.

You probably think that I always live like this, without care, gazing out of the window, like when I'm sitting in the kitchen at your place? When I've nothing else on my mind than you, [seeing] how you bustle around, when I eat up every movement of yours, every word?

I remember how you asked me if I didn't want to do some work?

You did well to notice it.

After arriving home, I rushed into work so vigorously that my heart began to pound. However, you were like a peaceful shade for me — when the heat was troublesome[;] and like the sun — when I needed to be warm: in short under your image I work well.

And now suddenly such reproaches? How could that have occurred to you?

Only she who so definitely wrote *Tvá* could take the liberty. It's possible that all sorts of things don't occur to me because from the age of nine I was left completely to my own resources and without the care and concern of parents, only among foreign people, hard people, and what's more, among priests.

I'm already waiting for Monday, when I'll leave here and when I'll write long letters – to Zdenka.

I want for once in kindness and without anger to explain to her calmly my relationship with you.

There will be such things that not even you yourself know much about.

I want to say openly what binds me to you and what will bind me right to the end – and what can't get in her way.

She's sensible; perhaps she'll acknowledge that to live like this is a torment for her and for me. I know that she'll even understand your strength and conviction and meaning for me, and that a more cheerful and intimate way of life among us all will be found! And then – you'll come to Hukvaldy, without excuses, with your younger son or your older son or with both.

Yours for ever

Dear Kamila

It's only that I think that you or your boy are sick, only because of this that I'm writing to you.

But do give me your word that if you're ever sick you'll tell me without delay! Then, when you're well, don't write perhaps. If you don't feel the need – don't write.

Recently I've had some quick jobs so that there were no free moments. Three things of mine are being printed:

1. *Taras Bulba* – I celebrate a prophet of Slavonicism in it.
2. *Lachian Dances*
3. *Nursery Rhymes*

I had to prepare everything for printing.

And on top of that the new opera *From the House of the Dead*.

And on top of that the nomination to the Prussian Academy, the appointment as 'knight', and on top of that your '<u>Tvá</u>'; well, enough for ten months!

Today the heat here was 38° Réaumur![1] Unbearable!

Brno, 2 June 1927

And on top of this your letter with the two pieces of cake and the three oranges – well, I've lived through quite enough of this.

And if I were sad at Hukvaldy, wouldn't your younger boy – like to live with me there? Ask him. I think he wouldn't be homesick.

Will a letter come from you today? I'm waiting.

Brno, 3 June 1927

No letter came. I think that you're ill but I can't be sure. I've thought that many times before – but you were well.

It will be like it was with the shepherd. He cried: 'Wolves, wolves!' and there weren't any; people ran to help unnecessarily. And once again he cried: 'Wolves, wolves!' People thought: 'but he's having us on!' and didn't go to drive them away. This time there really were wolves, they came, they ate up the sheep and the shepherd as well. And one day there'll be a real illness at your place, it will destroy you – and I won't be able to come and save you!

This is my last letter from Brno.

Keep well.

Yours for ever.

---

1 Janáček probably meant Celsius; 38° Réaumur is Celsius 47.5 / Fahrenheit 117.5. See however p.110, fn.2.

So nothing today either. Who can see inside your head! And yet you're the only one in my life who definitely said '<u>Tvá</u>'.
4 June 1927

456   Hukvaldy, 8 June 1927

Dear Kamila

So here I am in this seclusion; I walk to my forest, as you perhaps to your rocks. It's good that thoughts know how to fly so well and so persistently. In a flash they're with you, only they don't want to fly back again. You keep them by you, and you've been doing so for weeks!

Yesterday I wrote down for Zdenka what binds me to you. It was an open confession; I think she'll understand it. She imagined more than was remotely possible. For surely between us there's just a beautiful world, but what's beautiful in it, these desires, wishes, the <u>Tvá</u> and all, all just made up!

I told her that this imaginary world is as necessary for me as air and water is for my life.

I told her how your appearance released me from the clutches of that disgusting H... [Horvátová], and how over eleven years you have been, without knowing about it, my guardian angel on all sides.

I told her how in my compositions where pure feeling, sincerity, truth, and burning love exude warmth, you're the one through whom the touching melodies come, you're the Gypsy with the child in *The Diary of One who Disappeared*.

You're poor Elina Makropulos, and you're in my latest work as the lovable Aljeja. I told her that if the thread that binds me to you were to be broken, the thread of my life would be broken. I think that she'll understand all this and especially this eleven-year riddle of ours!

I'm not asking for an answer from her, because I'll not be able to live other than the way I've lived these eleven years. And now, I ask you seriously, why don't you write?

Yours for ever

Dear Kamila

I'm writing this letter to Zdenka:[1]

[']1. By the bright memory of my father and mother I swear to you that Mrs Kamila is an honourable wife and mother. Will you believe this now?

2. I ask you once and for all to leave this spying, this continual suspicion of my feelings. I'm tortured by the concealment of a perfectly ordinary sympathy, the covering up of an ordinary feeling of friendship. Will you believe once and for all in my mission in life which needs freedom of feeling, freedom which in no way detracts from my feeling for you. To these two questions give me a simple and immediate answer.'

With her I think that prudence will triumph over hot-temperedness. I'm waiting for her answer. For surely what is white is not black. And you, dear Kamila, just be patient until it's clear.

In Frankfurt they're giving my Capriccio[2] during the musical festivities. People from the Ministry of Foreign Affairs want me to go there; they're paying for my journey. I haven't decided yet. If I do so, I'd leave here straight for Prague on 26 June; there'll be a preliminary rehearsal there. The concert's on 30 June. In all I'd remain abroad about a week and on the return journey I'd certainly stop over at your place.

Really I'd only go because of this.

They're already rehearsing *The Makropulos Affair* in Prague at the National Theatre.[3]

How difficult it is to believe that apart from these 'desires' on paper – nothing has happened during the eleven years. With all other people something would probably have happened by now!

Yours for ever

---

1 Janáček wrote an exact version to Zdenka of the passage in quotation marks (Hukvaldy, 13 June 1927; BmJA, B 1394) and on 15 June 1927 also wrote to David Stössel (BmJA, E 445) about his 'innocent friendship' with Mrs Stösslová. In phrases recalling 456, he explained how she was the source of his 'much-praised melody'. As a token that she would continue to be his 'protector' until the end of his days he had implored her to write 'Tvá' just once. And so she had done, a gesture misinterpreted by Mrs Janáčková, though he was sure that Mr Stössel would not see it as any betrayal.

2 Janáček meant his Concertino, which was included at the Fifth ISCM Festival in Frankfurt later that month. The Capriccio received its première only in March 1928.

3 On 8 June Ostrčil wrote to Janáček asking his advice about the producer (Tyrrell 1992, VM72). Reseasrsals, naturally, began rather later and it was only on 13 December that Janáček heard by chance about the cast (VM74).

459 Hukvaldy, 21 June 1927

Dear Kamila, write!

I'm as if without a soul. I turn everything down, I sit around at home. I don't speak, I sit lost in thought. They ask me why and I don't know. Answer, let me know where my thoughts should go in search of you.

And that letter [to Zdenka] – let me know how I should act further. I'm as if cut in two. Not myself.

Devotedly for ever.

Today, 21 June, the Ministry is sending me to Frankfurt. I leave from Hukvaldy on 24 June; on 26 June I'll be in Prague (Karel IV., Smíchov). On 30 June there'll be my concert in Frankfurt.

Doesn't your husband want to come too – and you with him?

When I return I can stop by in Písek. I'll wait for news in Prague.

461 Frankfurt am Main, 28 June 1927

My soul

This is the theatre in which my Concertino will be played this evening.[1]

Today I had lunch in a garden of nothing but palm trees; it was magnificent!

I leave here at 5 o'clock on Sunday morning [3 July]; will I get a card from you in Prague? Greet everyone at home.

Devotedly

L.

463 Frankfurt am Main, 1 July 1927

My dear soul

So I triumphed here yesterday.[2] When they finished playing my piece the audience started calling for me. I was sitting on the ground floor among the audience – modestly. Now people began to turn to me; I had to stand up and bow on all sides. From all sides congratulations from quite unknown people. If only you'd been there, you my 'hoped-for' wife. I remember the mayor of Písek – how it struck you.

1 Janáček is probably referring to a rehearsal; the concert itself took place two days later, as is clear from 459 and 463.

2 The Concertino, with the piano part played by Ilona Štěpánová-Kurzová, was the success that Janáček described. Other works played in the ISCM concert on 30 June were chamber pieces by Mosolov, Pijper, Castelnuovo-Tedesco and Turina.

How even more so here abroad! When late at night, after 12, I was returning to the hotel alone, when everything was over and I remained only with my thoughts, I felt here that everything that I'm doing and that's going on with me, everything, is serious, good – but that you're nevertheless the dearest to me. I felt that I am happy only through you, that you're the most essential one for me, the nearest; I felt that I could give up everything else, but not you. So this triumph passed coolly from me and you came to me warmly, nearer and nearer. So it was clear that you, my soul, are nearest of all to me! I leave here on Sunday morning [3 July] at 5, I'll be in Prague probably in the evening and will await your letter there. Will 'Come!' be written in it?

Yours, for ever yours

L.

464   Frankfurt am Main, 1 July 1927

My dear soul

You know, there's something in one which lives independently, without our will. I walked around the town this morning just as the spirit moved me. I remained standing on the banks of the Main; my eyes wandered aimlessly from place to place; I looked at one house and I read: 'here lived Marianna von Willemer, Goethe's Sulejka'.

What was it that led me here to this place of Goethe's great love? You know there's something which leads one without one even wanting it.

I went on again blindly and suddenly I read: 'here the poet Goethe was born and lived'. I went into the house, I looked round three rooms on the first floor, the little garden on the ground floor.

So I found both without even looking for them! And now a cheerful lesson for you, 'my dear hoped-for wife'; on your house you'll now put up the sign: 'here lives Mrs Kamila "the hoped-for wife" of Drph. Leoš Janáček'.

And it will be sad one day when other people come, and those two 'hopeful' dear people, who loved one another – will be no more.

Such is life! Be well, my wife.

Yours, only yours

L.

On the way back from Frankfurt, Janáček made an expedition to Písek as proposed in 459. Details of exactly when the trip took place are not suggested by the letters that follow, though from his recollections a year later (703), it is clear that Janáček was in Písek on 5–6 July 1927. According to Cyril Vymetal, he attended an afternoon concert in Písek on 5 July, the eve of the burning of Jan Hus, followed by a bonfire in the woods that evening (see Glossary: 'Hus Eve').

465 [Brno, 9 July 1927][1]

My dear soul

Now, from your warm letter today, I know that I've done you good. And I take unutterable pleasure from it: I didn't have a moment's embarrassment: in fact wasn't my decision to leave Huk-valdy earlier a providential inspiration? I gave a message to people in the bank first thing on Monday [4 July] and I'm surprised that you knew about it only on Wednesday.

So, we are mutually necessary to one another. Go on living con-tentedly, I stand by you at every moment. And now Luhačovice. You're anaemic and I saw the outcome with my own eyes: the carbonic baths of Luhačovice do good in this respect; your doctor must surely know this. I'm a recluse at the spa, you don't go looking for showy things – so we'd get along very well. We'd get the baths over with, and then up and away into the forests or we'd take a trip in the surrounding countryside. Do you want that? So come. A day earlier, you'll welcome me; a day later I'll welcome you.

You're strong, you're not frightened of me; I'm even stronger – and you don't have to fear.

The barriers fell; we won't let our desires be taken from us. You'll say you're mine, and you know that I'm yours for ever. Can our world be any more beautiful? I believe your declaration; you spoke it to me as simply as a child saying its prayers, and I in turn said it as passionately as the two magnificent butterflies in my wood who found each other in joy and my eye couldn't tear itself away from their happiness.

You're beautiful through your youth – I'm admired only for my work. You are already giving me more, won't you regret it?

I will love only you to the end of my life – and you're making a sacrifice. You're already making it at home now. I know what you've gone through recently and, believe me, I've suffered no less at the thought of it.

God made one mistake: you should have come into this world a

1 According to the postmark, the letter was sent on Monday 11 July 1927. 'Saturday' at the end of the letter suggests that it was written two days earlier.

[125]

little earlier:[1] most certainly as the two beautiful butterflies we'd have flown and flown, and inexorably have found one another.

So, we'll make up for it.

I'll wait until you tell me when you're leaving. Otherwise at least write on a card: 'I'm well', for I get anxious about you straightaway.

Saturday

Yours for ever

L.

There is a gap in the correspondence of two weeks, bridged by six letters of which only the envelopes have survived. The first four (*466–9: 13–19 July) were postmarked in Hukvaldy, the next two (*470–1: 27 and 30 July) were postmarked in Brno.

472   Brno, 30 July 1927

My dear Kamila

So read this: you're also going to like it.

We'll divide the fee which I received for the article into three:

a third for the Gypsy children,[2]

a third for their new 'mummy'

a third I'll take myself for pens to write nice things about you. And do you know what is the very summit of my happiness?

And I know that I'm more to you than those friends of yours. But by how much more?

So get well soon, sleep and warm yourself up as you like to, contentedly: someone watches over you, won't allow you to be wronged.

And last night I dreamt about you all the night. Now I say to myself: calm down! I open my eyes: reality is indeed far, far away from dreams, however beautiful!

[To come] at the same time to Luhačovice? I hope they won't photograph us [together] straightaway at the station! So, one after the other. I'm looking forward to it.

Anyway, are you happy in everything? [...]

Keep well my soul

L.

I have freedom of thought and feeling, I don't hide what you are to me. It was terrible before, that secrecy! Unbearable! Now what's

1 Janáček wrote 'later'.
2 See Glossary.

necessary is known.

And you have your certainty behind you; you can firmly rely on it. And everything else will be in God's hands.

Yours for ever

L.

Apart from a brief letter (*473: Brno, 3 August 1927), there is another gap in the correspondence, this time unbridged by any empty envelopes. On 16 August Janáček arrived at Luhačovice for a two-week visit. The fact that he did not send Stösslová a card on arrival suggests that the plan to arrive simultaneously (472) succeeded; certainly she was there four days later.

474 Luhačovice, 20 August 1927

My dear, only Kamila

In my life I've not experienced more beautiful moments than those this afternoon! I'd say more exalted moments.

I knew you as emotionally deep, so honourably sacred, so sensible, so true, strong, quiet, devoted that I stand before you as before an apparition which only the good Lord could have sent me. I've found you on my journeys, where no woman could have followed.

How warming were your words, how warm was your little hand which, for the first time, did not draw away.

I can't get to sleep until I tell you that you're more precious to me than my life. Just stay by me, my good angel.

Yours eternally

Leoš

And it was Friday – our beautiful day![1]

475 Luhačovice, 28 August 1927

My dear one, my only Kamila

I kept a grip on myself more or less but as the train turned and vanished in the distance – it was bad.

Why is love also painful! I went to the grave of my good uncle[2] and

1 20 August 1927 was a Saturday, so Janáček's postscript suggests he was writing about the day before, but the opening of the letter contradicts this. It is possible that Janáček muddled the day of the month (the letter was delivered by hand, so that there is no postmark to offer support to this theory). It is less likely that Janáček muddled the day of the week, especially since he continued to celebrate this 'Friday–feast-day' (see Glossary).
2 Janáček's uncle, Father Jan Janáček (1810–89), who took responsibility for him after his father's death, is buried in the cemetery of Veselí nad Moravou, a short train journey from Luhačovice.

I remained there until the arrival of the train. On the way to Miramare[1] I looked round the whole time in case you were calling perhaps – but there was no longer any sight anywhere of my little devil. And from the 'budka'[2] I'd have gone on further right to Světlov[3] –

But so what, it isn't easy to write when one's eyes are full of tears. I look all the time at my watch – now it's half past five – and so I'm bound up with you into the distance. I don't know, don't know – these days without you won't improve my health. I can't think of anything now after all the beautiful things we've experienced here. The most beautiful of all was that they always saw us two, both of us [together], and that they certainly knew and said to each other: 'these two are a world unto themselves!'

[...] How one falls in love even with the paths when that dear black Kamila of mine pattered along them. Now you should rest yourself. I'll be up until 10.30 at night. And you also had tears in your eyes!

Yours for ever
Leoš

476   Luhačovice, 28–9 August 1927

Dear, only Kamila

It's 9 in the evening. You'll still be trundling along for another hour and a half.

I've passed on your greeting to the woman from the dairy;[4] she much regretted that [we] didn't look her up; and she praised you, and I – added kindling to the flames!

I've eaten on your behalf what we so liked to eat and after 8 o'clock I went to Světlov.

The windows were open, but empty darkness. Your little black head didn't appear! That was sad, you know. With a sob I passed by. Why does everything disappear so soon and why do these memories turn into tears? And tomorrow morning I'll go there again – and I know that I'll return all alone and the window will be open – but silence behind it. My chatterbox won't answer. And these few days will go just as they went with you. Certainly I'll have my eyes open – somewhere into the distance, and in them there'll be your

1 A local café.
2 The Slovácká búda, see p.72, fn.1.
3 The *pension* where Stösslová had been staying this season (see 476).
4 See Glossary.

image. And people will think: 'he sees her beside him'.

And I waited until 10.30 at night. You were glad to be home now and promptly into your feather bed and I also shut my eyes.

Today, 29 August, the sun woke me up again. At a quarter past seven I'll be in Světlov. The people inside will be surprised! What does he want [?]; she's no longer here, is she! And the window will be open – but she's not here, not here. But I've grown to love you, and so you are with me, my single dear joy!

Yours for ever
Leoš

480 Luhačovice, 1 September 1927

My dear Kamila

The window of your little room is already shut today; certainly my Kamila's no longer there. It's impossible to forget this little room; and the journey to it. Plenty of stars shine above it. But quiet all around. I buy a stamp at the kiosk. 'Has madam left already?' Reply: 'Yes, my wife has already left.' And in the dairy they put a fresh bunch of flowers for me on the table. I ask: 'Is it to decorate the table, or for me?' For you! So I went off with the bunch of flowers and you're too far away for me to give them to you. It's easy to say 'don't be sad', but hard to smile. Your letter cheered me up; I read it all the time and look forward to the 'laughing walls'.[1] And [do you think] that we'll be able to laugh any more? And to exult until our hearts want to leap! And the walls will want to give way and not be able to: they won't let go of us and we won't let go of each other! Will it be so? And now goodbye, dear places! There was love where we stood and sat. There, surely, fragrance breathed. And those who come to these places, let them have such strange feelings in their hearts as we had. And they won't know why they feel like that.

And thanks to all of you who smiled on us. We met no bad people and silenced the insolent.

And you, Kamila, remember these days for ever, as the holy day of two souls. I saw traces of tears on your letter and there'd be so many in mine, that you won't be able to read it. Keep well my soul, my joy.

Yours for ever
Leoš

1 A reference to Stösslová's cheerful character and tendency to laugh, possibly based on the expression (in Czech) 'even the walls were laughing'.

484 Brno, 11 September 1927

My dear soul

Pay the fine! I don't have stamps[1] and I want to thank you for everything good; for every smile, for every kind word.

You're my good spirit. Were it not for you, I'd have no joy, there'd be no smile on my face!

The telegram was already waiting for me: on 29 September I'll probably already be in Berlin – and I'll see you after that – earlier than you permit and earlier than I'd hoped. It's simply our fate now: to be often with one another, willy-nilly! Well, I'm glad of it – and you? I don't even have time now for reminiscing. We aren't bored together, we don't know sadness, we don't even speak an unnecessary word. So once again, I thank you from my heart for everything good.

I see and know more and more that I'd no longer want to live without you.

Yours, for ever yours

L.

Janáček had returned to Brno on 2 September but soon was off again to Hukvaldy, from where he sent Stösslová a series of postcards and short notes (*485–92: 13–24 September 1927). On the day of his return he wrote a longer letter (*493: 26 September 1927), complaining about her lack of communications and over the paintings that he was buying from Stössel, which he was now discovering were of indifferent quality (he nevertheless went ahead; see 502). Then, on 28 September, he left for Berlin.

495 Berlin, 29 September 1927

Dear soul

It was a pleasure to hear my little work.[2] I've signed contracts with Moscow[3] and a contract for my latest opera.[4] And I remember

1 There were no stamps on the envelope, so Stösslová had to pay the fine imposed for delivery.
2 The Sinfonietta, conducted by Otto Klemperer in Berlin with great success on 29 September 1927.
3 Janáček signed no contracts, but at his instigation Universal Edition began negotiations with Professor Yevgeniy Maksimovich Braud, who promised to perform the Sinfonietta and *Jenůfa* in Moscow. The Sinfonietta was performed in Moscow in 1929 under Klemperer, but *Jenůfa* was not given there until 1958.
4 The Berlin contract for *The Makropulos Affair* was of no avail; there was no production and the German première was given only in 1929, in Frankfurt.

you. Tomorrow, on Friday, I leave here. I'll be with you on Sunday [1 October].

Your

L.

496   Prague, 30 September 1927

Even if you don't invite me, I'll nevertheless come for lunch on Sunday!

Greetings

Invited or not, Janáček arrived. The stay was particularly memorable in that it was on this occasion that the Písek album (see Glossary) was inaugurated. The first entry was on 2 October and thereafter Janáček wrote something in the album each time he visited Písek.

497   Brno, 5 October 1927

< [1] > And I burn everything. At least I ought to collect the ash, buy an urn for it and put a label on it: 'This is ash from thoughts; it's a cure for great love. [...]

498   Brno, 8 October 1927

Dear, beloved

< top portion of letter cut away at an angle: one? word missing > [...] How vividly I remember our Luhačovice now. I'm pining for it so much; the tears almost burst from me! I see Světlov and your little room; I'm so sad. Why don't such moments last for ever? Why sometimes does everything one has lived through appear to one with such sharpness? I almost see myself with you, when we wrote on those photographs. And yet it's certain that it will no longer return *just as it was*! That's the sadness behind it! You, bending over me, I feel the warmth of your body; you're so near – and I can't write for bliss. Our dear beautiful Luhačovice! Was anyone so happy there at the time as we? No-one, no-one could have been happier. Oh, people don't know everything that's hidden in love. But Kamilka, tears pour down my face. Why? Painful love, you see. My dear soul, why do I love you so! Indeed one can hardly believe it.

1 This is a scrap of paper, cut from the middle of a letter, with a few lines on each side (see Glossary: 'omissions, crossings-out').

This morning I composed a lot, touching things – and into it your dear image now falls, that face of yours full of tenderness. < three? words missing > That's why I'm so unutterably sad.

It's necessary to calm down. Tears relieve grief, but at other times they devour. Will the post bring lines from you? Think of me often; keep your smiles and jokes for me. For me they're a necessary cure – and as for others, let them now do without them.

Today's Saturday; you'll be going to the cinema. And in Brno they're already saying how smartly and with what good taste you go about in Písek. What if they knew about that dress for the concert, and that blue-and-white dress when the aeroplanes were circling. You have no idea how you're watched in Písek. I'm glad that you arouse attention – and respect. On 28 October they'll award the state music prizes.[1] I ought to have a claim on the basis of my works; but the silence in Prague doesn't augur well for me. They'll think to themselves: 'nothing for him, he's got enough!' Yes, I have the greatest treasure, the greatest riches, but they don't know that you're that treasure, you're my wealth.

Keep well, my Kamilka!

Yours for ever

Leoš

500 Brno, 16 October 1927

< p.1 missing > It seems as if you came to meet me: I think that you were in a blue dress. And today I feel so bitter! What a life I live! How would a breeze feel if it could not fly to the ends of the earth, how would a drop of rain feel, if it could not fall on the earth and moisten the parched earth?

I'm the same.

There are people who sit down halfway through their journey – they can't go on! But what if one's not allowed to go on! That's the pain.

Well, enough of that Kamila. I'm feeling lonely again today. I'm finishing a big work – probably my last opera, so it seems to me. And I'm always sad when I take my leave of those whose lives I've lived for as much as two to three years. And you understand my pain and also my sorrow. You understand and you feel why it's essential for me to see you often!

< p.3 missing >

1 See pp.59, fn.1 and 139, fn.1.

[132]

So today, Sunday, I invited Ondrúšek for lunch. At least I could recall our happy days in Luhačovice. I gave him two pears for the journey – from your ones! But while [he eats] them he won't be thinking the thoughts I have when I suck into them!

Keep well, my soul.

I'll put this in the post, so that my letter will be with you in good time.

Yours for ever

L.

Sunday, ? [Janáček's query] October 1927

501 Brno, 16–17 October 1927

My dear Kamila

16 October, Sunday, evening, 10.30.

I didn't even know what the date was: it's all one when day after day you live the same, workday or holiday.

In the evening there was a ringing in my ear; I wanted to be a little superstitious and I thought to myself: I suppose Kamila's probably in the cinema and has remembered me! Ondrúšek sat around at my place until 3 – then I ran off quickly with the letter to get to you in time. I'd also like to receive something from you tomorrow. I have your picture before me; I think: she sits here with me, she can almost talk! Do you remember how we spoke in the park about that scale, that it continually rises higher and higher between us? I'd most like to jump right to the very highest note: it would be that exultant shout!! You're content, dear soul! I'm also, at least in the vicinity of the photograph, satisfied, restrained.

*

So, my dear soul, yesterday and today I've finished that opera of mine.

From the House of the Dead

A terrible title, isn't it? Also yesterday, at the end [of Act 1], one criminal described how when killing the major, he said to himself 'I'm God and Tsar!' And in the night I dreamt that in the eiderdown a dead man was lying on me, so [vividly] that I felt his head! And I cried 'but I've done nobody any harm!' The eiderdown fell from me; and I was so relieved. –

And then I felt your soft arm at my head and I ... oh, don't ask more... it was more delightful. These dreams, these dreams, just dreams!

[133]

Will a letter come today from you? I think so.

In the picture you're striding forward:[1] with that step you could already be in Brno in a little while. But I like it when you toss your head like that. Today you'll probably have two letters from me: I'll send this one only tomorrow; perhaps I'll hear something from you.

But now that work with my copyist! I'd rather shift gravel! And it will go on certainly right up to Easter, if not longer![2] Well, it's impossible to be only with my sweet Kamila! It's impossible to walk continually round the flame – and avoid it, so as not to burn up –

It won't do just continually looking into your black, bewitching eyes – and keeping guard over them –

It won't do not to let that delightful little figure of Kamila out of one's head at least for an instant,

but it is allowed, surely, always to think of her, always to want her, to want, to want – maybe six things!

And, after all, this letter will still go off today.

Yours for ever

L.

Brno, 17 October 1927

502   Brno, 19 October 1927

My dear Kamila

Didn't you get ill from the patronal festival?[3] Goose, chickens, pigeons!

And you were run off your little feet! Who brought those guests to you?

If you'd been made of oak, but you're like warm breath, which ought to be wrapped up and nursed, worried over, so that it doesn't disperse. And to pile guests on you?

Oh dear soul, I'd take care of you differently. I'm waiting to see you now. The man from Budějovice[4] didn't get in touch; but there'll be another opportunity soon.

And I don't like this changeable hot-to-cold [weather]. But you also go from the hot kitchen barefoot across the corridor, down the steps

---

1 The best candidate would be Plate 12, taken two months earlier in Luhačovice.
2 By Easter (8 April) only Act 1 had been copied out. Janáček went on working with his two copyists until 20 June (see 607 to 690 *passim*).
3 The festival celebrating the feast of a patron saint. In Písek the main church is dedicated to St Václav [Wenceslas], whose feast is on 28 September.
4 Jan Hubáček, the director of the theatre at České Budějovice, asked on 3 October 1927 (BmJA, B 1124) for the loan of orchestral material from the Plzeň Theatre and at the same time informed Janáček that the première of *Jenůfa* would be on 27 October 1927.

for water, and back into the heat! God, Kamila, do think of yourself more! Write to me soon to tell me how you got through it all. I'm waiting impatiently for your news.

Everything's smiling on me now: the *Frankfurter Zeitung* apparently made much of me, Berlin now wants that new opera.[1] Well it's lucky that I'm near the end of it.[2]

And you, my little soul, for me you're above everything, above all the notes that I write! You're my joy. It's only through you that I like the world. You're the holy calm in my soul, but you're also the little fire which gives warmth, which heats up desire. Everything for you. You're the source of tenderness in my compositions. You're so lovable that if you were even smaller I'd place you in a crib like the Christ-child and I'd cradle you into sweet dreams. I love you from my soul. Are you sleeping yet? It's 10.15 in the evening.

*

And at the beginning of November the Italian composer Mascagni[3] is coming here; they'll perform my *Cunning Little Vixen* so he can hear something of ours.

So many things are happening around me that my head turns.

And from that photograph, it's as if you spoke to me: better come to me! And I'd come running. Aren't you for me the highest thing for which I long! And the next thing is that it should grow, but in your sun.

You're so tiny and pretty – and you have such power over me! – Tomorrow I'll probably send you Kč 2000 for my picture debt; now those children[4] will soon be mine. Really – mine–yours! They came to me at your behest.

Are you well?

Always write, whether yes or no! I need your health for mine. I'm hurrying in order to send off this letter still [today].

1 After the successful performance of the Sinfonietta in Berlin, Janáček promised, without further consideration, the first performance of *From the House of the Dead* to Klemperer at the Kroll Oper, Berlin. In a letter of 5 October 1927 (BmJA, D 1058) Emil Hertzka, the director of Universal Edition, tactfully reminded Janáček that Erich Kleiber was equally deserving: with the Staatsoper, Berlin, he had given the very influential Berlin première of *Jenůfa* in 1924.

2 Janáček's announcement in his previous letter that he had 'finished' *From the House of the Dead* referred only to his first draft. There were another eight months of hard work still to go.

3 Pietro Mascagni (1863–1945); Janáček later described his encounters with him and his wife (see 513 and 516).

4 Two pictures by František Dvořák, *Laškující amorci* [Dallying Cherubs] (see Glossary: 'children' and Plate 37).

I always think to myself, will some inquisitive person turn up who will spy on this daily correspondence?

And it's only my conversation with you – when mountains divide us. A conversation without which I couldn't exist.

Yours for ever

L.

503   Brno, 21–2 October 1927

My dear Kamila

Today, Friday, evening, 21.IX [*recte* X].

This morning working from 7.30 until 12; in the afternoon to 4. Post the letter at noon, afternoon walk hopefully to the post office – but nothing.

So don't wonder that I'm cut up, as if a hamburger were to be made out of me!

You are far away, I like a fish out of water: it hurls itself about and thrashes itself to death.[1]

And just at the moment nothing's going on in the world, nothing calls me. I'm glad now that I've got your photographs from Luhačovice.[2] If you've got some where you're alone, send them to me. I have only that one that we 'cut off'. And mine? Wait until I get that Hukvaldy one.

And that fish which thrashes around on dry land, how different it is when it's in the Otava at Písek! Unrecognizable! Lively – and now I'm languid; chatty – and now I'm grudging with words.

But also that silver-foaming Otava; you have it near you, glance at its waves! As if you borrowed it for yourself: hands, breasts, your whole body ripples so beautifully too![3]

Well, in your vicinity, I'd not thrash around. *And I'll not let my internal pain be known!*

Are you well now? Don't you need that doctor any more? Aren't you going anywhere? Wait until it becomes clear when I'll be able to travel. That will be within a fortnight. That's my only consolation. If I didn't have you, I don't know what would become of me!

Nevertheless I have you – and nevertheless I don't! You know I'm not able to divert myself with anyone else; to trifle, to laugh – like you! I thought that now I'll be merry everywhere – it lasted for a

1 See Glossary: 'fish thrashing'.
2 See for instance Plates 9–12.
3 Janáček's first comparison of the river Otava with Kamila's body; see Glossary: 'Otava'.

while; but because you're so far away, that *separation* takes away all my laughter and at times I'm indescribably sad; like when I'm so alone, as for instance now! And I feel that if I had the 'whole scale' then I'd never leave you. So from it I have only what you called 'nothing', and how sad this separation is. Sleep in health!

Saturday.
The last pear! The largest! Oh, what kissing that was – of that pear! And it was juicy, and sweet as honey!

Today I did two numbers – pieces from the opera: a merry one – two rascals are fighting, having stolen sour milk and bread from an old woman; and a second one, sad, fateful.[1] I think that I succeeded with both.

I have a little devil who's sometimes naughty and sometimes is close to tears. Do you know her?

I've put her into my heart, and now that heart sings out such notes, now laughter and then crying!

Tomorrow's Sunday [23 October]. Boring. I'd rather bite into something else – instead of Sunday!

Yours, only yours and for ever
L.

504 [postmarked, Brno, 24 October 1927]

My dear Kamila
Do you know that it's known in Brno how I go shopping with you in Písek? A 'serious' gentleman, they say, and you in your red flowered dress! And amazingly, Zdenka told me this *without anger*!

How I laughed! In Brno, you know, I don't go to the market. That woman painter, God knows what she's called,[2] the one who was in Brno, told someone.

Well, we'll really start going out together now! And until she meets us somewhere in the woods! It's true that we fear this so much! And České Budějovice! Their theatre's going to Norway, and there they'll also perform *Jenůfa*.[3] So I'll have to go and see it in Budějovice – so they don't disgrace me abroad. I'd be in Budějovice on the 27th. So

---

1 The first number is an incident near the start of *From the House of the Dead*. The 'sad, fateful' piece is probably the arrival of Alexandr Petrovič Gorjančikov, the well-born political prisoner, whose dismay at the first sight of his new surroundings is brutally portrayed.
2 By 28 December 1927 Janáček knew as well (see 548).
3 The České Budějovice Theatre did not go to Norway.

you see, fate's always leading us together. I'm now so much looking forward to it. So invite me!

But I'm sad that you don't write. Today I wanted to read < about two lines cut out >

Does the way to Budějovice go through Písek? If not, it must be built, whatever it costs. I'll stop off for you, take you with me – and then I'd most like to abduct you.

I just think up journeys so they lead to Písek. All roads, they say, lead to Rome; that's not true any more! All roads lead to Písek.

How the world changes.

And you, my dear soul, what are you doing?

I enclose that photograph; however it looks.

Now you're probably taking a rest on the divan; it's 1.30 in the afternoon.

I'd sold this pig in a poke; I'd like to get it ready now.[1] But I'll hold on to it a bit longer. What of the pig when I have the little devil from Písek in my mind?

You, my dear little devil, be well. Thinking of you all the time.

Yours for ever

L.

< postscript? cut > 1927

507   Brno, 26 October 1927

My dear Kamila

Today Wednesday 26 October. I was reading *Národní politika* at 8 o'clock this evening and ... [I read České] 'Budějovice, twenty-seventh gala performance of

Jenůfa!'[2]

There was nothing in *Lidové noviny* and absolutely nothing in *Národní politika* before that.

Of course there was no longer time for the trip to Budějovice. So they spoilt it for me – not the going to them but to you in Písek. I suppose they were frightened of me; that's why the director didn't invite me at all.

I'll combine it with a trip to Prague, for I must hear it to know whether the Budějovice people can dare to go abroad.

I never complain about fate. If only because it's been so kind and

1 i.e. *From the House of the Dead.*
2 See 504.

sent me you. So I'm friendly with everyone and the journey to Budějovice will surely come my way.

For there's something fateful in our relationship. Just compare Luhačovice the first time and this year! And as for what will come, fate will bring it to me, and will be even kinder to me. The portrait < second half of page cut off >

As for that state prize – it was to have been a secret, a surprise for me. And already two or three people have whispered it to me as a secret which they weren't meant to divulge! And I always pretend to be astonished. How surprised I'll be on Friday![1]

If 'our state' were to say to me: 'Marry that delightful girl who's called Kamila. And be happy with her!'

That would be the recognition, the state prize, which would please me most of all.

I'm so indifferent to everything else. Ah yes. The state cannot say that. Only we can say it without apprehension.

But I've got a presentiment that nevertheless we'll say it one day. Openly, with firm vision, with decisive words.

You're glad that you've found peace again – and for me peace is boring. I don't like it except as relaxation after an enjoyable great excitement. That was the case with you, now you need peace. However, I've thrown myself into work.[2] You've regained your cheerfulness, humour – and I'm as if pressed down by a heavy stone. Your photograph alone must be enough for me! In it you're as if alive; you've given it to me to bring pleasure to me.

< second half of page cut off >

You slept again at my head! You laugh so much in the portrait that you always make me laugh!

508 Brno, 30 October 1927

My dear Kamila

What a sudden change! I'm curious what sort of 'rebuilding' you've done in your house! I'm already heating [the room] a little in the evening; cold nights, magnificent weather during the day!

Here at home I've also had some 'serious' talking. The crisis passed.

---

1 See 498. The state prizes were announced on Friday 28 October. Janáček received one for *The Makropulos Affair*.
2 After completing his first draft of *From the House of the Dead* on 17 October (see 501), Janáček had begun a full-scale revision, in progress by 22 October (see 503; Tyrrell 1992, 332–3).

We'll tell each other everything: we'll have quite a lot to talk about. If only I could see you soon!

For ever yours

L.

Between the letters of 30 October and 5 November Janáček visited Písek and together with Kamila and her mother attended there a performance of *Jenůfa* given by the České Budějovice company on 2 November. He left Písek on 4 November.

509   Brno, 5 November 1927

My dear soul

Just now I wanted to write 'tiny little imp' to you instead of soul.

But you're a nice little imp, a lovely little devil. I'm mindful that I haven't yet paid you for the tickets for *Jenůfa*, I didn't even ask how you acquired them. You know, I arrive at your place and I'm already a different fellow from the one in Brno. I forget about everything. I just want to stroke you all the time and find solace in you. How strange it is for me that I can say of you 'she's mine, all mine', that good soul!

When I was leaving I wasn't able to open the window in the train to take one more look at you. And so it was suddenly as if all those nice things fell into an abyss. You disappeared. And I so regretted it. In the train from the main station I closed my eyes so as to see only you in my imagination – and for a good three hours I was deeply lost in thought.

And how could I not be! You're like an open book, one just wants to read from it and not to stop until one's finished reading! I'd like this book to be so big that I could always read from it! I wouldn't put it down during the day, or even at night. And I'd read some pages in it several times, those pages about a big promise, and then those pages where it tells about mother and a certain father. About an adorable mother who has so many of these noisy children that she doesn't know what to do with them – and nevertheless loves them.

And then there are many other beautiful pages in that book, they breathe the fragrance of your body! And do you know what's just occurred to me now? When I stand close to you, your body breathes of pure water, fresh and refreshing, it breathes of that pure air in the Písek woods, of the silver water of the Otava! That's why your breasts swell like the tree tops of those woods, and undulate as

[140]

softly as when the little waves of the Otava run along. And we recalled that on the bridge! That's your charm.

And in the park the darling Kamila made that quiet promise – 'I don't have to go' (you've got little teeth like pearls) – and we'll be able to cope with a life of merry and sad memories. We'll bear that separation resolutely together. We'll not look for anyone else apart from ourselves.

Kamila, I believe that I speak also for you. –

I'll send you something in the next few days for your needs for the Gypsy children.[1]

So I'm living again in work blessed by the memories of beautiful days.

Keep well.

Yours for ever

L.

510   Brno, 7–8 November 1927

My dear Kamila

So have you put it on already? Have you got a warm back? That's why I took to it so. I was going past the Lyons silk house:[2] I saw a model nicely dressed and that shawl hanging so loosely around the neck and the ends on the shoulders. I thought to myself: for Kamila! I went in, bought it, sent it! To give her a little pleasure; for she was slaving away for me during those three days! She was cooking, making beds; taking fright. Her mouth almost swollen – from speaking. Surely that's the holy truth! But today, Monday, nothing at the post office! Dear Kamilka, I think that we'll begin sealing our letters. Wait until I start it. Today you ought to have been at my place so I could keep going into the night. I have had so much fast work. Now I'll look at my laughing one – [your] photograph and – good night!

Did you get pleasure from the shawl? Do tell me sincerely!

Tuesday (8 November). So have you got it on already? I seem to be like standing water, like a fish pond! Everything that lives in it must be within its banks that rise up all around.

And I'd so like to be a strong current which clears from its path everything that gets in its way.

Kamila, be also that strong current!

1 See Glossary.
2 Maison de Lyon, Masarykova 8.

[141]

I won't survive for long in the standing water! It's beautiful, pleasant. And the carp[1] even have little baby carp.

But, but! When later they're caught! And fate can catch even the prettiest creatures.

To escape that fate.

Today it's bubbling up in me so. You're in my thoughts as quiet as when you walk ever so quietly from place to place. But time is racing! I don't want to be in that standing fish pond.

And yet there's nothing else other than going from bank to bank. But how to get out of it!

And when you said: 'in the day? at night?' and I just said quietly – 'in the night' – and I'd have cried out 'even during sunlight!'

That already was the way out of the fish pond!

Today I can't wait now for your letter! After Friday [4 November], when I left [Písek], simply nothing.

What have you been doing all this time?

Yours, for ever yours

L.

511 [undated, Brno, 9 November 1927, postmarked 10 November 1927]

My dear little soul

It greatly pleased me [to hear] what effect *Jenůfa* had on your mother. I value that recognition more than the writing in the papers.

I'm now patching up *Káťa Kabanová* in two places: the stage-crew can't get the stage ready [in time], they need more music.[2]

I've done that now and take up my pen today to write to you.

You know it's like when children say their prayers before sleeping. Only they don't like doing it and I do like writing to you.

Children fall asleep at their little prayers and I wouldn't fall asleep until I'd finished writing.

< p.2 missing >

It's perhaps the sweetest tiredness, that tiredness from a great love. Sleep sweetly, my Kamila!

*

1 Carp is traditionally bred in Czechoslovakia as a common freshwater fish in reservoirs and fish ponds.

2 This refers to the extensions to the interludes in Acts 1 and 2 of *Káťa Kabanová*, which were first performed in the Prague German Theatre on 21 January 1928.

And dear Kamilka, when you were lying on that divan, you were like a little lamb which I had a mind to take, tie all up in the shawl and run far, far away with it. And then I'd untie the shawl and stroke and kiss the dear little lamb.

This bit of letter you'll cut out again. But what can I do! One doesn't forget what makes a fellow glad.

Otherwise, if he had to forget, he'd want everything at once ravenously.< p.4 missing >

And[1] that shawl just fold it from the corners [i.e. diagonally] and throw it across [your shoulders]; don't tie it. Have I got your colour right?

[...]

So my little soul, you are as dear to me as the spring sun! My Kamila!

512   Brno, 9 November 1927

My dear soul

So I earnestly beg you, don't go there alone to the wood and also avoid those rocks. There at the wood and near those rocks, you know the ground trembled under me, we'll go there only together.

I fear for you! Those murders in Písek[2] are terrible now! With your appearance you're striking, you go richly dressed, you're beautiful, my child. So many wretches wander around there. Don't go alone beyond the outskirts of Písek! I ask you for that, promise me. I myself was disturbed by that last event!

Today I read your letter once again and I beg you, calm down. After all it's not necessary for us to get excited: we put ourselves in the hands of fate. We'll take from its hands what it brings us. Believe me that I'll protect you. I know you, that you're unable to bear pain and especially spiritual pain. Don't I want you to be spared it at all costs? I want to have my dear laughing Kamila, and for her not to suffer. Surely you have to and will look everyone straight in the eye. So don't be frightened, Kamila.

You've such a dear, gentle nature; of such perhaps were angels [made]. Wouldn't I protect you? If your life were at stake, mine would be too. I've looked only for those two words[3] at the end of the

---

1 The remainder of the letter is written as a PS down the sides of pp.1 and 3; the missing pp.2 and 4 would presumably have had similar additions.
2 On 6 September 1927 Marie Lepešková (41) killed her husband, Vojtěch Lepeška (71), a teacher at the Czech State Gymnasium in Písek.
3 i.e. Tvá Kamila [Your Kamila]; see Glossary: 'Ty'.

letter! I found them: the first in haste; the second I deciphered. It seemed to me like your crossed arms. What more can I ask out of life! That second word hints at everything which is in my desire. I found your tears on the letter. But keep your head up, Kamilka! Again I look forward to seeing you! Until I'll be able to say that it could be at such and such a time, and until you'll say 'come'! How merry we'll be together! You won't have to invite me: 'come on, talk!'

So for today, 9 November. Sleep sweetly![1]

513 Brno, 11 November 1927

My dear Kamila

It's half-past two at night! Imagine, I've only just returned from that gala evening in honour of Mascagni.[2]

We got acquainted with one another in a friendly fashion; he's coming here once again in early spring, he wants to get to know *The Cunning Little Vixen*. But his wife! Only now do I know how happy I am that I've got you. You, this quiet, devoted, mild soul. She's loud, banged her fist on the table when she didn't get water. Yes, Kamilka, we complement one other. I look at you as if on quiet water; I have the time to see myself in you, to find peace and satisfaction in you. With you there's time to consider, there's time to love you < one word obliterated >

You've long been asleep. I'm sending you a message while you're in your dreams!

*

[...] And now let me tell you a funny story. Mrs Mascagni continually kept on interfering with what was going on on stage. When the producer had had enough of it, he took the lady into the auditorium and shut the doors on her so that she couldn't get out. How she banged!

So, contacts made. – And today I'm waiting again for your letter. Will there be again the 'two words'? You know those are magic words! They give you to me and I take you without embarrassment. It's so nice when two people give themselves to one another.

There can't be anything nicer!

[...]

1 This letter is complete in itself, but unsigned, which may suggest that Stösslová destroyed a continuation.
2 Pietro Mascagni conducted *Aida* in the Czech National Theatre, Brno, on 10 November 1927. He seems not to have seen *The Cunning Little Vixen*, given the evening before.

Keep well, my soul
Yours for ever
L.

514 [undated, postmarked Brno, 13 November 1927]

Dear, dearest Kamila

You gave me a nice surprise today! I wasn't waiting for a letter and hey! here it is! And only now will I begin to read it. What will be there?

And now I stop at one nice sentence: 'When I read those letters of yours, I blush so!' And I, when I read yours, I'm a man full of joy – and to have this dear Kamila here beside me! I always think this to myself. [Have I] burnt [the letter]? You know, today the letter didn't want to burn even with a flame. I was sorry that it had to become ash. So today I left it still half-burnt. I'll read it – and burn it for sure; so you shouldn't fear.

< about three words cut from bottom of page >

I don't know how to write to you in any other way. To write in another way wouldn't even give me pleasure. These are letters which only the heart writes – and reason, keep away from them! And the shawl? I just said that it was for work. In fact I couldn't help showing how I love you at least with something. And when it did give you pleasure – so, little shawl, lie on the breasts of my Kamila!

We're like little carp in stagnant water. This stagnant water, this is just our correspondence. But one day we'll thrash so much in that water that it will froth up and we'll fling ourselves over the dam wall!

And now I'm glad that you're also frightened of that isolation on the rocks.

I was always worried about it.

< second sheet of letter missing >

515 [undated, Brno, 13–14 November 1927; postmarked Brno, 14 November 1927]

My dear Kamila

'So I'd ask for those other ones to be a little different!'

Oh, how I laughed at that 'ask'! How on earth would I know how to write differently, to be a little different!

I imagined you vividly as you wrote that sentence. I wonder where you were? In the kitchen? Surely there because it's warm there. But I know that it was written calmly. You know how to control yourself. But it's so hard for me to control myself in this.

I just hope now that the two carp will thrash so much in the water that a wave will cast them out of the fish pond. [It's enough] now to think this far; [in] whatever happens next – may the good fates preserve us.

Today Sunday. [...]

I've got lots of work now, because things are coming to the end. This is when one hurries up with it. But your hunch was correct: not that I was perhaps ill, not that, but overworked. Little sleep. I miss having you near me, you who take my thoughts in another direction, and that's already a rest for me.

That's why I wait for your letters longingly; how immediately overjoyed I am when I take one [home]!

And you're calm now; for a short while that 'burning' doesn't harm – as long as you laugh again afterwards.

Today I put on my fur coat for the first time; it snows here at night, but [always] melts at once. And I wait again for the days when I'll be able to see you again. You like entertaining me and I so like being at your house! [...]

516   Brno, 15 November 1927

My dear Kamila

Don't hold it against me that I gave you a nudge then. Above all it was only a slight touch, a squeeze. I feared you'd cry out, not that I would have held it against you! God forbid! But because that operetta[1] was so extraordinarily *stupid as a whole* except for a few places where I'd also have laughed if the rest of it had pleased me.

And now, my joy, when I saw the fly's legs![2] At once I thought to myself 'something must have happened!'

I can imagine that the shawl suited you. As if I'd seen you with it. Did you have it thrown over your shoulder? Weren't you cold? So your husband[3] gave it to you? Perhaps your husband's kind! He certainly loves Kamila so much that his heart aches from it. And if he knew perhaps what gave you pleasure, he would now so like to be able to read it from your dark eyes, and certainly Kamila would not

1 Janáček attended an operetta with Stösslová given by the České Budějovice company during his trip to Písek in early November.
2 A reference to Kamila's spidery writing.
3 Janáček is here referring to himself.

wait long for it. And he would bring you joy only out of pure love.

So you, husband, remain now for ever the husband of that brown Kamila.

Oh you may well ask how I enjoyed myself. And if you didn't ask, you would have guessed it quite well if you'd said 'how can you enjoy yourself without me?' 'He cannot!'

I sat next to Mascagni; he's not a talkative man. I plied him with questions, in vain. He doesn't have an easy time in his own land. He's not in good spirits. He wants to get to know my pieces, he'll come again to Brno in the early spring. I myself would like to know what effect I am now having on the world about me. I needn't pretend, I'm lost in thought, sometimes deeply lost in thought. I have a smile on my face perhaps because I see you in the distance. It's a puzzle for the others because they don't see you.

They're preparing my concert now; it will be on 5 December.[1] If you can, listen to it somewhere where they have a large radio – a six-valve one. [...] We're still not quite finished but it will be in a fortnight.

And now that piano! I'm curious what you bought! So it's the firm *Blüthner*? And when it's in place, you'll let Otuš learn the piano.

[...]

And a comment: 'The piano should *stand away* from the wall a little'. Don't let it rest against the wall. And it would be even better if a carpet were to hang on the wall. [...]

And is the amount [Kč] 34,000 or 3,400?

And we have a lot to talk about, Kamila, happily and also seriously. You know how to do both. I won't budge from you.

Keep well.

For ever yours

And when you'll have a piano I'll certainly teach you how to play it. That will be fun!

517   Brno, 16 November 1927

My dear Kamila

I take pleasure from the fact that people in Písek now look upon you with respect. So were there many of these letters?

One went on Friday evening – and even that lay around through Sunday;

1 Jaroslav Kvapil was preparing the first performance of Janáček's Glagolitic Mass with the Philharmonic Chorus of the Brno Beseda. It was broadcast live on 5 December 1927.

[147]

on Saturday a second – it lay around through Sunday;
on Sunday a third – and all three met up on Monday at your place.
I'll put this right now so that there won't be [so] many of them.
[...]
Today I'm not myself. I don't know why.
I'll rather stop. You won't get any post today.
Nevertheless I can't.
You know, I'll teach you to play the piano within an hour.
Listen:
1. Sit at the piano
2. Look at the keys

[TAKE IN FACS 4]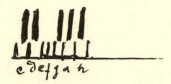

c d e f g a h[1]

3. There are always two and then three black ones raised up
4. The white ones are called c d e f g a h
5. Strike them with your finger and name them
6. Do it several times in order, up and down, with any finger.
7. You're a clever girl, therefore you know how to play with one finger
this order: a g f f e e
then this: e d d a g g
then this: a g f f e e
then this: e d d c
Play everything the same length of time. What song will that be?[2]

1 Czech nomenclature, like German, designates B natural as 'H'.
2 The song was 'Ach, není tu, není, co by mne těšilo' ['Oh there's nothing here that would please me']. It is curious that Janáček transcribed a song that was not in one of his own collections or a Moravian folksong, but one from Bohemia, printed in several well known editions. Janáček could have chosen it for its simple tune, or its words, a song of longing. The last verse in particular has interesting resonances: 'They keep on giving me [...] what I don't want. They're giving me a widower, he has only half a heart; half he gave to his dead wife; he would give half to me.'

And was it so easy for you to say 'my husband bought it for me'?
Yours for ever
L.

518   Brno, 17 November 1927

My dear Kamila

It's Thursday. I won't write to you tomorrow, nor on Saturday. It would pile up again and on Monday you wouldn't know what to do with them. 'How much this husband[1] of mine writes!' 'It's maddening!'

Would you say that?

Or, 'my husband wants me to lose my reason!'

I'm now at work like mutton on the spit.

You have no idea how one is now all just opera, all just song. You wouldn't recognize me. And I know now that I'll have to stop for a while; as soon as I go to the place where it's possible to do that.

[...]

And how's the piano? If it's really valuable, then be careful with the heating. Either don't heat at all in the living-room, or heat so that the temperature's always the same. Put a thermometer in the living-room.

[...]

Tomorrow I have to go to the first rehearsal, on Sunday to the orchestra for my 'mass'. I'm curious whether after two years I'll like what I wrote.

[...]

For me tomorrow's the day where I wait [to see] what my *'wife'* will write to me; if I'm a husband, then you're my 'wife'.

For ever yours
L.

519   [postmarked Brno, 22 November 1927]

My dear Kamila

You shouldn't have got annoyed. It's true that it annoyed me too – but I soon calmed down. I know that she[2] will bring about – what we peacefully want to leave to fate. If it happens like that – it will fulfil only what's predetermined. That's why I'm so resigned to fate.

---

1 i.e. Janáček, see p.146, fn.3.
2 Presumably a reference to Zdenka.

So everything rolls forward, no-one can stop anything – no-one can stop even our dear Otava.

And we two know one another. We won't hide anything from one another. Let people talk about whether we need anyone else or not. Your letter was serious; I felt it at the first reading. And I'll read it over many times more. I feel that a thought's ripening in you – as in me – into a decision.

< p.2 missing >

[...] Don't decide about the trip to Vienna until it's certain when I'll be able to come to you.

Either it will be before the holidays, but more like soon after the holidays.

Then I want to go to Hukvaldy to fix it all up there; I think that I'll see about raising [the roof of] the attic room.[1] Then I'll hang the pictures and the photograph with you sitting down.

So are you content then?

< p.4 missing >

520 [Brno, 22–3 November 1927]

My dear soul

Well, I won't disown even your photograph. In Brno I have two of your photographs on my writing-desk; in Hukvaldy I have none. Let's send it to Hukvaldy and I'll write to my sister [telling her] how to arrange it. Leave it at home now, we'll organize it when I come to Písek. I'll rejoice with you when you're sitting there so nicely. But now, my Kamila, your charm's in your liveliness. You're as enchanting as you're lively. Could your soft little hands ever be painted? Your fine raven hair – who on a photograph can toss it like a mane? I imagine your beautiful breasts; what little wave of the Otava can match them? Even if the sun should rest on it, it wouldn't have such brown gold! I just make it all up. Let fate give you to me alive like that! This is my 'Our Father', every day, every moment.

I've already written to you about my Sunday [20 November].[2] One work has fallen away: a great meditation on folksongs.[3] So there still

---

1 Janáček's first reference to the proposed extension to his cottage in Hukvaldy (see Glossary).
2 i.e. about the first orchestral rehearsal for the Glagolitic Mass (see 518), perhaps in the missing portion of 519.
3 A reference to his Introduction to the collection *Moravian Love Songs* (see Glossary). Janáček signed and dated a version of it '25 November 1927', i.e. two or three days later. However, he rubbed out the date on the manuscript (see Janáček 1955, 484, fn.2), and seems to have gone on tinkering with it (see 526). This 'meditation' remained in manuscript

remains that concert. And then a little rest will be necessary. Man isn't made of iron and my Kamila goes to the market, stands at every stall, shoes made of paper, stockings like cobwebs – and then ought she not to be cold!

Dear child, in general it's necessary in that damp cold to heat your bedroom and dry out the air. In the high mountains one can go out into the cold. And what, am I all there within a gingerbread heart?[1] And is there an empty place in that bloody heart which beats in your bosom? And about that heart, above it and below it, things could be said.

I don't feel my own heart; evidently a lady has taken up residence, and gently, with devotion just beats in it – they call her Kamila.

Sometimes there's a storm in it – it's the wild girl – Kamila.

But it's so firmly locked that she won't get out of it – that dear Kamila of mine.

It will probably strike people – that I'm so self-contained. If only they knew that I'm never alone, that with me, around me, everywhere and continually there's such a nice little creature.

If they believed in spirits – then they would have to see you: you're a spirit, a memory continually with me.

That's why we're enough for each other.

Now I kiss you in spirit – just in the way they say no-one has ever experienced.

Why doesn't blood flow at such recollections, too?

Yours for ever

L.

Tuesday–Wednesday

522 Brno, 24 November 1927

My dear Kamila

I'd say that mud, damp gets into a fellow and annoys him and poisons his mood. So now, is the piano tuned already? Don't let Mr Kodl bang on it! I'm curious what sort of tone it will have.

There was news from Prague that they'll give *The Makropulos Affair* at the beginning of January. I'll certainly go and have a look before the holidays and take a peep at Písek. And I'll dig out someone

---

(it is printed in Janáček 1955, 477–84) and was replaced by a briefer and more down-to-earth introduction (dated '14 June 1928') in the published volume (1930–6), signed with the co-editor Pavel Váša.

1 A reference perhaps to a traditional type of 'hard' gingerbread, decorated and made in the shape of a heart.

[buried] there even if she was hidden as deep as can be. But it won't be necessary. All of a sudden Mrs Kamila will quietly give me her hand. I always think that it's her ghost when I see you from afar. The greatest happiness approaches so quietly, unheard, and surprises one. Believe it or not? Stretch out one's hand for it? Won't it disappear?

Oh, I'll read your last letter – to get out of such a melancholy, overworked mood. – Yes, I did read it through and burnt it unwillingly. You don't even know how precious your letters are to me. These are moments, when I read them, when the sun just shines above me. All other time [seems] as if a nightmare were hanging in the sky.

My little soul, I'll still need two small carpets for Hukvaldy, under the writing-desk and at the doorway. When something turns up now buy it for me. We'll then send it to Hukvaldy with that portrait of yours. I'd like to have warmth there; you know that warmth which is felt when two people love one another, when two people understand one another, when two people have desires only for each other! When two people can be silent and understand each other's glances. That warmth when you don't have to put more fuel in the stove. Warmth which doesn't know a dull moment; when one is wrapped up in a fur coat and tightly hugging oneself.

I'd like to have a Hukvaldy paradise and would look for my Eve there all the time. Will the Lord God create it for us? Sleep sweetly; it's already 11 o'clock.

And what calm there is in my soul now. Now there is the thing that's been lacking all my life.

I'm not irritable, I answer calmly even to the sarcastic needling intended to taunt me.

I'm at peace with myself. Through you a reconciling angel has taken up residence with me. I know that I can rely on her. Nothing surprises me now; I'd wait calmly for the deluge. I know that I'll soon see you; I suspect that they'll summon me somewhere and I'll then call out to you 'he's off now!' And this dear spirit will again wait quietly.

You won't need to burn this letter? It's so calm that it could be printed. You'll be writing today. I'm already looking forward to it.

Yours for ever

L.

523   Brno, 24–5 November 1927

My dear Kamila

So tomorrow's Friday [25 November] – your sad day. With me Friday, feast-day – it's all the same.

[152]

Think of me, however, on Saturday! I'm invited to a social lunch organized by the Tenth Regiment 'Kozina'.

I promised that I'd go – convinced that I'll pay for myself. And now I've learnt that I'll be a guest. And the gossips say that the menu will cost Kč 150. Me, eat for Kč 150 and drink water!

It can't be changed now. If I could put things into my pocket for you to taste from the table, oh how gladly I'd run off with it – but it's impossible as far as Písek.

At least I'll describe it to you – and when I come to you we'll make a 'piano reduction' of it and will eat it with 100 times more gusto.

In this work, which will be given on 5 December, I try a little to depict the tale that when Christ was crucified on the cross, the heavens were rent.

So, I do the noise and lightning flashes, but what if in the heavens, in the portal, Kamila were to appear – I would portray that even better!

So you don't want to learn that little song on the piano? I'd hold you down at the piano so you couldn't escape.

That would be the easiest bit.

And you know, the person who says the worst things about himself – isn't bad.

The boasters are the worst.

Today I wrote a few lines about how I see my cathedral.[1]

I've set it in Luhačovice. Not bad, eh? Where else could it stand than there, where we were so happy!

And that cathedral is high – reaching right to the vault of the sky. And the candles that burn there, they are the tall pine trees, and at the top they have lighted stars. And the bells in the cathedral, they're from the flock of sheep.

The cathedral's the subject of my work for 5 December.

But now. Into that cathedral two people enter, they walk ceremonially as if along the highway, all a carpet – a green lawn.

And these two want to be married. And it's strange that all the time there are just these two. So, priest, come at last! Nightingales,

---

1 Janáček is referring to his article 'Glagolskaja missa' (dated 23 November 1927 and printed in *Lidové noviny*, 27 November 1927). This frequently reprinted article (there are English versions in Vogel 1981, Janáček 1982, Janáček 1986, Janáček 1989 and Wingfield 1992) has much in common with his account to Kamila Stösslová, except that in this private account the mass is presented less as a Slavonic or pantheistic mass than as a nuptial mass.

thrushes, ducks, geese make music! For their general[1] now wants to marry that little Negress, that small, tender – that dear Kamila. End of dream. You're already sleeping and I daydream about you.

Yours for ever

L.

10.30, 24 November 1927

25.11. So will you write something cheerful to me today? If only there were [written] there: come, come!

---

524 [Brno, 26–7 November 1927; postmarked Brno, 27 November 1927]

My dear Kamila

[...] So today I was at that banquet. They put me at the table of honour.

Generals on my right and left. Our conversation carried on without let-up.

Opposite me the regional commander General Vojcechovský,[2] next to him the Mayor of Brno,[3] next to the chief of the general staff, General Syrový,[4] next to him Minister Udržal[5] – and so just serious company – and I a terribly serious general from the musicians.

When we broke up, Major General Syrový came to me and said that he remembered me from the Demänovské caves.[6] They're in Slovakia and are terribly frightening. I was in them when there was neither footbridge nor even lighting. I went across the abyss on a plank. Slip – and [it's] the end. They called one cave after me. So you see, I'm not frightened.

[...]

And I must still tell you what the food was. My glasses were like a shop-display – full. I only touched them with my lips. There were six courses – all French names.

---

1 i.e. Janáček; with this rather odd designation he placed himself in the company of the military generals he would be meeting two days later, i.e. as the 'terribly serious general from the musicians' (see 524).
2 General Sergej Vojcechovský (1883–1950s).
3 Karel Tomeš (1877–1945), Mayor of Brno 1925–35.
4 General Jan Syrový (1888–1971), prime minister at the time of the Munich agreement.
5 František Udržal (1866–1938), Czechoslovak defence minister 1926–9, later prime minister.
6 Limestone caves in Slovakia in the lower Tatra mountains near Liptovský Mikuláš. Janáček had visited them in August 1922 with their discoverer, his former pupil Alois Král (1877–1972) and recorded his impressions of them in two newspaper articles (see Janáček 1990, 100, fn.).

As a memento I took a cigar from Major General Syrový – and kept it at home.

It's a beauty; and it's our pride that we're free in our beautiful republic.

Then I went to a rehearsal for the concert. On Monday, Tuesday and Saturday [28–30 November] there are still more. And it will be played as soon as Monday 5 December. Perhaps I've said something new. And I have lots of ideas. I have a contented mind, I can love someone from my whole heart, and it's mine, my black Gypsy girl who grew up, guess for whom?

And who now certainly sleeps contentedly and what if I wouldn't let her sleep, and what if I were to tickle her – and are you ticklish? That's something I'd like to know. See now, what occurred to me to ask about! And what if I were to stroke and kiss

and what if I'd hug and not let go – and what would she do? That's something I'd again like to know. But I haven't yet said all that I'd do.

Don't talk, and get on with it.

Yours

L.

*

And I've had three days so much on my own.

Zdenka had her brother[1] here – and she came home only at night – and late. At other times I wouldn't have put up with it – but now I'm indifferent to it.

The little article[2] enclosed is universally liked. That was Luhačovice the year before last – sad. This year's Luhačovice – it wasn't the mood for a 'mass' – I'll commemorate it as well – when I tell about that first kiss which seizes a fellow like a storm seizes a bit of paper and flies off with it. Where does the earth remain! A fellow's in heaven at once!

Really it's the shortest way to heaven. Without hills, without mountains – just a little blood and you're there.

Meanwhile today, on Sunday here, I'm far from that little heaven.

[...] Today I dreamt that we sat together at the piano! It was clear as if in real life.

Write lots about it to me!

For ever yours

L.

Sunday

1 Leo Schulz, see 170.
2 See p.153, fn.

525   Brno, 29 November 1927

My dear Kamila

[...]

And I as if in solitary confinement. Today, however, I had a glorious day! That French critic[1] was at the rehearsal for the concert [= the première of Glagolitic Mass]. Such praise from him! It is, he says, my greatest work.

After the rehearsals we sat together in the restaurant.

That work came about in Luhačovice, when I was at my saddest [see 407–8]. What I shall write one day from when I was at my happiest! The little angels will get up to such mischief, just like you know how to. There'll be no stopping them!

What's going on inside you? Untamable high spirits, uninhibitedness. It's evident that you're happy. I'd love to have seen you; you certainly didn't walk along the street; you floated. And those eyes! They danced. They sparked like fireworks!

And those breasts of yours! They weren't just the little waves of the Otava, they were the swollen sea just as I saw it on my way to London [see 381]. I stood up to it, but it affected my fellow companion.[2]

So, you wild girl, we're both happy! So now reply to my questions. Yes, yes, yes! I'd love to see. But there was a line and a T. Long <   > and ever <   >[3]

Yours for ever

L.

On Wednesday [7 December] I go to Prague. So you know that we'll see one another as soon as possible.

526   Brno, 29 November 1927

My dear soul

Today, you know, I'd like to sit with you again on that divan in 'my' little room. You'd lie down for a rest after all that cooking. And I'd stroke you and look at you all the time.

And again twilight, the fewest thoughts, the greatest feeling.

I'm tired, which is why I've so wished it.

Yesterday evening [I was] at the rehearsal; but it will be nice.

Then in the night I wrote the introduction to the folksongs; so it

1 William Ritter (see Glossary).
2 Jan Mikota, see p.87, fn.1.
3 The two partly obliterated words here are 'líbání' ['kissing'] and 'Tvůj' ['you', singular]. The preceding 'T' is enormous.

can be printed soon, I['ll be] in Prague, and then with you.

And that black opera of mine [*From the House of the Dead*] is giving me plenty of work.

It seems to me as if in it I were gradually descending lower and lower, right to the depths of the most wretched people of humankind. And it's hard going.

You're my comfort here and the ray of light which gives me stamina in my work. [...]

527   Brno, 30 November 1927

My dear soul!

I'm so sorry that I have to burn your letters. What nice memories there would be. You're in them with your character as if in a mirror. And some of them – like when you wrote about how your husband[1] gave you a shawl – always conjure up a smile on my face. We must think of something so that we don't have to burn [the letters] – and nevertheless can write what we want and what we feel.

And now to the point. On Wednesday [7 December] I've got a meeting in Prague in the morning at 11.30. Should I come on Thursday? And then return again to Prague to find out what's going on in the theatre? Or else settle everything in Prague and come to you for Saturday and Sunday? The first would suit me better.

I'm finishing works one after the other – as if I had to settle my accounts with life. We've prepared a thousand folksongs for printing. That's work from 1901; thus twenty-six years![2]

With my new opera I'm hurrying like a baker throwing loaves into the oven!

And do you know what peace I'd wish now for myself if it were in my power?

Three days and three nights I'd not let you from my embrace! I'd be as blissful, you know, as that beautiful butterfly about which I've written so many times. [see 465]! Where are the poor things? She laid her eggs. What will come forth from them in the spring sun? Certainly she laid them safely, hid them well – and then left them to their fate. And what about him and her? The first frosts burnt them.

And us people! Isn't it the same with us? Somehow I'm so sorry for everything.

1 i.e. Janáček (see 516).
2 See Glossary: 'Moravian Love Songs'. There are 150 numbered songs, though most of them in several variants and subvariants. The work dated back to 1905.

I'm always sorry when I finish some work – lay it down and never return to it in my thoughts.

And the two of us. How far we are from the life of those dear butterflies.

They were supremely happy.

Why can't I forget about them!

You know, that wild, rich green of my forest. The hillside, warmed up until it breathed a heavy fragrance. And on a stalk a little breeze cradles those two, united in love. I see their red and dark colour clearly – you've got that colour on your body – and they didn't even move in that bliss. I think that that was eternity for them. They didn't care that it was night, and they must have been surprised when the morning sun greeted them!

Let fate judge everyone the same – if with justice for them, for us too. I look forward to you.

And even your smile will be a dear gift for me.

— · —

The concert's awaited here with great excitement. That Frenchman wants to come again. He's in Prague now.

If it's as fine as he says, I can be satisfied.

And what about you? Does your head still ache, your ear? Were you both at the doctor's? Have you been such a cheerful girl all the time, such a little imp up to her tricks?

I'm curious about the photograph.

So sleep sweetly and without waking until morning. You know how to do that until 10!

Yours for ever

L.

528   Brno, 1–2 December 1927

My dear soul

If I didn't have you, so distant, desired and unattained,

    your cheerfulness,

the pleasure of your goodness,

if I didn't have you, whom I remember so gladly for all that – I'd have to despair of my life.

I'd not have a bright moment, a mind warmed by such great friendship. I'd have only this work – and otherwise oppressiveness.

The most terrible tortures are when someone wants to imprison the soul, when someone wants to chain up feeling, feeling from which every joy of my life wells up.

[158]

Here everything in me resists as if out of desperation.

And consider, a life's work – *about folksongs* – I've finished it.

What pleasure there should be from that alone. The second great work – about which I sent you that article[1] – finished. I could shout for joy at the way it's already appreciated. –

And perhaps [my] greatest work – that latest opera – I'm finishing – excited almost to the pitch where my blood feels like spurting out. –

And I must live through it all as if it had been swallowed up.

If I wanted to cheer – I must be silent.

But that's nothing, worse is the poison that's dripped into my blood.

Oh but I'd be sorry to make you anxious. You would suffer more than me.

Now I want only to see you, to relax in peace. To see joy and pleasantness all around.

So you see, my letter today isn't cheerful. On Wednesday [7 December] I go to Prague; I've got a meeting there at 11.30 in the morning. On Thursday I'd go to you in the morning. I'd draw a healthy breath, peace, and from your face, joy and cheerfulness.

After that, we'll see.

Will it be good like that?

I'm curious at your letter tomorrow. It's like a medicine for my painful body. Keep well and think much of me.

Yours for ever

1 December in the night.

I think that you were partly right.

There was anger that I wrote those beautiful articles about you and that we have that Gypsy child together.[2] As if you did everything for my articles! As if I were a journalist, who writes to order.

Well, it's all settled and quietened down. I don't want to hurt her, but I won't allow anyone to force me to what they want. [...]

531   Brno, 4 December 1927

My dear Kamila

So that's Sunday gone.

[...] The piano will give the room a whole new appearance. Also at

---

1 See p.153, fn.

2 Janáček is commenting on Zdenka's disapproving reaction to the articles that he published in *Lidové noviny* celebrating Kamila's good work in Písek among the Gypsy children (see Glossary).

Hukvaldy there will be something new to look at; electric light is being installed! At the end of January I'll go there to give instructions about everything in the house and where to place the bulbs. I think that on the first floor I'll also raise [the height of] the room and re-do the entrance to it. Then you'll come and see.

My work [the Glagolitic Mass] will be broadcast from here to Bratislava and also to Prague.

Anyone with a strong receiver in Písek could hear it. I learnt about it too late.

And what has my dear Kamila been up to on Saturday with the school director? Behind [closed] doors?

And what about Sunday? Did Mr Kodl come again? It's said that if a devil's hungry he even catches flies.

You're a dear little devil whom one has to cuddle the whole day. To bring to you whatever you wish, to occupy you every moment – but think, dear Kamila, that in the distance there's also someone sharp-tempered, passionate, who's become so isolated, who's so happy but only when thinking of you. He has nothing other than your quiet picture in his thoughts and knows that while he's alive it will never disappear from them. He's cheerful also – on the surface,
he talks with everyone – only a smile on his face
he's content – because he has another internal, secret life,
he doesn't long for anything – because he has a treasure beyond gold
– and they call it Kamila.

I know that my position at my house is easier. You're isolated – for such periods through the year.

What wouldn't you get up to!

The world would be too small for you.

But you'd then long for your corner by the stove again.

There you're the prettiest woman; I most like to imagine you there, and when I write to you I always see you in 'my' room, on that blood-red chair, on that small divan; or in the kitchen, as you turn about. But I also see you there in that wood where the ground trembled beneath me. Ah, don't forget those moments!

I'll write to you tomorrow again – and I'll send you a telegram from Prague on Wednesday.

Sleep well, my dear soul.

For ever yours

L.

532 Brno, 6 December 1927

Dear Mrs Kamila

Just the shortest letter – everything's in a rush – to Písek.

Your

L.

533 [postmarked Prague, 12 December 1927]

My dear soul

I know now that you're my soul! And I'm frightened only that you will fly away from me – you know, I would be left wretched.

< second half of p.1 and all of p.2 missing > [...]

You're young, blooming, I in the strength of spirit; it's a good combination!

I came to Prague half asleep. To < second half of p.3 and ?p.4 missing >

534 Prague, 14 [*recte* 13] December 1927

You my dear soul

So the day's at an end. I arrived, booked into the hotel, went to buy some sausages and then went to ask what singers will be cast in *The Makropulos Affair*. I gathered that they are the very best. Then to buy a ticket to Brno, have lunch and a walk in the Kinský park – I walked for nearly two hours. It's six in the evening. I met the administrator of the Society for Modern Music.[1] They also want to give my

Glagolitic Mass.

We agreed on basics.

It greatly cheered me that you're interested in Fibich and his Anežka.[2] Whatever's very learned in the book, skip it. What's there that applies to us, remember it well and then tell me. Anežka must have had something strange in herself for a strong man like him, a big fine

1 Mirko Očadlík (1904–64), who later worked for Czech Radio (1928–50) and became Professor of Music at Charles University in 1952.
2 In 1893 the Czech composer Zdeněk Fibich (1850–1900) presented his pupil Anežka Schulzová (1868–1905) with six piano pieces, part of a cycle that he began in 1892 and which by 1899 had grown to 376 *Moods, Impressions and Reminiscences*. In them Fibich purported to chronicle events in their life together with musical descriptions of various parts of Schulzová's body. The cycle and its programmatic significance was explored by Zdeněk Nejedlý in his book *Zdeňka Fibicha milostný deník* [Zdeněk Fibich's erotic diary] (Prague: Hudební matice Umělecké besedy, 1925).

fellow,[1] to fall for her.

And you have strange charms within you with which you bind me to you. You haven't thrown a net round me; Anežka surely threw such an enormous net that he couldn't break out of it. I found the charm of a body and a natural soul, he found a frump and the grammar of words.[2] He threw notes at a hump and sensuality, I would cover your beautiful waves of the Otava with melodies, your leg[s] as swift as pikes, your mouth like a little window into the sanctuary where things are burning. Into your womb I'd put the most beautiful things that would ever occur to me.

I'd even make a joke of your flexible toes and your big toe.[3]

But I'd not leave to the clutches of the common crowd the thing that would bind us irreversibly for ever. This is the way I'd do it – and will do it.

This evening I go to the concert[4] and tomorrow, [made] happy by you, I return to Brno. I've got a proper cold! I only hope you won't get it too! That wouldn't be surprising.

Thinking only of you,

Yours for ever

L.

I enclose what came into my hand during the concert.[5]

536 Brno, 14 December 1927

My dear Kamila

I was already thinking that the doctor would send me to my bed!

A proper cold; I have to inhale camphor dissolved in alcohol and take some sort of pills, five of them daily, in which one can smell menthol.

Otherwise I'm well! The heart's good, kidneys clean. Anyone could

---

1 At 5 ft 8 ins Fibich was certainly taller than Janáček; he was sturdily built and became quite corpulent during the last years of his life.

2 Anežka Schulzová was well educated and from her early twenties she published theatre reviews and translations from several languages. She also had a slight deformation of the spine which, uncharitably, could be regarded as a hump (private information from Fibich's great-nephew the composer Jan Hanuš). This is not apparent in published photographs which, furthermore, do not suggest that she was ugly.

3 A reference to Fibich's *Moods, Impressions and Reminiscences* (see p.161, fn.2).

4 Janáček took part on 13 December in a concert celebrating the twentieth anniversary of the publishing division of the artists' club, the Hudební matice Umělecké besedy. The programme was made up of contemporary Czech works published by the Hudební matice, including Janáček's First String Quartet.

5 The enclosure has not survived.

take me for a sixty-year-old. Well I'm still fit for life – and, a little, for my lady, for my Kamila?

So back to work – excited by reminiscences!

Oh, there were so many of them! You'll have a burden with me! But after this warning that I could sometimes think ill of you – I'll tame myself after that warning! A single warning glance from you – and I'll become tame. There was a wild animal in me – I'll storm out my passion in music! And then they ask where does that youthfulness in my composition come from! If it weren't for you, from whom the sparks fall on me and catch fire, I'd not be what I am!

And now our attaché in Vienna, Mr Vavrečka,[1] has invited me to talk about my work and method of composition in Vienna. He wants to invite a large gathering.

I'd have to say to them: 'my soul and feeling is warmed and comes to the boil only through a single woman – but you must understand that I cannot name her, nor even describe her to you!' And you could best tell them that: I'm at my writing-desk, I feel your foot on mine, I throw down my pen, I'd embrace you, and in a moment I scrawl on the paper. It seems even worse; as if the pen were fighting with something that can't be seen.

This is the reason: the notes would like to slide along the moist lips of my Kamila – and they have to sit on the paper!

That's why my compositions have become so wild.

And what about you now?

Describe everything to me nicely as usual, even tell who took you on the motorbike! But if you don't want to, I won't insist on it. Actually I don't even want to know. It's a shame to shade the sun when it's shining, and we both love it.

And Kamila, you're better off because for weeks you're just on your own, alone – better off than me, who steals moments for himself! You know what it is to get under someone's feet! It's only through my work that I [can] exact privacy for myself with you, while you can dream in comfort, in that fiery glow.

I carry a heavy burden. You must help me. Tell me if there's something about Fibich and Anežka in the second book.

If I could put those kisses into a box like live butterflies – now I'd let them go and catch them, catch them!

---

1 Hugo Vavrečka (1880–1952), Czech journalist and diplomat, who worked in Budapest (from 1922) and Vienna (from 1926). He was in contact with Janáček chiefly at the time when he was on the committee of the National Theatre *Družstvo* and an editor of the *Lidové noviny*. Vavrečka's letter to Janáček (BmJA, B 631) was written on 6 December 1927.

Keep well!
Write lots, nicely and openly.
Yours for ever
L.

14 December (Wednesday) 1927 at night

Thus I finish my day – every day.

Kamila Stösslová to Leoš Janáček, Písek, 14–15 December 1927

Dear Maestro

It's Wednesday and not a word from my husband. I just knew this [would happen]. In the morning I was in town I bought a doll and a pram for my brother and some sweets where I got held up quite a long time. I got home I had visitors from the castle Osek they wanted to talk to my husband. They stayed quite a long time until the car came for them. They also invited me to visit them at the castle and I promised but not until the summer for now I excused myself because of earache. I was scared but it turned out quite well one has to conform [...]. I'm still a bit flushed what was it perhaps the fear that I don't know how to speak to aristocrats. They were so specially nice to me not like everyone that I can't write about it. I'm pleased that I don't offend anyone, oh I don't even know how to. In the evening I was at the Pinc's so we remembered you. Today again the man from the *Prácheňské listy* [*noviny*][1] invited me to come tomorrow to the concert at the Music School. And then he told me that they'll be rehearsing operas here. I laughed at him – to be performing operas in Písek, that's a good one [...]

(Thursday evening). In the morning I got your letter and I hope that you'll be better already. Have about three onions boiled up a little marjoram and lemon peel and then drink it like tea with sugar. It did me good. This morning I was in the school with Rudi and that photograph of mine is more than one metre I don't know where it will be hung. Yesterday evening I went walking outside for a long time with my [girl]friend and the headmaster's wife. My husband will arrive on Saturday [17 December] he's got lots to do and would like to go to Strážnice for the holidays mother has also got a cold. I would like to be at home for the holidays and sometimes after the holidays go for a visit there.

1 See Glossary.

537 [undated, postmarked Brno, 16 December 1927]

My dearest Kamila

You've no idea how your letter cheered me. There was so much heart in it! Above all tell your 'mummy' that I was sorry that I didn't say goodbye to her. You know that I like her because she's your mother! And my little soul, if I'm sad sometimes, silent, taciturn, lost in thought – even beside you, never conclude from it that on that occasion I might not be thinking of you, that perhaps I don't love you so burningly, that you weren't the dearest person on earth to me at that moment – no, my dear child. In my head there lies so much you've no notion of and you would only get to know when we lived together permanently, and not just in those rare moments.

You said that during the first two days I wasn't the same person as in Luhačovice. Oh, in my mind I was the same: but sometimes one's drained like a well to the very bottom. But wait a moment – and there'll be fresh water in it again! And in my profession it often happens like that! And already by the third day you perked me up – sick though I was! I was healthy when I left Brno, in Prague I made speeches all the afternoon, took decisions – and suddenly in the night it all came over me. My only thought was to be with you as soon as possible!

These were moments which one doesn't experience often. So dear, so sweet.

[...] < second half of page missing >

I have something to celebrate, I know that. But tell the moon not to smile from the heavens, the sun not to be like gold – and I'd so like to be openly joyful, happy – and I must hide much, much, as if with a hand in front of one's face. Not openly celebrate so many things. It's painful.

How could I forget anything of all those sweet experiences! So now I've written out my pain, and I'm more cheerful now.

So I can come whenever I like! I hear your exclamation even here.

The meeting on 7 January clashes with the Leipzig performance of *Jenůfa*. That's also announced for 7 January.

I'll try to put off Leipzig for a week so that I can be free for you on 8 January. I've got three trips to Germany. Leipzig in January, Dresden in April, Berlin also in April.[1]

---

1 The Leipzig première of *Jenůfa* took place in Leipzig on 7 January as planned (though without Janáček's participation). There was a performance of the Sinfonietta on 16 March 1928 in Dresden (but see 619). In Berlin Janáček was counting on a production of *The Makropulos Affair*.

As you're not here with me now, it doesn't interest me. Zd... would like to go to Leipzig. I don't know whether I'll go there.

We'll be together somewhere. And we'll be happy.

'Heaven – you' [*nebe – tebe*] those go together well.[1]

So sleep sweetly. I know but < second half of page missing >

538   Brno, 18 December 1927

My dear Kamila

[...]

Today is the first day I'm better; I've got a more sonorous voice again. From my work [i.e. *From the House of the Dead*] there remains now only for me to finish the fair copy of the last act. Then a load will fall from me!

I'll write to Leipzig asking them to postpone *Jenůfa* by at least a week. I want to have a day or two for Písek and my treasure in it.

Today's Friday.[2] I know that it's the day for cleaning at your house – and for *buchty*! Have I guessed right? I've now also got an appetite for food. I was choosy at your house wasn't I! A guest – and choosy! But surely we lived those four days as if *in our own home, at home*! Sleep well, my dear soul!

How's that? For the signature neither ' / 'nor T. That was enough to make me sad.

How can my Kamila forget? I'd rather forget about death than 'for ever yours'.

I'll read it nevertheless –

Ah, I know now why it's like that! For I myself asked you for a cool[3] letter! I think that I'm now getting well. But those three onions![4] I'd tremble at the thought. I wound myself up with damp towels impregnated with camphor and alcohol. That also helps. So we have two remedies. Better not to need either of them.

[...] Now in a while I'll send you my operas – so at least something can lie around on the piano – and can be played from, when I come – and so that it can be known – that those are now rooms which can be called heaven – and in heaven a little music is also necessary.

1 Three weeks later Janáček had devised a more elaborate version (see p.185, fn.3; see also Glossary: 'heaven').

2 18 December, however, is a Sunday. The letter is postmarked 18 December 1927.

3 On 14 December (536) Janáček asked Stösslová to write 'nicely and openly', presumably so that it might be read by Zdenka too. The resultant letter was cool enough to be one of the few letters by Stösslová from this period to survive.

4 A comment on the cure that Kamila suggested to Janáček in her letter of 14–15 December 1927.

I think that I might come on 8 January – but I dare not until an invitation arrives.

I'm surprised that this letter came so late. I'll send this one on Sunday morning.

And yes, Kamila knows how to fit in; it's a nice quality of yours; straightaway everyone would like to be at home with you. You could be an excellent minister; all political parties would think that you were on their side!

Both that director Mr Kodl, and the man from *Prácheňské noviny*, and that man from the Gymnasium,[1] even that Kohoutek from the industrial school, and those from the secondary school, and Mr Pinc – well you've got the whole of Písek in your pocket.

But – but – the president knows that you belong only to him; he smiles blissfully that he has such an excellent minister. Do you know who's the president? Guess, guess, fortune-teller, my delightful imp!

For ever yours

539   Brno, 18 December 1927

You my dear dark dove

That's a nice greeting I've given you! Believe me, you're happier that you're on your own for long periods. I'm always waiting for that time, evening till night, when I'm with you in my thoughts uninterruptedly. Only then I do relax. Otherwise I'm as if cut up into two parts: that everyday domestic part gets in the way of that part which lies on my soul like sweet breath. It blows from so far away and yet I feel it from your hair and from your whole body.

It's freezing and snowing here; it's not possible to go out because of the wind. In the morning I just put a letter to you into the post; otherwise I was simply caught up with music. From Vienna (Universal Edition) you'll receive the vocal scores of my operas; I wrote to them that you should have them by the holidays.[2]

You'll also get something both from Brno and from Prague. When I come we'll have them nicely bound and then you'll put them on the piano; so that all who come will see that someone rules in this heaven[;] in the first place: my sweet Kamila, and beside her, the one who loves her infinitely.

On certain books of music I'll write who was in my soul when the

1 Possibly Josef Novák (see p.220, fn.1).
2 Janáček gave instructions to Universal Edition about this on the same day, 18 December 1927 (BmJA, B 2080).

music swarmed out of it, and that for these notes one mustn't credit just me, but you as well, my Kamila.[1] That's the indissoluble bond between you and me. Oh how many desires of mine there were there – put, for show, into somebody else's mouths.

I'll tell you.

What did you do today? A long Saturday, a long Sunday! What a pity to experience life to so little effect! I know what life could give, and know that I'm not getting anything.

And yet I know how happy I am with you – and how terrible my life would be if I hadn't known you.

Your second last letter was the warmest I've ever received and known in my life. I couldn't take my leave of it for a long time – until finally last night. I'd have put my hand into the flames and still grabbed from them what was nice in that letter.

And how I was taken aback at the 'cold' letter! I couldn't believe my eyes; I read, I read, could Kamila have signed something like this? And at that moment I remembered the reason. I really breathed a sigh of relief. On Tuesday I'll then await a warm letter again. Before you send it off put it on your heart, yes? Then put your mouth to that '/ ', yes? The letter will then be for me like a little rosary in the hands of the pious.

I don't know what news I'll get from the world. I'm very unlikely to go anywhere.

I belong so much to you now that without you I've got no interest in what's going on around me. Well, we'll see. Chin up and make sure that she'll be with you. My little soul, sleep well, and please, please write to me on Monday. And what about the [Christmas] holidays? What will you get under the tree? What will you give [and] to whom? I'd most wish to see you – but in the summer – under the highest fir tree in my wood; I'd lie down there for you and say[:] I'll give everything I have for you! Would you run away? Would you be frightened?

Yours for ever

L.

18 December 1927 (Sunday night)

(This is my happy time with you[2] [lasting] an hour and a half. But what's that against the whole day!)

---

1 In the score of *The Cunning Little Vixen* Janáček wrote: 'In every work of mine there is at least a shadow of your soul. It is in this work when they cry *chcu*!' ['I want', i.e. when the Vixen capitulates to the Fox's advances]. For *Káťa Kabanová* see pp.201–2. The score of *The Makropulos Affair* is signed by him but has no further message.

2 i.e. the pleasure Janáček had in writing to Kamila.

My dear soul

So I thank you for the letter today – at least a joyful smile broke over my face. And now about those journeys.

Our attaché[1] wrote to me from Vienna that he'd like to organize a gathering of critics, reviewers and musicians at the Embassy. I'd address it about my method of composition. Bits of my works would be played. I answered: that I wouldn't give a thought to [trying to] convince anyone *through speaking*; that Vienna ignores me altogether[2] and that I don't want to force myself on anyone.

I have, however, invited the attaché to come and see me for a chat should a journey take him to Brno. I don't know when that will be.

But, however, *be prepared if I should send you a telegram from Vienna at any time* to come.

The second trip, to Leipzig.

First they didn't invite me *in such a way* that I have to go there. I'm used to warmer invitations. And then Z. has a good mind to go, and I've a good mind not to go.

[*Jenůfa*] should be in Leipzig on 7 February [January], but on 7 February I badly need to be in Prague.

The third trip[3] on 7 February is vital for me; I can't put it off. And now your trips.

So off to Strážnice? It goes without saying that I'll wait for you at the station.[4] And then to Vienna for a fortnight? That would be possible during my Prague stay.

Anyway always let me know your address, where you'll be and I'll always inform you where I'll be.

A lot can still change before that time.

'Not go' – is the 'cleverest' for me, but for my darling Kamila –
– also!

And don't take it badly about that motorcycle! It gave you pleasure, you returned healthy – so it's fine.

Yes and a single glance – that's sometimes a salvation!

---

1 See p.163, fn.

2 Janáček was certainly correct as far as operas were concerned: at the time of writing only the famous German première of *Jenůfa* in 1918 (revived in 1926) had been given in Vienna; the next productions there were *The Makropulos Affair* in 1938, *Jenůfa* again in 1948 and *The Cunning Little Vixen* in 1956.

3 This seems to have been Janáček's folksong meeting in Prague on 11 February 1928 (see p.201), thus postponed by four days.

4 To get to her husband's family home in Strážnice in southern Moravia, Stösslová would have had to travel via Brno.

And now about Fibich's Anežka.

In what way was she able to attach someone to herself, she who was just a poor cripple? [...]

Between us there's just innocent feeling; the sort that ignites regardless of what flares up from it!

Fibich–Anežka were different: they were warmed up by what they had forged [between them] – their work – librettos – and really didn't warm themselves! They had no children! But many stupid and unnecessary operas.[1]

How would I know should it flare up with us, whether children would come into this world, or into this or that opera? With me everything possible could arise from this feeling of love for you.

You're my sacred fire: in it gold will get shaped into a ring and God knows what else.

With us it's simple: we want to live in love and they lived in dry work and got warm only during that – and with what they didn't tell. And what will you now reply to this?

Soon, and lots and lots – even though there are holidays. You'll be getting lots of music! At least read the text under it.

Yours for ever

L.

And what else to ask than for love from you? God forbid! Just you as you are! And you yourself are my treasure on whom one can draw continually and never use up!

543 Brno, 21 [*recte* 23?] December 1927

My dear soul

So enjoy the holidays. I hope you've received a good number of my paper presents.

The nicest presents would be:

give yourself to me and

I long ago gave myself to you!

I'll write – I think – only on Sunday [25 December]; so don't worry if one day a letter doesn't arrive. I go to Prague on 6 January in the

---

1 Anežka Schulzová wrote the librettos for Fibich's last three operas. They include his most famous one, *Šárka*, which was also the subject of Janáček's first opera, written a decade earlier but not produced. Janáček expressed himself forcibly about Fibich's and Schulzová's first opera, *Hedy*, which he saw during the period of the rehearsals for the Prague première of *Jenůfa*: 'it's so dry that one's tongue sticks [to the roof of one's mouth]!' (Tyrrell 1992, JP97).

morning; on 7 January I've got a meeting; on 8 January I'd rejoice in Písek.

I think that after my departure for Hukvaldy I'll have to organize everything there. I'd hardly be able to get there again in the winter.

I probably won't go to Leipzig; a fellow has to spare himself – when he has a golden treasure, by which to stand, watch and live – that's the greatest experience.

And that golden treasure, who is it? It's that black-eyed, dark, intimate, dear, sweet Kamila of mine.

And when you have your Christmas meal remember that you're taking the first mouthful for me; I'll remember that [I'm doing the same] for you.

I finish one work after another – but it's strange, I'm not thinking about a new one. That's because I'm doing the sweetest work – remembering you. Even though you say that it's unnecessary to remember you the whole time. But what about when it's impossible!

I'll write into that music which bits you did with me.

Not the silly libretto – but warm feeling, a warm, faithful picture of you in the background of every page. The warmth that breathes from my pieces, that's your warmth.

So keep well, my little soul

Yours for ever

L.

544 Brno, 24 December 1927

My dear Kamila

You noticed a nice passage in my *Diary of One who Disappeared*!

You know, it would be like under that fir tree of mine in my forest.

And there's another nice one! At the end – Žofka[1] with the child in her arms – and he follows her.

And I always thought about you in that work. You were that Žofka for me! [...]

And this night of mine today. It was all just Kamila! And your 'yes, yes, yesses' how many of them I counted, without end!

So it's the holidays[2] today. It will pass off here at my house. The hours will pass pointlessly just as the waves run along in a little stream – unnecessary, unnoticed. As if deserted, they whisper and

1 The Gypsy in *The Diary of One who Disappeared* is called Zefka (a diminutive of Josefína); Žofka is a diminutive of Žofie [Sophia].
2 As a Catholic country Czechoslovakia traditionally celebrated Christmas Eve more than Christmas Day, so that the Christmas holidays started on 24 December.

nobody listens to them, they run, and no-one stops them. Cold fate.

You'll be like a shining shadow, colourful, cheerful. I'll look for it and perhaps I'll see it continually before me.

It's nice too, even beautiful – perhaps almost marvellous! But behind it there still stands always the desire for that Negress whom I will not and cannot fear, who with her smile and everything about her has put a spell on me!

Be cheerful today and I'll try to do the same.

Yours for ever

L.

545 Brno, 25 December 1927

My dear Kamila

The holiday's over and so I'm writing to you now with joy. Today your beautiful present arrived, today, on Sunday. Well, I'll take pride in it.[1] I ask you, those ties must be the most expensive ever! I understand these things!

The present aroused attention, but was appreciated.[2] Now in addition [send me] that tie-pin through someone else, so that our friendship will never be punctured.[3] But pinned to be sewn together.

You had a goose, a hare and still more goose. I: fish soup, black fish with an enormous dumpling, fried fish with your [potato] salad, fruit ice cream, black coffee, sweet biscuits, fruit, tea![4] So much food! But you should have been at the table – then merriment would have been a guest. And so there was only blessed peace.

I gave and I also received presents, to general satisfaction. I kept on waiting for your gift – and nothing until Sunday. Then at once, apparently, cheerfulness shone from my eyes! It's no wonder, is it!

So you were generous on all sides; I sent at least something to you for 'our' boy; give it to him when he'll have need of it.

[...]

My Kamila, although a fir tree grows quite quickly, it would have

---

1 With these words ('to se budu pyšnit') Janáček perhaps consciously echoed those of Jenůfa when she picks up the discarded flower from one of Števa's admirers.

2 This doubtless refers to Zdenka's reaction.

3 From Janáček's comments in a letter of 20 December 1927 (*541) it can be inferred that Kamila had bought him a tie-pin for Christmas, but superstitiously did not want to send it. It was eventually presented to him at the time of the Prague première of *The Makropulos Affair* by David Stössel (see 600). Janáček had received a tie-pin the previous Christmas, presumably from Zdenka (see 419).

4 It is clear that the Janáčeks observed the Catholic avoidance of meat on Christmas Eve, whereas the Jewish Stössel family did not.

to hurry up to catch up with love! So you've received four operas; leave the binding now until I come. It must last for ages!

And the trout which I chose, what did one cost? I'm curious. [...]

Next time we'll cook and bake them together – if they're cheap in Písek. Professor Vymetal[1] sent his wishes for the holidays; I wrote to him that we now see one another very often.

I'm finishing the correction of that last opera of mine; I sweated over it. But after the pleasure from your gift today it went like roasting in an open fire! It's like that because this Mrs Kamila is a living fire.

[...] And what did you get apart from those four operas? I think *that you were not alone* during the holidays! What sort of father is it who's uncomfortable with his children around? Greet your mother. Be well and spare yourself and write and write!

Yours for ever

L.

And it's pointless to speak about this night! How did you appear with me?

546 Brno, 26 December 1927

You my dear Kamila

For two days now I couldn't get to the post; it was shut for the holidays. Have you written? Were you alone at home? I don't believe it. That would be gross behaviour.

And today we had pheasant and baked potatoes. If you don't know I'll teach you how to bake it. I'm at home in your kitchen.

If holidays are for lazing about in – I didn't get much out of them. I'm rather like a painter. He's finished and yet he keeps tinkering with it the whole time.

Ondrúšek wrote to me that he'll sign and send the pictures after the holidays.

Today that Frenchman W[illiam] Ritter wrote to me. The letter's full of praise.[2] If the newspapers print it, I'll send it you. Today you've got some words of mine about Brno.[3]

Well, wait until I write about Písek! So there'll be my dear Negress,

1 See Glossary.
2 Ritter's letter was published in the original French in JA ix, 261–2 and in English translation in Susskind 1985, 116–17.
3 Janáček sent Kamila the feuilleton 'My Town', published in *Lidové noviny* on 24 December 1927. It had already been published in a German translation on 4 December 1927 in *Prager Presse*.

so there'll be our 'heaven'. And tongues of fire will flare up from the stove. And there'll be darkness and in it those fiery tongues will run around. And the little tongues will be sought behind hot lips. And the hot lips will be hidden in the palms of hands. But that won't help them.

They'll be found; they won't even be able to cry out. And they'll flow with blood and they won't feel any pain, only a pleasure never felt before. Well, that feuilleton will be gobbled up! And everyone will guess at once: well it's those, those two in no.17, in Přemyslová ulice.

They don't have enough of it. All the things they get up to! Where do they get it from? Who taught them? No-one, no-one – it comes of its own accord. In heaven it falls on its own from heaven![1]

And they themselves don't know what they'll still think up. They don't go to learn it from anyone, and they'll know everything.

Kamila, and also our 'yes, yes, yes'! So now you know all the things I'll write about Písek.

And also about the tom-cat that walked with us, that accompanied us. And now that Sunday [25 December] of yours, [and] your Monday? Were they boring, did you get any pleasure in anything which would have pleased me?

And now what should I wish you for the New Year? What should we wish one another?

Health, my dear soul!

Even in sickness there's love, and in work, love's everywhere in what happens to you.

But the most blessed of all is in health! Take care of yourself and I'll do likewise. We'll watch over ourselves.

And now still this: bring us together, fate, give to us those moments about which we don't talk, in which there's forgetfulness, in which a new world opens – and a new life grows!

Be happy and well.

For ever yours

L.

547 Brno, [27–]28 December 1927, at night

My dear soul

Today's Tuesday – and no letter from you. I think you're ill. With you that wouldn't be anything strange – sometimes there's no

---

1 The first 'heaven' is Kamila's home in Písek, a designation Janáček had begun using a month earlier (see p.155; see also Glossary: 'heaven').

advising you. I'm worried; I'll wait until tomorrow – then a telegram will fly to you.

After all, the post was already operating on Monday morning.

How it instantly spoils my mood! People must think that I've lost a treasure or I'm looking for one! I know that there must be a serious reason why you don't write.

I'm getting better; I'm not coughing any more. But I was in a bad way. A fellow forgets about himself – when he meets with a bewitching presence. That was you. If it weren't for you, perhaps, I would certainly have fallen ill. And because of the stronger flow of blood, that passion swallowed up the sick bacilli.

Perhaps I won't cough at night any more beside you. And how much I concealed so as not to wake you[!]

Now I sit in the night at a loss. Were you alone over the holiday or not?

I feel as if my head is deserted. You're always there alive, in the certainty that you're happy, you take up all the space – and now I don't know how to imagine you and, if it were necessary, how to help you.

And in the morning I can't go to the post, some official has announced a visit. And to wait until evening – that's already a day of life wasted.

If I knew that you were well, then perhaps don't write – but at least I know that you're my chatterbox.

But this uncertainty! It was agreed for Monday, wasn't it? – and no message from you.

I won't go to Leipzig although they invited me. I don't want to go myself, I don't want to go without you. I don't want to write anything until I know how you are.

I'll send this letter only in the afternoon when I'll find out what's the matter with you.

And I don't want to wake you up with a telegram during the night.

Perhaps everything's alright – and these are just unnecessary fears.

And the new year is just outside the door – I'd like to think of it as *our year*, but I get frightened when I don't know that my Kamila is well and flourishing.

After all, you're more than everything that's dear to me. I feel that my reputation, the adulation in the press, even this note-scratching, will not compensate for a single kiss of yours, a single promise of yours! That's the truth, that is. Nothing will change that now; that's why you must stand beside me; then I'll look with pleasure on the

[now] unimportant things, at the things which I used to regard above all.

You're my one and only joy.

Just that you're well, just that you're happy,

Yours for ever

L.

548   Brno, 28 December 1927

My dear Kamila

So that was the sort of holiday you had?! I foresaw it. The infection must have come from me and a chill on top of that – and it could have been bad.

Don't think that I was well when I was with you! Only your being near kept me on my feet; here at home I'd certainly have gone to bed.

And now promise me that you'll follow what I advise you as a cure. It helped me too.

1. into a quarter-litre of *pure alcohol* put

2. fifty hellers-worth of *camphor*.

The camphor dissolves quickly.

With this you rub your chest and have somebody also rub your back. It quickly evaporates on the body. Lie for a moment in bed and pull the quilt over your head and *inhale that camphor vapour*. Keep on inhaling for one- to four-minute intervals. You'll see that it will soon relieve you and you'll get better. Do that at bedtime and once during the day. That's the prescription of my doctor here in Brno. Will you do that? Will you obey? I'll hold you to the word of our promises!

In your very next letter write to me: 'I obeyed, I'm inhaling camphor!'

I was troubled all that time. Just think, from Friday until today, Wednesday, I didn't get a letter from you.

I suspected you were unwell. I know you, you don't know where to stop when you launch into those preparations with the food etc.

That nice gift of yours gave me lots of pleasure. It will remain as one of those presents to one another at Christmas. I'll always look forward to them and I'll give you pleasure too. The [tie-]pin of course has still not come. Don't think of going out of the house now; with these frosts and with your tendency to get catarrh in the throat and lungs – it could be really bad some time. I pity you, dear soul, in your isolation; you need devoted company. I, on the other hand, seek out isolation – because only with you do I have the spiritual companionship which has to compensate me for so very much!

So don't go out now until you're completely well.

That woman painter from Brno[1] is called Miss Prošková; she has a villa in Písek. But nothing about her is important to us.

I've recovered, but I'm also taking care now. But that time in Prague it came on me out of the blue.

And Kamilka, even our < one word cut out > would not have been necessary – the air was already infected. Well, we both went down with it. But just get well!

And now in the New Year! To yours at home, to each of them, I wish every happiness and to you once again, really to both of us, I wish that the good Lord grant that we would never have to part, that *we could never part*, never have to leave one another! And if so, then to go from here together. So, let us live for one another, with one another; let us wish good to one another. Well yes, I'd also mention what's my special wish for myself. You know that. But now be well, well.

Yours for ever

L.

550   Brno, 30 December 1927, at night

My dear Kamila

I went sadly from the post office; no news from you and I'd so like to read that you're a lot better now. Well, tomorrow, on that last day of the year 1927, of our year, perhaps something will come. I remember fleetingly what we've gone through in this year of ours.

On that place where the earth trembled when I said 'Ty' for the first time, on that place we'll have to sow at least the little seed of some flower of the field.

They'd pull up the tree,

they'd tear off the roses,

and no cultivated flower would survive there. So some ordinary little flower, a blue cornflower or a red poppy! Yes, that's it! That won't get lost! It has so many seeds that no-one would weed it out, and it's easy to buy, to get poppy seed! So my Kamila, during the first thaw, when it warms up a little bit in the early spring and I'll be there with you, we'll sow poppy seed!

How many flowers there'll be! If at least one remains, the seeds

1 Marie Prošková (1874–1928), teacher of drawing at the girls' gymnasium in Brno. Janáček mentioned her in October 1927 (see 504).

[177]

from it will be a large – large family! Do you agree? And now, just think, what hard work I still have with this difficult opera![1]

There's a sad story there, about the marvellously beautiful Akulka.

Oh, a big story! The man who took Akulka's life tells, broken-hearted, his whole life story and the whole tale [of Akulka]. How he loved her! I'll tell it to you some other time, that story of theirs.

He tells it during the night, in whispers. Many sick men are lying all around.

And now to hear a confession from him like this –

to hear – and know that it's night,

to hear – that he's speaking furtively,

to hear – that the sick men around them are sighing deeply,

to hear – and to feel his terrible suffering during his speech!

It's not easy, Kamila! But already I've had a good idea. It will be as if it were painted.

What about us! We too put out the lights,

we too don't cry out to make the house shake and bring it down,

we too talk to one another in intimate voices.

But my Akulka – Kamila – and I are merry. There's much laughter and fooling around and meanwhile the light burns red in the stove and spreads its glow. And I had a similar idea! Except it wasn't the light – but the heavy breathing of the sick prisoners.

So you see how you get mixed up with me! My little soul! Let's celebrate this year of ours! It's going out, but we'll remember it as long as we live!

Sleep well today, sleep well tomorrow and wake up into the new year already well – very well.

Thinking of you and /

Yours for ever

L.

Brno 31 (really still 30) December 1927

And give a present to the postman!

And you mustn't sleep any longer in an unheated bedroom. In summer yes, but to go to bed *in a damp quilt* in the winter is just asking for illness! That's why it gets you at once. And what about the alcohol and camphor? Did you obey me?

---

1 One of Janáček's most elaborate descriptions of his work on *From the House of the Dead*. The passage he refers to is Šiškov's monologue in the hospital scene of Act 3, telling how he murdered his wife Akulka.

You, my darling little Kamila

That silver cock and the black hen[1] would be glad to be merry and happy together! They'll certainly find one another. They won't get a moment's peace until they find one another!

And what should I carry, you'll tell me another time? [You say] that I know what I should carry? It would pass from hand to hand, everyone would kiss it, cherish it, stroke it. Is that so?

And you as well? And it would be so like you. A spitting image of you. Is it that?

Oh, that hopeful year of ours! If only that wish of ours would come true, the wish of both of us! So I'll wear the tie tomorrow for the first time and with it I'll then come to you.

Only don't make any preparations in our heaven. Just the heating, no more. And if you're not wholly and completely well, stay in bed. I'll get myself to your place from the station and at least nurse you for those two days. But not for free, my little soul, oh no. A big payment from you! And you don't have to reach into your handbag, not even turn your little head; you won't make excuses, or even be afraid! No! While you're sick, I'll just fondle you! So today is 'merry' Silvester.[2] From 9 o'clock in the evening I've been sitting here alone, but gladly! Your letter today is such a darling one that I'd kiss it the whole time.

It's just as if we were now definitely promised to one another. The feeling I'm getting from it [the letter] is right, isn't it? Yes, now to be with you, I'd implore you, Kamilka be mine! And I'd ask so that you'd not refuse – and that would be that.

I'd tremble with pleasure, I'd call you until my heart burst. I'd kiss you until you burned with love and said: 'Be mine, be mine!' And that would be that.

And it would be a delight such as no-one's ever experienced. We'd both burn with passion in it. To have you, just for that measureless love for you. A love which cannot abide our still being two alongside one another. A love which wants to drown spiritually and physically and merge into one. You don't know where you'd begin and where I'd end. I knew a picture like that,[3] I saw it, but now I sense how it would be if it became true.

---

1 i.e. the silver-haired Leoš and the black-haired Kamila.
2 31 December is the feast of St Silvester. The day is still known in the Czech Republic as 'Silvestr' and, as in Scotland, vigorously celebrated.
3 Janáček may be referring to *Splynutí duše* [Coalescence of the spirit], a well-known painting (1896) by Max Švabinský (1873–1962).

Such longings for the New Year. Oh that darling letter of yours, how I'd like to keep it for ever.

But the time will come when your letters won't be lost in a cleansing fire.

And now I'll go to bed with your reassurances and my single life's wish, that you'll be wholly mine, and God grant that with new life in your sacred womb – in this hopeful year and the sooner the better – yes soon, if I were to see you very soon ...?

Oh sleep well too – do have the same thoughts –

get well, but wait upon your health – stay in bed even longer if it's necessary.

Sometimes lying in bed is pleasant – and one sort – waited for, longed for.

For ever yours

L.

552   Brno, 1–2 January 1928

My dear Kamila

I hope you had a better first day of the year than I had.

Forgive my wild letter of yesterday; it surely flew straight into the fire.

I don't have the words today to tell you all I went through.

On the one hand I see myself wretched, on the other [I see] a woman [i.e. Zdenka] who cannot control herself.

I don't want to frighten you; you have enough of that yourself.

And how much there is that oppresses me, and how difficult it is![1]

If you don't get a letter on Tuesday [3 January], don't be alarmed.

Brno, 1 January 1928

So my dear soul, calm again after the storm. I kept the peace through self-discipline. But I know and she knows too, that this excitement cannot ever repeat itself.

I'm sure of that.

Despite that, no-one in the world will tear me from you.

In my life you're my only dear delight, my only peaceful rest; were it not for you what would I have here still!

Fate marches on so peacefully, the end is surely already settled. We'll submit to it.

1 Janáček was revising Act 3 of *From the House of the Dead* and, as is clear from 550, was finding Šiškov's long story about murdering his wife Akulka particularly demanding. By 3 January (see 555) he had reached the end of this monologue.

I just want to be with you now as soon as possible.

Don't be frightened by my letter. One has to get used even to storms now and one has to survive them.

I think that even I am excited at the moment — by my work. Otherwise I wouldn't perhaps write so irritably.

So please forgive me now — I forgave you your illness; you my irritation.

I'm only yours[,] for ever

Brno, 2 January 1928

554   Brno, 2 January 1928

My dear Kamila

What a comfortable time the post has in Písek! In Brno it was working all Saturday.

However, today, Monday, you must have received letters that you won't read through until evening.

But the last two, in those I wrote in total confusion.

I just want peace at home; that's surely not much. When she didn't provide it, she heard what you are to me. After all I don't hide what's evident from my face. Today there's now blessed peace again, for she knows that every string breaks when it's stretched beyond its limits.

I'd so like to be already finished with the last bars of my work. It's so exciting, that last act. And I'm pleased now that you've recovered. But I know you! Sitting at home! That's still in heaven. I'm so pleased about your health, but also about mine. Only now, in the last few days, I'm so like my normal self 'that I don't feel I'm a silver-haired gentleman'! You little black chicken! And you were showered with gifts so generously!

To your ruler — your husband,[1] say that I congratulate him on his escape from great danger. A tragic end is beautiful, but unenviable.

You had a bad New Year's Eve, I an even worse one; so we'll make it up to ourselves!

I'll get ready for Hukvaldy [Písek?] as soon as I've finished the last note. You know I'll be already looking out for you in the train from the second last station; but if you're not as right as rain you'll look out [for me] from the window — a closed window.

I'll thank Ondrúšek in your name, by my right as your husband,

---

1 An increasingly rare reference to David Stössel as Kamila's 'husband'. A few sentences later Janáček is referring to himself in this capacity. Stössel seems to have met with some accident on the train (see 555).

who stands behind you, guards you and looks for you, and who's glad to serve you because he knows that he has a clear sun behind him, which warms him and which he's so pleased to have.

Now it's Monday 9.30 in the evening. Have you read everything already? Even that letter about fees? That went straight into the fire, not so?[1]

But I don't mind. Those sort of fees are not forfeit; in the worse cases they get stolen, as in Luhačovice.

But one lesson to be learnt; don't boast anywhere about health and happiness!

Make use of both and worry about both – then they'll last longest.

Sleep well, my little imp.

Always thinking of you

L.

555   Brno, 3 January 1928

My dear Kamila

[...]

I'm finished with this difficult story about Akulka in my opera.[2] In the last few days I sat up working from 8 in the morning till noon, and in the afternoon until evening. I myself was excited until I [almost] bled – and for me there was no pity and understanding.[3]

And the hand of fate intervened directly in that train accident of your husband. What if the very worst had happened? That occurred to me at once – and I don't want to talk about it or even think about it! He was lucky. That struck me.

So let's meet up joyfully. We won't make any plans.

We're glad that we'll see one another and make each other happy; that we'll say lots to each other such as has never been printed anywhere. Or we'll be silent – just as God grants. Now I always take higher powers as witnesses.

Sleep well and get completely well.

Yours for ever

L.

1 If Janáček is referring to 551, with its mention of a 'big payment', then it survived the fire.
2 See p.180, fn.
3 i.e. from Zdenka.

556 Brno, 4 January 1928

So my beautiful girl, au revoir!
Opera finished.
The work finished.
I just want to see you now and have joyful moments.
Yours for ever.

557 Prague, 6 January 1928

I'm in Prague and on Sunday [8 January] I'll be in my beloved Písek.
If you're even a little bit ill don't go to the station. I'm looking forward inexpressibly to the pure transparent air and kind words.
Devotedly
L.

558 Prague, 10 January 1928, 9 a.m.

Dear darling Kamila
That you want to acknowledge publicly that you're my
only love –
for that
a most happy fellow
thanks you.

Yours for ever
L.

My only desire and my future wife!

Janáček had to be in Prague on Monday 10 January for a meeting about the printing of *Moravian Love Songs*[1] and took the opportunity of spending the weekend before in Písek, returning to Prague early on Monday morning. Over the weekend Stösslová seems to have expressed the wish for the relationship to become public knowledge, as is clear from Janáček's brief note from Prague (558). He wrote a postcard on his arrival in Brno (*559: 11 January 1928) and wrote again later that evening.

1 See Janáček's notes published in Janáček 1955, 538.

My dear Kamila!

So — two days as if snipped out of a fairy story. Two people met; they came from quite different regions, they made paradise for one another. Then they put it obediently into a little box and stored it. When they meet again they'll open the box. They'll find everything in order there: < one word erased > in order, unnibbled, the velvet [tenderness?] of stroking. But look! A little ring lies there nicely! That's something new! Which imp hid it there? Oh, I know him! But which one will take it? I know her too![1]

Just imagine. I go to Hukvaldy as early as Saturday [14 January]; they already have a commission there about the installation of electric light. Write so that a letter goes to Hukvaldy u Příbora, Moravia — and *sealed*.

And a second piece of news. On 21 January the German Theatre in Prague is giving *Káťa Kabanová*.

I'm going there by express that day in the morning via Olomouc–Česká Třebová. So I invite you and your husband. Come for sure and we'll go to the theatre. I'll organize a box; I'll stay a day or two in Prague and then return again to Hukvaldy directly via Olomouc. So good health! Away with the iron corset from off your body! Away with your suspenders! Free your body altogether, it can't take such constriction! You'd get even more ill! What were you doing at the market today? I fear that you got frozen again! Weren't you worse after accompanying [me] to the station in the early morning? Write to me about it.

I was at the doctor's, Dr Výmola,[2] in Prague. If only I could give you my medicine! We have the same illness. I take something in which there's bitter quinine and also some sort of syrup. Well, we'll get well and comfort each other in Prague!

The theatre is inviting me urgently.

I didn't find Dr Brod[3] at home. My dear, dear soul! Don't be afraid, the world will learn what you are to me! And it will learn that we

---

1 The gender of the two imps is not revealed in Czech; the pronouns refer to the word *šotek* [imp], which exists only in a masculine form. Since Janáček had already received a ring from Stösslová in the earliest days of the friendship (see Glossary: 'ring'), it seems more likely that it was he who brought one for her this time.
2 See Glossary.
3 As Janáček soon revealed (see 574), Kamila wanted Janáček's biographer and translator Max Brod 'to know everything' about the relationship, perhaps as a means of telling the world, though Janáček seems to have jumped the gun by writing about it himself, in an article for the magazine *Venkov* (see 561 and 567).

both take pleasure in it.

You know that by your wanting it to be known, you've bound me and yourself so strongly that there can be no firmer bond! I thank you for it with all my soul.

And you, little gold ring, I'd kiss you without ceasing.

What about the alcohol–camphor?[1]

Don't imagine that it will help you at once. Just look after yourself and don't act foolishly so that your illness doesn't get worse. It's no joking matter! That Tuesday morning[2] was already a sin. But your obstinate little head!

And Kamilka, don't forget that we belong to each other and to no-one else.

We confine ourselves to our heaven. There I've no other saints but you. You see how nicely it rhymes.[3]

What about your mother? Is she also recovering?

You could wear the same clothes that you had on for the photographs. Were they a success? I'll learn that only in Hukvaldy.

Thinking of you

Yours for ever

L.

561   Brno, 12 January 1928, at night

My dear Kamila

I'm travelling from Brno on Saturday morning [14 January] and will be at Hukvaldy by the evening.

Then certainly a week after, on Saturday 21 January, I want to be in Prague for that performance of *Káťa Kabanová* at the German Theatre.

You know that it's your work. You were that warm atmosphere for me, in which, in my thoughts, you were continually present in all parts of the opera where expressions of love occur. You know, even during that time when we still knew each other so little – I already felt myself linked to you so closely.

It's possible that I'll go to Prague as early as the day before, on the Friday.

I'll certainly be waiting for you to come there too. I'll ask for a box

1 A treatment that Janáček described and urged Kamila to take for curing her bronchitis (see 548).
2 10 January, when Kamila saw off Janáček at the station in the early morning.
3 *Omezujeme se na své nebe.*
  Tam nemám jiných svatých než Tebe.

so that we can listen to it in peace. And then to chat about everything somewhere. So [come] for sure! Just don't get ill! A letter didn't come from you today. I'm waiting for it tomorrow.

You can't imagine how the last visit to you has preoccupied me! Those were such serious things which I experienced, I got to know such serious sides of you, so dear that I'm deeply lost in thought under their influence.

Yes, I feel that I must say publicly in some way what you mean to me. I can't even wait for Brod. I'll tell it in a way that will convince everybody. You'll be elevated, raised above all slander.

My dear Kamila, sometimes jokes themselves fall silent and quiet truth reigns. As Dr Hostinský[1] vindicated Fibich, so will people see good in us. I'll write about you, and will write beautifully and truthfully. You're half of my soul.

[...]

And that gold ring, it has brought us close. There's no longer a hair's breadth between us. Just be well. Seal the letter! I'll wait for it impatiently in Hukvaldy.

Yours for ever.

Only your

L.

562 Kojetín, 14 January 1928

My dear Kamila

I'm off, and writing in the train. I got your dear letter. There was complete peace at home. My friend Těsnohlídek, who wrote *Liška Bystrouška* with me, has shot himself.[2] He prepared for it for a long while. When his young wife learnt of it, she also took her life! Terrible! At home we said that we'll avoid arguments completely. I continually think of our little ring. So we belonged to one another! Not so? It's a strange thing. Where burning desire leads. We already belong to one another and will do so for ever. I'm so happy at your place; I don't think of food. And I'm glad that your dear ones like me. You've been bequeathed to me. I'm your husband. I'm waiting for

1 Although the aesthetician and writer on music Otakar Hostinský wrote extensively about Fibich, he was discreet about the composer's relationship with Anežka Schulzová; Janáček probably meant Dr Nejedlý, who wrote a book about the couple, see p.161, fn.2.
2 Rudolf Těsnohlídek (1882–1928), whose novel *Liška Bystrouška* Janáček used as the basis for *The Cunning Little Vixen*, shot himself in the editorial offices of the *Lidové noviny* on 12 January 1928. His third wife, Olga (1893–1928), committed suicide when she heard the news.

word that you're coming to Prague. They'll send you a [ticket for a] box. I'll probably be staying in Prague at the Karel IV., Smíchov, from Friday. You could also stay there.

Yours for ever

I'll bring the photograph!

The next day, Janáček wrote from Hukvaldy (*564: 15 January 1928), repeating all the travel arrangements, and adding that on Friday 20 January he had an appointment with the doctor and one other unspecified meeting, but that on Saturday and Sunday they would be together. The next letter (*565: postmarked 17 January 1928) may have been more personal; only the envelope has survived. A postcard from Hukvaldy (*566: 19 January 1928) reminded Stösslová of the première, and mentioned that he had written to Dr Brod ('he'll get a shock'). Janáček had done so the day before,[1] mentioning his friendship with Stösslová in oblique and guarded terms. By his next letter Janáček was back in Hukvaldy, having met up for the première of *Káťa Kabanová* at the German Theatre on 21 January, the first time that Stösslová had seen 'her' opera. David Stössel perhaps came too, as Janáček suggested (560) and as decorum dictated, not that one would guess from Janáček's reminiscences of the event:

567   Hukvaldy, 23 January 1928

Darling Kamila

The more I know you, the more I respect you, [and] the more sincerely, if it can still be said, I love you.

Into the café – you didn't want to go with me,

In the theatre – you hid yourself,

at Burian's[2] – it's a wonder you didn't split your sides laughing,

in the street on the way home, at night – they could almost have said that you'd drunk a brewery – and you took [only] a sip from my glass; and then you came to the station while it was still dark and immediately waved merrily to me, yourself bringing a bit of cake –

And you went away. I go, and tears cover me. And I write this, and where on earth have these tears come from in me, they are tears of joy! You are my dear soul, be, as you write now, that faithful woman for ever.

The late Těsnohlídek – now his son's[3] turned up! Through all the

---

1 JA ix, 231–2; English translation in Susskind 1985, 119–20.
2 The Theatre of Vlasta Burian (1891–1962), a popular Czech comic actor.
3 Těsnohlídek's son from his second marriage, Dr Milan Navrátil (1910–86), was adopted by his mother's second husband.

newspapers he thanks all who were at his father's funeral! What life sometimes hides in itself. Poor fellow!

I got home alright; I was at Hukvaldy only at 5 in the evening. A pile of letters was waiting for me.

I'm sending you two of these. If only they'd let us live now as we want to!

So I had pleasure at least for a moment on my arrival. I really do want to take a rest now; but something's pecking its way out of my head again. That article will be nice now. Wait, little imp, [in that article] I'll also make you go tearfully on a lead.[1] You're probably asleep already. All wrapped up?

You know, you didn't rush around excessively as in Písek: from warmth to cold – you were therefore coughing less in Prague.

Keep well. I'm looking forward to your letter. In April they'll give my 'merry mass' in Prague.[2]

I'll lure you out of Písek again somewhere, although I know that nothing's better than our Písek paradise!

Yours for ever

L.

And my little cook, black-eyed, black-haired, bronze, darling – what does it mean when the *buchta* has a kiss mark?

I wanted to send you a letter from Zdenka too. She writes that she's content, that she'll no longer disturb the peace, yes, even if she has to take shares in this fame of mine. She says she didn't mean harm with the cuttings. Let it be as it all is. We don't set much store by the fame. It's enough for us just to love one another!

568   Hukvaldy, 25 January 1928

My dear Kamila

How did you get home?

Did they pump you for information about how you got on in Prague? Did you brag about it? Were they in ecstasy over you? What about your mother? I was hungry in Prague; you know for what? I

---

1 In a letter of 3 December 1927 (BmJA, B 632) the magazine *Venkov* had asked Janáček for a feuilleton for their Christmas number. Janáček failed to meet this deadline but nevertheless supplied an article entitled 'It's dusk', dated 24 January and printed on 5 February 1928. In it Janáček discussed the sources of inspiration of his work, and used this as a pretext for mentioning Kamila Stösslová (though not by name) in connection with *Káťa Kabanová*. It also mentions an incident Stösslová must have told him, recounting that, as an unwilling schoolchild, she was led to school on a piece of string by her grandfather.
2 See Glossary: 'Glagolitic Mass'.

bet you don't know!

So your first fee for *Káťa Kabanová*[1] from 1 August to the end of December 1927 brought in – don't faint –

Kč 240!

[...]

I've now had workmen for two days wiring the electric light. The dust, the dirt, the mess! I look at it – and keep sneezing.

I've now sent the article to *Venkov*.[2] You go there on a lead to school, and two further incidents [...]. Well, they'll know you, you naughty girl, in Písek!

I've also sent a trifle to the *Prácheňské noviny*[3] – since they keep on sending it to me. Tomorrow I'll be waiting for a letter from you for certain. In March and April I'll be continually on my travels. I think that the carpet and the photographs are already on their way too.

I can't look enough at our photograph [see Jacket], you're that true woman, yes, and [in comparison] I'm just a little fragment.

Always thinking of you, and very much loving you

Yours for ever

L.

I'll leave here most likely on *31 January*.

569   Hukvaldy, 26 January 1928

My dear Kamila

The carpet, the sweets, the photograph with the children [see Plate 3] and your dear picture arrived.

It's already hanging above my writing-desk! I've shown it to my sister; she was delighted with what you are to me!

Today a marvellous review of the Prague performance came out in *Lidové noviny*.

It also concerns you. Now it's known how love helps a composer to make his work dazzle.[4]

And now to get you better, my soul! I know your illness, bronchitis, I also had it and it plagued me a long time! Compresses,

1 Janáček had determined that Stösslová would receive the royalties from performance of *Káťa Kabanová*.
2 See p.188, fn.1.
3 See Glossary.
4 The review by Boleslav Vomáčka appeared on 24 January 1928 and made the point that for all its originality *Káťa Kabanová* speaks dramatically to its audiences 'in the language of the richest feeling'.

nothing else will cure you. In Gleichenberg, in Cukmantl[1] I took a cure and was cured. Neither sun nor inhalation will itself help. If you can survive until morning in that compress, well-made so that *the wet bandage won't show anywhere*, so that it's covered by the dry one, and in between put a waterproof cloth (it's reddish, you can get it at the chemist's), all the better. Otherwise two days in a row for two hours in bed, rest on the third day!

So to it! Before it's too late! You know we *must be* well!

Here I've got lots of work; the lighting's already finished. The builder was here the whole day measuring. I'll get an estimate in February; if it's reasonable, I'll build. It must be finished by 1 July.

I leave here *on 31 January*. An awful lot of work awaits me in Brno! Our heaven's the most beautiful; the Lord God doesn't have such a heaven; because he doesn't have a little imp like you.

Just spare yourself, spare yourself!

Yours for ever

Leoš

That carpet, what did it actually cost? Your royalty's coming at the same time.

571 Hukvaldy, 29 January 1928

My dear Kamila

I believe, Kamilka, that the draught made your ear worse – but, I tell you, you're just going to have to go to Výmola!

I don't believe anything your doctor says. He was terribly wrong with me. And I'm glad that your back has stopped aching – and that Kamila will be well!

And now to business:

1. Yes, I and I and I – am guilty of everything. I'm glad to take that on myself and will bear it gladly to the end of my life.

2. Your photograph hangs in a gold frame above the writing-desk and will continue to hang there, and the other photographs are not hidden in my home and will not be hidden.

---

1 Janáček was cured of bronchitis in the Styrian spa town of Gleichenberg in 1884 (see Helfert 1939, 327); in 1887 he went to Cukmantl on the Moravian–Polish border after a general breakdown in health probably caused by overwork (it was from there that he sent Dvořák his first opera, *Šárka*, for an opinion).

3. Věra Janáčková[1] spoke insolently, because she's an insolent woman and because there's nothing else in her except empty pride, conceit. For that I've rebuked her so openly that I believe no more will surely be heard from her. With this the matter's settled – and also for you, and for ever.

4. I don't set store by fame, you'll not take shares in it. You have me entirely, with absolutely everything, including my importance! That's because you have such a big share in my importance in the world. It's not necessary now to talk about it, that will be known at the proper time.

5. I'll never hide anything. I don't know how to, I don't know such hypocrisy. There aren't lies in my compositions, there's no lie in my life. You're so dear to me, so good, you're half of my soul! It's impossible to hide anything. The world must recognize it as a fact, just as when the sun shines, one says 'it's shining'! In the same way it must be recognized, and said, that he loves and must love Kamila with all his heart.

There's no getting away from it.

And travelling to you? If you say come! I'll come. And if you don't say, I'll also come; I'll look through your windows – and go away.

6. You don't lure me. It's like when you let go of something it falls to the ground and doesn't fly to the ceiling. So I fall to you.

7. You soften my nature, you make it better; everyone around me feels that. I'll wait impatiently for your letter in Brno.

6. [*recte* 8.] And I want to see my heaven and my saint in it. And how again and again one moment you shine through, you warm all around with love, and how immediately afterwards it's as if you'd faded!

But I believe only the first! And may your letters only be warm ones; and surely they'll be so?

Will there be written 'faithful unto death'?

Will there be, as you said on the Prague streets, 'I'm yours, and will remain yours for ever'? – because I want to hear it continually from you – regardless of the bad world which we now know how to deal with!

---

1 It appears that Janáček met his niece during the trip to Prague and that Janáček reported her words to Stösslová (see 576). The basis of Věra's 'insolence' may be inferred from points 6 and 5 of Janáček's letter, that Stösslová was 'luring' him away from his wife, and that he should be more discreet. Janáček's hope to have silenced her permanently was a forlorn one; a month later both Věra and her mother were writing vociferously to Zdenka about 'die Jüdin' (e.g. BmJA, E 1138–9).

Keep well!
Yours for ever
L.

572   Hukvaldy, 29 January 1928

Dear Kamila!

I was sorry that you wrote me such a sermon. But I cannot be angry with you!

I'd thought that I'd give you pleasure when I invited you to Prague and meanwhile it didn't turn out that way.

You attach too much weight to the impudence of that woman – and I don't lay any store by it at all, because I know her.

And haven't I tamed her?

Why isn't that enough for you?

It's been no pleasure for me either. It wasn't much to find a moment during those two days [to say] two or three words coming from the heart! I'd just want to be with you < small part of letter cut out > [...]

But I know that you'll come to yourself. For at the end of your letter was the familiar line of dots.[1]

And me? I'm sad. I don't know why, but very sad. The reason is probably your letter and those terrible pieces of advice!

I fight for that little bit of your love and instead of kind, helpful words from you – advice like that!

Don't come! Work hard!

I was waiting for a joyful letter – and I was hardly able to read to the end of it. I was waiting for you to draw even closer to me – and an incident like that concerning me rather than you was capable of muddying the water. And yet you said, there at the clock, as we waited < small part of letter cut out >

Kamila, what's the matter with you?

I'm calm. I know you're everything to me. Don't torment me with dry letters. I don't cry much, but today and at this moment I'm crying.

Yours for ever
L.

1 More familiar in Stösslová's surviving letters are endings with several horizontal lines.

Dear Kamila

I don't know how you could have sent me such a letter after Prague. I've read it now several times, and if it weren't for your signature, which says much to me, I wouldn't understand it. Perhaps I don't understand it. It's possible that in this isolation of mine I don't understand it. In this isolation one needs a warm heart nearby. Today, it's Sunday, I'm especially sad. I've begun to work on a quartet; I'll give it the name *Love Letters*.[1]

I'm now able to write about them even in music.

Yesterday I explained about those Gypsy children[2] to my sister. She was moved, she cried. I'd like her to know you. You'll come here.

It's unlikely I'll be building; that single room would come to about Kč 20,000![3] She said when she's no longer in this world I'll have enough rooms downstairs and a housekeeper would be content up in the loft.[4] She's right.

Today I went to my 'hill' as they call the woods in the hills here. It's 29 January and I've already found a daisy blooming in the grass. I'm enclosing it for you as a little harbinger of spring. And although your cough still hasn't gone you went at once to the wood again?

What stupid words: that [your] ear ached from exasperation. Put all the blame on your nerves.

I die of fear for you, and now you go into the wood in the frost!

Today I got an invitation to Prague; they're giving my composition Capriccio (*Defiance*)[5] in a concert there on 2 March.

So I've been away from Brno for a fortnight. What one has lived through here. You say you were pleased how you differed to your advantage from the Prague ladies. Yes, to great advantage, except for one thing.

'When the truth is spoken to someone it angers him.' I'll tell you the truth, don't be angry. I don't know how to be angry with you, similarly don't be angry with me.

I regretted that after the theatre you left the company before I did.

---

1 The first mention, anywhere, of Janáček's String Quartet no. 2, the piece most directly inspired by Kamila Stösslová. The progress of its composition is described in the next few letters.
2 See Glossary.
3 In the event he paid Kč 22,500 (see 597).
4 Janáček's sister Josefa Dohnalová lived in his Hukvaldy cottage as housekeeper. Since she was eight years older than him, she expected to predecease him.
5 See Glossary.

The whole company guessed our relationship, and you go away, in spite of my pleas. You've already done it once before. I'd fear it [happening] a third time. And now I'd like to have your promise that you won't leave – without me.

No, I won't be in a good mood until I read your next letter. Nothing pleases me, everything's the same for me. I'm held above the water only by a straw – your signature. It's a nice straw, however, and I believe nevertheless that it will sustain me.

Keep well. I'll send you the next letter on the way. From here it would go only on Tuesday [31 January] anyway.

Yours for ever

L.

Don't be angry any more.

574 Hukvaldy, 30 January 1928

My dear Kamila

I'm sitting here for the last evening and I could get accustomed to being here and working.

I came here a fortnight ago in the hope that I'd see you in Prague within a week. How I was looking forward to it!

I'll no longer mention it. You see, you wanted Dr Brod to know everything; he knows it, and in *Venkov* there'll be quite a lot about you perhaps.[1] And that woman's slander has spoilt your mood, has upset your equanimity! Well, there'll be other such slanderous women! But surely they won't get into our heaven! They'll immediately fly away from the door just as that one flew away. Don't think that I don't know how to smooth your path! To save you.

But my Kamila must stand behind me, I must feel her love and her affection; my strength and determination lie in this.

When I look back, I must feel her black eye upon me.

It wasn't comfortable in Prague; I felt as if I were able to speak to you only through a wall. Except that I felt your breath and your closeness. Nothing more. I was pleased at least with that – but I knew that it was too little. Just to look at the sea – and not bathe in it; full dishes – but no spoons, forks, knives, not even fingers! To want to sing – but just croak. To drink – and an empty glass. Then add an insolent woman to that – oh yes, that was the end of my joy! And I paid for it.

1 See p.188, fn.1.

No, it will never happen again like that. But still something hurts me; someone knows more than he ought to know. –

And so I sit here the night before leaving and think to myself 'you're a sorry fellow!'

And I finished reading the diary of a great Russian composer.[1] He made entries day after day – until his death approached; and not a word about love! How's it possible? I need it so much! He, Tchaikovsky, got drunk day after day and I've a single picture in my mind, it's my bread and my wine. I get drunk on it.

So many dark clouds lie on my soul! Will you disperse them in the letter which I'm waiting for tomorrow! I think that you've got well again. [The stay] helped me too; only a little more joy wouldn't do any harm.

I'll put this letter in the post on the journey.

Yours for ever

Leoš

575 Kojetín, on the journey, 31 January 1928

I'm on my way now. The mountains are covered with snow, but it's warming up. My sister thanks you once again for the sweets.[2] On St Andrew's Day[3] you'll get something from the local bakery in return. I'm terribly sensitive. Did you take my letter badly perhaps? Forgive me now, I couldn't write otherwise. Perhaps I'll find my cheerful mood when I read your letter which will be waiting for me.

Yours for ever

L.

576 Brno, 1 February 1928, at night

My dear Kamila

I came to my post, I saw your letter lying there – and I sighed aloud with joy! I'm writing now before opening your letter. I know that without you my life would be a dried-up meadow. At every step, I'd be saying, here this flower bloomed, there that one – that would be

---

1 Janáček probably read the Russian edition *Dnyevniki P.I. Chaykovskovo*, ed. Ipolit Ilyich Chaykovskiy (Moscow: Gosudarstvennnoye, 1923), though this volume has not survived in his library.

2 Sent with the carpet and the photographs (see 569).

3 A local chapel in Hukvaldy is dedicated to St Andrew, which is probably the reason why his feast-day was celebrated locally with special delicacies. But Kamila would have had a long wait: the feast of St Andrew is on 30 November.

sad enough to choke one. I'll read it now! I think that I'm going to be pleased – if only because you're writing! – –

I've read both letters – and I'm immensely glad that I recognize my Kamila again! No, Kamilka, do write. When you write simply 'I'm well', I think of you with joy – it makes me well, and you also. Not to write, that would be worse. I haven't said a word at home about what happened in Prague;[1] I've told my sister everything. It was my fault that I told you, but I thought that when two hold something [together], they bear it better. I dealt with it, and I'm at peace; you paid for it; I know that your nerves are filaments of fire; they burn. Next time I'll think of that and spare you. But I ask you, at least take two tablets daily from that small tube which I gave you in Prague.

Only tell me the truth, whether you're coughing, whether your back aches, whether you have twinges. Then, when spring begins, you'd have to look for spa treatments. I'm just glad that you've forgiven me. My letters, I know, became embittered. Now it will be different. Now I've begun to write something nice. Our life will be in it. It will be called

'*Love Letters*'.[2]

I think that it will sound delightful. There have already been so many of those dear adventures of ours, haven't there? They'll be little fires in my soul and they'll set it ablaze with the most beautiful melodies.

Just think. The first movement I did already in Hukvaldy. The impression when I saw you for the first time!

I'm now working on the second movement. I think that it will flare up in the Luhačovice heat < one word inked out >. A special instrument will particularly hold the whole thing together. It's called the viola d'amore – the viola of love.[3] Oh, how I'm looking forward to it! In that work I'll be always only with you! No third person beside us. Full of that yearning as there at your place, in that heaven of ours! I'll love doing it! You know, don't you, that I know no world other than you! You're everything to me, I don't want anything else but your love.

And how bitter it was for me when I read from your letter how you wanted to forget everything nice that had happened between us!

I thought to myself, how could my Kamila forget everything?

1 See p.191, fn.
2 See Glossary: 'String Quartet no.2'.
3 Janáček did indeed write the quartet substituting a viola d'amore for the viola part, proudly writing the name on every page of his manuscript. A viola d'amore was available at the first rehearsal and was tried out, but was found to be impractical. Janáček reluctantly agreed to substituting a regular viola (see Tyrrell 1982, 159).

Would it be possible? I now know that it wasn't! We've reached that stage in heaven where to go back is no longer possible, one can only go higher! Take strength in that; you'll surely find peace. If I'm something, if my work's something, *then surely you're also something with it – and higher and more important* than that common niece of mine, who will never stand before me again. So it is, my dear Kamilka! Don't blame your nerves for everything; that bronchitis creates a terrible mood. It will also pass.

And don't be ashamed of your own character. It's so dear to me, so very dear. You're a cheery person 'leavened' with tears. It's just that your character – and I already understand it well [–] is almost pathologically sensitive. You're difficult to understand. The people around you are hard and – Kamilka [–] heartless. Better to avoid than to fall between hard stones.

So, my beloved Kamila, do write; even two or three words will be enough to satisfy me.

And when you write 'I'm for ever only yours', you open heaven to me with it!

That carpet is more valuable – and the rest is your share which you've unwittingly but rightly deserved.[1]

At Hukvaldy I now have electric light installed; the 'children'[2] are delightful. I've a fine building plan. I'll see what the estimate comes to. So we stand where we've reached –

    no thought of going back –

    dear fate be kind and lead us forward!

Yours for ever

L.

577   [Brno,] 2 February 1928, at night

My dear Kamila

I know that without you my life would be a scorched desert. I also know, however, that you need the gentlest handling. I'll speak and deal with you as if you were wrapped in cotton wool. Tell me truthfully though, I was surely never rude in word or deed to you. You said to me yourself that I am good. Only that letter after Prague, that second one, was like a sharp change in the wind – and at once I desperately defended myself. I enclose a letter for you so you'll know

---

1 The carpet that Stösslová sent Janáček arrived in Hukvaldy on 26 January 1928 (see 569). Stösslová was to receive the royalties on performances of *Káťa Kabanová* (see 568).
2 See Glossary.

what other people think about that article that's coming out now. Keep the letter. Don't be frightened of it in advance! You know that I'm unable to harm you.

I'll write to you daily – for my consolation – but I'll send the letter to you every other day. So don't wait every day. On Monday [6 February] that virtuoso from Prague is coming to see me.[1] He'll play for me here that piece of mine he's going to play in Prague on 2 March. I think I'll be able to hop over to see if you're well again. This time I won't even wait for an invitation from you. You might forbid me! – And I wouldn't listen.

And now I'll tell you what happened today. Don't be alarmed!

I had to make a list of possessions for the tax office – and one [savings] book for Kč 100,000 – couldn't be found! I ran to the bank. I thought that I'd lost it, that the money had gone. But in the bank my money was untouched. So it wasn't lost. I was amazed at my calm. I didn't burst out with a single word. Gone? So it's gone. But it's not gone, and it's alright. Tomorrow I'll send you my debt.[2]

So I'm working hard – it's as if I'm living through everything beautiful once again – working on these *Love Letters*.

So sleep well. I feel that I love you more and more. Even more is possible!

Wasn't that trip to Topělka[3] too much for you?

580   Brno, 6 February 1928

My dear Kamila

[...]

Today that one-handed virtuoso came from Prague to see me. He'll play my piece nicely. I'll go to Prague earlier for the rehearsal; the concert's as early as 2 March. How I'm looking forward to seeing you!

That article of mine was in *Venkov* (the Sunday number, 5 February).[4] Order it at the bookshop for yourself; they haven't sent it to me yet. But people like it!

Don't go out much; the weather's raw now. After my medicines, I already feel well now, but nevertheless for safety's sake I'm having myself x-rayed on Thursday [9 February]. They can see at once for

1 See Glossary: 'Capriccio'.
2 See p.189, fn.1.
3 Topělec.
4 See p.188, fn.1.

sure where there's something diseased. I thank you warmly for your decision over Luhačovice;[1] it'll be decided soon, won't it – and we won't miss out on a spa, whether this one or some other. For me not to be there and be thinking of you there – I'd get ill anywhere else.

If I'll build, it's only really for you, so you'd be comfortable.

I'll make a little sketch how it will look afterwards

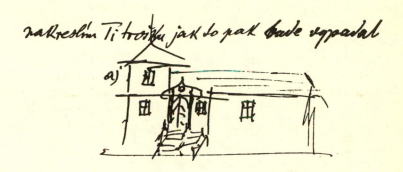

The living room at (a) will be for you; that would be the new extension. I'm waiting for the estimate. It would all have to be finished by 1 July!

So sleep sweetly! Oh, if only you were m[y] w[ife]!

Yours for ever

L.

I'm going to be x-rayed now. What if your picture were suddenly to be found in my heart and were to leap out?! That would be fun!

581   [Brno, c8 February 1928]

< all but one side, 'p.3', destroyed >

[...] So let's sound a cheerful note. I'm writing the third of the 'Love Letters'. For it to be very cheerful and then dissolve into a vision which would resemble your image, transparent, as if in the mist. In which there should be the suspicion of motherhood. It's night now. Sleep well.

Yours for ever

L.

1 Stösslová had presumably agreed to take a holiday at Luhačovice at the same time as Janáček (see also 583).

My dear Kamila

You have no idea what an impression your letter yesterday made on me!

I woke up in the night, couldn't sleep till morning. A whirl of thoughts in my head! How will you answer tomorrow? Will you avoid direct speech again? You know, don't you, how to speak as in the saying — what's on the heart is on the tongue![1]

You're like a savage and that's why I love you so! One moment one's carrying you in cotton wool, then the frosty wind wraps you up and bears you away! Have you been taken ill again?

I wouldn't run after you; but were the ice to break I'd jump in after you.

Today I wrote that sweetest desire of mine in music. I fight with it, it triumphs. You're having a child. What fate in life would that little son have? What portion would you have? It sounds just like you are, turning from tears to laughter.

They invited me by telegram to go to Vienna for Sunday [12 February]. They're giving my Military Sinfonietta[2] there.

It's not a first-class orchestra playing it and I don't even know who's conducting it. So I won't go there. I know that I wouldn't find my heaven there.

I hope it will be warm already around 2 March; I hope we can sow that poppy seed.[3] For our enjoyment and the adornment of that field.

I'm simply waiting for your answer now. What will you do so as never, never to go back again?!

Come what may. I have never known what it is to go back. What's done cannot be undone! Let a new day dawn, a new sun! That's you! It will always dawn for someone; for another it's behind the clouds. I'm not forcing anything for myself, in any way. I'll wait devotedly, trustingly. I'll break through those clouds — and perhaps you'll be mine. It would be a strange fate — to fight for a single bit of happiness and not to win it! I need to have you near; that's spring. Otherwise many, many times I become lost in thought. I feel so today. Well, when you write, [say] how we'll do it so that we could

1 Here Janáček unconsciously echoed the words of Kamila's letter of 11 January 1923.
2 The Sinfonietta was performed in Vienna on 12 February 1928 by the Vienna Symphony Orchestra under Jascha Horenstein. It is interesting that Janáček was still referring to his Sinfonietta in this way, although the word 'military' had been dropped from the title on publication a year earlier (see p.87, fn.2).
3 See 550.

never go back! I'll reach for that letter as if for fate.
    Yours for ever
    L.

Your letter took me into my seventh heaven. Let me stay there, and you with me!

583   Brno, 8 [*recte* 9] February 1928

My darling Kamila
    So they x-rayed me – and from my heart there jumped out – Kamila, and chirruped: 'I'm at home here. I fill up every corner! How do you do!'
    That's how it was. Everything healthy. But Luhačovice came out of it; [doctor's] orders. At the end of June I'll already be there – we'll be there.
    Look out on Sunday [12 February] in case you see me somewhere in Písek around nine. They've called me to Prague for Saturday.
    Yours, yours!

The meeting in Prague on 11 February was of the folksong commission on which Janáček sat. He described it to Zdenka in a letter written that day from Prague,[1] saying that he would return via Písek and would be back on Monday or Tuesday morning at the latest. Janáček and Kamila had last met in Prague for the première of *Káťa Kabanová* at the German Theatre, and now that Kamila had at last seen the opera she had inspired, Janáček inscribed the vocal score that had been sent to her for Christmas (539):

Janáček's inscription in Stösslová's copy of *Káťa Kabanová*, Písek, 12 February 1928

Mrs Kamila!
    And it was in the summer sun. The slope was warm, the flowers almost fainting bowed towards the earth.
    At that time the first thoughts about that unhappy Káťa Kabanová – her great love – went through my head.
    She calls to the flowers, she calls to the birds – the flowers to bow to her, the birds to sing to her the last song of love.

1 BmJA, A 5049.

'My friend', I said to Professor Knop.[1] 'I know a marvellous lady, miraculously she is in my mind all the time. My Káťa grows in her, in her, Mrs Kamila Neumannová! The work will be one of my most tender!'

And it happened. I have known no greater love than with her. I dedicate the work to her. Flowers, bow down to her; birds, never cease your song of eternal love!

Dr Leoš Janáček

Similar warm thoughts overflowed into Janáček's first letter on his return, and not all of it survived Mrs Stösslová's scrutiny. What is left, however, is wholly characteristic of Janáček's abrupt switches from the sublime to the mundane:

584   Brno, 14 February 1928

My dear Kamila

Well I've read the letter – that Friday one. It was very much a Friday letter. But that doesn't matter. I know that you're a child who wants to be happy. Who'd like to be pampered the whole time, who in that terrible isolation sometimes strikes herself and doesn't know where to turn. How I'd like to be near you all the time. And now, Kamila, let's be enough for each other. You know, you're not just you, but I'm here too, I, who need you. I'm also so much a child by nature, a child sustained only by the image of you, good soul. I give myself up to you entirely! The two of us together want to be such so that others will say of us they weren't united in vain. So that they honour us, respect us. We want to belong to each other, but only to each other.

< one page missing >

it will remain our undisturbed happiness.

I'll probably write to Belgrade that I'd leave the trip to them until the early spring.[2] Now's the worst time. One doesn't know what to put on. You had a rest today. On the journey I enjoyed the smoked meat from you. I travelled well, almost alone right up to Brno.

Now sleep well! I remember your soft plumpness! It's no wonder your skin itches. Have your back massaged with alcohol; so that the

1 It has been suggested that 'Professor Knop' could be Alois Kodl. If so, it would be the only occasion that Janáček got his name wrong. Furthermore, Janáček's words here refer to the period of the composition of *Káťa Kabanová*, several years before he met Kodl.
2 The première of *Jenůfa* in Belgrade was given on 24 February 1928. Janáček did not go later either.

blood circulates. Scratching it with your nails isn't allowed, it's dangerous.

So sleep sweetly.

Yours for ever

L.

[...] < at least one page missing >

585 Brno, 15 February 1928, at night

My dear Kamila

So you see that I'm writing now on large-size paper and there'll be lots so you'll have something to read and to laugh at, and so that your smile will please everyone. Little flower, the prettiest I could choose, 'a spring flower, for a light, lilac-coloured spring robe'. She [the shop assistant?] kept on giving me something grey; there weren't any violets yet. So at least you have buds about to flower. It seemed a bit small to me; there weren't any bigger ones. It's already in the post. [...]

All the time I have in my mind's eye the way you liked to lie wrapped up in that shawl, buried in the eiderdown. One could hardly find you in that soft valley. But I wouldn't have to look long; I'd fish you out at once and find the little waves of the Otava, the red corals of your lips, and in them a little tongue as active as a little lizard. And I wouldn't let go!

I'm in some sort of good mood now. I won't go to Belgrade; it's a foul time of year. I could easily catch cold. The concert in Prague on 2 March is already announced.[1] I'm waiting to hear when the rehearsals will be.

I don't know what to wear. A fur coat already feels heavy on one but on the other hand it's too soon for the light-coloured raglan.

You know, I'm so glad that there's now no turning back. I'm so sure of you, that you're mine, and I'm as overjoyed as when the sun stands high over the field and the farmer knows that his crop will be good and looks forward to it. He is perhaps as pleased with the warm sun as I am with my own little sun – Kamila. But I have an even greater joy! I can fondle my little sun. I can stroke it. Always when it's close it nearly sets [me] on fire. And whilst this happens one feels strong, powerful. And one need only stroke that sun. The sun must also be glad that it shines; that it makes somebody's life pleasant,

1 See Glossary: 'Capriccio'.

[203]

even the sun must know that. I know that it never wants to cause that person grief.

That dear little sun – Kamila [–] must always remember that it shines not to cause pain [but to give joy]. No, it knows that, it doesn't want pain. Well, I left Písek as if I had bound that dear, beloved, plump little lamb in a silk kerchief, not with rope, just with soft little bows. And I whispered to it: 'You're mine!' And will it be pleased at this? Sleep well my dear child. Thinking always of you

Yours for ever

L.

586   Brno, 16 February 1928

My dear Kamila

Your letter pleased me very much. I'm glad that you're [']blooming like a rose now[']. And those 'little madams' know that women often bloom like that when there's another life in bud. And they think to themselves – that's certainly the case now – and they laugh foolishly. What an idea! They judge after themselves; with them it would be – on meeting.[1]

But what's true is that you appear [big enough] now for two; but you're pretty at the same time, and that's the main thing.

And not speaking with anyone? For what reason? Of course now you're Mrs Doctor[2] and Mrs Doctor doesn't get into conversation with everyone, especially when you're the Doctor's wife – the wife of that artist!

[...]

Those few hours were so beautiful! You know, you have so much about you that it's impossible to satiate oneself with it. It's still sweet in my memory. Everything about you is soft, round; even the words which I hear from you seem as if they're rounded; they would never cause harm!

I'm happy and wish only to give you lots of joy.

I'm happy when I'm with you, near you, and that happiness will remain with me even when I'm very far away from you. You alone are all my joy. I don't look for any other – and in my work you elevate and strengthen me!

Today I got a letter from Vienna from an unknown lady,

1 i.e. other women would have let themselves get pregnant at the first opportunity.
2 At the time Czech wives were often referred to in terms of their husband's occupation or title. Once again Janáček imagines that Stösslová is married to him.

seventy-six years old, a letter in which she describes the effect that my work, the Sinfonietta, had on her. That letter's worth reading.[1]

Have you got the little flower on the light-lilac cloak yet? When I see something better I'll send it. Tell me whether it suited you.

I'm pleased that you don't cough much now, that you're looking fine – and that you love me.

Yours, for ever your
L.

587 Brno, 17 February 1928, at night

My dear Kamila

How everything has now piled up on me! I've already received an invitation from the National Theatre in Prague.

Rehearsals [for *The Makropulos Affair*] are

23–4 February

27–8 February.

The première will be on 1 March.

I'd come to you on 25 *February*.

I'd take you to Prague for the 28th and for the dress rehearsal. That would be nice. I'll have tickets sent for 1 March to your sister,[2] as promised. You must still write her address for me. Zdenka is coming for 1 March. I won't turn up at the première. Is it alright like that?

I'm leaving for Prague as early as Wednesday morning, 22 February.

On 29 February I have things to negotiate with the ministers[3] and will have a rehearsal with that one-armed man.[4]

So is the little flower growing even in Písek? They haven't yet got spring decorations. I'll show them this label.

Oh, I'll bind you hand and foot! And you won't untie yourself. And I'll close your little lips so they won't bamboozle people. I'd even put shells on your eyes so that sparks from them won't set fire to things. And I'd put all of you into cotton wool so no-one could harm you.

Today I've been reading about a great French writer. I'll tell you about him.[5] He's called Zola.

---

1 The letter does not survive.

2 Helena Hřebíková, see Glossary.

3 On 29 February 1928 Janáček negotiated with Dr Kamil Krofta and Minister Dr Milan Hodža to secure financial support for a folksong edition and research (see Janáček 1955, 538–41). The outcome was announced in Janáček's letter to Stösslová of 29 February 1928 (597).

4 Otakar Hollmann; see Glossary: 'Capriccio'.

5 He did so in the next letter.

I'm happy – although one shouldn't say that, and only on the quiet to cheer oneself up. Strange that on my last visit it was as if I'd caught the most beautiful little bird in a cage, so it seemed to me. And I'll take care that it won't fly away from me. Only when it's nicely domesticated will I then open the door for it. You dear little bird of mine!

So you'll be having guests, again you'll be rushed off your feet, you'll get a chill!

And laugh, my dear Kamila must only laugh! It's healthy.

Changeable weather. I'll take my fur coat to Prague and also my overcoat in reserve. I'd so like to see you in that light-lilac cloak. I'd just like to see you. And I'd like it to be warm enough already for us to go to the places where the earth trembled with joy. I'm now putting the finishing touches on those 'Love Letters' so that everybody will understand them; here they kissed; there they longed for one another; here – here they gave change[1] to one another, here – here they said they belonged to each other for ever! Perhaps people will guess this.

Keep well my beloved Kamila.

Yours for ever

L.

They want to give *The Diary of One who Disappeared* at the theatre in Plzeň. We'll be there.[2]

588 Brno, 18 February 1928, at night

My dear Kamila!

First of all, if a letter from you won't go off until Monday morning [20 February], send it to Prague (Smíchov, hotel–pension Karel IV.)

It wouldn't get here before my departure: I leave Brno on Wednesday morning. You've got cooking today, preparations; guests tomorrow – and I've got dull days today and also tomorrow and the next day without any signs of life from you.

I don't believe it; perhaps you'll find a little time and perhaps I'll receive something from you on Monday. Really today I'm like a dry stick lying across the path. It's not even worth someone's picking up.

Today I was successful with that movement 'When the earth

1 See Glossary: 'change'.
2 In his letter of 16 February 1928 (BmJA, D 622) the director of the Plzeň theatre Karel Veverka asked for permission to stage *The Diary of One who Disappeared* and for Janáček to orchestrate it. The performance, in the orchestration of Ota Zítek and Janáček's copyist Václav Sedláček, took place in Plzeň much later, on 26 June 1943.

trembled'.[1] It will be the best. Ah, that was an amazingly beautiful [time]! And it was true. Only the most beautiful melodies can find a place in it. I just hope I can still bring off the last movement. It will be like [my] fear about you. You know, such fear that I'd bind your feet like a pretty little lamb's so you wouldn't run away.

Today I'm so downcast after work – and no refreshment! Sadness in my soul.

And I don't know how they'll perform my piece [i.e. *The Makropulos Affair*] in Prague. They're not even putting a word in the papers in advance; even the *Prager Presse* is surprised by this.

On the other hand that one-armed man[2] is pushing my *Defiance*.

I'll go to the ministers[3] with whom I have things to negotiate perhaps on 29 February or 1 March.

And on Saturday [25 February] I'll hop over to you for a moment. And that famous writer Zola had a love; and two children with her. And it was all kept quiet. And she poor thing died, and when he died – his so-called real wife took over the children![4]

These are strange – and beautiful events. It moved me. *She* and *he* shouldn't have died. But the twig blossomed, became green! And when a fellow's like a dry, broken-off branch and just lies in the way, no-one even picks it up. Oh, in my forest I see that so often and start thinking. I prefer to remember my beautiful butterflies![5]

And what will you say about this letter? Will it also please you?

And I know that you're as sensitive as I am. I think that when I have some quiet pain now, that you'll feel it too. And it would be good if we could laugh. After all we hide so much with laughter. And don't burn this letter. It will be good when one day it's known that every life has its heads and tails.

And I have this rough tail-side.

Just make it smooth! – And what about coming to the dress rehearsal [of *The Makropulos Affair*] on 28 February? It will probably begin after ten o'clock. We'd listen to it in semi-darkness. The

1 The third movement of Janáček's String Quartet no.2.
2 See Glossary: 'Capriccio'.
3 See p.205, fn.3.
4 Svatava Přibáňová (Janáček 1990, p.304, fn.) traced the source of this information to a news item in the periodical *Zvon* (edited by F.S. Procházka), published on 16 February 1928. The news item was based on the preface by Zola's daughter Denise Le Blond-Zola to a new edition of *Contes à Ninon*. This states that from 1888 Zola, already fifty at the time, had an affair with the twenty-year-old Jeanne Rozerot, who bore him two children, Jacques and Denise. The relationship was hidden from Zola's legal wife, who nevertheless adopted the two children after the death of Rozerot's husband.
5 See 465 and 527.

première gives me no joy. No matter, no-one will see it in me! That's why I feel so sad and almost aching. You my dear soul.

Yours for ever

L.

589   Brno, 19 February 1928

My dear Kamila

It flashed through my mind how you said that you're not [made] of plaster! I laughed at that. You, being plaster! You're [made] of the fire which blazes up, you're as if [made of] india-rubber, you could surely put your feet behind your neck; already you sit like a Turkish woman. You're as if [made] of pure butter, touch you and a little valley remains. You – you're a witch.

So today you've put a difficult day behind you. You must have been cooking as if for a wedding.

Today I recounted that incident with my niece.[1] She [Zdenka] began to speak about it herself – and it was discussed in peace and in quietness, and reprovingly. She knows that I've finished my

'Love Letters';

she knows that it's now impossible any other way. That last movement doesn't sound fearful about my nice little weasel but [sounds] with a great longing – and as if it were fulfilled. I'm curious what effect it will have.

On Wednesday morning [22 February] I leave for Prague, already in the evening I have a rehearsal for *Defiance*. And on Thursday it all begins;[2] how they'll scrape and distort it, and I'll just laugh.

In the magazine *Die Bühne*[3] there's said to be much talk about me and pictures from the production at the German Theatre in Prague which put on *Káťa Kabanová*.

I said [to Zdenka] that you had to be in Prague for it, since you have a close relationship to Káťa. She acknowledged it!

On Saturday [25 February] then, I'll fly off to Písek – for three or four words.

Perhaps the violets will already be blooming by then. Now that I'm finished with those

'Love Letters'

1 See p.191, fn.
2 i.e. rehearsals for *The Makropulos Affair* that Janáček was invited to attend at the Prague National Theatre (see 587).
3 On 15 February 1928 the Viennese magazine for 'theatre, literature, film, fashion, art, society and sport' *Die Bühne* published an enthusiastic 850-word review by W.M. Essers of the German Theatre production accompanied by a single photograph of the 'finale'.

I have an empty head. I'm like a completely ordinary man in the street – except for you. It's always bubbling in your little head and [sometimes] it boils over.

My head's strange – now nothing in the brain – and then all at once a flood. But that flood always takes you with it. I'm glad. But I remember your witty idea to go and get change.[1] This time I'll take only large denominations and I'll always be needing change – but I know that often you'll not be able to give it. But we'll never be short of ideas.

The weather's mad. One has to have everything for winter and for spring. I think that it will be spring in Písek – so that the violets will greet me. Sleep well, dear soul. It's 10 o'clock, you'll probably be already tucked up. You looked like a little devil in those white sheets. But the wine was already gone! Not good for weak nerves!

Keep well.

Yours for ever

L.

590   Brno, 20 February 1928

My dear Kamila

My letter today won't be long; after some sort of concert[2] they dragged me out to a meeting and it's now 12 at night as I take up my pen.

Today the whole day without work, after work really; and here I'm always like a string on a violin which hasn't been drawn tight. Around me people that I don't care about; everyone now wants to be terribly exalted – and they're not able to be. What's it got to do with me!

At home it began to freeze again today – and I picked up some violets and sent you a bunch. It's worn with stalks on top, the violets hanging down. How will you like them? I told the seller never again to give me something that can be bought in Písek.

What a look she gave me! But until it's a warm spring don't wear the spring cloak just because of the flowers! I'll still travel in a fur coat. [...] I pine everywhere. Everywhere someone's missing for me. I walk round the room – but where are my thoughts!

What did you do on Sunday?

---

1 See Glossary: 'change'.
2 Janáček attended the third Members' Concert of the Club of Moravian Composers (see Janáček 1990, fn.).

It's Monday and tomorrow Tuesday I'll already be buying a ticket so I can leave. I feel restless at home. You know there's not that warmth here, that heaven. There's no-one here I can caress! And I so need affection!

Now I know how it could be – and I don't have it at home!

That's why I get so lonely.

And do you think I'm lured to Prague by these things of mine?

Not a bit of it! When you're not around, it's all one to me. I don't care about them.

It's as if it weren't mine when it's yours at the same time.

Oh, do dispel my sadness! Will I get a letter from you tomorrow?

I walk about like a lost sheep; it bleats and bleats, and stands around. Not like an eagle which looks round, soars and finds the way! In short, a sheep. I'm not myself, I'm not completely yours! Oh one day I'll look up and find the way! How I'd so like to write cheerfully, but I can't now. You know I can't after tiring work. I've called the piece 'Intimate Letters'.[1]

I won't deliver my feelings to the tender mercies of fools.

You're sleeping now! Keep well my dear Kamila.

Yours for ever

L.

591 Prague, 22 February 1928, afternoon

Dear Kamila!

What's happened that you haven't written? I'm very anxious; write back at once!

How can you bear not to write since last Thursday [16 February]!

Yours for ever

Leoš

592 Prague, 23 February 1928

My dear Kamila

The fact that you don't write – there must be something serious in it.

I can't explain it any other way – only by illness; and you would have let me know, wouldn't you? You can surely imagine, can't you, what anxiety you're driving me to! No, I can't explain your silence in any way. I'd send you a telegram this evening – but I don't want to

---

1 See Glossary: 'String Quartet no. 2'.

spoil your night. Tomorrow morning I'll certainly send a telegram, and if an answer doesn't come I'll be with you on Saturday morning. No, you surely cannot and could not torment me like this with an easy mind.

I'm only half here – and half with you. Although work occupied me from 10 till 6. What can you be thinking of, what are you up to! Surely you can only be seriously ill! Strange, during the night I myself got the same sort of earache as you. In the morning Dr Výmola discovered inflammation in the left ear. But that won't prevent my coming to you. What on earth can you be doing not writing!

Yours for ever
Leoš

Janáček arrived in Prague for the first stage rehearsals of *The Makropulos Affair* on 23–4 February and over the weekend visited Písek as announced (587–9), arriving late on the evening of the 24th. He left early on Monday morning in time for further rehearsals. The most serious incident that occurred during his stay in Písek was his proposal to burn the album (see Glossary). Stösslová prevented him from doing so, evidently to his gratification:

593   Prague, 26 [*recte* 27][1] February 1928

My dear Kamila

So I got to Prague with thoughts only of you.

In my memory those serious, beautiful words 'You would destroy me!' And your tears then, and my pity that I could have caused you pain, although the picture of a burning album went through my mind only as if in a flash. I know that it would have been inhuman to destroy that witness of our beautiful days. Never, never more will it occur to me. I would never do it. Now, only now, do I know for sure how dear to you are those lines which I < part of letter torn off > with joy <   >. You yourself have understood by now why in hot-headedness, blind pain I could have wanted to do so. [...]

You're like a mirror with me; no-one must cloud it even with a breath. I know that I draw closer and closer to you. I know that it's unthinkable: me without you. The more you're in my thoughts, the deeper your soul seems. I respect you, I love you, you're like a fierce torrent which falls from the mountains and in which everyone likes to

1 It is clear from 594 that Janáček spent some part of Sunday 26 February in Písek and from 600 that he left on Monday morning, presumably very early. According to the postmark this letter was posted in time for the 8 p.m. post.

see their reflection. You're so pure even in your hot-temperedness. I don't want to and cannot harm you.

< part of letter torn off > [...]

I came back for lunch after the rehearsal only at 3.30. No letter had come for me by then. It seems to me that the post has forgotten where letters should be sent.

Keep well, spare yourself and love me!

Yours for ever

Leoš

594   Prague, 27 February 1928

Dear Kamila

This evening I'm sitting at home alone. I remember everything that Saturday and Sunday, 24–5 [*recte* 25–6] February, brought us. That beautiful walk beside the five fish ponds! One day we'll go there alone. I feel more and more certain all the time that things are moving towards a serious decision for us. An image stands before my eyes that you'll leave what has bound you till now and I'll break what binds me. I've got such a strange premonition that it must come to this. As if some sort of flood were rising which would sweep us both away. I've got a premonition, Kamila, that the little games, however nice, will have to make way for a serious decision. You see, that incident on Sunday, your tears, your fear and the memories in the album – and altogether as if something hung in the air: we won't keep up that secret world of ours, we'll have to acknowledge 'we want one another'! Our premonitions seldom deceive me or even you. Tell me, how long can it go on like this? In this isolation of mine that thought bores into my mind.

No post has reached me; not even that first letter of yours! Well, no matter.

And I'd so like everything to be acknowledged, to be untied in gentleness; without anger and hate.

These are my thoughts before the première! I hear my work as if from a distance. In spirit I'm already further on. Write to me also frankly on Sunday [4 March]. Give yourself time for it, a calm head, deliberation – and draw on love for every word.

Yours for ever

L.

My dear Kamila

So the main, final rehearsal is over. I think that it will turn out well. Mrs Kejřová,[1] who is taking that 300-year-old woman, has movements like you. You know that time when you told me about your childhood adventures, those 'four fingers' — that lady seems just like you in her gait and her whole appearance. Well, you're now my dear woman, my dear wife, you won't be an actress any more. You'll be only her — that dear wife of mine. But what a waste of your out-of-the-way life. And, on the other hand, no harm. Where would you have landed up in the world! And fate has turned in such a way that it's brought us together.

It just annoys me now that up to this moment I've not had a single letter from the Brno post office! Yesterday I wrote express to the Brno post office and to this moment, it's 4 o'clock in the afternoon, not a line! And surely it's out of the question for me not to have got a single letter for a whole week, when that first letter of yours must have been in Brno as early as Wednesday!

You see, you could have been here at least today! Already, my little soul, you must be more Janáčková than Stösslová. Altogether now only Janáčková!

No, a premonition keeps on whispering to me that times of decision are coming.

We both must bring them about. What do you get out of that life of yours, such as it is! And I, from those few nice moments when I'm with you, and those weeks torn apart when I'm far from you!

[...] I'll write to you again tomorrow. But no more on Thursday, Friday, Saturday [1–3 March]. On Sunday again and on Monday I'll wait for your letters.

Yours for ever
Leoš

596 Prague, 28 February 1928, evening

My dear Kamila

You're no longer for me anything other than Kamila née Najmanová [Neumannová]. See, already I'm sitting a second evening in Prague – at home, in a hotel! I still have a supper from Písek, and an orange to go with it. And I write to you and am content. It went

1 Naďa Kejřová (1899–1983) sang the title role of Elina Makropulos/Emilia Marty.

excellently in the theatre. I didn't insist on your being at the rehearsals. The impression isn't pure; costumes and stage sets are missing, mistakes are made, things are repeated.

It would be too much for you to imagine what's missing and to disregard what still has to be corrected and what stands out as bad. I'd like us to be *together alone* once in the theatre when they perform it. And altogether often and often *together alone*. I feel too strongly that in that atmosphere you wouldn't feel free. I don't want to drag you into it. In our *heaven* we would fulfil our longings and our wishes. And I would come out from that heaven into the world only when life and social standing urgently required it.

I in Prague – and sitting at home! And I don't need anything else. Thinking of you, I'm quite content in the company [of your thoughts]. And my Kamila must also live in it now that she's the wife, the commander, the adored woman, the sun and the stars, the first wish and the last, the only desire – of mine!

Now I bury myself in the white sheets with these thoughts. I know that often in the night, and as soon as I wake up in the morning, you'll again jump up before me: blooming, with a nice smile; at the hot oven, with lots of mugs on it. You'll carefully break the eggs, pour the coffee – and I'll look at you as if I were a cook's apprentice. Oh no! Panting for your first kiss – which isn't dry. It will certainly be like this tomorrow. – Today they filmed me going out of the theatre![1] Just think when it will be shown in Písek in the cinema! So tomorrow yet another letter.

Yours for ever
Leoš

597   Prague, 29 February 1928

My dear Kamila

Today I eventually got all the post of the last fortnight! Including your first letter. It's so nice! Zdenka writes that she's been taken ill and is unlikely to come to Prague. I'll send her a telegram saying that she should come if it's not too bad.

If she doesn't come I'll probably go home via Písek. I'd send you a telegram saying when.

---

1 There is only one known short footage of Janáček captured on moving film (see p.69, fn.2); the film of his coming from the theatre has not survived.

They photographed[1] me today about ten times. I was always thinking of you. It will be seen in my eyes! And in the small hours! Your
beautiful breasts, and I kissed you at your heart! It was a strange dream!

And I've got on excellently in the Ministry. They've given
Kč 56,000 straight off for printing the songs[2] and Kč 50,000 for
uninterrupted printing every year.

The house with its extension will cost Kč 22,500. I'll build it. I still
want to show it to you.

What a lot of running around I had today! So in brief only [a little
done] – but well.

You are my gold.

Your silver

599 [postmarked Prague, 2 March 1928]

Tremendous success [of *The Makropulos Affair*]! Even the people
from Luhačovice were here.

Greetings

Drph L.J.

600 Brno, 3 March 1928

My dear Kamila

It seems to me as though months have passed from that moment
when I was with you!

So it was a week ago on Monday we left Písek; I still wrote to you
daily then; then only a card, and this evening I'm sitting down in
order to write so much to you that you might get a headache.

So listen. When I got here on Monday [27 February], I splashed
myself with a little water and [went] straight to the rehearsal in the
theatre. I was needed there.

On Tuesday, the second and last rehearsal.

On Wednesday with those ministers. I've written to you already
how well it turned out for me there.

They filmed me outside the theatre, they photographed me about
ten times at Langhans's. Apparently Mrs Horvátová would be coming to the photographer to see me! 'Is that so!' Apparently she'll be
celebrating her twenty-fifth anniversary in the theatre in Prague. 'Is

1 Janáček was photographed by the distinguished Prague photographer J. F. Langhans for
a collection of photographs of members of the Czech Academy of Arts and Sciences; see
also 607.
2 *Moravian Love Songs*, see p.205, fn.3, 520 and 526–8.

[215]

that so?' Apparently a display of her theatre portraits will be put on show. 'Is that so?' Indeed for her work as a singer she deserves that the theatre remember this [anniversary]. But it didn't remember; the display went up, it had to be taken down. She'd thought up this celebration herself!

Zdenka recovered and came to the première. As I've already written to you.[1]

And there was the première. I had two boxes, no guests in them! So I invited the Kretschmers; they came and brought me a nice little picture as a present. The première began; success mounted to unprecedented storms.

Someone knocked on the box; I went out and was greeted by the couple from 'our' vegetarian restaurant[2] in Luhačovice! I was very pleased that they hadn't forgotten! They asked after you. I lied a little, that you were poorly, that this year, soon, we'll come to Luhačovice! And I got a present from a woman shopkeeper in Luhačovice – a pretty inkwell! Just imagine! Well, I was immediately with you in my thoughts and not in the theatre!

The performance finished and about thirty of us went to Šroubek.[3] I imagined you all the time, I looked for you there! Home late at night. On Friday 2 March a rehearsal again and a concert[4] in the evening. It went well. The Kretschmers invited people to supper at their house. By now I felt a kind of stupefaction. I just wanted to get home. Early morning, got up, to the station, and now I'm sitting here and writing. And here comes the most interesting bit. Read it well.

On Friday morning they called me to the phone. Your husband! He had a present for me, he said. We agreed to meet at 3 o'clock in the afternoon at the café. He didn't know that Zdenka was also in Prague. He came; he showed me *Die Bühne*,[5] and gave me – a

1 He had not written this (in any surviving letter). In a second letter from Prague of 29 February 1928 (*598) Janáček had suggested that Kamila might like to come instead of Zdenka and he would send her a telegram accordingly; if no telegram came, then he would not be 'alone'.
2 See Glossary: 'dairy'.
3 A well-known restaurant in Prague's Wenceslas Square, later the Café Europa.
4 The concert, organized by the Organization of Czechoslovak War-invalid Officers, was the occasion of the first performance of Janáček's Capriccio (see Glossary). Otakar Hollmann was accompanied by members of the Czech Philharmonic; at the concert he also played solo works by Bach–Brahms, Schulhoff, Jaroslav Tomášek, Reger, Skryabin and Chopin–Godowsky.
5 See p.208, fn.3.

magnificent tie-pin.[1] I pinned it on my tie at once – and he took my Kč 3 one [i.e. cheap] for the 'Janáček Museum' in Písek! Well, it's beautiful – and who to thank? You? Certainly you, and him for choosing it so well. Everyone likes it. Mrs Löwenbachová[2] couldn't keep her eyes off it. Well, it will be quid pro quo.

And we [the Janáčeks] went to the Brods. Mrs Brod told of her relationship with her husband, they had been on the point of separating. With these artists,[3] she said, it's a real tribulation, and impossible any other way!

We came home and had a frank exchange of facts.

Do I say *Ty* to you? Does your husband know about it? I tell her [Zdenka] the truth. You will give your life for me, I for you. But although we're so close to each other, even so we're also honourable! That wasn't the case with Br[od]! My relationship to you will remain for ever. It's impossible to tear it apart. I related this calmly, it was listened to calmly.

[She reported] that you were said to be in Brno! I said that must be a lie. 'That you'll be going to Luhačovice!' Yes. To Luhačovice and then to have a look at Hukvaldy. 'When?' In July. I'd go for a while to the Tatras with you (i.e. with Zdenka) in August. So everything was said. The words of Mrs Brod were appropriate, sensible.

Get ready, then. At the end of June I'll go to Luhačovice; you'll arrive: according to the doctors' advice both of us need this spa. Both of us need cheerfulness, good will, and it will do both of us good because we like going there. So make arrangements accordingly. I'll go tomorrow to order a room.[4] I'll be in Prague again probably in a fortnight. So don't go to Vienna until afterwards. It will be warmer then. In Prague the wind was like ice.

I'm happy that there are no secrets in my life. You're said to be 'a woman in bloom'!

So it's said here.

I was happy when I was able to speak openly. I said 'You, Kamila,

1 This had been waiting for Janáček since Christmas, but had superstitiously not been presented (see p.172, fn.3). Though Janáček said he was not superstitious (*541: 20 December 1927), he gave something in return as a way of preventing his friendship with Stösslová from being 'punctured'.
2 Wife of Jan Löwenbach, a copyright lawyer with Hudební matice, to whom Janáček often turned for advice.
3 A reference to Max Brod's relationship with an actress; Janáček described it in more detail on 5 March 1928 (602).
4 Since the Augustiniánský dům belonged to the Augustinian Monastery in Old Brno, Janáček was able to order a room directly through the monastery (see Štědroň 1939, 22; see also 607).

suffer for me, but I also know that you too, Zdenka, are suffering'. But I can't live without you, Kamila, and I told Zdenka that I won't until my death. We are bound together now and will remain so. Is it all alright like that, Kamilka? I'm looking forward to Luhačovice now and also to Hukvaldy. I can be cheerful now. And we'll be cheerful together! And happy, terribly happy. And I'm looking forward now to when I go for your letter on Monday. Keep well my soul! Now I need a rest. Of course I'd rather have 'repaired' myself with you. Well, it can't be any other way now!

Yours for ever

L.

601 Brno, 4 March 1928

My dear Kamila

So now we can be cheerful. Now we can make plans! Three solid weeks in Luhačovice; then to Hukvaldy. In Luhačovice to cure weaknesses: with water, merriment, Russian eggs, and fun and games.

One day take a trip as far as Velehrad. 'They've got lost! They're not here today anywhere! Well, what's up? Where are they? They've disappeared! Well, goodness!' Sharp tongues will say: 'But we know now why they went off!' 'As if we couldn't guess!' And we'll laugh. Everyone will gaze at you to see if you're already broader than you're tall! 'But that's strange! Unbelievable!' 'But it seems to me that she's not walking so firmly any more!' 'Well, we'll see them soon!' There'll be talk, won't there? So we must be there to confuse their conjectures even more.

Well, then to Hukvaldy, to take a look at the residence.

We'll drive up in the coach[1] to the little cottage. Kamila will get out, look round. 'Oh my!', she'll exclaim. 'So this is the cottage at last? So this is what it looks like?' And will you feel at home there in a short while? The cellars will be opened – and still empty! Pantry – empty, chickens in the courtyard, vegetables in the garden. Well, one day Mrs Kamila will make me a real wife in my own home! But it won't be so bad. The cellars will get filled, the chickens will get roasted – yes, and to go with them the kisses[2] we've gathered will taste best. We'll go for them together, we'll remain a long time there where they grow the most plentifully.

1 Transport from the nearest station was horse-drawn (see Glossary: 'Hukvaldy').
2 A charming culinary pun: Janáček writes *hubičky* [kisses], which could also be a dialect form of *houbičky* [mushrooms].

That's how it will be.

And the tie-pin has given me much pleasure; I like wearing it. I now have you – a tie – around my neck, and a tie-pin – at my heart.

What's still to come? Your letter tomorrow. I'm so hungry for your words already. There'll be lots of them! Above all I'll get ticked off! For that album! It's forgotten now. And then there'll be an indecipherable little picture. And then – what have you been doing the whole time? Today's Sunday, it's fine again, just like a week ago. The conversation with Mrs Brod had a good effect. Dr Brod's going to Palestine for the whole month of April. I'd rather go to heaven [i.e. to Písek]; and I'll probably go there soon. So don't go away from Písek for the next fourteen days. You'll have lots of time for [buying] clothes when it gets warm. I've carefully studied the plans for the rebuilding. He wanted to knock down my whole cottage! I'm waiting for an answer now. Otherwise I want for nothing other than to breathe your warm air; to feel your burning lips, to see your blooming appearance, which they talk about even here. I recovered again in a day. But I was already a martyr – who was on the verge of going to heaven.

Keep well.

Yours for ever

602 Brno, 5 March 1928

To you, dear, darling Kamila

The first lines on this paper, the like of which even a minister hasn't got.[1]

[...]

Zdenka's arrival[2] was a good thing. Mrs Brod told her her life story. She told her that she puts up with everything, that with artists there's no other way. They wanted to get divorced; but – here I know more about this – it didn't come about because of that actress's character. Now each of them – the Brods – live in a different room. She and Zdenka understood one another. I was pleased about it; Mrs Brod is clever, educated. It's better to listen to her than to those old hags with whom she's gone around up to now.

1 Janáček received note paper and envelopes headed 'Dr· PH. LEOŠ JANÁČEK, BRNO' as a present from the Stössels.
2 Zdenka went to Prague for the première there of *The Makropulos Affair*. The visit of Janáček and his wife to the Brods took place during the day (Friday 2 March); Janáček mentioned it in his letter of 3 March (600), which also describes the ensuing conversation between himself and Zdenka.

Brod and I didn't know that in the third room Zd. and Mrs Brod were getting on famously with one another.

Our relationship is different. It's certainly more elevated. I extol you only in your beauty. That I long for you is simply a natural extension of the fact that spiritually we've belonged to one another for many years now. [...]

And you haven't read the album for a whole week! No, that won't do. There's not a word in it that's untrue. Both of us would have pined for it. There would have been nothing else but to live through it all once again! And I wouldn't have done it, to burn, to tear, to torture my own heart and to destroy your love for those beautiful moments. Don't think that I could have done it! And do read the album again. I always like to read it. And I can imagine life with you; we're living it now already, really, aren't we – and I love you infinitely. I think that I'll surprise you again in the next fortnight. [...]

Yours for ever

L.

And I'll still reply to the nice sentences of the big letter. I'm happy, happiest of all with you where there's no glory, but instead the good soul of my Kamila!

Kamila Stösslová to Leoš Janáček, Písek, 5 March 1928

Dear Maestro

I got your long letter and I'm glad myself that everything ended so well for you. [...] Yesterday there was a big concert of the Foerster Choral Society from České Budějovice. It was very nice they were very pleased that I came I sat next to the Mayor and Professor Novák[1] spoke to me he wants some autographs from you. Everyone asked me whether I'd been in Prague and asked after you. I was surrounded on all sides it gave me great pleasure. Everyone greeted me and all those little speeches. Well it's all over and I'll go there frequently now. My husband's gone off now, he left everything at home the rail ticket and passport in his suit I get so angry that he never wants to get up [in time]. He'll be arriving from Vienna by express in Brno on Thursday [8 March] at 10 and needs a few lines from you for the political administration[2] you said that you knew someone so if you'd be so kind. I hope your wife will also look at

1 Perhaps Josef Novák, teacher at the local Gymnasium and chairman of the local choral society 'Hlahol' (see Mácha 1985, 20).
2 See p.223, fn.4.

everything correctly. So the tie-pin is nice and the paper too I hope. As for Luhačovice I can't say anything more definite today as I don't know how it will be with the children. It pained me how you write that your wife is suffering on my account perhaps you could devote a little love towards her too. Don't be so reserved you know well that I don't ask it of you. I make no claims on anything. But she's your wife and she has claims on everything. You know well how it is when a person suffers? Why can't you prevent it it's your character. What does your wife think when you say that we're bound together do you know what that means? This way you've given me no pleasure. It's your open character it doesn't matter to you even if you wound.

Keep well

Kamila

603 Brno, 6 March 1928

My dear Kamila

I'm returning again to your first letter. You're imprudent, you're impetuous, but you're good, you're better than I am. I love you from my whole soul, you should be loved, you deserve it, and you need it.

I don't care about glory, but I do care about your love. Have you told your husband that you love me? Zd... knows that I love you, and that I'll love you to the end of my life. If the two meet on Thursday [8 March] let them speak to each other about it. The plain truth is dearer to me than keeping it a secret.

Kamila, we'll speak openly when there's a serious reason for it; we'll declare it. There's no other way. I'll come and meet your husband on Thursday at 10 o'clock. It goes without saying that I'll help him all I can. To your last letter: I'm pleased to hear you're now welcomed everywhere. Just go everywhere where you know that I'd also go.

I know what it means that we're bound together. That is, that I can't be bound to any other until death. I'm like water – I know how only to make things wet; like fire – I know only how to burn. I don't know how to do two things at once. If I love you, I can't love anyone else. I can do good to someone but to burn with love on two fronts that I can't do. We're bound together; we have the same desire for each other, if only in thoughts. But according to some apostle it's already enough that we're bound together. And I said this is how we're bound: that I won't allow you to suffer, and you won't allow me to suffer.

We won't noise it abroad, but in certain circumstances and with certain people we cannot keep it a secret. And these people are those who are closest to us. Otherwise we wouldn't be able to go on living. We wouldn't be able to defend ourselves. It must be known: 'they belong to one another!' To what extent, let everyone think what they will. Then we'll be a mutual shield to one another; no-one may lay a finger on us. With us the doors are closed; they must knock politely before we'll say 'enter'. With the assurance that you're mine I've found such calm that I've never had in my life.

How your husband and Zd. sort it out – is all one to me.

And you my tasty morsel, you dear little Negress, you keep on writing 'my head aches, I've got a cold'! How to help you? Either the Glagolitic Mass will be in Prague on 8 April or you'll come even earlier with me for a consultation in Prague. And you'll take a treatment decently in Luhačovice. I'll tell the doctor what you're lacking. That lying about in the sun won't help much. [...]

604   Brno, 7 March 1928

My dear Kamila

So I enclose a photograph of Ondrúšek's picture.[1] Such sleepy eyes, so many frowns on the face, crooked lips. Fingers like a thief. That's a sleepy one! He must crawl into the old women's corner. He mustn't raise his eyes towards the fire which comes from Kamila. Where did Kamila put her eyes? Either she's blind, or doesn't see the ruins? As an everlasting memory of me put this among my innocent letters.

[...]

I praised you [to Zdenka] according to my inclination and according to the truth!

She went silent. She said I'm cold! My God, I was never anything else towards her. And I can't be anything other – than calm. And can do her no harm. After all it's possible to be content with this! Enough of that.

I still think of you at the concert![2] How they opened their eyes! Mrs Kamila now walks among us!

An excellent Frenchman [William Ritter] also announced that he's coming to see me at Hukvaldy. He's writing a book about me, [as are]

1 of Janáček (see Glossary: 'Ondrúšek, František'). Janáček is evidently describing the oil painting of himself which, unlike Ondrúšek's pastel portrait (see Plate 32), depicts the composer standing, left hand in pocket, right hand revealed with fingers gripping something. It is an imposing portrait, but the eyes do seem dreamy.
2 Janáček is referring to the 'big concert' of the Foerster Choral Society Stösslová described going to in her letter of 5 March 1928.

that Englishwoman Newmarch, and Dr Brod and Dr Arne Novák.[1] Well, if they like! But I will still steal a little time for us.

And they have begun building.[2] I don't want to be around during it. It will be necessary to get that junk – the writing-desk [–] from the corridor of Mr Kretschmer's mansion. Mr Kretschmer said that no-one wants it; so I hope he'll give it [to me] for Kč 50.

And then, Kamilka, I need a terribly big carpet; you can help look for it. You can't go barefoot now on anything other than a Persian carpet.

Now you have an enormously long letter from me. Well it's classy paper; the post office will know it in the dark. I remember you joyfully.

And the fact that we're bound together – didn't it give you pleasure? But it would give me great pleasure. I know that there'll be that relentless calm – until blood can't be distinguished from blood.

Yours for ever
L.

605   Brno, 8 March 1928

My dear Kamila

I don't know whether I've done everything the way you wanted when you announced that your husband was coming.

Since Monday [5 March] they've been painting at our house. Furniture moved around, like a warehouse even in my piano room. I said that breakfast should be prepared for your husband. So it happened. During the conversation I told him, completely calmly, what binds me to you. The conversation ended without greater excitement. Lunch couldn't be prepared at our house, therefore I wanted to take your husband to lunch in the Zemský dům.[3]

However your husband refused everything. So we went to the café. There I wrote a recommendation for him. I don't know how he got on; he sent me a message not to wait for him any longer. I didn't know that he's actually domiciled in Lwów.[4] And so you with him? And the

---

1 Of the four only Max Brod wrote a book about Janáček – he had already done so, in 1924. Arne Novák, dean of Brno's Philosophy Faculty, had made the oration about Janáček on the occasion of his receiving an honorary doctorate from Brno university (see p.63, fn.1). Rosa Newmarch was the moving force behind Janáček's trip to England in 1926 (see p.86). For Ritter, see Glossary.
2 A false alarm; the extension to Janáček's Hukvaldy cottage began only in early May 1928 (see 645).
3 See p.111, fn.1.
4 David Stössel's father, Marcus, had moved to Moravia from Lwów, then ruled by Austria. The family was technically regarded as being domiciled in Lwów (part of Poland 1918–39) and in danger of being repatriated.

children? Why didn't he tell me that he's keen to get Czech residence? I could surely have helped him more substantially in such matters!

At 1 o'clock he apparently left for Strážnice. And at home he forgot everything he needed for travelling! He didn't tell me that.

And dear Kamila, today, now in the evening, these longings go through my head once again.

I've now received the first sheets of those *Nursery Rhymes* from the printers. It will be nice; it's even got pictures.[1] Then I finished the fair copy of our *Intimate Letters*. I said to Zd.: 'if this work is recognized as exceptionally beautiful then you ought to be convinced of her influence on my soul, on my work!' Oh little soul, we'll flicker together in that cinema! We won't go there now in vain. I can't say which incidents I communicate in these 'Intimate Letters'.

Whether those, where the earth trembled –

whether when you slumped in that chair as if cut down

whether then, when you had our < two words inked out >

All this feeling as if it were piled up on itself –

as if it had lifted you and me from the earth, as if everything around was joyfully, longingly hovering; and in that feverish mood these *Intimate Letters* were born.

I'm so glad at how my pen was burning when it wrote it! How quickly, how pantingly it wrote! How it didn't want to stop!

So you've got something new for the album, something which can never be destroyed. I ask fate, or, if you like, God, for these moments of our life never to fade away in us. And I have tears in my eyes at these words. I love you so much; and how happy I am for that reason –

Today I'm writing to you again on ordinary paper. Not that I wouldn't want 'Dr L.J.' to be read daily on the envelope. That wouldn't worry me. But there again I've come to know what a thorn it is in some people's flesh 'that we two are bound together'! Oh, if it were only true! – Apparently you've still got a cold?[2] Will it affect your ear again?

Look after yourself!

Yours for ever

L.

---

1 The publication included line drawings, mostly by the Czech artist Josef Lada.
2 David Stössel presumably reported on Kamila's health.

My dear Kamilka

I came across the administrator of the Augustýnský dům. Well: I'm booking a room in Luhačovice at the beginning of July. Will that be alright? So hurry up with that too. And from the Good Lord we'll also book a little sun and good weather and we'll make a deal between us not to stir from one another, not to look at anything but each other, not to think about anything but each other, not to smile at anybody but each other. And as a joke I'd add, to walk beside each other, to eat beside each other and – – – can you guess the last?

Now that I've finished those *Intimate Letters* I've got a head as if swept clean by the wind. You could jump around in it alone now.

What do you think that the Hor[vátová] woman wanted with a registered letter?[1] She wrote nothing to me. During the whole of those ten–twelve years I didn't even brush against her in my thoughts.

They'll begin building as early as 1 April.[2] It will turn out nicely![3] Everything will be upside down there, sheer madness! Oh, no. There'll be joy there. I'm building it only for joy and for love. I'd wish for sadness never to reign there. During the day the sun will go round the whole house. Whenever anyone looks into the window, may that person always see a smile there; and I'd wish to have lots of your laughter, your contentment.

In the upper living-room I want to have those two children,[4] a writing-desk, a communal table, a comfortable bed, perhaps of brass; a wardrobe with mirrored doors; a marble washstand; *four chairs, each from a different part of the world and from a different period –* and the wish that Mrs Kamila would often sit and lie there contentedly.

In the last *Pestrý svět* [*týden*] – it's a picture magazine – I have a little musical article; to which they've added three pictures.[5] Those photographs at Langhans[6] didn't turn out well. I thought of you during the session; so the eye was dreamy, I was tired of myself; it's a wonder I'm not sleeping in those pictures. What different sparks you've got there in your eyes where we're together! So sleep well. It's

---

1 Gabriela Horvátová sent a registered letter, presumably to Zdenka, which was returned to her (see Janáček 1990, 318, fn.)
2 This was an optimistic estimate; by 30 April (643) he still had not heard whether the building had started, though it seemed to have begun soon thereafter (645).
3 This is intended ironically; the Czechs also celebrate April Fool's day.
4 See Glossary: 'children'.
5 Two photographs of Janáček were published in *Pestrý týden*, iii, no.10 (10 March 1928).
6 See p.215, fn.1.

as if I were making a warm and soft bed for myself with these evening lines.

Saturday, 10 March at night

And yesterday with those copyists of mine I worked hard for five hours and my head began to go round.[1]

It's because I don't have anything here that would occupy me in any other way apart from work. You're far away and I look in my work – for relaxation. If only there were that diversion – with your laughter, your ideas, your darting around me – as if in heaven, then I would be rested. So today's Sunday and I'll hardly drag myself about the house. Snow has fallen here as if in winter. I remember you earnestly. As for my head, which ached a little yesterday, I think it came from my left ear. Now in the evening it's already gone away.

What have you done today, Sunday? Here it snowed the whole day and there was one degree of frost! I didn't even step out of the house. It's slowly becoming more or less clear what will be happening each month. In March Prague – and a leap to my beloved Písek, which has a special heaven; in April a leap to Hukvaldy, when they will begin demolition with an axe; 8 April Prague – *my mass*. In May Berlin perhaps. May–June at home, work with the copyists. July Luhačovice and you in Hukvaldy; August also there; lots of visits. Perhaps the Tatra Mountains. September – Italy perhaps. And where's Kamila? I'd like to have her either in Prague on 8 April or in Berlin in May. We'll talk about it. Most of all I'd like to have you with me always. Let's be healthy and let's have fine weather – when we'll be together.

Today you're probably sitting by the fire? Does your ear ache? Must we even have the same pains! Well, since we have the same joys. We know what we would like – and we know at once what gives pain to the other. I wait to see what nice things you'll be writing to me. My Kamilka, I love you from my whole soul.

Yours for ever

L.

Brno, 11 March 1928 at night

608   Brno, 12 March 1928

My dear Kamilka

Thank you for writing on Saturday [10 March]; I had the letter on Monday. I've read it many times. Yes, now I can be cheerful. No-one

---

1 Copying of Janáček's autograph of *From the House of the Dead*, in which Janáček worked closely with his two copyists, had begun (see Tyrrell 1992, 335).

knows how empty it was in my mind before; just like an empty house with open windows. A cold draught whistled through it, it was lonely inside, one didn't want to linger for a moment in it, it drove one away. I was always looking for something, was discontented, irritable. And now? My Kamilka has sat down there; it rings with her laughter; it breathes with her warmth. My mind is suddenly full of it all.

[...]

I sent you *Pestrý týden*.[1] I'm sitting in that carriage like a pasha; they stuffed me [with food] in London so much that I was ill from it afterwards. Whereas at the seaside,[2] my Kamilka, I would so like to have sat with you. The hot sun on the warmed-up stones: you would have enjoyed lying down there; the white swish of the sea would have made you a bed. And for once I would have experienced being a happy man.

I'm cheerful now; but let no-one think that it's for this reason or that! The only reason is you, my black, velvet Kamilka. Your good heart, the impetuousness of your feeling, your appearance, which fascinates me, your whole naturalness – with all this you dazzle me, captivate me. That I have you, and fate will grant that I'll have you for ever, that thought is the reason for my contented cheerfulness. I'm glad that I live in you! You're mine. [...] And [other] people? Their eyes are out on stalks; I've nothing but success; vigour in my compositions. Where does that fellow get it from? A riddle. They burrow into it like moles in order to decipher it. I'd so love to cry out, to raise you up, display you: 'Look, my dear beloved riddle of life!'

Keep well.

Now you'll come with me when the night is dark. What wouldn't the night see even in the dark!

Yours for ever

L.

609   Brno, 13 March 1928, at night

My dear Kamila

Why didn't you write on Monday? I thought that Saturday's letter was just an extra and meanwhile – [.] I think that it was bad weather and you didn't even go out.

---

1 See p.225, fn.5; the photograph to which Janáček refers to shows him sitting in a railway carriage, on the way home from his trip to England in 1926 (see Plate 34).
2 The seaside photograph, taken by his companion on the English trip, Jan Mikota, shows Janáček on his way back at the Dutch port of Flushing, notebook in hand, listening to the waves (see Plate 35).

And how at once it made me sad! I go around as if looking for something which can't be found. Perhaps your letter will come tomorrow. It's easy to say, be cheerful! It's easier to lapse into sadness and harder to get out of it. Sometimes a good little word would be enough, but I won't hear it now, will I; that's why I prefer to run away into seclusion and complain to you that you ought to have written! Don't forget to write! Don't write much if there isn't anything special to write, but let me know about you even if it's just a few squiggles.

When I wrote those *Intimate Letters*, you were alive beside me. I lived through fond memories, at a faster rate, perhaps rather like a flower in a hothouse. I lived more vigorously, just as my blood demands. Now it's finished. I've grown calm, as if I've come into the cool. This doesn't suit my character: I can't bear lazy calm! And now I don't know what to take up. I'd take you up – but you're far away. You would ruffle my thoughts as if a brood of ducklings had descended with noise and splashing on to a fish pond. And now there's nothing of all that; that's why I'm so sad, almost bad-tempered. Now you know what you've done by not writing to me on Monday! Now I sit here all alone! [...] If at least I'd kept your last letter! *Now I will hang on to each one until the new one arrives.* I'm like on a boat without a rudder. To go to sleep – if I can fall asleep. I'm like a child, when it has to have a dummy. [...]

I want to write to Horv[átová]: 'that I commemorate her twenty-five years' work in the theatre because she created the role of the Kostelnička in an exemplary way'. I don't know whether I'll do it; whether the thought of her disgusting life doesn't exceed the thought of her purely as an artist!

I ought not to have written those [the above] five lines to you. I fear that she will make use of that letter publicly; and I don't want to be linked with her for ever.

I'd like to be with you now. To lose myself looking at you, to forget myself; this would be the longed-for rest. Why didn't you write! I'm so lonely now – and you know that you're my sun. You must never set when around me.

Keep well.

Yours for ever

L.

Kamila Stösslová to Leoš Janáček, 14 March 1928

Dear Maestro

[...] In town today two ladies came [up to me] [saying] that the violets[1] are very pretty and that in general I always have pretty flowers. I said that I have a good gardener whatever he sows always blooms nicely. They laughed and said they'd like to have a gardener like that too. But I won't say anything about him let them roll their eyes and keep on guessing. I really don't know what I'd have done during this bad weather if it weren't for your letters. I asked you not to go away anywhere why didn't you listen? I won't move away an inch I'll be obedient. I read your letters many times, they're nice and even if I didn't want to I'd have to think of you all the time. I'm so glad to be alone[2] that I can't even write to you. Every day I go to bed as early as 7 o'clock. And the quiet is just like that with you. Reading your letter today I thought so much of everything past of all I've lived through and I'm happy. You remind me of it when you write how your life was before and is now. And what about mine I've not known anything else I've not longed for anything else my life just went by without love and joy. But I always went along with the thought that that's the way it had to be. Now I think that God was testing you and me and when he saw that we've been good and that we deserve it he has granted us this joy in life. If you told anyone he wouldn't believe that I've perhaps waited for you that all my life I'd found no-one who would offer me his love. I steered clear of everything I didn't look for anything and you were the only one in all the years you've known me and that really is the truth. Someone would just smile and ask how it was possible, but yes it is possible you are much dearer to me than if you were young. I can assure you that my life is pleasant that I don't wish for any better. And for that only you are guilty. I thank you for it also. [...]

611 Brno, 15 March 1928

My dear, my very dearest Kamilka

Your letter today is lovable like none before it. May I keep this one? Keep it for a long time at least, and safely. It's your confession and no-one can see anything ill in it. We're together here just like when full light falls on a picture. Everything can be seen in it. All is clear, distinct. People would simply say let them take each other's

---

1 The bunch of artificial violets that Janáček sent her on 20 February (see 590).
2 David Stössel was presumably on his travels.

hands for ever! I think that everyone would wish us that. I'm over-joyed today. Anything particularly nice I always underline with a red pencil. And today's letter is completely red! So that gardener is competent! Never mind the gardener, but what a delightful garden! All by itself it wears many things that a gardener couldn't produce. It's his living flower which he wants to look after with love and devotion. So as to be always fresh, always there for pleasure. Always to sprout in the early spring, to be clothed with blossom, to boast the very sweetest fruit! That's you, Kamila, you're the fantastically beautiful garden! How glad I am that fate has made me its gardener. And you've related that comparison nicely, too. And the ladies laughed! And just think! Yesterday I went to the post office and I didn't want to walk on the pavement but on the snow-covered and frozen avenue. I slipped – and picked myself up quickly from the ground. I fell on my right hand and on my right side. It's lucky that I had a fur coat on. But today I'm feeling it; nothing bad happened. And then today I went to Professor Ninger,[1] to have a look at my left ear. It was like the sea hissing in it. Also nothing bad, it will go away. And on top of that twelve visitors came to see me! You would have had a jolly time! If you'd been with me, there wouldn't have been enough chairs. And that doctor and professor searched out a nice pretext – to chat with Mrs Kamila. Well, no bad thing. I know you're my representative, and I'd get rich even on autographs.[2]

You came into my life like a bright vision. You can be felt every-where, you're in harmony with everything, you conciliate, you stroke, you tame. Your letters come to me like a warm ray of spring. At once I smile, at once I see everything in a welcoming light. And when there's no letter, straightaway it's as if I'm in twilight. I grow sad. So, dear soul. We belong to one another. I think that some day I'll send you my manuscript of those *Intimate Letters*.[3] After they've played it to me, so that I know if it's worth something too in terms of music. You know, often the *feeling itself* is so powerful and strong that the notes hide under it, they run away. Great love – weak piece! And I'd like to have: great love – great piece! And with me love is great, constant – wide fields and the sun above at night just as in the day. Here that rich musical harvest could also come about. And don't compare yourself with me. For you're such a dear good soul that you

1 Professor František Ninger (1885–1966).
2 A reference to Professor Novák's request to Stösslová for Janáček's signature (see her letter of 5 March 1928).
3 In his will Janáček bequeathed the autograph to Stösslová.

can be compared only with other women. And I'd always choose you among thousands. I won't compare you with the chestnut-tree flower – it's a slightly famous composer.[1] You now stand beneath it; he's glad that you're in his shade and you're glad he's full of those flowers – full.

I don't value them;[2] I'm a plain fellow beside my brown Kamila, no adornments at all, that's my full happiness. So it will remain between us. Sleep well, as well as I sleep; and when I wake up I'll think of you at once. This is our joy – the only delight of our living.

I'll obey, I won't go – because they're not inviting me to Prague. If they send an invitation, I won't obey, I'll travel – to see my Kamila. I'll look after my health – and you do the same.

Yours for ever
L.

612   Brno, 17 March 1928, at night

My dear Kamila

[...] So an invitation lies before me [asking] whether I can be in Prague on 23 March at 10.30.[3]

Joyfully I answered yes.

And 24 March in Písek – if God grants; and on the station a red shawl will appear and shine, violets from a good gardener and all of it on that delightful Kamilka.

Let the sun shine and let it get warm at last now! So we can wander somewhere on Sunday [25 March]; yes and on Monday, strengthened, rejuvenated by black eyes – back to work. I now have two copyists so that I'll be finished with everything by the holidays.[4] [...]

What pleasure I had from the invitation to Prague! Never mind about Prague! I'll cope with that easily. But with Kamila, it's not that easy with her. She's like the wind, she slips through the keyhole. She's like fire; blazing on all fronts. You think you've got it now – but then

---

1 Evidently Janáček himself.
2 Janáček's 'flowers', i.e. his compositions.
3 In his excitement Janáček temporarily got the date and time wrong. The invitation (BmJA, A 1358) was to a gathering arranged by the Minister of Education and National Culture, Dr Milan Hodža, at 8.30 p.m. on 22 March 1928 in the Rohanský Palace in Prague. On the back of the invitation Janáček noted the names of other participants. They included some of the top names in Czech culture; among the composers were Suk, Foerster and Ostrčil. Janáček also noted that he got home at 1 a.m.
4 Uniquely in *From the House of the Dead* Janáček used his two regular copyists simultaneously for the primary copy of the opera. One copied Act 1 and half of Act 2, the other the remainder (Tyrrell 1992, 335).

it turns in another direction. Only once it turned [to me] of its own accord! Then in the doorway of the house, when we went the last time to the station and I begged < a few words inked out >. That was nice and dear. So what will you say to me! And again I think it will be your 'Speak!' And I'm glad that I can silently devour you with my eyes.

I enclose that Viennese letter for you.[1] Hang on to it. I wrote to Horv[átová] that, remembering her splendid Kostelnička, I wished her continued success on top of her twenty-five years![2] I enclose a draft. And you must be sleeping nicely now. I'd give you no peace meanwhile until you called out, Am I [made] of plaster?[3] That would be nice.

Yours for ever
L.

Of plaster, plaster! And I'm laughing!

613   Brno, 18 March 1928

My dear Kamila

I've sent you many [letters]; you'll have lots to read on Monday [19 March]. Today was a nice spring day here; I threw off my fur coat even though I was going to freeze. They're building fair grounds here;[4] you'll have to take a look at it on the way from Luhačovice to Hukvaldy. Otherwise a long Sunday, little work done. Useless life – that day. And you? With you things will get moving tomorrow when you learn that you'll have to get heaven[5] and yourself ready. On Friday [23 March] I leave Brno; write so that I'll receive a last letter from you on *Wednesday*. I'm waiting for important mail from all sides.

I'm looking forward to hearing your warm words; to talking avidly, as with no-one else. For the whole of the last fortnight I've really not gone out of the house, have spoken with no-one other than at work with the copyists, or at home 'what have we got for lunch?' Can this be enough to satisfy a man! If I didn't have this 'life of ours', its expectations [–] I don't even want to say fulfilment – it would be enough to choke me. It's such a relief for me when I'm on my own; I can at least imagine what I want.

1 See 586
2 See 609; Janáček's brief letter to Horvátová (16 March 1928) is reprinted in JA vi, 90.
3 See 589.
4 See Glossary: 'Exhibition of Contemporary Culture'.
5 See Glossary.

And I don't know what I'll want from you! Never anything in advance; only take what the good fate provides. And will it give abundantly?

Would that it would give this much, for lips to burn, an eye to sparkle; so I can go out 'for change'; so it would give all at once what it's given me so far [only] piecemeal.* Nothing would remain of the plaster. And Mrs Kamila would only burn.

I'm glad that the hissing in the ear is stopping; it tormented me. And it seems that with the winter even all sorts of chest pains and catarrh have gone away. I tell you, to be a man again who doesn't worry about his body and lets his soul fly wherever it most wants to; where she would most like to sit down, to look everywhere with curiosity, to stroke everywhere, kiss everywhere. And you promise that you'll tell me lots of things! I'll listen pantingly to all that comes, what I'd most like to hear and now would like to know. I'd like to shake off the many things which occupy me, so that I could listen just to you alone.

You know, my little soul, that I'm glad that I like my new opera, now that I've been 'cleaning' it after a year. That's a good sign. I'm curious how the Prague gentlemen will thank me for those Kč 56,000 + 50,000.[1] Those two things[2] are the cloud which you must shine through, so that I can see you, hear you, feel you alone. And you know how to. That's your power over me. This is your dominion; the kind rule of the little Negress. I'll obey her, I'm completely devoted to her. She's bewitched herself from all sides so she won't escape. Even I must tie her up, bind her strong hands – no, she, Kamila, also knows how to fold her hands submissively – really she could do so. But I love her so much, infinitely – as she is.

Sleep well.

Yours for ever

L.

*And it gave nothing! 24 March 1928.[3]

1 See 597.
2 Janáček's two major preoccupations: the completion of *From the House of the Dead* and the edition of *Moravian Love Songs*.
3 The date suggests that this addition was written during Janáček's next trip to Písek. If so, it would seem that Janáček reread his letters kept by Stösslová there.

Janáček's next communications were a letter (*614), postmarked Brno, 19 March 1928, of which only the envelope survives, and a postcard (*615: postmarked Brno, 22 March 1928) telling Stösslová not to wait for him on Friday as things were uncertain. Nevertheless he made his way to Písek on Friday 23 March, somewhat the worse for wear after his cultural party in Prague the night before. He seems to have had a wonderful time in Písek over the weekend and relived some of it in his next two letters to Stösslová:

616   Brno, 26 March 1928

Kamilka, my darling

At least a few words. I got home safely, but expensively! Instead of a second-class compartment I sat in a first-class one and fell asleep. The inspector came – so I don't know what they'll charge me for this 'fraud'!

Thank you for all the pleasures. For your storms of laughter on Sunday. As only you know how. As I sat down in the carriage, I wetted my cheeks a lot until the Písek towers vanished from my sight.

They weren't expecting me at home; my letter still hadn't arrived. But it was hot! I'd have liked to have thrown my fur coat out of the window. I'm now 'rejuvenated' – by you and the spring clothes.

But ... but! I forgot my long grey silk scarf at your place. It will be hanging in the lobby. Write to me to say if it's there. Tonight again I'll write lots to you. We'll see one another again soon, won't we!

Yours for ever

L.

617   Brno, 26 March 1928, at night

My dear Kamilka

You know, dear child, I came to you on Friday like a puffed-up bellows. Add that fur coat of mine and it's really true. The visitors who arrived on Saturday were wholly to my taste. We all conducted ourselves well. You know not only how to eat a lot but also how to lead a discussion well. On Sunday morning going shopping together; lettuce for four – and I ate it all up myself! Well I'll make up for it! Then that concert,[1] that worry of ours during it and again a good conclusion. And in the evening that laughter of yours! In the night we

---

1 On Sunday 25 March 1928 Janáček attended a concert in Písek in which the Prague Teachers' Choral Society performed Otakar Jeremiáš's choral cycle *Zborov* (1927), first heard in Prague on 3 March 1928. After the concert Janáček met Jeremiáš and Písek acquaintances such as Otakar Ševčík and Cyril Vymetal.

were even sweating from it. And on Saturday afternoon – you were even pale [from it]! It was all so nice.

Whereas today, Monday, it's hot! In Brno 25° Réaumur. I wouldn't have been able to walk round Prague. Today straight after my arrival, I wrote diligently with the copyist and sent you a few words about myself.

The train ran ahead quickly; your white scarf waved – until suddenly as if all dropped out of sight. And that's the picture which frequently repeats itself in life. You, in your hand a white waving scarf, as if a little dove were flying and fluttering – and suddenly all gone. And that touched me greatly. Just let nothing change! Let nothing drop out of sight! [...]

618 Brno, 27 March 1928, at night

My dear Kamila

I've got that reddened hand bandaged,[1] so I'm writing badly; it's the right one. I'd even write to you with the left, if it weren't possible otherwise. [...]

That 8 April is approaching.[2] I want to invite your sister[3] as well. What's that village called? And then you can get your outfits ready without delay. The weather here has suddenly changed.

Already I walked round the garden today. On 3 June they're laying the foundation stone for Brno University, of which I'm a doctor.[4] They asked me for a piece for the occasion; so I scrawled it today.[5] [...] Will you take the red dress to Prague again? The journey would soon be over; I'll come for you on Saturday evening [7 April] and we'd leave Písek on Sunday morning. On the homeward journey we'd have a look at Karlštejn. So you wouldn't do the journey in one go. And, dear soul, we'll rather have that writing-desk from the Kretschmers fixed in Prague; one has to know how to do it, and I don't know whether the Hukvaldy joiner could cope with it. So you, my dear ruler, take care of it. Were you at that operetta? A good man is never harmed and an evil man is repulsed by the good. Every person is

---

1 For Janáček's accident see 611.
2 The Prague première of the Glagolitic Mass.
3 Helena Hřebíková (see Glossary), then living in Nezvěstice.
4 See 281 and 285.
5 *Chorus for Laying the Foundation Stone of the Masaryk University in Brno* for male voices to words by Antonín Trýb. A sheet with Trýb's typescript text, covered with Janáček's sketches, has an added date (24 March 1928) though not in Janáček's hand; Janáček dated his autograph score 2 April 1928. The date of the ceremony was postponed to 9 June (see Janáček's account of the event in 681).

complete when he's born. Education simply sews a cloak for him.

You, my little soul, did they make you what you are at school? Certainly not, and similarly no-one helped me make sense of a tangle of notes. Together we act through inner compulsion, did anyone teach us that? No. It must be that I'd never leave you, and I believe steadfastly that you stand by me and won't go away. No-one taught us all that; therefore I believe in myself, I believe that everything that comes, comes like a ball of wool unravelling itself. Let's have peace of soul and joy. – I'd have pills and syrup for your cough, but I'll look after you in Luhačovice. Have you got an answer from there yet?

I remember how your white scarf waved farewell; and tomorrow I expect your letter, so that there'll be lots of scrawls at the end. Sleep well.

Yours for ever

L.

619   Brno, 28 March 1928, at night

My dear Kamilka

Today was endless drudgery. I got up at 7 o'clock in the morning; towards 8 I'd had breakfast. I was preparing sheets for the copyist and, in the middle of it, in comes, flies really, the Prague conductor of the Glagolitic Mass, complete with score.[1] He said that there are lots of mistakes in the music! We corrected it until 12.30! A quick lunch; the copyist came; he pestered me until 5 o'clock. Notes danced in front of my eyes as if they were drunk. I then took a walk to the post office; it added to my bad mood: no letter from you. It put me off my supper. I read the newspaper – and now I'm pining here. And what has my Písek imp been doing? She was certainly better off; she got a letter and even liked her meal. I can only have a rest when I get away from Brno. In Brno I bury myself in work until I drop – because I don't find such whole-hearted moments of rest here.

They are only in Písek, in heaven. When you stop heating, move out into heaven for the night. I'll certainly sense that my little black angel will be there.

I got a letter today from that Frenchman W[illiam] Ritter from Switzerland. He wants to write a book in French about me. He greatly extolled my *Mass*. What doesn't he want to do with it![2] It

---

1 The conductor of both the Brno and Prague premières of the Glagolitic Mass was Jaroslav Kvapil (1892–1958), the chorusmaster of the Brno Beseda.
2 In a letter to Janáček (BmJA, D 1363: 24 March 1928), Ritter proposed that the Mass be performed annually at various memorable locations (see Janáček 1990, 330, fn.).

wouldn't occur to *our* people, oh no! You can see what sadness and memories about you, of places where I used to see you in Luhačovice, you can see what sort of influence they had on this venerable work. Well, love is a wizard. Submit to it faithfully and it gives a person joy. It intoxicates, it envelops, it isolates. It creates fragrance from the air, ardour from coldness, it beautifies everything around it. Everywhere you see and want only black eyes, raven hair, the silk of the body, soft, smooth like velvet – in short, everywhere you want just your Kamilka. And I feel good on it, I'm content. [...] Dear little soul, there was a row during the performance of my Sinfonietta in Dresden.[1] Some clapped, others whistled. But the first group won. It makes me feel good that people fight over the value of my work. It's good I wasn't there; I'd have probably got involved. Dr Brod is said to be often at the Russian embassy.[2] Somehow try and talk Rudi out of going to that Communist physical training group. *He won't hear anything good there!* We need peace at home and honest work, and not fire and murder! So sleep well.

Yours for ever

L.

620   Brno, 29 March 1928, evening

My dear Kamilka

Yes, they were two beautiful days; especially beautiful because we could even laugh heartily. But behind that laughter there was always something else, something hidden; that we belong to one other. I think that even our crying wouldn't be painful because at the same time there'd surely be again the sweetness of mutual belonging – yes, of being related.

So you've crossed out 'mouths!' once again. So you don't have a moist mouth any more, only sweet little lips for kissing? Surely no-one's going to understand these letters, or will only think up something even nicer there. [...]

On Saturday week [7 April] I'll arrive by the evening express; of course first thing on Sunday morning I'll be off again to Prague.[3] And

1 Fritz Busch conducted the Sinfonietta in Dresden on 16 March 1928 in a concert which included Mozart's Sinfonia Concertante K364 and Brahms's Second Symphony.
2 Like most artists and intellectuals in Czechoslovakia up to the Stalinist trials of the 1930s, Max Brod was on the left, though not the extreme left. Charles Susskind, author of *Janáček and Brod*, believes that Brod's presence at the Russian embassy was most likely explained by 'a preference for good vodka and caviar, not for Soviet-style politics' (private communication).
3 i.e. for the Prague première that day of the Glagolitic Mass.

I just hope I succeed in taking you with me. Zd. is not coming.

[...]

Today I looked at the Luhačovice photograph of you taken years ago. It drew me to you as firmly then – as it has drawn me close now after many years.

Dear God, 'don't allow a bad end', as we two say to ourselves. For that *It* which weaves all fates will also tie up our fate – so as not to hurt, neither us nor others – not to hurt too much.

You're probably already sleeping. Today I sent off the last correction to the Mass; it will already be out next week.[1] Again the piano will be more festooned [with music].[2]

Don't go anywhere; it's poisonous weather now. Until the warm weather settles in. So the scarf[3] was found. Keep it until I come. Must I write to the Kretschmers about that writing-desk?

Yours for ever

L.

621   Brno, 30 March 1928, at night

My dear Kamila

Believe me, I feel as if they've scraped me against a grater. What sort of life would I have now if it weren't for the carefree moments with you? There isn't a conversation that she [i.e. Zdenka] won't twist into some sort of taunt. And I leave her in peace, don't I?

I went out into the country for two hours today; the shrubs are now sprouting vigorously; the grass is turning green. I'm hurrying with the work simply to have it finished certainly by the beginning of July.[4] So that nothing would tie me to Brno; so that I could leave at any moment. Instead of holding time back, I make it fly. With you it flies by itself and we hold it back; we want to enjoy it.

Just think, I got Kč 3031 royalties from those performances of *Jenůfa*[5] in Prague. It surprised even me. And believe me, when I finish work I just want to get away from here. The emptiness here would drive one to desperation. And I need to put down my pen for a while;

1 The vocal score of the Glagolitic Mass was published on 6 April 1928 (Wingfield 1992, 18).
2 The piano would presumably be festooned with sheets of *From the House of the Dead*, temporarily put away while Janáček worked on corrections for the Glagolitic Mass.
3 Janáček had left his 'long grey silk scarf' at Kamila's house on 25 March; see 616.
4 i.e. the revisions of *From the House of the Dead*; Janáček achieved his aim, with both copyists paid off during June (see Tyrrell 1992, 338–9).
5 Two performances given by the Prague National Theatre, 17 and 24 March 1928, the first in honour of Gabriela Horvátová's twenty-five years as a member of the company.

I need to forget completely all that I've written recently. Only Luhačovice will help; and there's still such a long time until those moments. I feel in myself that I'm already terribly irritated. And it's not really necessary. What I wanted fate has bestowed upon me – I have you. So I must just calm down; I'll read your last letter – it will be my lullaby. When I returned from my walk such hunger overcame me while still in the street that I bought a roll from a street vendor and ate and ate whether people were looking at me or not.

The incident in the train[1] with the first class turned out well. I heard what he said down the phone: 'but it's a man with an international reputation' – 'throw it into the bin'. But from now on I'll never sit there again for the shame of being interrogated.

And how is it with you? Has your cough calmed down? It's good to treat it with a compress. Of course you're a little fish who won't lie peacefully even in bed. But what's to be done when *in the first place* you never take care of *yourself*! It's treacherous weather now, it makes you sweat so as then to give you a chill.

I remember the fun on Sunday. Who knows how to be so heartily happy? It's a good tonic; we'll take it.

I've come out a little now from my bad-tempered mood. What if I didn't have at least someone to open my heart to. [...] < one word inked out > [...]

Sleep well.

Yours for ever

L.

623 Brno, 1 April 1928, at night

My dear Kamila

You see, with me Sunday's a long, tedious day. There's much time for dry talk. Today especially your illness came to mind continually, so that those few bright thoughts were as if under a cloud. In the afternoon I went out beyond the town; it was warm, but the wind was throwing hats off. I didn't get far. Worries about you mingled with worries about that Sunday concert [8 April] with my Glagolitic Mass. A young conductor and few rehearsals. On Sunday the orchestra is to have the final rehearsal in the morning, the first concert in the afternoon, and that one of mine in the evening. Who'll suffer for this? So, Kamilka, I'll come to Písek on Friday evening [6 April]. At least I'll see you and make sure with my own

1 See Janáček's account in 616.

eyes how you are. We'll decide accordingly what to do next.

April and June, I'm not sure if I won't go completely crazy because of these two months. Just yesterday both I and the copyist flung down the music. The notes danced before our eyes as if possessed.

How one can be a slave to oneself! And it's so with me.

What have you been doing the whole day? Dosing yourself? The wind certainly picked up lots of Písek dust; I hope you didn't go out in that 'clean' air of the town? You don't really know how it grieves me that you can't get rid of the after-effects of when you bought fish for Christmas in that bitter winter! You were already getting on so well, and here you are throwing away the health acquired in Luhačovice.

I won't reproach you any more about it. I know anyway that it annoys you. I'll see what there'll be in your letter tomorrow. All jokes have faded in me. And you've told me so many of them. Right from the one with those two 'Kamila's darlings' and whether the big one or the small one will get a hiding if he isn't quiet at night! But the big one won't give up, he's got 'gigantic strength'. And although he's got a bad hand,[1] he'll nevertheless know what to do, won't he. Especially when that 'weak' woman will raise both hands and cry out 'I'm frightened!' And the scrawl at the end of the letter was as if it were an eiderdown and out of it peeped the name Kamila. And underneath, again a scrawl; I was certainly wrapped up in that one. So everything would be fine – if only I already knew that my darling Kamila was well now! But, my soul, to go to Luhačovice earlier, particularly April or the beginning of May, is out of the question. You'd have to look for a different cure. But I'm troubled. Even you believe firmly in *premonitions*; and I'm almost fearful. It's because you're left on your own. And one always has to watch over a sick person. Illness isn't lightly borne. A little better – and already one thinks, I'm well. And it's not like that. My Kamilka, be well for me!

Yours for ever

L.

624   Brno, 2 April 1928, at night

My dear Kamila

There's hope for improvement when one's being treated. It was horrible for me to think that you made so light of that cough and that

---

1 This clue provides the identification of Kamila's big 'darling' with 'gigantic strength': on 27 March (618) Janáček reported that his right hand was 'reddened' and 'bandaged'.

pain. I enclose for you the pills prescribed for me by Dr Výmola. There's quinine in them; that will prevent further spreading of the catarrh in your lungs. You must have it just like I did. The pills are very bitter; take them with water. Best to take them after meals, noon and evening. They soon helped me. Have them made up according to the prescription as if for me; and use them. Keep the prescription until I come.

I'll arrive, then, on Friday [6 April]; I'll travel by express at 4.10 to Zdice[1] so as to be with you at 8. I don't know if I'll be able to remain on Saturday; if I had to leave on Saturday I'd come again on Monday morning.

[...]

So after such a jolly Sunday, what a Monday![2] Why didn't you say anything to me about it! But we didn't do anything that would have disagreed with you. In the concert certainly not, in the cinema also not. And that little bit of a walk? You already must have caught a chill earlier. In your signature there's lots of scrawl. I'll imagine things in it: kissing you, yours for ever, and still more of that.

The builder's also not writing to me; he's hardly likely to begin demolition now before the holidays.[3] I'd already like to have it out of the way, and in good order.

April, May, June is a long time; I won't hold out in Brno. One surely needs more than eating, more than not quarrelling.[4] One needs this: to fade away through feeling into another dear being so much that one forgets oneself. It's just like having a heavy burden carried by someone else. And when I'm with you I certainly forget about myself, I live only in you, I live just as you live. That's why it relieves me so. And at home? I'm always *me*, I always pass by, keep out of the way. Living's therefore difficult for me despite the comfort. Everything tires me so quickly.

So just dose yourself obediently. It won't be good by Friday, but I'll take care of you. When I saw the letter written in pencil, I knew that things were bad. Thinking of you all the time and suffering with you.

Yours for ever

L.

1 On the Prague–Plzeň line; at Zdice the line branches with the west fork going through Písek to České Budějovice.

2 The 'jolly Sunday' refers to the Sunday of Janáček's last visit to Písek, 25 March, about which Janáček reported (in 616) Kamila's 'storms of laughter'. The next day, however, Kamila fell ill. Her sudden decline in health was presumably offered as an excuse for her not wanting to go to Prague for the première of the Glagolitic Mass the following Sunday.

3 i.e. before the Easter holidays; Easter Day was on 8 April that year.

4 A summary of Janáček's life with his wife.

My dear Kamila

Today people from *Lidové noviny* asked me to write something for the Easter number.

What else, when I haven't finished writing all the good things you've done?

So I wrote something.[1] Let *Prácheňské noviny* print it.

The rehearsals in Prague[2] are on Saturday from 9 o'clock and on Sunday.

I'll arrive on Friday at 8 in the evening for certain; I'll travel to Zdice and then to Písek.

[...]

Today we [i.e. Janáček and his wife] discussed how to spend the summer. It's better to talk about it. Luhačovice and Hukvaldy are firm. Z. knows that we don't have much to say to one another. She's looking for company so that she can also go off somewhere.

We spelt it out to each other peacefully.

I just wish that you were now yourself again; the thought haunts me continually that last time I didn't notice anything amiss about you. And so suddenly! Try those pills of Vymola. They helped me very quickly. After quinine illness doesn't spread and in this way things begin to get better.

Otherwise I'm like a squeezed lemon. Anyone could throw me away as useless. No ideas occur to me. Anyone who meets me will certainly say to himself, who's that person lost in thought shuffling away there!

Haven't you got an answer from Luhačovice yet?

It's a nice retreat there – and near.

Perhaps you've got an answer already.

And so, my soul, I don't know how to imagine you. Are you lying ill in bed?

Are you sighing [from pain]? Or are you again in the kitchen, again not giving yourself any rest? Is it worse, is it better? I sit here as if at the crossroads. I don't know which way my thoughts should go. Everything's knotted up in me. Like when there's little water and the

---

1 Janáček sent 'Pepík and Jeník', the last of the four pieces concerning Gypsy children, Kamila Stösslová and Písek, to *Lidové noviny*, which published it on 2 April 1928 (Janáček's assertion that he was asked for it on 3 April 1928 is clearly incorrect). Janáček quotes the final words of the article towards the end of this letter.
2 for the Glagolitic Mass.

dam wall stops that little. There's none of the usual ebullience bubbling over in me.

And my article ends thus:

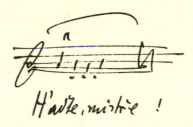

See now, Maestro! They caught the Gypsies again but put the children into 'care'.

Will the Písek people guess who's praising them? Will they guess that it's Kamila?

It will be widely known who can take credit that the children in Písek no longer die of hunger and cold.[1]

So now let me hear again soon your soft 'see now, Maestro!' and your 'there's nothing wrong me with me now'.

And your playful laughter and joy in living. Otherwise I'd be like a fire which has gone out except for the stale smell. It doesn't glow, it doesn't warm – better pour water on it.

With all my thoughts on you, yours for ever
L.

626   Brno, 4 April 1928

My dear Kamila

I wanted to come on Friday [6 April] for the following reasons:

1. to see how ill you were

2. and, if you were just a little healthy, to talk you into coming to Prague on Saturday to be looked at by an important professor so as to decide how to cure you properly.

I didn't think of myself or of the fatigue.

And now you write that hardly have you improved a little, you've already gone to town!

And after the holidays they'll be dragging you off to Vienna and then perhaps to Italy.

Do you think there are no sick people in Italy? Don't you think that

1 See Glossary: 'Gypsy children'.

[243]

the journey to Vienna and going here and there in Vienna — that it won't be tiring for you, who's only just left your bed?

Here, in our country, the most beautiful time is beginning now; everything's putting out shoots and breathing with health. Why go off now when you didn't go off in the hard winter, muddy spring and autumn? And you're scared and frightened of the journey to Prague! Kamilka, don't go anywhere now; don't go until the weather changes to being warm all the time, until your headaches disappear! It would be a gamble with life, with your health.

You've surely got time enough [to get] outfits.

If you don't want to come to Prague on Saturday, if you can't come, if it doesn't give you pleasure, if I can't persuade you — if you feel healthier, if I don't need to nurse you — *then I'll be sad on Saturday, sadder on Sunday* and would come to you on Monday morning.

Wouldn't your husband like to come up for the Sunday concert? I've got three tickets ordered. On Saturday and on Sunday I'll be at the rehearsal in the Obecní dům from 9 o'clock in the morning; he can look me up there without any fuss.

I'll write to the Karel IV. [Hotel] that I'll arrive on Friday afternoon. Write to me there too; and if you decide to come to Prague, send a telegram.

I was looking forward to staying in Prague just you and me — and I've been let down.

I know that to come to Písek only for the night, that it's too short; but if you'd been seriously ill, I'd have come even for that [one] night.

I'll await your decision in Prague. But — and you'll listen to me now — you won't go to Vienna nor to Italy now! First of all you must be x-rayed, so that it's *known* where the root of the illness lies, and then be examined by a top-notch doctor. No-one can be allowed now to drag you round Vienna and bore you abroad.

A healthy person can take any sort of weather; you ought not to go *to town straight after leaving your bed!*

It's true that you've caused me concern but that's no crime; it would hurt me more if you'd wanted to hide something from me; especially something which hurt you yourself.

Have you got any news from Luhačovice yet?

You've had an empty head, and I also. These past days seemed to me as if there were no need for me on earth.

I wasn't able to be with you, to help you, to advise you, to drive away boredom. So why are you here! And now suddenly to read that they wanted to drag you through the world for no good reason, senselessly, unfeelingly! And you'd let yourself be talked into it, and instantly start taking clothes with you – not objecting to anything! I was determined to be with you on Friday evening, just to see you and [to travel] from Písek to Prague on Saturday morning again. Would I have survived this? – I'd have endured it to be of service to you.

I'll be sad if you don't come. I'll miss you very much. Someone whom I love won't be standing by me at a nice moment ...; then what's this stupid glory for!

Yours for ever

L.

But this time Kamila changed her mind. She arrived in Prague on Saturday 7 April. Her visit took in both the Prague première of the Glagolitic Mass on Sunday 8 April and various other trips, described in **628**. When she left on Tuesday, Janáček wrote to her that evening, before he returned to Brno the next morning:

627   Prague, 10 April 1928

My dear Kamilka

At your departure I felt that love, my love, is painful. That it forces tears, that because of it I suffer so much. The longer I'm with you the worse it is for me. It's always as if I'd fallen from a height on to a hard road.

How lovely it was at Karlštejn, there where we had lunch, when you leant your head on your hands and passionately I related my morning dream to you – and how sad it is for me now when I sit here so forsaken and in tears! All the things we've experienced from Saturday in those concerts, how everything's useless, empty. It didn't provoke a smile, not even a tear, and now – you're going off and I'm drowned in tears here! No, there must be an end to it, it can't be endured. But I'm nevertheless glad that I've got tears here for my love. Glad that I still thought of – the post by which your lips went to my lips, through your little fingers.[1] If it weren't for that, the tears would have turned bitter! You mustn't promise things, Kamila, and then – not fulfil them.

I live only in you, I believe in you, my dear little angel. You must

---

1 There was apparently no appropriate moment for Janáček to kiss Kamila goodbye (see **629**). It seems then she devised a 'postal kiss', perhaps by blowing him a kiss.

devote yourself entirely to me. I thank you for everything nice in the last few days.

Yours for ever
Leoš

Do remember [this], I [will] even more!

628   Brno, 11 April 1928

My dear Kamilka

Without you I wasn't able to remain any longer in Prague. After all our being together on Saturday, Sunday, Monday and Tuesday, where we were together as if we belonged to one another, where everyone probably believed that we belonged only to one another – what would I do in Prague without you? When you were leaving I wasn't in control of myself. You disappeared; my joy went down with you. I had supper silently in the Obecní dům, I wrote a few words to you, packed and waited for the morning in order to leave. I didn't even feel the need to see my own work.[1]

I'm home again, like a fish on the sand. It remembers the fresh water; it will soon choke without it.[2]

The most beautiful time was in that garden in Karlštejn when we ate together, spoke quietly.

What a honeymoon trip that would have been! What was still needed to make it so?

And how foreign, how cold was my one forty-five years ago![3] Yes, I undertook it then without need. Not a single warm memory of it remained, because there was nothing.

And now us two! And how quietly time ran by for us, how warmly, contentedly, how full of longing. How nice it was. Just us two. You unkempt on the stone bench; the hours passed by, both of us without tiredness.

And the Chuchle races.[4] Not even the horses were much of an attraction for you, yet, those that went past [asked]: 'Why are these two sitting for hours at the judge's box? [Going] to Chuchle for the races and they see only each other!' And in those concerts! He's just

---

1 There was a performance at the Prague National Theatre of *The Makropulos Affair* on 11 April 1928.
2 See Glossary: 'fish thrashing'.
3 Janáček married Zdenka Schulzová on 13 July 1881, i.e. almost forty-seven years earlier.
4 Velká Chuchle, a village near Prague (incorporated in 1968), was a popular place for excursions from the city. It became particularly fashionable after 1906, when a racing track was built, creating one of the few venues for horse-racing in Bohemia.

her shadow, just her echo. At the Castle[1] Kamila whimpers, in Bertramka[2] she shows off! They like her everywhere.

And nevertheless she ought to have stayed longer in Prague for that Wednesday! I'd have received – what belonged to me[3] and without it it was suddenly so sad for me that I couldn't find words. And everything that was experienced here would have lost all its charm for me!

You can't imagine how it pained me when I realized that I had nothing from heaven for all those days.[4] Now, when I know how you saved Karlštejn for us,[5] how resolute you were, I place a higher value on everything. Without that day how much more sad it would have been!

All the days were like that; here everyone sees that we're together. Remember this, that it was 7, 8, 9, 10 April 1928. We've given our joint visiting-card to everyone. He who wants to read it, let him go to Karlštejn, there he'll find it in the [visitors'] book. It's clear there: Drph. Leoš Janáček and Kamila, i.e. Janáčková.

The book's no respecter of persons, it's impossible to erase anything from it. For that postal kiss[6] you'll get a flower on the violet spring coat. In Prague there was more choice; we didn't get round to it.

I'm glad that your worries about your health are over, I'm glad that Kamilka is as plump as a 'village beauty'. Glad that she takes pleasure in life and that she will give me one.[7]

Yours for ever

L.

No-one reading this letter or any of Janáček's subsequent accounts of these four days (e.g. 629, 631) would guess that Janáček was not entirely alone with Kamila. Yet the photographic evidence (Plate 26) shows otherwise: they were joined by David Stössel at least during the expedition to the Bertramka.

1 The Prague Castle, a major tourist attraction in Prague.
2 The villa in the Smíchov suburb of Prague where Mozart stayed in 1787, completing the score of *Don Giovanni*; it is now a museum of Mozart memorabilia. See also Glossary.
3 Perhaps the farewell kiss that Janáček missed (see 629).
4 i.e. although they had been together, he had missed receiving letters from 'heaven' (i.e. from Písek).
5 Perhaps a reference to Kamila's agreeing to attempt the steep flight of steps up to the Karlštejn castle (see 631: 'up those steps to Karlštejn – that was a big feat for you, I know'). Alternatively this may mean that Kamila had persuaded her husband not to go with them to Karlštejn and did so 'resolutely', thereby allowing Janáček and her to spend the day on their own.
6 See p.245, fn.
7 Another reference, perhaps, to 'Kamila's baby' (see Glossary).

This perhaps explains why it is a part of the four days which is least mentioned. From the references to 'these two' or the 'honeymoon trip' it appears that they were on their own at least at the Chuchle races, at Karlštejn, and at the doctor's. David Stössel perhaps joined them on the first day, but had business commitments of his own and so left his wife and Janáček to their own devices.

629   Brno, 13 April 1928

My dear darling Kamilka

Don't wonder that I had no words during parting. I was inexpressibly sad that you were going off already! That after those beautiful times you were to leave me and no moment was found for me to be able to touch your lips, although painful. And you know that for me it's the single proof that you're mine. Everything was so beautiful! But what sort of sun would it be that kept its warming rays to itself? What sort of warm rain would it be that didn't dampen? What sort of dear Kamilka that didn't know that her moist lips are not only hers but also mine?

This so saddened me as soon as we came out of the hotel. So I was different at once, when I thought of our post,[1] and you understood it so well! Nothing will ever change any of this. Tears wiped everything away and I remember our Prague stay with joy. It couldn't have been more beautiful.

And now those letters! It's a mystery to me that you aren't receiving at least one every day! I tell you, I put them into the post by about ten o'clock in the morning; why then aren't they with you the next day? Day after day I write and one went from Prague even on Wednesday evening. Write whether they've all arrived.

Dear Kamilka, I'm also now as if newborn! I'm forthright, enterprising; a smile on my lips, and hardworking! Desire for you is an enchanted strength. That I love you so much, love you with all my heart, is the reason why I don't look for anything other than you and for work bewitched by you. Therefore I'm strong, I don't get distracted. Oh no, my little soul, we'll often be together, and together for a long time – longer, continually longer, so there'd be no pain from it, but that greatest pleasure! That's so good to write. So everyone in Písek knows that we're inseparable? And even they know that we'll be constantly inseparable in the future? I'm also uncommonly glad of it! No secrets. Straightforward and truthful. And your [dear] ones at home are also pleased? You see, we made no plans for those days and

1 See p.245, fn.

it turned out so nicely – well, until that kiss. But we can make up for that; and everything else that took place – that lunch of ours as a 'married couple', that thirst of ours! From those 'five'[1] our heads didn't ache even a little! The sun burnt us in a trice, it liked us so much! And how we stepped out along that steep footpath! Your raven hair was fragrant and waved victoriously. And nowhere was there even a little thorn which would have given pain. Pleasure the whole time that we were together. My eyes fixed only on you, and how gladly! No, there were no happier people at that time on the whole earth! I remember it so fondly! But Karlštejn was high, impregnable like ...?

Oh, Kamilka, your words 'am I made of plaster?'[2] flashed through my mind. Even if you were made of granite like that rugged castle, even then you could have said 'am I made of granite?' And you wouldn't have been? And you won't be? Will you be dear, soft, silent Kamilka? Oh, let's allow the greatest pleasure to come by itself; let it come as if it were blind, as long as it finds us: unexpected, sudden, unsought. We'll fall into its arms, overcome. It will be as beautiful as the moment when the earth trembled, as when you cried out 'I've never experienced this until now!' As everything awaits us so unexpectedly, leading us closer and closer to one another. With holy calm I wait for that most blissful moment. It will come!

And now that *new quartet of mine*: 'Intimate Letters'.

Today the leader of the Moravian Quartet[3] said that it was a magnificent work. That's the main thing. They'll play it for me in a week's time. *The première will be in Písek.* And who'll perform it? If it were to be the '*Czech Quartet*',[4] which has an international reputation and which will spread the work over the whole world, then that's surely not to the disparagement of the Ševčík people[5] and Professor Vymetal! We'll arrange it that Professor Vymetal will invite the *Czech Quartet* himself. The Ševčík people, i.e. the pupils of Professor Ševčík, don't have two instruments: the viola d'amore[6] and the cello. It will be impossible to borrow these players from somewhere else during rehearsals! *It will be rehearsed in Prague, it will be played for the first time in Písek.* So Kamilka, pass on this

1 Five drinks, perhaps cognac (see 632).
2 See 589; the words are remembered slightly differently here.
3 František Kudláček (1894–1972).
4 See Glossary.
5 See p.58, fn.4.
6 See 576.

message to director Kodl. When the right time comes – that wouldn't be until the autumn – then we'll make up for it.

And now, my little soul, I'm pleased that you're already getting involved in the musical whirl. Well, drink the wine of the one you belong to.

[without signature]

631 Brno, 13 April 1928, at night

My dear darling Kamilka

I can't read your last letter enough. Joy and contentment from those few days breathe from it – just the same as I had. I have every moment in my mind! From the instant when you arrived at the station. The journey with the cases to the doctor.[1] His demeanour as he measured all of you! Wasn't he thinking of something too? Why did he think that I so feared for your health? I wonder what he'll say to me? I'm ready to tell him the truth. And now cheerfully in health, you to the hotel, I to the rehearsal. And then to lunch with the not-completely-cooked fish. Freezing at the concert, getting a cold in addition. Then next day I to the rehearsal, you with the eggs. To the Castle, to Bertramka and you, still untired, telling me fairy stories. What a memory you've got! Up the hill to Karlštejn – and you remember a poem about the death of Charles IV.[2] Well, we were so glad and happy together! And a walk in Stromovka,[3] looking at pictures, and at the afternoon concert that curious glance from H[orvátová], wanting to examine you through and through – but she didn't put a spell on you. We were safe together, we were as one, we were faithfully devoted to one another! That's a power which no-one can overcome. At least she [Horvátová] must have said to herself: now he's happy! And is happy! Those were days so lovely that no-one can imagine them. It was a blue sky, we saw no clouds, we didn't even think of them.

I won't forget your words, soft as a warm breeze:

'So it's a year since we've loved one another!' [See Facsimile, p.251]

You said it and I was so glad to hear your confession! It was the most beautiful conclusion to those red-letter days. Were there any happier people in Prague during those days? Surely not!

I'm glad that you got home safely, that you haven't been bothered

1 Dr Výmola, see Glossary.
2 Karel IV. (1316–78), Czech King (from 1341), Holy Roman Emperor (from 1355) and founder of Karlštejn castle. The identity of the poem about his death has baffled Czech musical and literary experts; it is perhaps another instance of Janáček's unreliable memory.
3 A large royal park in Prague, founded in the thirteenth century.

by having to attend to others. And that you could rest. Our walks –
Bertramka, over the Castle, to the races, up those steps to Karlštejn –
that was a big feat for you, I know.

But twice Kamila grumbled, at the Castle and when in the train[1]
she squeezed through half a dozen carriages! Until I had to say to her:
'Will you be quiet, Kamilka!' Well, a cross child. But that certainly
belonged with everything else. So thousands of people knew who that
black-haired woman was, brown like a bronze bust! Who does she
belong to? Well, I won't give her to anyone. You thanked me for
those beautiful days. I just said to myself: you'll make those days as
dear for her as you can. That was [done] without orders, it was [done]
out of love for you. I can't help doing good to you, giving you
pleasure. It could have been still more beautiful – but those tears of
ours at parting – they were rain from heaven. After them everything
will be fruitful. As much as they hurt, I liked them. You wrote about
them before you knew about mine. They'll be a blessing. I thank you
for them with all my heart! I'll always remember them in difficult
moments.

And what a pneumatic post[2] for kisses we've found! We'll now
always use it in front of people. The nosey will never guess!

And now, has your cold gone yet? Do you do exercises morning
and evening? When I come I'll teach you. What about Luhačovice?
Have you had an answer yet? Today by chance I met the administrator of the Augustýnský [dům] again. I've got July [reserved] for
certain now.

It's cold here again. You'll take care of yourself at least, and you'll
be in front of the safe, warm oven.

Yours, completely yours and for ever

L.

---

1 They would have taken a train to and from Karlštejn, a journey of 33 km from Prague.
2 See p.245, fn.1; 'pneumatic post' was propelled in special cylinders through tubes,
mostly underground, by means of vacuum suction. Systems for transporting post in this
way, often to and from big users such as banks and newspaper offices etc. where speed was
important, were set up in London (1854), Paris (1860) and Vienna (1875). Prague followed
in 1899.

Dear, darling Kamila

I've read [your] last three letters again. I see that you're happy; that pleases me. It comes across to me. I wait dutifully as in front of a church before it opens! It was beautiful! I remember how he [= Stössel?] wanted to cure you with that 'fatty pork'! How he feared cognac! And you turned the goblet to yourself hopefully – and it was good. We never lost our appetites. Well, we want to live and we have a reason for living!

I'll now speak more about those *Intimate Letters*.

Professor Vymetal probably thinks that it's a piece for the whole orchestra which he'd rehearse and conduct. That's a mistake.

It's my second *quartet*; a work for four players (two violins, viola d'amore and cello). These players will rehearse it themselves. There are several such groups of four players in Czechoslovakia. The best, with an international reputation, is the so-called *Czech Quartet*. They play the best, they travel the whole world. They also took my first quartet into the world.

In Písek there aren't four such players; you know that the last time they had to borrow a cellist from Plzeň. Unfortunately, on top of all that, the Plzeň man got repeatedly drunk.

Therefore I turned again with that *yours–mine* composition to the Czech Quartet. They accepted it with joy; they'll start rehearsing it as early as the holidays.[1]

I made a condition that the première, i.e. the first performance, would be in Písek.

There's nothing therefore directed against Professor Vymetal! *So Kamilka, kindly give him the message and straighten it out with him.*

Today was Sunday. I worked in the morning; I posted the letter. Tomorrow you'll probably get two: from Saturday and from Sunday.

There's a famous stage play: *Cyrano de Bergerac*![2] A lover, an ugly man with a long nose, has the power only of beautiful words – and great hopeless love. Because of his long nose no-one wants him.

He writes love letters for someone else, beautiful letters, one or even two daily! Here I thought of myself. When will she, the beautiful lady, realize the mistake? Too late. He's mortally wounded and recites by heart to her the last, most beautiful letter. Amazement!

---

1 Nevertheless it was the Moravian Quartet which rehearsed Janáček's new work and played it for him the following month (see Glossary: 'String Quartet no.2').
2 At the time of Janáček's letter Edmond Rostand's verse play *Cyrano de Bergerac* (1897) was in the repertory of the Brno theatre.

How does he know it? He reveals his burning love to her – and dies. So it is with our letters. They race between Brno and Písek and back. Many a concealed longing, however, races with them, but ardent, constant love is always their conductress.

What is this love of ours? It boils and seethes like strong wine. Take care that it doesn't boil over. And I stoke up the fire so that it boils over! But no, it's a volcano! You don't know where its fire comes from. From deep eyes, from every curve of your body. Well, God's fire which will never go out.

Today there was rain in the morning, clear sun in the afternoon. I'm curious how my *Intimate Letters* will work. It's my first composition whose notes glow with all the dear things that we've experienced together. You stand behind every note, you, living, forceful, loving. The fragrance of your body, the glow of your kisses – no, really of mine. But the softness of your lips. Those notes of mine kiss all of you. They call for you passionately.

It's said that they're very fine.

But everything's still only longed for! You yourself said that I've not yet experienced everything! Well, this is only a presentiment. How will it be after everything comes true that was longed for in the work!

And what did you do today? Your cold has gone, a clean bill of health from Dr Výmola and by now surely healthy sleep has hunted you down!

Yours for ever

L.

633   Brno, 16 April 1928, at night

My dear darling Kamilka

The last three letters of yours I know off by heart.

In the third there's that comedy with Mr Kodl and the *Intimate Letters*.[1] In the second there's the nicest thing you've ever written: your quiet weeping when the train carried you off from me.

It was as if we said to ourselves: see, this is how we are. What will you do with us?!

And then that first letter, when you recall that afternoon in heaven. The afternoon which was the nicest. In fact, where it was burning

1 Presumably about the misunderstanding over the fact that *Intimate Letters* was a quartet and not a piece for string orchestra which could be performed by amateurs in Písek. Janáček's comments about this in 632 appear to be a response to something in a letter from Kamila.

[with love]! Today I was waiting for word from you; well it will come tomorrow and will give me pleasure.

I'm glad, my little soul; work [on *From the House of the Dead*] moves swiftly to its conclusion. No worries on my mind about new journeys, yet tomorrow will be a week after our one to Karlštejn! The dear Lord conjured up beautiful weather for us then. 'Because you love one another I can look on you with a full sun!' That's probably what he thought. And we showed ourselves to him a lot. We didn't hide ourselves. Even I caught the sun. He who hasn't experienced it wouldn't believe it. [It will be nice] when one day we'll tell how just the two of us wandered together into the distant countryside. Just us together! Well, now. What did they do! Mischief! Listen world! It hasn't happened here yet!

[...]

I've already got a mind to see you again. Some sort of premonition is now growing in me.

Only don't let anyone think if I've got a smile on my face that Brno has conjured it out of me! My contentment has faraway roots. And just imagine. I take some old magazine into my hands and I see the title

Lullaby

to the words of Jan Amos Komenský by Leoš Janáček.[1] It will be a magnificent little piece. At that time, years ago, I'd already composed a lullaby. Well, for stock.

And now you, my little soul! Are you well? Have you stopped worrying that it would be bad even when you cough? I'm so glad that we've chosen Dr Výmola. And what did you do on Sunday [15 April]? Have you got an answer from Luhačovice? Are you exercising your body? Even in Brno someone told me that you're putting on weight! They're all looking for something on you![2] Let them wait, they'll live to see. It torments them that it's not happened yet. They think that both [of us] are worth nothing. Eyes measure you up both in Písek and in Brno.

Slowly but surely. And otherwise how are things with you at home? Did you relate everything in detail?

---

1 Janáček's piano accompaniment to a well-known lullaby by the seventeenth-century Czech educationalist was first published in a commemorative book on Komenský in 1920 and reprinted in the March–April issue of the magazine *Hudební besídka*, iv (1927–8); see also Glossary: 'Kamila's baby'.
2 i.e. to see whether she is pregnant.

I'm now drinking Karlsbad water domestically; I do it every year.[1] But I have to get up early. So for fourteen days I'll have this torment. It rains here often, not good for my building. You're sleeping already; my eyes are also closing. Come, come now, oh little letter of yours! It's on the way now.

Yours for ever

L.

634   Brno, 17 April 1928, at night

My dear Kamilka

I wrote to you yesterday that I had a premonition that I'll be seeing you again soon. And this morning an express letter arrived [asking me] to be in Prague on Monday [23 April] at 10 o'clock.[2] Those premonitions of mine are always fulfilled!

If I'm through quickly with the important meeting, I'd leave by express at 4 o'clock to Zdice and by slow train to Písek. At the very worst by the express which you took.

I'm not to the liking of someone from Písek. He[3] is writing anonymous letters to Z. If he were writing the truth I wouldn't bother about it, but these lies and rumours!

You're said to be getting parcels through the post from me every moment. I'm said to be sending a whole garden to you. I've concealed nothing. After all I give something for something and I give less than I receive. Even Z. has acknowledged that.

But the evil intention is to give no peace. I don't even want to repeat some of the other lies. It's impossible for us to stop the work of this hidden scoundrel. One time he sent a letter from České Budějovice, another time from Plzeň; but he's certainly sitting in Písek. We'll go on living as before; in such a way that everyone sees us. What is clear cannot be maliciously coloured.

And with those autographs! Whoever wants to, let him turn to me directly; don't let them trouble you. So turn away every one.

[...]

1 In her memoirs Janáček's maid Marie Stejskalová recalls: 'At six in the morning he'd get up, drink his Karlsbad water – every year in May he'd take a Karlsbad cure at home' (Trkanová 2/1964, 99). Either Stejskalová got the month wrong or Janáček seems to have begun early this year. The 'cure' evidently consisted of drinking Karlsbad water early in the morning, and avoiding certain foodstuffs such as radishes and lettuces.
2 in connection with the printing of *Moravian Love Songs* (635).
3 or she. The Czech does not specify the gender here. In his next letter Janáček spells out both possibilities.

Today I wrote to the Bertramka; I applied to become a member.[1] I'm curious [to see] the photographs.[2] I know Mozart's biography; [it will be] good if you'll know it too. You can tell me what I don't know. [...] I'm looking forward to seeing you again. Who's interested in muddying the water with insults? Is it a man, is it a woman?

I'll leave Brno on Sunday morning [22 April] at 10 o'clock; I'll be in Prague at 3; I'll sleep over at Karel IV. [Hotel]; [go] to the meeting in the morning. And then on to you; to see that you're well and cheerful. After Karlštejn all days now are like workdays. So you liked the meadow flowers after all? Despite the poisonous gossip I'll send a whole garden to you. You'll certainly be surprised by this letter. Within a week again [I'll appear] out of the blue!

Yours for ever

L.

635   Brno, 18 April 1928, at night

My dear Kamilka

[...] And now the author or authoress of these pointless anonymous letters knows well what your place looks like. Where there's 'some sort of' back room. There the writer probably has our heaven in mind. There, apparently, is our snug little room. As if he'd looked in on us. So we should invite him. I'll tread on his patch; I'd drive him away from mine.

[...]

Just fancy, on Saturday *Jenůfa*, on Tuesday *The Makropulos Affair* at the National Theatre in Prague. Only your *Káťa*[3] is not making any money.

Today I had an exhausting day. I got up at 6 o'clock on account of that Karlsbad water. I went for a walk, I worked. But in the afternoon I'd had lots to do, from 2 to 7! Anyone who'd met me in the evening on the street, eyes on the ground, tottery gait, would certainly have thought to himself: 'that man's having a nightmare'. And it wasn't a nightmare, but that dark little devil from Písek who was sitting in my

1 of the Czechoslovak Mozart Society (Mozartova obec), which administered the Bertramka.
2 See 639.
3 *Jenůfa* was performed at the Prague National Theatre on 21 April; *The Makropulos Affair*, however, was not performed on Tuesday 24 April (there were no performances of the opera between 1 April and 4 May). After its initial run of ten performances (1922–4), *Káťa Kabanová* was not performed at the Prague National Theatre until a new production in 1938. For Stösslová's royalty, see p.189 fn.1.

head. I'm telling you, if I don't throw out these copyists soon, I'll go mad.

If at least slippers were walking round me here, if a mane of black hair would toss so that I'd have somewhere to look – but nothing other than the copyist reeking of smoke and beer!

The folksongs[1] are already going to the printers; that's why they've called me to Prague. Kamila, twenty years of work is ending with that. Everything, everything ended! I'm even coming to an end in my operas. Because what's liked now is terrible! In the operetta *No, No, Nanette*[2] Nanette plays the trombone. What she does to it I don't know. But everyone's in ecstasy over what she does! That's the taste now. Today it's warmed up a bit. Let there be sun above the Písek heaven. And what about [going to] *The Makropulos Affair* on Tuesday in Prague? I'd need

    a continual Karlštejn,

    a permanent Bertramka,

    continually being with my Negress Kamila;

otherwise it's a desert around me. It's like reaching for grapes which are too high. Their sweetness attracts, they're full of juice, they burn with dusky redness, they glow with ripeness – they aren't grapes, they are the burning lips of Mrs Kamila. Sleep well.

    Yours for ever

    L.

636   Brno, 19 April 1928, at night

Dear, absent-minded Kamilka

You have presentiments which come true; I have a will which everyone must carry out. So many times something that I've wanted has come true! Today for example I wanted to talk to two professors: I go out, I meet one at the gate, the second half an hour later in the town. The day before yesterday I happened to ask why that daughter of General Podhajský[3] doesn't send news of herself. Today a picture postcard arrived from her from as far away as Florence, from Italy. I write to you that I've got a premonition that I'll see you soon and this

---

1 See Glossary: 'Moravian Love Songs'.
2 Vincent Youmans's musical *No, No, Nanette* was given its Brno première on 13 April 1928.
3 Zdeňka Podhajská (1901–91), daughter of General Alois Podhajský, regional commander in Brno. She was the model for the original front wrapper design by Alexander Vladimír Hrska of the vocal score of *Káťa Kabanová*.

morning[1] an express letter arrives which summons me to Prague — and naturally also to Písek! Are these coincidences or what?

I've got still other premonitions — I'll see whether they come true for me. Why did I come across that lullaby?[2] I did it years ago and yesterday it fell, by chance, into my hands!

I'll now carry that cross myself. It weighs about eighty kilos, but it's soft and doesn't oppress; one can rest with it, one can put it down for a moment. It sleeps from 7 in the evening to 10 in the morning. A strange cross! It has hands which are without bones and a little body like foam. It's a joy to hold it. It's not a matter of carrying the cross but whether this cross is carrying something?[3] So just do exercises so that there's enough strength in you. You're like a little ball; there'll be somersaults! You naughty thing! [...]

Those notes [fashioned] after you![4] If we hadn't had so many honestly experienced moments together, without delusions, without pretence, the notes wouldn't have sprung out just like a spark springs out when I strike flint with iron. They are born of what the kissing was made of. They burn as if they were burning lips. And then the notes fly faster, they sing with a presentiment of blissful moments, they already sing a lullaby — and there's still no child anywhere! At Hukvaldy I'll show you where, as children, we thought that babies flowed out into the world. It's a little stream springing from the mountain, from Babí hůra; pure water. You can drink it; it gurgles merrily and falls from the gully and runs off, it runs down quickly into the stream — so that the parents would have them soon, would have those babies! I've looked many times with such wonder at this fairy-tale place! We'll see it. And if a child swims to the surface just then — we'll catch it at once! So careful! Be well then, dear soul — and strong — so that you could carry a cross!

Yours for ever

L.

637   Brno, 20 April 1928

My dear capricious Kamilka

You won't go to Vienna on Saturday [21 April]. I'll be in Písek on Monday. If I don't catch you at home — — Send a telegram to Prague

1 Unless he received a second express letter, this letter had in fact arrived two days before (see 634).
2 See p.254, fn.1.
3 See Glossary: 'Kamila's baby'.
4 i.e. the String Quartet no.2.

(Karel IV., Smíchov) [to say] that you're at home.

I'll wait for that telegram on Sunday and on Monday morning.

If the telegram doesn't arrive — well then I won't come.

Yours for ever

L.

Kamila did not go to Vienna on Saturday and Janáček's plan (outlined in 634) was realized. He left Brno for Prague on Sunday 22 April, stayed at his Prague hotel that evening, and after his folksong meeting the next morning went on to Písek. He left early on Wednesday morning, sending Kamila a card from Tábor on the way back (*638: 25 April 1928).

639 Brno, 25 April 1928, at night

Dear, darling Kamilka

So you said to me that you love me! I've said it to you countless times; your once outweighs my countless times. We walked together alone along the streets of Písek; we met serious people; they thought to themselves: 'Now they walk by themselves; they're certainly engaged!'

Let everyone think what they will; what's written about us in the book of fates will come true at the right time. We go straight on, we don't avoid anyone.

I slept a lot during the train journey; since, Kamilka, it was 'going swimmingly' for me from Sunday morning at 5 o'clock to Wednesday morning at 5 o'clock! Without stopping.

You've probably now also received the photographs from Dr Blažek[1] of the Bertramka. They've come out well [see Plates 25–6]; you're pretty there; we stand beside one another. And they'll remain in that house as a memento. So link is added to link until there'll be a chain from it by which a certain Leoš will be bound with a certain Kamila. I wish the chain were very short but tough; so that they'll be bound closely.

[...]

1 Dr Vlastimil Blažek (1878–1950), Czech musical archivist, founder and director of the Czechoslovak Mozart Society (Mozartova obec) and responsible for the exhibition in the Bertramka. Blažek, whose father had been an older colleague of Janáček's at the Brno Teachers' Training College, had ordered the photographer himself, as he discloses in his memoir of the occasion (see Bibliography).

My Kamilka

Now it's all go again at my place like a mill. From morning to eve. Did you read yesterday that a certain American offered the heirs of the composer Antonín Dvořák

200,000 dollars for six manuscripts?[1]

That was yesterday's news. Today the newspapers say that it's [just] a rumour.

I thought to myself, what would Kamilka get for the quartet *Intimate Letters*? I calculated it yesterday to between two to five thousand perhaps; and today I tell myself that it's a rumour.

[...]

I now live on lettuce; day after day I eat a lettuce scalded with [fried] bacon. Instead of vinegar, lemon juice is used to make it bitter; otherwise I might get rheumatism from the vinegar, if I took so much of it.

And you, my little soul, aren't frightened of this. Your little round body needs proper exercise; of course in your soft bed, made up from top to bottom with eiderdowns, this sort of exercise won't be of much avail. You'll 'lose weight' after just one big turn in your body.[2] You know what I mean... I'm speaking as if I were a doctor and I'm not one. You've got a 'talent' for getting fat and other women for making planks out of themselves. But I like your talent more.

I haven't heard whether they're building at Hukvaldy or not. You know, there are those people who say 'what goes slowly can't escape'. That saying is rather apt for us too. I believe it now; except that what goes slowly with us is also nice; it's never yet escaped from us. This is why I put up with it; you're very dear all the time, I love you unutterably. Only now am I a complete man, i.e. a person on whom no-one will be able to have any effect, only that dear small pretty Kamilka of mine. So you'll think now of that usual addition of yours: 'I'm enough for you.' It rang in my ear now; was it because you too were thinking of our little moments?

I'll write to Mr Kodl when the Brno people play [the quartet] for me; that will be any moment now.[3] – I now remember you during our

1 The statement was published in the newspaper *Ruch* (26 April 1928), p.3: 'The family of the composer Antonín Dvořák has sold six of his manuscripts, including that of "The New World Song" [sic] in E minor, to America for 200,000 dollars, i.e. 6 and a half million Czech crowns.'

2 See Glossary: 'Kamila's baby'.

3 See Glossary: 'String Quartet no.2'.

last parting when the word 'lips!' were uttered. And you were dear like a child.

Yours for ever

L.

642   Brno, 29 April 1928, at night

My dear Kamilka

So the snap's enclosed here [see Plate 26]. We stand close to one another. The lodge behind us pleased Mozart too and perhaps the same family of birds sang to him and to us too. It's well captured; you're laughing and I've got contentment on my face.

A nice memory.

[...]

Today's Sunday; it's a day without end for me. It's warm, but clouding over. I'll go out into the forest countryside. What will you be doing? [...]

*

I'm looking again at the picture [Plate 26] for pleasure; you're happy there. Only we two have hats on our heads. It's clear who's with whom. Today I was in the Brno vineyards. Full of flowers, fragrance, the budding virtually audible. Every bud was now stretching out its own leaves; it didn't want to be bound up any longer as if under an eiderdown, constricted. It's already unclasping its little hands. Only I went without my dearest flower, that black rose of mine. She would have showed off here, laughed. The footpaths wouldn't have been enough for her, the sun wouldn't have burnt enough. So one thing can send you jumping around for a hundred paces, and at another you stand like a worm that's been trodden on. It's lucky that at least every other moment different views open out. You can look far into them. As if the sun had specially gilded them; the sun had made a little path for a fairy tale. And in the fairy tale there should be just two people; one of them you and the other me.

And in that fairy tale they should be able to love one another to their heart's content, just live for one another unconcerned, guarding their happiness, enjoying it.

Can you imagine it? In that fairy tale they'd have a cottage; they'd bolt the gate. They'd open it only now and then so that people could see that they still love one another, and that they can never have enough of one another. I can't have enough of that portrait. You must also keep it carefully; we came together in a special place. Did Mozart love Mrs Dušková[1] as much as I love you? I think I love you more.

Sleep well.

Yours for ever

L.

643   Brno, 30 April 1928

My dear Kamilka

[...]

So Luhačovice's alright. Good. The rocks are warm! But you mustn't go there alone, Marta[2] will keep guard so that the bogeyman won't come. And Kamilka, I ask you this earnestly: don't overdo the sunbathing, especially wrap your *head* with something *light*. Not with a red scarf or a black one; they eat up the sun's rays, they absorb them into themselves, whereas a white one deflects the sun. You can take lots of warmth, but too much of it does harm. I'd like to be that bogeyman who takes you off sunburnt, all warmed up, into his hidey-hole and never lets you go. [...] You've probably got the picture from Bertramka now. Nice, isn't it? And do you know why I've got black teeth? That's from the red disinfectant with which I rinse my throat every day! Everything it touches turns black. I'm throwing it away now.

News has come from Berlin that *The Makropulos Affair* will be there as early as May.[3]

The exhibition[4] in Brno will be inaugurated in the theatre with *Káťa Kabanová*. Ducats will be falling into your lap after all![5] And your lap will be golden!

The electricity is already on in Hukvaldy; but I don't know whether they're rebuilding my cottage.

And now that conscience! So people seek you out 'much more than I think'? For what, why, how so, to what purpose, what for? You know, so many questions. Why this looking when I've already found you? Let them be sure to come to me, to the one who already has you since he's found you. I'll never return you, I won't give you to anyone. It was a heavy ballast – my life – which went with you. So don't

---

1 The singer, Josefa Dušková (1754–1824), wife of the pianist František Xaver Dušek (1731–99; see **645**). The Dušeks owned the villa Bertramka in which Mozart stayed while completing *Don Giovanni*.

2 Servant in the Stössel household.

3 Janáček was under the impression that *The Makropulos Affair* would be performed at the Berlin Staatsoper (but see **670**).

4 See Glossary: 'Exhibition of Contemporary Culture'.

5 See p.189, fn.1.

overdo the sunbathing; two hours at the most. And Marta, on guard!

Keep well.

Yours for ever

L.

644   Brno, 1 May 1928

My dear Kamilka

Today's the first of May. Everything's blooming, everything's green. On this holiday [in celebration] of work I've been hard at work. I have – perhaps successfully [–] got round one very complicated passage in the opera. Skuratov tells of his Lujza, about his love for her, and at the same time unshackled prisoners are getting drunk, are shouting, dancing.[1] You know, it's like someone wanting to cross the mud without getting dirty.

Well, it's done.

Then I went for a walk on my own; what do I mean on my own! With you!

And now this evening I've written 'Sounding the alarm'[2] on four sides.

It's those few words about the Bertramka. I celebrate you too there.[3] How could I avoid you!

What have you been doing? It's warm here, overcast, a light rain falls at times. That's why I think you've not been on the rocks. I've got no fears about you, at least. Are you on your own? Have you written to me today? I'll believe so. I'm terribly tired today. I'll rush to bed and call you into my dream. I hope I'll have a very good time with you. You know, only in my dream! But at least the dream's lively. It doesn't need to bother about anyone else.

---

1 Skuratov's tale of his German sweetheart Lujza (Luise) and how he killed the bridegroom forced upon her provides the central narration of Act 2 of *From the House of the Dead*. It is interrupted from time to time by a drunken prisoner, and finally overwhelmed by the rest of the prisoners, exuberantly enjoying the rare feast-day entertainment.

2 This article, which appeared in *Lidové noviny* on 20 May 1928, draws attention to the plight of the villa Bertramka. Janáček's formulation in the next sentence ('those few words') suggests that these were words already discussed, possibly solicited by Dr Vlastimil Blažek (see p.259, fn.) during Janáček's visit to the Bertramka. Blažek wrote to Janáček on 22 April 1928 (BmJA, A 1349) answering questions about the Bertramka (some of which Janáček incorporated in his article), expressing pleasure that Janáček would be aiding the Mozart Society with his 'powerful influence', and looking forward to news where and when the article would appear.

3 The 'celebration' is restrained, confined merely to the opening of the final paragraph, which is addressed to an otherwise unidentified 'Madam'. Janáček explained to Stösslová who 'Madam' was when the piece was published (see 661).

So come into the dream. I know how to call up, through my own will, whom I want!

I'm calling now and I want [you]: Kamilka, come! Oh, I'm afraid. For you're also so over-sensitive. [I'm afraid] that you won't be able to sleep! And your little soul had to travel to me!

I'm overworked and I don't have any congenial relaxation, that pleasant time with you. Very often it's so hard for me to endure it, this love far beyond the hills! You know, the Germans in Salzburg are asking for Kč 345,000 for the Bertramka and they got it for nothing![1] That's greed. And they let the historic building fall apart.

I'm now eating nothing but lettuce. The lettuces have already got hearts. And I take out the hearts. And there's one that I'd stroke and listen to how it beats, and the more passionately it beats the more I'd hold it tight. It's the little heart of my Kamila. Keep well! Don't get sunburnt unnecessarily! Healthy skin, healthy body.

Yours for ever

L.

645   Brno, 2 May 1928, at night

My dear Kamila

[...] Today I got news from Hukvaldy that they're already making the rafters for the house and that if the weather's fine they'll be finished in May. I'm glad of it, the building will get dry.

I need devils on stage;[2] I just cannot find the thread to pull them out of my brain. I keep on throwing things into the bin. Well, it's spring now and it drags me outside from the writing-desk.

You're reading that book on W.A. Mozart;[3] perhaps you'll get to the place where it deals with his stay in Prague at the house of the virtuoso *Dušek*.[4] Perhaps there'll be something more about his wife

---

1 The building had been bequeathed three years earlier to the Mozarteum in Salzburg by Ema Popelková, who inherited it through her husband's family. The Czechs wished to buy it back, but the Mozarteum had set a price of Kč 345,000 for it.

2 For the plays in Act 2 of *From the House of the Dead*.

3 Perhaps a book or guide bought on the trip to the Bertramka (see also the reference to 'Mozart's biography' in 634).

4 See p.262, fn.1. Josefa Dušková's mother lived in Salzburg, and the recently-wed couple visited her there in August 1777 and several times later. A friendship between the Mozart and Dušek families grew up from this time, documented by many references in the Mozart correspondence and by the fact that Mozart always stayed with the Dušeks on his trips to Prague, most famously during the preparations for the première of *Don Giovanni*.

there; she was a *singer*, and Mozart wrote arias for her.[1] There's nothing about it in my encyclopedia.[2] I think there was a friendship between them.[3]

Today they sent me more than 200 printed pages of the music of my dances.[4] I have to look through it, find mistakes – and my head's already dropping over it.

If only I had at least these devils out of the way! This is always the worst thing. Well, a little devil like you, I'd not want that sort out of the way. On the contrary, I'd even want to embrace it and hold it however much it might wriggle.

And about Marta. Here, they let the maids go on paid leave – without food [–] when the gentry go off for the holidays. I'm sure you'll think up something. You won't get a better one. [...]

You know what I'd like to do most of all? I'd lay my empty head on your lap and you'd tell fairy tales. We could manage that. In every one they would have to marry one another. Otherwise I wouldn't go along with it. And my players[5] have still not got in touch over the *Intimate Letters*; and I'd like to write now to Mr Kodl.[6] [...] I now get up at sunrise. And yesterday I called you into my dream for the night, however a swarm of notes descended upon me. You of course were in and out of the swarm – well, a wild, confused dream. Tiredness. I know the cure for it. It's in your blood-red lips.

Yours for ever

L.

1 Mozart wrote two concert arias for Josefa (essentially an artist of the concert hall and salon rather than the opera house): *Ah, lo previdi* K272 (1777) and *Bella mia fiamma* K528 (1787).

2 Janáček possessed *Ottův slovník naučný* [Otto's encyclopedia] (1888–1909). Its six-column article on Mozart (vol.17) mentions Mozart's stay in Prague in 1787, but not the Dušeks or the villa Bertramka. However the article on the Dušeks (vol.8) states that Josefa Dušková was a singer and that Mozart wrote arias for her.

3 Presumably Janáček meant something more than the family friendship between the Mozarts and the Dušeks. Speculation about a relationship between Mozart and Josefa has been fuelled by their nearness in age (Josefa was twenty-three years younger than her husband) and by a ring allegedly given to Josefa by Mozart but later found to be given to Dušek (Sýkora 1958, 50–2).

4 Janáček is referring to the proofs of his *Lachian Dances*, published later that year by Hudební matice. The 'more than 200 printed pages' was an exaggeration: the total was 123, of which only 108 have music.

5 The Moravian Quartet (see 640 and Glossary).

6 See Glossary.

My dear Kamila

[...]

I went this morning, Saturday, to the post office to get into a different mood but there was still no letter for me there.

I've had news from Hukvaldy that the extension is coming on fast. I'll go off there at once, just as soon as I've finished here tidying up the opera.

I really feel that it's high time to put down my pen – and walk from the Augustýnský [dům] to Alojzka,[1] not to think about anything other than listening to you, looking at you. I'm much exhausted now. What will you be doing on Sunday? Preparing already for the journey?[2] What will you do with Rudi now? It makes you worry, but time hurries on. Let the lad decide himself and you must all stick by his decision. [...]

They're[3] playing *Intimate Letters* for me on 15 May. If you weren't in them I'd have already forgotten about them. I've been deprived of Kč 5000 from the Academy. I put in my application too late. I'd certainly have got it for *The Makropulos Affair*.[4] It will wait a year. And Berlin! It's already May, let them rather leave it until the autumn.[5] I don't want to hear any more music now it's May! You're blooming while I'm drying up in all this hard work. And no pleasure! Only those memories beyond the hills and dales. They must be strong if it makes up for my sadness.

[...]

Kamila, the copyist has just gone. You can't imagine what a load will fall from my soul when this *House of the Dead* is finished. This is the third year it has oppressed me, night and day.[6] Only when I was with you did I forget it. And what it will be I still don't know even myself. Now notes upon notes just pile up into a mountain; a tower of Babel grows. If it collapses on me, I'll be buried.

1 i.e. Aloiska, one of the springs in Luhačovice, discovered in 1883 (see Plate 16).
2 From Janáček's letter of 1 June 1928 (670) it appears that Stösslová was planning to go to Vienna to buy clothes.
3 See p.265, fn.5.
4 Janáček won a prize from the Czech Academy in 1924 for his First String Quartet and *Mládí*. Unlike the State Prizes, Academy prizes (top award Kč 5000) were won on the basis of competitions for which specific works needed to be entered. Janáček had already received a state prize for *The Makropulos Affair* (see 507).
5 A reference to the promised Berlin production of *The Makropulos Affair*. Janáček had been anxiously awaiting news of it since 30 April (643).
6 There is no evidence that Janáček began considering his Dostoevsky opera before February 1927 (see Tyrrell 1992, 326–7), i.e. sixteen months.

I'll dig myself out of these ruins in Luhačovice. And we'll rejoice! Tomorrow, Sunday, I'll go off somewhere beyond Brno. I'll bend down over every little stream to see if I can see your image in it; I'll always be beside it.

We look fine in that [photograph] from Bertramka! [see Plate 26]. Well, a fiery life stood next to me and enchanted me.

This evening I'll make an inspection of your letters; I'll read those which I've kept.

So enjoy yourself in the sun tomorrow. Let Marta keep watch. Bogeymen away!

Yours for ever

L.

648 Brno, 5–6 May 1928, at night

My dear Kamila

And you were alone on those rocks? Won't you take advice again? When it gets about that you lie around there on your own, it will be bad. [...]

Today I was coming from the post office; a letter in my pocket, lost in thought at that moment, I was looking at the ground. Someone passed me, I sensed him turning round behind me, and he addressed me (in German): 'Are you Mr Janáček?'

Yes.

'I bring you greetings from America. Haven't you got the courage to go there?'

I've got the courage; but only if it would be worth it.

'I recognized you from the photographs in the American newspapers!'

Whom do I have the pleasure of addressing?

'I'm Čermák, the brother of the local architect [Gottfried] Čermák'. What pleasure it gave him that he recognized me. He said goodbye and hurried to the railway station.

[...] So you'll sleep well today. I'm still waiting for an idea from above about the beautiful miller's wife.[1] Before leaving, the miller gives orders: 'Don't let anyone in!' No sooner has he gone than a neighbour knocks; she lets him in; flirtation.

At that very moment someone else knocks. A clerk; she lets him in,

---

1 This is the second and last of the two plays that the prisoners enact in *From the House of the Dead*, Act 2. In essence it is the folktale elaborated in Gogol's story *Christmas Eve*, set as an opera by several Russian composers (e.g. by Tchaikovsky in *Vakula the Smith*).

having first hidden the neighbour. Flirtation. At that very moment someone else knocks. A bearded monk – the devil [–] enters after she has hidden the clerk. Flirtation.

At that very moment her husband knocks furiously. The doors fly open – what happens next you can imagine for yourself!

I must finish that tomorrow. And then I'll throw down my pen and be off!

So, sleep well! (Saturday, 5 May, in the night)

So my little soul, today, 6 May, I've done it! From 8 in the morning to 12.30, from 3 to 5 – and the devils have taken off the false miller's wife. A load off my chest, emptiness in my head. Open the gates, let me live like any other man. Now you'll sit down on the throne and I'll bow down before you. For such a long time, for the third year,[1] it was being shaped inside me unceasingly. You were the only shining cloud with which I liked to run about to have a rest from my work. All finished!

It was cold here today; I didn't get out of Brno. I went out only during the evening to the café to look at the picture magazines.[2]

[...]

Don't overdo it with those rocks! I beg you. People know 'that pretty lady from Pražská ulice',[3] but wretches also know it. I fear for you.

Sweet dreams.

Yours for ever

L.

Brno, 6 May 1928 at night

In June I am to give a lecture[4] in Prague.

649   Brno, 7 May 1928, at night

My dear Kamila

You're a lively one today! But thank you for the letter, I'm glad that it came today.

1 See p.266, fn.6.
2 Cafés used to keep current issues of daily and illustrated papers for the benefit of their patrons.
3 Stösslová's address was 17 Přemyslová ulice, but this street was on the road to Prague and thus known informally as 'Pražská čtvrt' [Prague Quarter].
4 The lecture was for the First International Conference on Folk Arts (Ier congrès international des arts populaires), which took place in Prague 7–13 October 1928. Janáček's contribution was at the request of the conference secretary, Dr Zdeněk Smetáček, who wrote to him on 4 May 1928 (this letter has not survived but is referred to in further correspondence). Two days later (650) Janáček mentioned that the lecture was in October, not June, but nevertheless began working on a draft entitled 'What results from the notation of colloquial speech?'

[268]

Yes you're well,
  you know that someone loves you more than himself,
  that you're mouthwatering.

No worries oppress you, you can relax. The sweetest pleasure can alight on you. Mastering oneself is like piling up still more wood on the fire. There's pleasure in it which not everyone will experience; we will, and to the full. It's like believing in eternal life; where it will be full of joy, happiness, where every wish will come true. And let our dearest wish also come true!

Today the builder wrote to me. The beautiful, dry weather will enable him to be finished in May. There wasn't even a drop of rain when the roof was dismantled! I'll go off to Hukvaldy when he has connected the electricity. So I'm counting on those three Turkish rugs from you. I'm curious what impression the cottage will make on you. [...]

650   Brno, 8 May 1928, at night

My dear Kamila

So why was it that a little devil got into you the night before last? Then at 5 o'clock you couldn't sleep any longer. The reason is too much sunbathing. It affects the head. So take care! When I'm finished with work now I've nothing serious to do – and for me boredom's worse than work.

Something will turn up. Together we'd enjoy ourselves. In heaven time always passes for us as if there were no clock there. It will be necessary to get that alarm clock fixed by the watchmaker; it lost a quarter of an hour during the night. Ever so reliable in Hukvaldy!

If only it were warm now! I wanted to force a change [in the weather by going out] only in a short coat, but it still isn't possible. Today the brother of my 'secretary'[1] was here from Prague. He told me that *Walter*, the distinguished conductor, will conduct my piece *Taras Bulba* in Leipzig and in London.[2] Yesterday I learnt that I'd made Kč 6000 on a National Bank bond. It was for one hundred dollars, which have so risen in price. A shame it wasn't possible to get more than one of those bonds. And not everyone got one. Have your [Kč] 10,000 risen again already? With me it now goes slowly – but

1 Václav Mikota (1896–1962), director of Hudební matice, and brother of Jan Mikota, who accompanied Janáček to England in 1926 (see p.87, fn.1).
2 Bruno Walter (1876–1962) conducted Janáček's *Taras Bulba* at a concert of the Leipzig Gewandhaus orchestra on 25 October 1928, the first German performance. It was Sir Henry Wood, however, who gave its first performance in London, on 16 October 1928.

surely. The cottage will empty my pocket; but on the other hand it will be evident what [the money] was spent on. The world's now boarded up against me; no 'presentiment' that I might get to, and would be able to get to, my beloved part of the world in Písek. But just you wait, you little black ball! What will become of you when your little legs can't carry you? Well, your mouth won't get overgrown; it takes the most physical exercise. It's clear what's necessary for that little round body too. – More this evening.

And now it really is as if I'm caged in. From nowhere [even] mildly stirring news. Universal Edition has taken Kč 996 from my receipts for *The Makropulos Affair*.[1] I've written to them today for the third time [asking them] to explain it to me.

If it weren't for you I'd bury myself like a mole in the autumn. But you, my sunshine, you warm me; that's why I run to and from the post office; my eyes just rooted to the ground. People greet me, I thank them when they've gone.

And my lecture[2] in Prague will be only in October! So I'm sad. Perhaps something will change, and I'll appear on the Písek bridge.

Dr Löwenbach[3] also wrote an opera with someone. Last night [*recte* 5 May] they played it for the first time; the second time there was an empty theatre!

And I'd love to be with you; to lay down my tired head somewhere. To forget the whole world. Simply to gaze into your eyes, at your buxom little figure. Not to want anything else but you, not to hear anything else but you. I know that I'd revive at once. And so after much work, indifferent boredom; as if flails were hitting an empty threshing floor, as if water were going through a mill-wheel in vain. So now day after day trickles by like tar.

You're happy, cheerful! I, on the other hand, am glad only that I can think to myself 'She's mine, that dear Negress!' But it's as if I'd said that that little star in the sky is mine, that the little white moon is mine or that golden sun! But reach for the stars, the moon, the sun! But just wait for the day when that little star falls to earth! I'll run to

---

1 In his letter to Universal Edition of 7 June 1926 Janáček mentioned that he had already asked twice about why the firm had taken 2% of his royalty for *The Makropulos Affair*. The reply on 11 May 1928 stressed that these were not royalties on performances, but on performance materials, which were very costly (Janáček 1988, 353–4). The firm later conceded Janáček's demand (see 655).

2 See p.268, fn.4.

3 Under the pseudonym of J.L. Budín, Dr Jan Löwenbach (1880–1972) wrote the libretto for Bohuslav Martinů's opera *The Soldier and the Dancer*, first performed under František Neumann at the Brno Theatre on 5 May 1928.

20 (*below*) Zdenka Janáčková in 1924.

21 (*top right*) The singer Gabriela Horvátová in 1925, in one of her last roles as Eve in E. F. Burian's opera *Before Sunrise*.

22 (*bottom right*) Kamila Stösslová in 1927 (photograph from the studio of J. Souhrada).

23 Janáček in Písek with the renowned violin teacher Otakar Ševčík and his American pupil Arthur Bennett Lipkin on 8 September 1927 (see **266**: 2–3 November 1924).

24 The Janáčeks and the Stössels in Písek, a group photograph taken before the Janáčeks set out for Venice on 1 September 1925 for the ISCM Festival.

25 'Ah, to descend the stairs looking for the reason why one has to live? It's not empty notes which are liked. Passion gets into them from somewhere else.' Janáček's inscription on the back of this photograph of him (7 April 1928) standing at the first-floor entrance to the Bertramka, the house in Prague where Mozart lived during the première of *Don Giovanni*.

26 'We stand close to one another. The lodge behind us pleased Mozart too and perhaps the same family of birds sang to him and to us too. It's well captured; you're laughing and I've got contentment on my face' (642: 29 April 1928). A photograph taken during Janáček's visit to the Bertramka with the Stössels on 7 April 1928. Dr Vlastimil Blažek, director of the Czechoslovak Mozart Society, stands on the right.

27 Janáček's Hukvaldy cottage, acquired at the end of 1921, with the upstairs room added in 1928 for Mrs Stösslová.

28 The 'Hotel-Pension Karel IV.', the modest hotel in Smíchov, Prague, where Janáček regularly stayed during his visits from 1919 onwards.

29 A Hukvaldy postcard (c 1930s) showing Janáček's 'villa' (cf 27), his birthplace (the school where his father taught), and views of the ruined castle.

30 A Brno postcard issued during Janáček's lifetime: 'A picture postcard is being printed here in Brno. Views of Brno, my music, some words about the Glagolitic Mass and then my head' (661: 20 May 1928).

31 'In the evening we'll go to the French restaurant.' Janáček hoped to take Kamila Stösslová to the nearby French restaurant in the Zemský dům [Regional House] to celebrate his knighthood from the Belgian King and his 'eleven-year friendship' with Stösslová (see 441: 6 May 1927).

32 'However it's raining here now. A sculptor [Julius Pelikán] is sculpting me, the painter Ondrůšek is painting; and I sit for them at home! (396 15 June 1926). Janáček's friend František Ondrůšek completed and dated his pastel study of Janáček at Hukvaldy the next day.

33 'Am I listening to a woman or a tree? I think it's a woman, like Mrs Kamila': Janáček's comments on the bookplate which Eduard Milén, the stage-designer of the Brno *Cunning Little Vixen*, had made for him (see **247**: 2 August 1924).

'I'm sitting in that carriage like a pasha; they stuffed me [with food] in London so much that I was ill from it afterwards. Whereas at the seaside, my Kamilka, I would so like to have sat with you. The hot sun on the warmed-up stones: you would have enjoyed lying down there' (**608**: 12 March 1928). Janáček's comments on the photographs Jan Mikota took of him on his return from England, May 1926 (34, *left*) and notating the waves in Flushing, Holland (35, *below*).

36 Otto and Rudolf Stössel aged four and seven respectively. Kamila Stösslová sent Janáček this photograph on 8 June 1920.

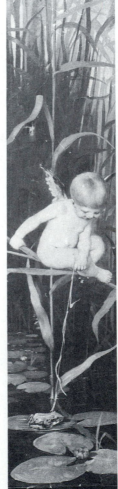

'In the upper living-room I want to have those two children, a writing-desk, a communal table, a comfortable bed, perhaps of brass; a wardrobe with mirrored doors; a marble washstand; *four chairs, each from a different part of the world and from a different period* – and the wish that Mrs Kamila would often sit and lie there contentedly. (**607**: 10–11 March 1928). 'Those two children' were František Dvořák's *Dallying Cherubs* (37) which he acquired from the Stössels in 1927.

the place and pick it up – that dear little Negress of mine. Then I'll reach her. I'm sad today in quiet happiness.

Sweet dreams.

Yours for ever

L.

651 Brno, 9 May 1928, at night

My dear Kamilka

Yes, yes to take care of oneself, not to work. She gives advice to others and doesn't carry it out herself. It's good that it's got a little cooler now because I know that you'll not bake yourself too much on the rocks.

Today I dreamt a lot about you. We were together in some sort of large room; full of young people dancing. I said to myself that's something for us. Then again on the Hukvaldy footpaths; I still see one of them, the one on which we ran down the hill to avoid some sort of large group. Night at least makes up for what the day doesn't grant. I'll recover somehow. Now, after work, I'm like a violin whose strings have been loosened. So still be cheerful for me too. – Then when I catch you up there'll be another wedding.[1]

Keep those garnets until there'll be time to read them to me.[2] But I know that I'll rather gaze at your mouth; rather let my longing thoughts wander over your little face. I'll let it go in one ear and out the other. And let it end how it will. I don't care what the others think when I've got my love story which is simply impossible to bring to an end. And if the end does come perhaps only the two of us will like it. So what have you really said about our photograph where we're together? You must surely have said something; what?

I know, I know, where it would all stop hurting. Well, the time will come. I can't move now. I'm waiting for a telegram from Berlin[3] at any moment, from Hukvaldy to say that they've now built the staircase, [I have to go] to Sliač, somewhere in Slovakia in search of some folk musician and here in Brno [I have] these copyists, stinking of beer and smoke!

And in the distance that little Negress of mine is smiling. You know where my heart would most like to go!

I'd like to have seen that butterfly on your round ankle on the

1 A pun: *veselá* (cheerful) becoming *veselka* (wedding).
2 This is obscure, but could be an allusion to love stories (in Czech, 'red books'; garnets are also red).
3 About the proposed production of *The Makropulos Affair*, see p.266, fn.5.

rocks! I'd have caught it. Or rather, I'd have gazed on that burnt ankle and I'd have thought to myself how sometimes a butterfly has it better than a person! Well perhaps Baker[1] won't go to Písek. Surely she'll just appear in the pictures at the cinema? You'll laugh a lot. Now there are the icemen;[2] today it's freezing here. No thought that you should go off somewhere!

I'll promise you *yes* three times that I'll look after myself. What will you give me for it? Yourself? Again, in the same way that I have the moon, the little star, the sun? And a sky nearby? Oh, I'm a fish out of water; it dreams only of the fresh water, its fins dried and stuck to its body, its mouth beseechingly open! – I've got white teeth now![3] But not such little pearls as you have!

Keep well!

Yours for ever

L.

652   Brno, 10 May 1928, at night

My dear Kamila

I'm already puzzled by what's going on with the post. Day after day I go myself with a letter to the station post office.[4] I'm there at 10 o'clock in the morning. The express train from Brno departs only at 4.30 in the afternoon. How's it possible then that you wouldn't get a letter the next day!

I'm not ill; I just want to sleep and sleep after that hard work!

[...]

And Luhačovice! 'We' wouldn't need more than that single room – your husband, for those moments when he comes to see you, could sleep on the divan; you'd need only a single bed for your own comfort.

It's therefore a daily saving of Kč 15 and for three weeks 15 x 21

Kč 315.[5]

But where will the bedroom with the single bed be? It's not healthy on the ground floor; the attic's for doves. So still get that settled. It's

1 The black American singer Josephine Baker (1906–79) was making a tour of central Europe, and arrived in Prague on 16 April 1928.
2 The 'icemen' (*ledoví muži*) were the cold days after the first warmth of spring, sometimes coinciding with the feasts originally of SS Pancras, Servatius and Boniface (12, 13 and 14 May respectively).
3 Janáček had 'black teeth' on 30 April (643) from his red throat disinfectant.
4 The large Brno post office beside the railway station, where Janáček had a postbox (see Glossary: 'post').
5 Janáček's multiplication digits omitted.

impossible for you to stay alone in Luhačovice. I'd worry and you'd not have peace or quiet. They'd ask why you're there alone. And there'd be conjectures by the sackful.

Now fix it up with Rudi in good time. For him it will be downright miserable to be in a strange place, among strangers. So if he can get useful employment with your sister that would be pleasanter for him. On the other hand, the harder the bread – the healthier. I remember myself how sad I was when they took me in my ninth[1] year from my home to Brno. But I was among students, I soon got used to it. I think that you [must] have received both letters today, because I wrote on Monday [7 May] and on Tuesday. Generally I write every day; except I join Saturday with Sunday, since the post office doesn't deliver on Sunday.

Today my players told me that they'll play me those *Intimate Letters* on Friday (tomorrow) week. I'm curious about your influence on that piece. I've already reminded you once that either it will all burn and even the music will flare up, or that only my love will burn and it will burn up everything beside it.[2] Then I'll write to Mr Kodl.

It's cold here, as in winter. Today it snowed and the north wind blew, cutting like a knife. And you with the washing? Aren't you afraid of catching a cold? [...]

653   Brno, 11 May 1928, at night

My dear Kamila

And you write about Hukvaldy in June.

I'll see how it is with the building there; I'll know again on Monday [14 May]. I'd go and have a look there and see to what's necessary for living in it.

But how could you be in June in Hukvaldy when you've got doubts about July in Luhačovice? However, it would be better in June; from Luhačovice, after the spa, it would be more difficult to travel somewhere else with used underwear, dresses. It is better to sort oneself out again at home. We'll see how best to arrange it.

On 9 June I still have to be in Brno; they're laying the foundation stone for the university;[3] my chorus will be sung during it.[4]

1 Janáček left home soon after his twelfth birthday.
2 If the reminding was by letter it has not survived.
3 The Masaryk University in Brno was founded in 1919. Teaching began in temporary buildings; the foundation stone laid on 9 June 1928 (see 681) was for the Law Faculty, which was ready for lectures in January 1932.
4 See 618.

And that accommodation in Luhačovice. Above all it must be healthy, dry, light. The number of beds is beside the point. Rather pay more than live badly. You'll get over those extra Kč 300. We can afford it now.

And now a joke. If we were to live there together, I'd say that one bed would be enough!

Sometimes two people need amazingly little space, and at other times they need to be about half an hour away from one other!

I fear that in Světlov[1] they've got single rooms on the ground floor. That on no account! Do you now have all my letters? Should someone or other read some of them he'd think to himself: 'Oh-ho, he's now talking as if a single room would be enough!' How many times someone could get the wrong impression from written and even spoken words! As for us, we'd huddle up together like birds in a tiny nest. How many flowers sometimes stick out from it! I love you, Kamilka! –

[...]

Oh, my little sun's still so high! But I'll go there one day to that place where it sets, where it's near, where I'd catch hold of it in my arms. And I'll catch it and make up a bed [for it] and not let go even if it were to burn, cry out, sigh, thrash around! No, my little sun, I won't let you go when you fall into the black night and rest until the morning. So you know who's my little sun? You know where I'd make a bed for it? And it may or may not cry;

but it would burn; it's full of red burning blood. It's my Kamila! You're so good that you want to write more often; I need it. Those are the only pleasant warm moments of conversation, by letter with you.

I was happier today with my copyist; when he could do no more it's a wonder I didn't overturn the rocking-chair.

[...]

I feel that only true love creates warmth in the home; otherwise even at best it's only habit – which is always cold, indifferent. – From Berlin they wanted a *Song of Peace*[2] from me. Four express telegrams

---

1 One of the *pensions* in Luhačovice. Stösslová stayed there in August 1927 (see 475, 476).
2 In a letter of 26 April 1928 (BmJA, D 640) the editor of the Berlin newspaper *8 Uhr-Abendblatt* asked Janáček to contribute his view about the conditions in which a 'Hymn of Peace' might be created. Two further telegrams urged his reply, which was published on 26 May 1928 in the *8 Uhr-Abendblatt* alongside those of eleven other composers including Respighi, Schoenberg, Zemlinsky, Charpentier and Bruneau. Janáček's brief reply pointed out that the hymns of the French and Russian revolutions had been 'born in rivers of human blood' and that a hymn of peace would arise only when the killing of people ended (see Janáček 1990, 365, fn.)

back and forth scattered their wishes. Idiots! Can one nourish love where there's none? Is it possible to drum up enthusiasm when one gets goose pimples from all that one sees? I'm already looking forward to Friday [18 May] when they'll play me my *Intimate Letters*! I'd send you a telegram, but it would wake you in the night. I won't do that to Kamilka!

Sleep well!

Yours for ever

L.

[...]

654   Brno, 12–13 May 1928

My dear Kamilka

I felt something unpleasant at the same time as the visit of that sergeant.

I didn't want to ask you who's lending you books when you won't say so yourself. You've said so and sorted it out yourself.

How could he himself simply dare to go to you on your own! To bring you books, to sit down and for a long time!

Now at last, Kamilka, make short work of such people.

You caught cold at the dressmaker's, therefore your head and eyes started aching.

And your little white teeth certainly know how to bite well. I on the other hand would like to bite into you, but not bite through, not wound. Just like my little dog when out of joy and devotion he wants to bite and his teeth simply tremble.

[...]

That Luhačovice Friday–feast-day[1] is proof that I don't belong among the 'icy'. But I don't know that story about the cook. Tell it to me. I thought that Baker[2] would be only in the cinema. For you the sun alone is everything! And for me you alone are everything. Now that you're writing often, for me it's like a hot bath. I hardly get dry when I plunge again into the warm, fragrant water. They would be sad moments if I couldn't speak to you in this way. I don't know what would remain of me!

[...] Do you know why I'm sad when I don't have work? I have lots of vacant time then, only you near me could fill it joyfully with your presence. No-one else. And now you're so far. I'm not someone who

1 See Glossary: 'Friday–feast-day'.
2 See p.272, fn.1.

simply sighs. I want to have a keen word, I want to taste blood, I want to catch a sparkling glance, to feel your firm arms, your hot lips; your movements supple like a little lizard. And now I'm missing it all! That's why I go around out of sorts. So I must get over these bad moments. Pleasant dreams come to you and to me too!

Yours for ever

L.

12 May 1928 at night

[...] You wrote that the visit of that sergeant annoyed you. And – now that I've thought it over, it annoys me even more than you.

If a policeman comes into the house, he's always two-faced. You never know what he really wants. He has the job of fulfilling secretly, unobtrusively, what he was ordered [to do].

During Austrian rule a decent man kept miles away from a policeman. Nowadays on the one hand he protects the state from all sorts of unsavoury people. But he has yet another duty which I can tell you only in person.

So for us he's now more congenial than during Austrian rule, but even so – there's no need to have contacts with him! Why exactly did it have to be him who lent you books, how did it come about?

You know well that that male is hanging on your every step – why do you still borrow – books from him!

You like reading, you like reading your love stories; I don't hold this against you. But so that you don't have to borrow books from anyone, I'll pay for a subscription for you for the magazine *Zvon*. You'll get an issue every Friday and in it there are serializations of about three novels. You'll have more than enough for a week. Will you do it for my sake? The whole morning that incident weighed on my mind. It annoyed you and me still further. – I'm making preparations so you could come to Hukvaldy perhaps in June before *Luhačovice*. Keep well.

Yours for ever

L.

13 May 1928

[...]

655   Brno, 14 May 1928

My dear Kamilka

I thought that a letter would come from you today, on Monday. It didn't. And I could have done with it. What was going on at your place on Saturday and Sunday? Next week, either on Monday or Tuesday,[1] I'll hop off to Hukvaldy for a day. To measure the windows for curtains and see for myself how it's all going. They're already doing the staircase; they say the work will soon be finished now. I have parquet flooring, but who in the village will polish it! I'll now make arrangements somehow so that from the second half of June everything will be in order – for a dear guest, Mrs Kamila. I'm curious what it's going to look like now. Just don't think that you'll be walking into a little castle! Think more of a cottage so that you'll have a rather pleasanter surprise.

But prepare those three carpet strips. You're able, of course, to run around barefoot on the tiling [and] pick up a cold; but at my place I want you to go about warmly and softly. For you to be as if at home. I really don't know how you'll arrange your departure from Písek. I'm curious. Have you decided yet what to do with Rudi? It will depend on that.

No news from Berlin.[2] I'm also no longer waiting for any. Universal Edition have acknowledged that they took 2% more for *The Makropulos Affair*.[3] They'll reimburse me.

Today I was 'gladdened' by the hasty visit of a young lady (allegedly), who gave the servant something wrapped up 'for the Maestro!' and quickly disappeared. I open it. Poems. One on me, 'L.J.', a second 'after Janáček's *Šárka*'. Altogether there were perhaps thirty poems, luxuriously printed. Those poems about me show that she knows more about me, that she knows me quite intimately. The name of the poetess:

Božena Fmarja Věrná
from Brno![4]

It's some sort of assumed name. Perhaps I'll get to know what lies behind it. People run after you, run after me. Just let us be together at our own place without noticing all these people running around! No-one will make us run away from our heaven.

But one thing I know, is that I'm the reason why they run after you. And I don't like that.

Thursday [17 May] is a holiday[5] again; they don't deliver mail.

1 By his next letter (*656:15 May 1928), he had settled for Tuesday 22 May, returning to Brno on 24 May.
2 About the proposed production of *The Makropulos Affair*, see p.266, fn.5.
3 See 650.
4 Božena Věrná (1901–67), teacher, poet and translator. She published most of her poems privately. She sent her first poem dedicated to Janáček on 24 January 1925 (see Janáček 1990, 369, fn.)
5 Ascension Day.

One thing I'm surprised at is that so far they haven't printed those few words about the Bertramka!¹ I don't know what's behind it and don't want to ask.

I'm getting my lecture² in order for – October in Prague! Isn't that rather soon? But people from distant parts will be at it³ – so that Janáček's intellect must be displayed too. At your place I always hide it. That feeling is more pleasant; especially when we like someone, when that feeling is as vital to us as bread, and also when we've found it in someone for ourselves.

Forgive me if in yesterday's letter I preached a lot to you. I know that I won't put anything right by it and that Kamila knows well that we two must be without any social stigma. 'They're made just for one another!' – so people must say.

Keep well, my little soul. Sleep well.

Yours for ever

L.

Kamila Stösslová to Leoš Janáček, Písek, 15 May 1928

Dear Maestro

I didn't write yesterday because from morning till evening I was chopping wood and now [...] it's so sore that I can't even write. [...] However I slept like a bagpiper [i.e. like a log] from evening till morning I was so tired. [...] Reading your long letter I think to myself in spirit that sometimes I make you worried with every silly thing I write. Don't send me anything none of that *Zvon*⁴ I have so much to read that I won't read it all even during the summer. And reading doesn't interest me that much now except in winter alright? With Hukvaldy you've misunderstood I thought only in July instead of Luhačovice in June I can't move. [...] This evening I'm going to a concert but on my own. I don't want to go with my friend she's boring I'll sit somewhere on my own and listen. [...] Wouldn't you like to come to me as a governess? The whole time it would be you can't do that what have you done this time?; I'd often get a spanking

---

1 Janáček wrote his article about the villa Bertramka on 1 May; it was published in *Lidové noviny* on 20 May (see p.263, fn.2.).
2 See p.268, fn.4.
3 The music section of the conference had speakers coming from as far as South America and Japan. England was represented by Douglas Kennedy, Hungary by Bartók.
4 Janáček had offered to pay for a subscription to the magazine *Zvon* (see 654).

wouldn't I? [...] So that magazine only in the winter alright? Now I simply want to talk with you all summer long alright? Keep well.

Greetings

K.

657   Brno, 16 May 1928, at night

My dear Kamilka

I've got your letter to hand – and I'm not opening it. I'm frightened that you're angry in it because of the policeman, because of those borrowed books![1] Will I be right? Now I'm opening the letter. Ah, not at all! 'I didn't write – because I was chopping wood!' Splendid exercise. Only that once I got injured. And you got a blister! So still no anger! What further? 'And I slept like a bagpiper'. And do you know how a bagpiper sleeps? I've never seen that myself. So I must come and have a look at you one day. But I'll see how a little devil sleeps. It's already coming now. 'You make me worried with silly things you sometimes write...' And you're right. So then no anger! So then [you'll get] *Zvon* when the new subscription year starts. Well, good. My little soul's content now. You know well how to calm storms. You don't know how to be angry with me. And what you now write about Hukvaldy! I understood it just the way it was written. I wouldn't want to be in Luhačovice, and you in Hukvaldy, would I? And don't you know yet what to do with Rudi? And I still don't know where that room up six steps is. Is it *next to* your previous one? Is it *above* it? Is it below? Just as long as it's not on the ground floor!

I go off on Tuesday [22 May] to Hukvaldy; I stay there until 23 May, 24 May at the latest. And then back to Brno at once. Over the holidays[2] they're giving *Káťa Kabanová*[3] on Saturday [26 May], *Jenůfa* on Sunday and the Sinfonietta on Monday.

On 9 June the university foundation stone is being dedicated.

On 10 June I want to go off to Hukvaldy to put everything in order for the comfort of my Kamila. On 1 July I'll already be in Luhačovice for three weeks at the most.

And now my dear Mrs Kamila, make arrangements as you can. But write to me clearly. When I arrive from Hukvaldy I'll know when it will be possible to live there.

---

1 See 654.
2 The Whitsun weekend.
3 The performance of *Káťa Kabanová* on 26 May 1928 was to mark the ceremonial opening of the Exhibition of Contemporary Culture in Brno (see Glossary).

[...]
Yours for ever
L.

[...] And in connection with the photograph: did you say: that would be my future husband? I'd have said that I don't want any wife other than the one you see beside me!

658 Brno, 17 May 1928, at night

My dear Kamilka

That was a real holiday today![1] The copyist pestered me in the morning, and again in the afternoon.

And then I went to the Špilberk[2] for a walk! Guess with whom?

As soon as I left the house a pleasant spirit suddenly attached itself to me out of nowhere. Right then; so we'll go together. I won't be lonely.

And at once the spirit [said]: 'So go on, say something!'

I caught sight of her; she trotted along prettily beside me the whole time. We went through the streets quickly and were soon in the park. I looked at her furtively. She was almost as big as me. I thought to myself: 'I ought to know you well!' As if I'd once perhaps confessed my love to you. Yes, I remember. It was a hot day; one's blood heated from walking. And she about ten paces in front, was also bowed to the earth. Then out of the blue she simply threw in: 'and what would you do with me if I were yours?' And at that moment the mists cleared. Suddenly the thought flashed through my head like lightning. Suddenly I was standing so close to her. I was swallowed up in looking at her and wanted her to look at me; and a golden bridge suddenly sprang from her eyes to mine and going along that bridge I found my – Kamila! So you know now who I was with for the two hours of the walk. I didn't even look at the magnificent view, at the distant countryside. Lost in thought, my eyes turned to the ground, I walked quite slowly and that dear spirit of yours always beside me. I was glad of it and content, even in my deserted state. And what were you doing? It was in the afternoon from 3 to 5. And I always complain to myself, 'how sadly year after year goes by for you!'

1 An ironic comment on the way Janáček spent Ascension Day, a state holiday in Czechoslovakia at this time.
2 German Spielberg: a hill in Brno with a fortified castle at the top. The medieval royal castle was a notorious Habsburg prison from 1621 until 1862, when the buildings were turned into barracks and the slopes made into a public park. It is a fifteen-minute walk from the Janáčeks' house.

Another life is flowing past here within reach. Perhaps a hectic one, but nevertheless life and not stagnant water! –

So tomorrow they'll play through at least part of my–your *Intimate Letters* for me. I can't wait for it now. Mr Kodl will know about it at once.

Otherwise I feel a bit like pickled herrings in a barrel. How can they dream of the distant sea when they're crammed together? But I want to dream and I want to be in the waves of the sea! I want this, even if it's only the silver waves of the Otava! You know them? But I think you don't. For you're always saying: 'but they're nothing!' But you're wrong. And it was like plunging into a submissive little wave. What if it were the sea of all your charms! If only once the dam wall, as somewhere in America, would give way,[1] and that sea would drown me! – That's the end now of today's little talk. Sleep well.

I want to have such wild dreams as last night.

Yours for ever

L.

659   Brno, 18–19 May 1928

My dear Kamila

When you're pleased about something, how would I not be pleased [too]? So now it's all sorted out with Rudi to general satisfaction. In particular you won't be deserted and isolated. Believe me, I'm always anxious to think of you so deserted, all by yourself for whole weeks almost! That's [alright] for a person who has his own weighty thoughts in his head and they are sufficient for him. But you, full of feeling, good little lamb! It's a torment for you. So you'll have something to think about, and you'll see, at least, what the lad's up to, how he's getting on. Now, at 3 o'clock, the Moravian Quartet should be coming to my place to play *my–your* composition! I'm already panting to hear it. –

So they played me the first and the third movement! And Kamila, it will be beautiful, strange, unrestrained, inspired, a composition beyond all the usual conventions! Together I think that we'll triumph!

1 Although it took place thirty years earlier, Janáček was presumably referring to the widely-publicized Johnstown flood, the only instance to that date of a dam breaking in the United States that would have been news in Europe. Johnstown, Pennsylvania, then a leading steel-making centre, is a city about seventy miles east of Pittsburgh at the head-waters of the Conemaugh river. The city was practically destroyed on 31 May 1889 and 2300 persons were drowned when a major upstream reservoir burst. I am indebted to Dr Glen Bauer for this information.

It's my first composition which sprang from directly experienced feeling. Before then I composed only from things remembered, this piece, *Intimate Letters*, was written in fire. Earlier pieces only in hot ash.

The composition will be dedicated to you; you're the reason for it and to compose it was the greatest pleasure for me.

I wrote at once to Mr Kodl.[1] Get Professor Vymetal to invite the Moravian Quartet, whose leader is Mr Kudláček, professor at the [Brno] Conservatory, to play it in Písek in the autumn. They'll be glad to do it on account of Mr Ševčík[2] if for no other reason. We'll both be happy when it goes round the world. –

I'm glad that you've got everything decided now. So first to Luhačovice, then to Hukvaldy. So these are our plans. Who knows whether everything will soon be decided differently. This evening Z. came up after me saying that she wanted to have a few words with me. I said: 'Alright!' She said not until the morning. I went to my room upstairs in total calm. I don't know what she wants. After all, our relationship is such that no-one can have anything against it other than that we two live in the closest friendship with one another. We won't let anyone prevent it.

I'll go to sleep calmly and will finish writing the letter tomorrow. Sleep well too.

Yours for ever

L.

Brno, 18 May 1928 at night

Today, 19 May, morning. Two months ago Z. wrote a letter to my sister[3] full of false statements. When she knew that I was going to Hukvaldy – she told me about the letter. My sister of course answered her appropriately. That was the exchange of views today! It's all over.

Yours for ever

L.

1 Janáček's letter to Kodl (18 May 1928; see Janáček 1990, 373, fn.) virtually repeats this letter to Stösslová, though suggests 'a nice programme' for the autumn concert in Písek: his two string quartets together with the Violin Sonata and the *Fairy Tale* for cello and piano.
2 See p.58, fn.4.
3 Josefa Dohnalová (see Glossary).

660 Brno, 19 May 1928

My dear Kamilka

It was when those anonymous letters came from Písek.[1] In hot haste Z. immediately informed my sister about them; it was lie upon lie. And now of course she's afraid that I'll read her letter in Hukvaldy. So she told it me today from memory. Whereupon I gave her my opinion calmly, and by all appearances my sister also gave her a piece of her own mind. The affair is thus disposed of — again for the time being. I'm absolutely delighted with the quartet composed 'after our stories'. I was anxious whether I would climb higher with that work. And I went higher.

How could I not revel in joy at that time when it seemed to me that the earth was shaking beneath me, that the sun was rocking, that everything around me was turning in confusion? How was that furnace possible < two? words obliterated > [...] ever to be cooled? It makes every note glow. Then they flow like steel radiates heat when it's hot. You'll certainly obliterate these lines. Well, do what you will. And some places whisper so tenderly — well, a confession of love and a language of longing, the language of longing never satisfied. You'll certainly obliterate this too. Do what you will. It's the truth. On Friday [25 May] I'll certainly be already in Brno again. In the afternoon they'll play the other movements of the work for me. I think that they won't fall short of the ones I've listened to.

[...]

One Friday is the dearest of all Fridays for me.[2] Do you remember where that table stood? That you were seated at it against the wall and I against the window. But do you remember where that low couch stood in [our] heaven? That it was near the mirror and behind it that glass case with the decorative knick-knacks? Ah, lips, my fiery, blood-red lips! If only I were allowed to kiss you! You'll also obliterate that?

If that room's upstairs,[3] then it will be dry. If it's enough for you, it will be fine. If I'm in Luhačovice earlier, I'll have a look there at once. And Rudi? So nothing changes at your home; you'll have fewer cares. He'll set out then on a commercial career, in which there's not so much physical labour as there is with those electrical machines.

And I'll be completely happy only when I really will be your shadow all the time, when that shadow will breathe your warmth,

---

1 See 634.
2 See Glossary: 'Friday–feast-day'.
3 i.e. the room that Stösslová was planning to take at Luhačovice (see 653).

when it will feel your soft hand, when you'll intoxicate me with the fragrance of your beautiful body. You'll certainly obliterate that too. But why bother when it's true.

I leave early on Tuesday morning [22 May]. Write then to Brno so that I'll get a letter in Brno on Thursday evening. I'll always give you news about myself.

Yours for ever

L.

661 Brno, 20 May 1928, at night

My dear Kamilka

You'll get this letter on Tuesday[1] and the next one I don't know when. Believe me, I've grown so listless that I wouldn't be able to stand it in Brno any longer.

I enclose those few words about Bertramka.[2] 'Madam' is of course you. Everyone will take it so although it doesn't specifically say so.

A picture postcard is being printed here in Brno. Views of Brno, my music, some words about the Glagolitic Mass and then my head [see Plate 30]. When I find out where it can be bought I'll send you one too. Today's Sunday and I haven't been out of the house the whole day! Only now in the evening I went to look at the pictures[3] in the café. That's rather like you at the cinema. There was one picture there: a head with black hair turned against the sun. It calls out: 'Oh sun, sun!' and I exclaimed 'It's Kamila!'

My dances[4] are coming out in print now; the printer[5] from Prague came to see me in the morning. You were surely on the rocks today! It was hot, but windy here. Now I'm reading all your letters which I haven't yet burnt. With a heavy heart, I'll sacrifice to the pure fire the most intimate, which many people would take the wrong way. I'll keep the rest.

Today I learnt from that Prague gentleman more about Anežka[6] the hunchback. She was the youngest of four sisters. One of the sisters

---

1 Since the post was not delivered on Whit Monday.
2 See p.278, fn.1.
3 i.e. in the newspapers and magazines (see p.268, fn.2.)
4 The *Lachian Dances*, published 'by July' (Simeone 1991, 243) by the Hudební matice in Prague. Janáček's introduction 'My Lašsko' is dated 22 May 1928. Since Janáček went to Hukvaldy on 22 May, it seems that the first thing he did, before writing to Stösslová again, was to write the preface.
5 The dances were printed by the Průmyslová tiskárna, Prague.
6 See 534.

was the wife of Professor Daneš,[1] who was recently run over by a car in America.

Fibich died at the right time; it's said that he'd had enough of the hunchback and that their relationship was to have been broken off. As is well known, he went out of the theatre to the island[2] in a sweat, caught a chill and was dead in three days. So he'd had his fill! What's that? That's something I don't understand at all. He surely didn't love her enough for it have been a great love, unto death. I foresaw it. The Schulz family was well regarded in Prague.[3]

No, to have one's fill is something I cannot and don't know how to imagine. I've got some sort of presentiment that tomorrow, Monday [21 May], I'll get an important letter.

I'm simply overwhelmed by the passion of that work of 'ours', that quartet.

Hasn't Mr Kodl been to see you yet? I wrote to him about it at once.

The whole of this afternoon I sat out in the sun in my garden. And my thoughts kept on stopping like a heavy lorry when it goes uphill. So now I'll receive no news from you; instead I'm going to remember you so warmly that it will ring in your ears.

Sleep well.

Yours for ever

L.

662 Hukvaldy, 23 May 1928

My dear Kamilka

So they've built it well for me. I think that you will also like it here. A comfortable staircase, the sitting-room on the first floor is

5.70 [metres] long

5.25 [metres] wide

so you'll know what size carpets to get. The room has nice, light-coloured ash parquet flooring.

It's beautiful here; the sun shines; I'd like to stay longer; but on Friday [25 May] in the afternoon they're coming again to play through more movements of 'our' quartet. So I'm leaving here tomorrow at noon.

1 Dr Jiří Daneš (1880–1928), professor of geography at Charles University, died in Los Angeles.
2 Fibich had a flat on the Žofín island (now Slovanský ostrov) in the middle of the Vltava.
3 Anežka Schulzová's father was the literary critic and historian Professor Ferdinand Schulz; her mother was the sister of Edvard and Julius Gregr, prominent political figures of the time and co-founders of the newspaper *Národní listy*.

Today they'll connect up the electric lighting for me.

What about you, my little soul, have you been warming yourself on the rocks?

Over the holidays I've got lots of my music in Brno.[1] What will happen after that I don't know.

When it's all painted here, I'll need to come here and arrange the furniture, curtains, carpets etc so that before I go off to Luhačovice everything will be prepared and ready 'for my black queen'.

Keep well.

Yours for ever

L.

663   Hukvaldy, 24 May 1928

My dear Kamila

At least a few lines before my departure. The electricity's on; tomorrow they start painting; then the parquet and putting everything in the right place.

So now the carpets, and don't let Mr Kretschmer forget that writing-desk. There are enough eiderdowns here. After all, it will be hot then. My sister's already thinking about chickens. And for the rest we'll go and feast wherever it will be best. Already tomorrow I've got a rehearsal in Brno again; I hope they'll play through my quartet to the end.

That is what really draws me away from here.

Greetings

your

L.

664   Brno, 25 May 1928

My dear Kamila

So I've got back. I was needed there; the bricklayers were just leaving, the electricians have finished.

[...]

My sister was scared of the cooking; so I say you'll cook a bit more of what you cook for yourself and for desserts etc we'll always send to the hotel. The main thing is for you to like it. Around 15 June I'll take another look at Hukvaldy and arrange the furniture.

Today they finished playing the whole of the your—my work. The

1 See 657.

players are bowled over by it; they begged me to be able to play it first at the exhibition in Brno.[1] I consented. Universal Edition's interested in it; they'll probably print it.[2] I'll invite them for the main rehearsal on 11 June.

And now Kamilka, decide how it should be printed: Either:

Dedicated to Mrs Kamila S.

or *Dedicated to Mrs Kamila Stösslová,*

or *Dedicated to Mrs Kamila Neumannová S.*

I'd like to have your maiden name.

[...]

From Prague they requested the manuscript of what I wrote about that 'little bell'.[3] They've put it into a nice little frame and will hang it in the Bertramka. People will ask there 'which lady? What sort of lady? Mrs Dr Janáčková?[4] Is she young, dark, with dark eyes and hair? Sort of chubby?' Yes, yes it's her!

I'll send this letter to you *express*; you'll get it separately on Sunday [27 May]. Just don't let Mr Kretschmer delay; by 15 June I'd like to have everything in order.

So keep well!

Yours for ever

L.

666 [undated, postmarked Brno, 29 May 1928]

My dear Kamilka

I didn't have a good day today. I caught a chill – and got lumbago. What if it were a sort of black gander,[5] then I'd be able to bear the pain. But so what!

It's so like the pain you get from lying on the damp earth.

I'm glad that those 'gala' theatre and concert openings are over. It was a disgrace.[6] [...] < [7] >

Oh I wish that this month was already over! Oh no, it mustn't run away. The following one would run away too and that ought to be

---

1 Janáček had originally wanted the quartet to be first performed in Písek (see 629); for performance details see Glossary: 'String Quartet no.2'.

2 It was not Universal Edition but Hudební matice which published the work, ten years later. Universal Edition published none of Janáček's chamber music.

3 i.e. Janáček's article 'Sounding the alarm' (see p.278, fn.1.)

4 A central European style of address for a wife which included her husband's title(s) (see also 586).

5 A pun: *houser* = (1) lumbago; (2) a gander.

6 Attendance was poor.

7 The bottom portion of all four sides of this letter has been cut off.

the very nicest, after all! Did you cross out lots of what I wrote to you of that wild mood?[1] I don't know what boiled up in me. In fact I know: it's that infinite love for you, which is everything to me, everything about you, everything which is you, which lives in you < > [...] Oh that such a moment would come as in yesterday's dream. Will it ever? Will it be, although at the last moment we would have perhaps to remember ourselves? Let's get at least to that moment! Let's get right to the very foretaste of that infinite happiness! Don't resist until that moment, when I'd cleave to your lips, to feel your hot body, until that passionate < >

You'll certainly burn this letter.

But no fire will destroy what was felt when it was written. How eagerly I wait for your letter. You again will avoid the answer that I'd so like to read.

And there'll be no end to my longing for you, there'll be no end even if it were to be fulfilled. I feel so much that you're the beloved child which the good-natured fates have sent, which I had to know < > [...]

667 Brno, 29 May 1928

My dear Kamilka

Why have you got something into your head again! You know that I'll never betray what lives in me to anyone, not even to my sister.

I'll see to it now that you'll have a good time in Hukvaldy, that it will be nice and warm in our little house. I'll tell my sister in good time what you are to me, that you have been and that you are my consolation in the bitter moments of life. She'll invite you herself and will know how you've been maligned. That's past now and we won't dwell on it.

She gave me the slanderous letter herself;[2] I've got it with me, but I don't even want to read it – if only because it was written about two months ago – at the time when that anonymous letter came from Písek. So let's not talk about it and only when we'll be sitting contentedly in our cottage will we say so very many other things to each other. I'll write to my sister when I've finished all the work with the tradesmen. Then write to her too. Remember that she's getting on for eighty-six years old. It's difficult for her to understand everything.

I'd most like to dedicate it to

1 Stösslová in fact destroyed the whole letter, leaving only the envelope (*665).
2 See 659–60.

Mrs Kamila Janáčková!

That is true and God grant that it be real and unalterable. Would you be content too?

And what you hear here and there – what gives pain and no relief?

And don't think that at home anyone should dare allude to you even with a single word! God protect everyone!

Mine, wholly mine, heartily beloved Kamila! In that letter it apparently said that anyway one day, and soon, you'll leave me! You know then what she looks forward to. I thought about it and said to myself that you're truer, deeper, more serious than these gullible people think. I smiled at that wish. It's often possible; it was so with my sister; her husband was twenty-five years younger, he left her and married another woman.[1]

I don't think of it, I love you too much. And the two of us won't think about it. We want to love one another, we want to belong to one another, we want to experience with total passion the fact that we'll declare we belong to each other and for ever, inseparably.

I know that those are your thoughts too. Write back saying yes, yes!

Yours for ever

L.

I did nevertheless read through to myself that letter of Z. to my sister. As a result, I've revealed to my sister 'my happiness at home', about which I've not said a word to her up till now. I also wrote to her [saying] what binds us together. What you are to me! More about it some other time.

668   Brno [30 May 1928], at night

My dear Kamilka

I thought that a letter would come from you today; it's Wednesday.

Yesterday and today I've been in a terribly serious mood. I didn't suspect up to now what I am in the eyes of Z. Only from her letter to my sister did she show me what she really is and how cruelly she slanders me. I, who never talked about her, who concealed all her rudenesses, who did nothing bad to her, even in words! The die is cast. She has no notion that her letter is in my hands. I didn't even want to read it, just to keep it and yesterday, without thinking, I stretched out for it and read it. Well, enough of that! —

---

1 See Glossary: 'Dohnalová, Josefa (Adolfína)'.

Kamilka, today I ordered a washstand with a marble top. But some sort of mirror will be necessary. I'd like to have at least a reproduction of a small Venetian mirror, the type that has that gold frame with all sorts of twiddly bits. Will it be possible to find one? Now, my little soul, you must see to that with me so that we'll have it nice and comfy in Hukvaldy. I know what size curtains are needed; I'll buy them here and send them on. We'll put them up there.

I've got you in my mind all the time and if I could carry you off and always have you with me from now on, that would be the proper conclusion to everything. And so I'm like a bird which cannot fly and which simply runs around on the ground.

I'm hurrying up with everything here so that nothing would keep me in Brno. So that I could close the door behind me.

Here also nothing gives me pleasure; they perform my things and I don't even go along.[1] Perhaps it will pass, soon perhaps I'll calmly sort everything out for myself well and truly.

How she offended even my old sister, put the blame on her! She can't come any more to Hukvaldy; that's why I now organize everything myself. –

And a funny incident. A forest vandal, otherwise a decent fellow, cut down six fir trees in my forest. I think I've already written to you about it.[2] Today he asked me by letter to forgive him, not to take him to court. I'd already arranged beforehand merely that the mayor would have him summoned and would reprimand him. –

I'm now curious how you'll answer my yearning letters. [I think] that Kamila will avoid an answer? That she'll say 'when the time comes'! Would what was promised now come true. I'd like now to forget myself – on your burning lips!

Yours for ever

L.

669 Brno, 31 May 1928, at noon and at night

My dear Kamilka

Today I was given a chance to talk about you, to praise Písek! I went into the district archive. I had work there;[3] a Dr Šebánek[4] introduced himself to me. He showed me all the riches of the old documents. When I was going, he told me that he was from Písek,

1 See 657.
2 If he had, then the letter has not survived.
3 Possibly in connection with his edition of *Moravian Love Songs*.
4 Dr Jindřich Šebánek (1900–77), historian and professor at Masaryk University, Brno.

also musically educated. That he knew that I often travelled to Písek. Among other things, I said that I was often a guest in your house; he knows you and also your husband. So we chatted on; each of us was pleased. Well, I said: let's meet there soon. He says he goes to Písek for the holidays. So now you know everything. In the morning I still didn't have a letter from you; now I'm going there [to the post office] in the certainty that there'll be a letter! It's Thursday, 31 May, noon.

And even this evening a letter didn't come from you. You must be alright, you must be cheerful. At such times one forgets about another person. Today [*recte* yesterday] I ordered a washstand. It's strange that such things are no longer in stock! Everywhere, they say, people are building bathrooms now, so what use are washstands! A top and a surround will be made of grey marble for all those sorts of brushes, especially for your beloved rough one, and for soap.

The worst thing will be when I go to buy curtains. I don't understand these materials at all. Shall I leave it until we're in Luhačovice?

Otherwise I feel like a fish pond from which they've let out the water. A swamp out of which you can't pull your legs. The little fishes don't splash around in it, they don't dart about; the breeze doesn't play with the little waves. Even the grass doesn't grow. That's what I'm like when you don't write for a long time!

Here it's all concerts and theatres; I don't go anywhere. Just pack up and disappear – that's what I'm like when you don't write for some time.

Surely you know that I look for nothing on earth but you, that's why I need signs of life from you. When there are none, it's deserted and empty in my mind. And to throw myself into a new work, I don't want that now. Nerves aren't made of iron. My relaxation is to read through a letter from you, to pick out from it those places where one feels the beat of a heart. And when the longed-for letter doesn't come, how sad I am! Tomorrow's the first of June; thus in four weeks release should come.

It's warm now. You've surely been on the rocks. It's said to be good to rub a little oil or Vaseline on the skin; it won't get burnt. They say one shouldn't overdo exposing the body to the sun. But you're a cool little mouse; you can take a lot, therefore you don't listen. Now I've got this thought: you know, throw a stone into the water. You can't know how it will rest on the bottom? So it will be when I prepare to go to sleep. You ought to have written!

Yours for ever

L.

Brno, 31 May 1928, at night.

670 Brno, 1 June 1928, at night

My dear Kamilka

From morning to 6 o'clock in the afternoon burn your back, [get a] cold, jump into water.[1] God with us and away with evil!

So the letters are burnt, but 'indeed, we'll deal with that face to face!' It's good that you jump into the water! Just to have an ample net for you; to catch, pull you out – and whatever next just as it happens. But your little teeth won't bite through my net, your hands won't tear through it.

Yes, even in sleep you give me no peace. Today again; useless to talk of it. Who can help it if you come into a dream? What would there be of that sleep if you, my little Negress, weren't in it! But at least I see you in a way that I never see you, that I've never ever seen you! But it's that burning desire which has conjured you up for me in my dreams so that one dies of sweet pain. I'll look forward to seeing you healthy, buxom. I'll have a look at your room. And I'd like to become a little mouse which could hide in it and which wouldn't let itself be caught or driven away. Kč 90 for a bathing dress isn't much; in Prague in Celetná ulice,[2] as we passed by, it also cost as much.

I'm going to Hukvaldy on 14 June. They laid the parquet first and then painted! That will be a sight! I'll arrange everything so that you'd know at once where to sit, where to eat, where to lie down and sleep. I wrote to Mr Kretschmer today. You probably won't go to Vienna now? It's no longer worth it. I suppose you've had clothes made in Písek?

On 18 June, on the way back, I'll stop over in Kroměříž. They're giving my *Amarus*[3] there. *Amar* is the child of love – and dies when he has seen two lovers, and the desire for love in him sprang to life, in vain: he was a monk.

They thanked me from Prague, from the Bertramka. They say that the little article will have a good effect.

---

1 This, and the phrase in quotation marks in the next paragraph are presumably references to the long-awaited letter from Stösslová, who had been enjoying the sunshine (in the Kč 90 bathing dress? see below) rather than writing to Janáček.
2 A main street in the Old Town full of fashionable shops.
3 Janáček's cantata *Amarus* (c1897) is based on a poem by Jaroslav Vrchlický (see p.99, fn.1). An illegitimate child, Amarus was sent to a monastery, where he leads a miserable life. He dies when he sees two lovers embracing and realizes both what has been denied him as a monk, and also his own origins, which had brought him to the monastery. 'Amarus' is Vrchlický's invented name for a love child (from the Latin *amare*, to love). 'Amar' is Janáček's fanciful form of the name, not used in the original poem, nor in his setting of it.

When we're in Prague again, we'll go there once more. So you want only health from these operas of mine?[1] –

In Brno the theatre is in the town and the exhibition[2] beyond Old Brno. Why would anyone want to come from the exhibition? He'll sit there tired, eating and drinking in the evening. In Berlin there also won't be anything now, no *Makropulos Affair*. It's too late [in the season] now, although the newspapers continue to announce it. Well, what goes slowly can't escape. Now I'll conjure you up for myself. But what's the point? You burn letters – and so don't know what to write! You made short work of it. Still, it's nice of you at least to come into my dreams. It's too little; it's like showing someone a crust but not giving it him to eat. And he's so hungry, almost dying of hunger.

Keep well.

Yours for ever

L.

Kamila Stösslová to Leoš Janáček, Písek, 2 June 1928

Dear Maestro

We've come from the chief doctor arms legs shaking. It's all over mummy[3] has got cancer she's got five or six months to live the end might also be within three months. On Monday she'll be operated on they'll take water from her. I'm already sick myself. Now my brother-in-law arrived so that mummy could travel but it's now too late for everything. I'm now writing to Luhačovice that I won't go. Don't worry if I don't write you know what sorrow I have.

Keep well

Kamila

671   Brno, 2 June 1928, at night

My dear Kamilka

Your letter came like an attack of the plague. If there's a tumour in the womb then it's no joking matter. Then [she must go] only to a reputable doctor, to the hospital, or to the *sanatorium in Podolí near Prague*. Your mother's probably had it for a while and concealed it. I'm heartily sorry for her; tell her that I wish her a speedy recovery. I

1 A response to something in one of Stösslová's letters, perhaps indicating that she would prefer good health to the royalties from *Káťa Kabanová*.
2 See Glossary: 'Exhibition of Contemporary Culture'.
3 See Glossary: 'Neumannová, [Henriette] Jetty'.

can't imagine her being ill after my last stay with you. She didn't complain of anything, did she? And now you! I can imagine your situation. Alone in these distressing circumstances. Without help, without advice.

Don't lose your head. I think that an operation will probably be the right remedy for recovery.

Your sister must be there to help you in these difficult moments.

Don't lose hope. Just let the illness be identified, then a cure will be found. It's an internal disease; therefore Dr Libenský in Prague, Myslíková ulice, is the most reliable.

And think of yourself too. You can't take too much, your nerves are too jittery; it has a bad effect on you.

Write to me daily; at the worst send me a telegram. Don't think any more about Luhačovice now. It's still a long way off to that time. Don't cancel the room. In such circumstances one can cancel it at any time.

I believe in your mother's recovery, I believe that everything will turn out for us as we wish it.

I believe that fate won't be cruel to us.

Don't bother about that mirror;[1] I'll get some sort of reproduction one here.

All I'm concerned about after all, is that you can look at your head. There's a large, full-length mirror on the ground floor.

Act sensibly, don't do anything in a hurry. You can't stop fate if it's settled for someone, whatever it is.

Your mother didn't look well; but just that sort of bony person has sound health. I didn't notice a malignant disease about her; if it's early days, she'll get over it.

A tumour in the womb can be from inflammation of the kidneys. Didn't she get a chill?

You know, I continually feared that with you. To burn your body with the sun and then into the cold, fierce Otava; that was always a gamble at the expense of your health. Remember, illness strikes a person when he least expects it. Thus that fear of mine about you.

And don't make yourself sad about Luhačovice; if it's the worst, God forbid, you'll need it and you'll need Hukvaldy too. Let's leave that aside now.

The first thing is to do everything for your mother to get well; the rest can wait for us. Greet your mother, I love her for your sake and I wish for her recovery from the bottom of my heart. Don't let her

1 See 668.

[294]

resist good advice and the doctor's orders. If it's necessary to be away from home to get well, then get away from home! Even I will do that. In the hospital, in the sanatorium there's help on hand at every moment.

I feel sorry for you, my little soul. Many hardships have suddenly intruded on your joy. Greet your sister. I don't think of the worst. Write daily, and if necessary send a telegram.

I'm standing by you at every difficult moment.

Yours for ever

L.

Dr Blažek from Bertramka was with me today. He sent you the portraits, the pictures – and the packet came back! Addressee apparently unknown! He was surprised. Now he's written your whole address and will send it to you. How cheerful were those moments and today how sad!

672   Brno, 3 June 1928, at night

My dear Kamilka

I think that you must have had a bad Sunday [3 June]. Did your sister arrive? I'm impatient for a report whether your mother's any better. I also cannot imagine you quite alone in that house. Perhaps she'll get better; for she's not yet of such an age, when it's difficult for a person to be cured. I was also lost in thought the whole day. In the morning there was copying and in the afternoon I went to the exhibition. If all turns out well you'll have a look at the exhibition too. It's worth it. The furnishings of rooms that I saw there were marvellous. Bedrooms like fairy tales; one wouldn't want even to get up from them – especially – but let's leave joking aside now while illness threatens. The most beautiful and complete is the arrangement of the picture gallery. In it there's my picture by Ondrúšek[1] and my bust by Štursa.[2] I went through the exhibition on my own. Věra [Janáčková] from Prague has now avoided my house. She was here at some sort of congress. Those people know how to offend, but not how to ask for forgiveness.[3] She has her reward. Did you want to leave on Monday [4 June]? Now time will fly – and let it bring with it health to your mother, to us the hope of seeing each other soon, to me the hope of a good rest in your company, and to

1 See Glossary: 'Ondrúšek, František'.
2 See 352.
3 See 571.

us our joy, to me that 'indeed, we'll talk about it face to face!'

This exposing, this opening wide of the heart. How sometimes something that was already absolutely certain all goes wrong in a moment.

If your mother's in a really bad way, I'll come to you. Don't leave me in uncertainty; write even if just a few words. I'll make preparations for the Hukvaldy visit; whatever else happens, you'll always come and visit there.

I wanted to begin on the piece which they asked me for from Berlin;[1] but I'm not up to it. My thoughts remain standing; they won't go on. Just like a little stream barely trickling and a little further on [it becomes] a dry river bed. I'm overworked. It's necessary to pump more blood into the brain. Your nearness will stir it up, your blood-red lip.

Everything will change in me. Even fields, when they've produced a harvest, have to be ploughed over again. Otherwise only weeds would grow in them.

Will everything change for the better? Will health return to your mother? To us those few heavenly moments of ours? Will that first Friday of ours come again?[2] I think that a note will come from you tomorrow. What happened with you the whole day today? Which doctor came to the house?

I don't like to think what I would do if you couldn't stir from Písek. God forbid it be so. Think of yourself and spare yourself. You can't take much. I'm with you constantly in my thoughts. Greet your mother; your sister too.

Yours for ever

L.

Janáček wrote two letters the next day (673 and *674). Despite their numbering, *674 would appear to be the first written, promising a second letter later that day. It is a short letter in which Janáček made concrete proposals: that he would go to Luhačovice at the end of the month and to Písek on 12 July, then take her with him to Hukvaldy. Janáček probably took this letter to the post office at the same time as collecting one from Stösslová, on which he comments in his next letter:

1 On 8 May 1928 (BmJA, C 132) the German director Gustav Hartung asked Janáček to write music for Gerhart Hauptmann's *Schluck und Jau* (published in 1900), scheduled for an open-air production at the castle in Heidelberg during the summer.
2 See Glossary: 'Friday–feast-day'.

My dear Kamilka

Believe me that I can't get over your report. How's it possible for
your mother suddenly to be in such a bad way! I still don't want to
believe it, to talk with someone cheerfully a month earlier and suddenly to think of that person sacrificed. I'm so upset that I ask the
whole time: 'speak slowly to me!' I'd like to hop over to you to see
the terrible change with my own eyes. I've got work here on 9 June
during the laying of the foundation stone for the university;[1] on 11
June our quartet is being played and people are coming here from
Vienna for its printing.[2] This week by express post the director of
the Berlin theatre gave notice of his arrival.[3]

On 14 June the builder's handing over the house to me, on 18
June I'm committed to Kroměříž.[4] What a mad house it is for me
here!

But in any event I'll hop over to you; I can't hold out. I'd come by
the evening express from Brno. It will be either 12 June or 20 June.
I'm not fit for work; I have only your sad thoughts. Unutterably
disordered. It's as if the mirror in which we've seen ourselves smiling
is shattered by a stone. But if it suddenly got bad, if you yourself
couldn't stand it any more, just write the word 'come!' and I'll come
whatever may be happening any time. This is how things which
called so temptingly break down. At first I didn't want to believe it.
Today's letter, while I still hadn't opened it, seemed to bear better
news. I open it, and see the worst.

You mustn't be alone; did you write to your husband that he should
also come back? Your nerves can't cope with such excitement; you too
would have become ill very soon. I think that when I come you'll have
at least a little support. And then, take care of yourself. After contact
with your mother, always wash your hands well with soap. Wash the
cutlery separately. It's painful advice, but they ordered it during the
illness of my mother and also in other cases.

Why did it have to come like this!

I'll give you my Hukvaldy house for you to use for your recuper-
ation whenever you want it.

I can't get over this.

1 See p.235, fn.5.
2 This was wishful thinking on Janáček's part since Universal Edition had not yet responded to his invitation of 1 June 1928 (Janáček 1988, 355–6) to attend the rehearsal; see also
p.287, fn.2.
3 Hartung wrote to Janáček on 3 June (BmJA, D 644).
4 For a performance of *Amarus*.

Give a sincere greeting to your mother.
Yours for ever
L.

Kamila Stösslová to Leoš Janáček, Písek, 5 June 1928

Dear Maestro!

I'm sitting so listlessly as if there were no life in me. [...] I can't go into the street everyone knows everyone's sorry for her. Only now do I see how much people liked mummy how good she is. I really don't know how I'll get through it I've never experienced anything like this and now so suddenly. I'm desperate I can't even believe it I'm so afraid and I don't sleep the whole night. Today they were to have operated on her. [...] Don't hurry with anything for me everything happy is over. I do my crying upstairs granddad[1] downstairs he keeps on saying that he'll kill himself and so I really don't know what to say to him since I no longer have the strength. [...]

675   Brno, 5 June 1928

My dear Kamila

What sad letters we have now! I'm also somehow unsuccessful at the moment. I've had information today there's some sort of hitch with *The Makropulos Affair* in Berlin.[2] On the other hand a contract's been signed in Frankfurt[3] for the selfsame *Makropulos Affair*. Our quartet has been accepted for printing by Universal Edition.[4] On the other hand the same Edition tells me not to be caught out by that offer from Heidelberg, that it wasn't successful in the theatre.[5] And I've already begun; it will be music and action about two drunk beggars, one of whom shows how he would rule!

---

1 i.e. Kamila's father, Adolf Neumann (1864–1943).
2 Janáček had evidently learnt that Berlin would not be giving *The Makropulos Affair* (see p.266, fn.5). Barbara Kemp (1881–1959), the wife of the Intendant Max von Schillings, had refused to sing the role of Emilia Marty.
3 The Frankfurt production went ahead, though after Janáček's death. The première there, conducted by Josef Krips on 14 February 1929, was the first production of the opera outside Czechoslovakia.
4 In his letter of 4 June 1928 (BmJA, D 1657), Hertzka expressed 'great interest' in the quartet. Since he would be away in Paris, none of his directors would be able to leave Vienna during his absence and hear the work in rehearsal. But he was grateful for any work by Janáček and would accept this one anyway.
5 See p.296, fn.1; Hertzka expressed this view in the same letter of 4 June 1928.

When he's dead drunk, they persuade him that he's a prince.[1]

And so all joy at Luhačovice disappeared for good. Must I walk around there like an orphan? Around your windows? Along our little paths? Into our café? Surely I'll dry up with loneliness there. Why has this happened now! You must arrange it somehow so that you could come to me for at least a week or two, to have a break from these sad conditions. Arrange for your sister to stand in for you. I'm unutterably sorry about it all. A whole year of looking forward and now the tears burst out. As if the well from which I've drunk healthy water had suddenly dried up. I feel my abandonment weighing ever more heavily on me. If only your mother had learnt long ago that she wasn't in a good state! It would have been possible to prevent it. — —

I was buying curtains today; Kč 130 for one window with hand embroidery from a village factory from the Krkonoš mountains. Dear? In this way I get everything all by myself. I wonder why I'm condemned to live so forsaken! I know that I'll bring that to an end in the holidays this year. In the letter about which I wrote to you she [Zdenka] showed her true face. This is where it will start from. Well, I won't get you excited about it yet. You've got enough pain of your own now. And I've also received only unpleasant news today. In Berlin it's somehow precarious over *The Makropulos Affair*. I write, write this – and on the first page I've already mentioned it! I'm so unlike myself because of this sad event at your home. And now you, how many times have you run down the stairs from top to bottom? You're tiring yourself so much that you'll fall like a fly. You'll have to take on someone to help out with the night nursing; some sort of nurse. You'd exhaust your strength so much that an insidious disease would take root in you unobserved! It's not without reason, is it, that your lungs start hurting at once! I'm so low-spirited! But a stay in that isolation in the big house is still the pleasantest for me. Think about coming to Hukvaldy while your sister does the nursing for you for a while. Don't take away my hope and do it for your own sake. I wonder what you're doing now? It's getting on for 10 o'clock at night!

Yours for ever

L.

---

1 Hauptmann's *Schluck und Jau* is a free adaptation of the Induction to *The Taming of the Shrew*, in which Christopher Sly is replaced by the tramp Jau; his associate Schluck is dressed up as his 'princess'.

676   [undated, postmarked Brno, 6 June 1928]

I'll arrive on Sunday [10 June] by the express from Brno.
With greetings
   Drph. L.J.

677   Brno, 6 June 1928, at night

My dear Kamilka

I've decided to see you and your mother. You, because I'd like to ease your pain however I can.

You can't suspect yourself how your pain and that of your mother have upset my balance. I'm not myself; to see you at any price!

Add to that the pondering over Z.'s letter to my sister. I decided to separate from Z. I thought about my position for a long time; I wanted to carry it out in the holidays in peace and quiet. As always, an avalanche grew from a mundane incident. I won't upset you with this; I couldn't talk in any way other than [this], that what binds me to you is so strong that no-one on earth can tear it asunder. That I'll not allow myself to be constrained by anyone in this feeling. That I won't stand for low and continual suspicions of myself and you. I spoke of the illness of your mother and that I considered it my sacred duty to see her again and to comfort you. Everything calmed down. –

Today your letter opens up some sort of hope. In these terrible moments we always wait for a miracle. If only it would come, I hope you won't fall ill! And that we be granted at least our moment. Everything came so fast, unexpectedly. I thought to myself what would you do in that isolation, without your mother.

Today the weight fell from my chest. I'm completely determined to be with you at every difficult moment of life. I'm glad that I'll see you as soon as Sunday, that we'll tell each other of our pain. In fact we'll not talk even about that; I'll simply be glad that I'll be with you. And then I usually forget to talk. I've already written to you about those curtains; at Hukvaldy everything's said to be ready and clean. Now just go there and take a rest after these difficult days. Perhaps even Luhačovice will see you after all? But I know you. You'd rather die yourself than your mother. That cough, that's your overwrought nerves and heart. I just want to see you now. I think that all weight will fall from us both.

Greet your sister. She must help you out now; she's calmer. I knew that I had to come and see you, even if I had to go through hell and purgatory. When would there be that real place for me beside you if not in your sufferings!

Yours for ever

L.

Kamila Stösslová to Leoš Janáček, Písek, after 6 June 1928

Dear Maestro

I've just received a telegram from Plzeň that mummy won't have an operation and that the doctors hope that she'll be better. I can't believe it but God is mighty. God only knows what I've been through these past few days. [...] I really don't know now whether it's all a dream and if I'm dreaming.

I can't believe it perhaps they're just cheering us up.

She'll return tomorrow perhaps God grant that she's well. [...] Yesterday the one wanted to operate on her and the other not. [...] Please don't be angry that I give you pain but I've got no-one else to complain to no-one to share my joys. You've got enough problems yourself and so few pleasures. I'd like to give you only pleasure if only that was possible. [...] I'll write to you every day as soon as mummy arrives. I don't want you to worry on her account [...]

678 Brno, 7–8 June 1928

My dear Kamilka

Today's a half holiday; Corpus Christi. I couldn't stir from the house in the morning: the copyist – meetings. I don't even know whether there's a letter from you at the post office. So tomorrow I'll go for it quickly. I think that today you had at least a little rest? I've calmed down a little; I had more than a man usually bears piled up on me.

There was an excursion of the Prague Conservatory to Brno.[1] You'll gather how they bring them up, these hopeful young people, from that fact that neither the rector,[2] nor the director,[3] nor the conductor whom I helped to get a place,[4] still less of course the pupils,

1 As part of the Exhibition of Contemporary Culture the Prague Conservatory arranged a series of six concerts in Brno (2–9 June 1928), amounting to a small festival of contemporary music. Particular attention was devoted to other prominent Czech composers whereas Janáček was represented only by the piano cycle *In the Mists* (see Janáček 1990, 388, fn.)
2 Vítězslav Novák (1870–1949).
3 The administrative director was Jan Branberger (1877–1952).
4 Pavel Dědeček (1885–1954), a former teacher at the Brno Organ School.

[301]

knew, during a stay of more than a week, that some sort of composer lives here; one, when all's said and done, who has rendered some sort of service to Czech music. As if I weren't in Brno, either socially or even musically!

You've probably already had a card from me; you must have been surprised who was coming to cheer you up! But I'm also coming to you, even if in sadder circumstances, for a little comfort for myself. It will be only for a short while, but even so. I'll finish writing this letter to you in the morning; I can hardly see now for tiredness. Sleep well, sleep at least! That's the best remedy. And when, as one sleeps, one dreams about something nice, that's a miraculous remedy.

[8 June 1928] And it was truly. And how about you? Today quite a lot lies upon me too. Taxes rain down upon me; I protest. They remember about a person everywhere — when he has to pay the tax office.

And don't come to meet me on Sunday evening [10 June 1928]. You know that I'll find you in the dark. And I think I'll certainly find you here. Without your having to announce yourself. I'd go like a little dog by the trail, by feeling.

So let's try it.

I want to see you as soon as possible.

Yours for ever

L.

679   Brno, 8 June 1928

My dear soul

Promise me that you'll not go to Plzeň,[1]

    that you'll eat and sleep.

It can be only a tumour and not that terrible disease.

Promise me that you'll come to Luhačovice

    and to Hukvaldy.

Promise me that if it gets worse you'll send me a telegram immediately.

So then I won't come on Sunday [10 June]. I wouldn't be finished with the copying and it could be only for the day. It's nothing to do with sadness. Even with you I know how to bear sadness.

Yours for ever, for ever

Leoš

---

1 i.e. to Nezvěstice, where her mother was in hospital (see p.305, fn.4).

My dear Kamilka

After your letter today in which I feel confidence in a turn for the better in your mother's illness and at the same time the acceptance that you must also think of yourself, and that you also need peace and a cure – in short that you have need of Luhačovice, I decided not to travel to see you on Sunday and to wait for you – in Luhačovice.

If your sister will be so good and take over caring for your mother for a while, then you can get away.

I know from experience that such illnesses last long. It was the same with my mother, and with a certain female relative.[1] The doctor gave her three months – and she lived another six years! So Kamila, you also need your strength; you need to gather a lot of your strength. So make arrangements so that your stay in Luhačovice would be possible.

I would have been able to come only for the Monday [11 June]. I'd like to have seen you, to have calmed you, but I have faith that you'll go for a rest just as we'd wanted. I'd be away from Brno 10–19 June but that damned copying wouldn't be finished.[2] It would spoil all my joy to think of unfinished work!

So I ask you, take care of yourself, eat lots and don't worry any more. There is one single consolation: everything is in God's hands! It means that everything is left to inexorable fate!

Now I've come from a rehearsal for my song for the laying of the foundation stone for the university.[3] It sounds fine. But it began raining, who knows if tomorrow's celebration won't be 'drenched'. Kamilka, despite everything I'd rather have sat with you on that Sunday and Monday! It would have been warmer, I'd have driven away bad thoughts from you. But just that short while! We would have agreed that you would certainly come to Luhačovice. God forbid that I might have *seen* on you [i.e. from her appearance] that you needed to go! No, not that. You can go because they'll manage without you for that time, but you must go, I can just imagine what you've been through, what has to be put right. Without you I'd remain there for a while – and slip away. The doctor told me, just go if the spa will give you pleasure. And what can give me pleasure

1 Janáček's mother Amálie died of cancer of the stomach on 16 November 1884; she mentioned difficulties with her health in a letter to Janáček written around Easter 1883 (BmJA, B 1399). It is not clear what other 'female relative' Janáček had in mind.
2 The copying of *From the House of the Dead* was completed on 20 June 1928; Janáček shortened his stay in Hukvaldy to 14–18 June.
3 See 618.

without you! Nothing on earth. There at every step something would call out for you; I wouldn't go out of sorrow and longing – I'd slip away. I feel from your letter that, ever so secretly, timidly, you are also longing to be there. Perhaps it will come true for us after all! [...]

I look forward to your letter tomorrow. I've written twice already to Mr Kretschmer,[1] but he hasn't replied.

Your passionately loving

L.

So book that little room in Luhačovice again!

681   Brno, 8 [*recte* 9]–10 June 1928

My dear Kamilka

I should really have gone to you tomorrow![2] No letter came from you today; I won't know anything about you for three days.[3] But I think that things will be better with you, there will be more hope and a meeting in Luhačovice!

Today it was a furnace in Brno. 22° in the shade![4] But there was also a furnace in my room the whole day. In the morning, by 10, the copyist finished Act 3; part of Act 2 still remains to be looked through and the thing will have already been given its 'first rinse'.[5]

At 11 o'clock the foundation stone[6] was laid. They sang my [chorus] quite well.[7] I stood only five steps away from the President. 'High' society around me; I was hidden by a palm tree and by laurel trees and I had eyes on everything.

In the afternoon some madman photographed me; then the copyist came again. In the evening I went to the theatre and then to see the illumination of the town.[8] People everywhere as if it were day. Only

1 Presumably about the writing-desk (see Glossary: 'Kretschmer').
2 Janáček announced his plan to visit Kamila and her mother on Sunday 10 June in his first letter of 6 June (676), but after news from Písek he abandoned this plan on 8 June (679).
3 i.e. not until on Monday, when the post office would be open again; Janáček was writing on a Saturday.
4 Janáček was presumably giving the temperature in Réaumur, i.e. Celsius 27.5 / Fahrenheit 82.5 (see also p.110, fn.2).
5 Copying of *From the House of the Dead* continued until 20 June (see 690), by which time a complete, copied-out full score existed, needing a little more checking and a few last-minute additions.
6 of the Law Faculty of Masaryk University (see p.273, fn.3).
7 See 618, 653; the chorus was sung by the Philharmonic Chorus of the Brno Beseda conducted by Jaroslav Kvapil.
8 The town was illuminated in connection with the Exhibition of Contemporary Culture (see Glossary).

my Kamilka [wasn't there], I wonder what she was doing then? I'll wait until you write 'today at last I slept well!' That will be very nice for me too. And when you write 'I'll go to Luhačovice!' – that will be the nicest of all. And what if you were to take Otuš with you to Hukvaldy?[1] He'd have fun in the garden, at the stream, in the game park, where there are deer. He'd be miserable in Luhačovice. At Hukvaldy they'd think that he was 'our' son. Think about it. I'm 'worn-out' now. One cure would revive me. You carry it with you – it's red like coral, hot – nearly burning, touch it and the mouth bursts into flame, impossible to pull away! You'll give it me, you'll give it!

Sleep well.

9 June at night

I sleep like a log, you know. I'd willingly make half of my sleep over to you. Nowadays you have a house empty as the grave. I know what your dear mother is to you. She's the only other person in whom you confide everything, who's a firm support for you without your thinking much about it; who cries and laughs with you. Apart from the children, all the others round you wouldn't really need to be there, would they? And now to lose her! You were shattered; unprepared. The fact that you didn't write is, I think, because you went off to Plzeň?[2] I shouldn't wonder. You also worry being at home in [such] uncertainty. I was sad yesterday that the letter didn't come.

If only I could read again, 'I've booked the room'.

Yours for ever

L.

Brno, 10 June 1928 morning

That thought occurred to me about Otušek because you wouldn't know what to do with him. I think that he'd like to go.

Kamila Stösslová to Leoš Janáček, Písek, 9 June 1928

[...] Thursday was a holiday[3] I came home from town the husband of my cousin was waiting for me and said that he would take me to Nezvěstice[4] to see mummy. [...] The journey lasted a little over two hours. It was so beautiful I remember how we'd driven to Hodonín

---

1 This suggestion was taken up; see Epilogue.
2 To see her mother in the sanatorium (see Stösslová's letter of 6 June 1928).
3 Corpus Christi, a state holiday in Czechoslovakia at the time.
4 A village near Plzeň, where two of Mrs Neumannová's children, Helena and Karel, lived with their families and the location of the sanatorium to which Mrs Neumannová had been taken.

how jolly those journeys were [–] and now! We arrived there mummy cried as soon as she saw me all us children were there [also] plenty of strangers. I was so cheerful that everyone simply laughed at me and I cheered everyone up but at the same time I felt terrible mummy is in great pain looks poorly. [...]

682   Brno, 10 June 1928, at night

My dear Kamilka

Today's Sunday. This morning finish writing the letter to you, get vexed by the copyist. Put the letter into the post and think and think of my dear Negress. Think about her so much as if I were wrapped round, like that little caterpillar wrapping and turning itself from a caterpillar into a pretty butterfly. I've wrapped myself up too and what I'm wrapped up in is my Kamilka. In her I'm complete, with all the joys of life.

In the afternoon we went to the exhibition. It's magnificent and I'll show you round it too. After the walk we went into a wine bar where the Myjava musicians[1] were playing; among them two Gypsies. My thoughts were immediately in Písek.[2] I waited for the evening because of the illuminations. It looked like a fairy tale. We'll also go and have a look at them together.

Now I'm sitting and writing to you. What have you been doing? Were you in Plzeň?

On Thursday 14 June I go to Hukvaldy; on 18 June I'll be at my concert in Kroměříž[3] and then it will only be a few days before the journey to Luhačovice.

Will you come? Will happiness smile on us? Will it be possible?

If only an answer would arrive saying that you're coming! What a welcome I'd give you there! What will your letter tell me tomorrow! Will I be merry or even sadder? Now it's 10 o'clock at night; I'd already have been with you.[4] I tell myself you didn't want me to come, to come into a sad house! But I ought to have come even into a sad house. Perhaps I'd have cheered it up. Perhaps we'd have got

---

1 A group of folk musicians from Myjava, Slovakia, led by Samko Dudík, played with great success at the Frankfurt Exhibition 'Music in the Life of the Nations', 1927. They were organized by Janáček's colleague the folklorist Hynek Bím, and Janáček introduced them when he went to Frankfurt for the Fifth ISCM Festival, which ran there concurrently (see Janáček 1955, 67).
2 Presumably because of Stösslová's charitable activities among the Gypsy children there (see Glossary: 'Gypsy children').
3 See 670.
4 See p.304, fn.2.

everything settled and everything would have been certain – and so now only wishes!

At the exhibition I bought for Kč 520 a fine plush divan cover for Hukvaldy for your room. Tomorrow still [to get] that mirror for your dear head and everything will be prepared. If only you were there already! And what about your mother? How's she getting on? Did you pass on my regards? If only it were tomorrow now, for me to know already something for certain. – And today I had a bad dream. A steamroller ran over me on the road. I experienced every moment, right up to unconsciousness. I woke up at once. It's the result of this continual agitation now. I just wish that Luhačovice calm of ours would come. Not so much the calm but those moments from last year. It was on Thursday in the year when I was with you – 'and the earth shook!'

Keep well
Yours for ever
L.

Kamila Stösslová to Leoš Janáček, Písek, 11 June 1928

[...] After lunch I went to the rocks but such sadness came over me that I ran home [...] I still can't get used to the idea that one day I may be alone. That's why I'm not thinking about Luhačovice [...] I don't go anywhere now people annoy me I walk from room to room and I can't find a place [to be alone]. It's so difficult to tell someone who has not experienced it. Go to Luhačovice when you think right. I just long for peace and I'll find it only at your place in Hukvaldy. For the time being mummy will be in Poděbrady.[1] [...] Otoušek is lonely no wonder for she brought him up. I'm glad that the school will be over soon I'll take him with me. He also needs a rest he's weak. [...]

684   Brno, 13 June 1928, at night

My dear Kamilka

That letter of yours today! All at sixes and sevens! I see now that it's high time for you to get into a different environment, to other thoughts! So, I beg you, make arrangements according to what I propose to you now.

School's ending, the boys have got the holidays. As for Otuš you

---

1 A spa town to the east of Prague. Mrs Neumannová would have had a long journey from Plzeň (to the west of Prague), and would have been even further from Písek.

know that he'll come to Hukvaldy. What about Rudi?

You don't need Luhačovice so much as just a change of surroundings.

So come to Luhačovice just for a shorter time, perhaps a fortnight, and while I'm there. What would I do there on my own, and yet I need treatment[1] this summer.

You'd come straight after 1 July and could get to Hukvaldy sooner. You can remain there as long as you please. I'd go to Brno only for fresh clothes and I'd come straight to Hukvaldy to you.

That's my plan.

You, on the other hand, are thinking now of travelling immediately to Hukvaldy and from there in August (!) to Luhačovice! What's led you to such an arrangement? You without me in Hukvaldy, without me in Luhačovice? And I similarly without you here and there?

So I beg you, book a room immediately in Luhačovice for the beginning of July.

The day after tomorrow I go off to Hukvaldy and will organize everything so that you could live there comfortably.

I'll expect you in Luhačovice straight after 1 July.

So please, fall in with my plan. You can't be alone either in Písek or in Luhačovice.

Isolation puts your nerves on edge; you must be managed and diverted to cheer you up.

And the third idea that you should not go to Luhačovice at all and stay only at Hukvaldy would also be good for you. But I'd be sad not to have you around in Luhačovice even for a short while.

So, dear little soul, sit down in our heaven and read carefully one idea after the other.

I think this one: *Luhačovice after 1 July for a short while and then Hukvaldy for a long while is the best one for both of us.*

I'll write to you immediately from Hukvaldy; I'll be there at noon on 14 June and leave there in the early morning on Monday, 18 June. I'll certainly be in Brno already on 19 June.

Write openly to my sister; I'm glad that she wrote to you. You must bring to me, at the Hukvaldy house, bring and find an open heart.

---

1 For 'rheumatic pains from all that sitting' (702). The treatment is mentioned in 701 and 705. When it appeared not to work (711), Janáček then went on to 'the cold water treatment', described in 712. Janáček also mentions 'gout' which he treated with a vegetarian diet, losing eight kilos in the process (716).

Mr Kodl wrote to me.
Yours for ever
L.

[...] Why didn't your mother stay in that Plzeň sanatorium? What's there in Poděbrady?

685 Hukvaldy, 14 June 1928

My dear Kamila
   I arrived safely. I'm setting it in order so that you'll like it here.
   Now simply decide how, when and where.
   I'd prefer to know while I'm still here.
   Thirteen and eleven chickens,
   six ducks are hatched. There'll be vegetables. The rest from the hotel[1] and from the butcher. Your room will be a fairy tale.
   How well I feel here in the sun; in that clean air, in this dear quiet! Brrr! Brno!
   That's a prison for me. Now I'll make much use of this dear freedom and will continue to [do so] from now on.
   My copyists will be finished with me on Wednesday next week.
   The folksongs are being printed, after a twenty-two-year battle![2]
   And what about you, my little soul! Don't take the pain to heart any more. You won't change anything. And we still have to go on living.
   I can't imagine that Poděbrady would be the spa for such an illness. It's for heart trouble. But Dr Libenský, my professor from Prague, treats people there.
   I'm looking forward to seeing you soon – and pampering you. At least that's what I wish.
   Yours for ever
   L.

Kamila Stösslová to Leoš Janáček, Písek, 14 June 1928

Dear Maestro
   You can't imagine how calm I am today and how differently I already see everything now. Such was the effect the chief doctor had on me today. Yesterday they brought mummy back half dead. We were with him as early as 8 o'clock. [...] He was so persuasive with me

1 Mičaník's hotel, which still exists in Hukvaldy, rebuilt and modernized.
2 See Glossary: 'Moravian Love Songs'.

telling me that he knows that I've never had anything to do with someone seriously ill before and therefore he's taken upon himself this work with me so that I went away quite a different person than from when I arrived. [...] My sister-in-law and brother arrived from Prague today and are taking mummy to a sanatorium in Prague.

She's got much worse they'll have to take water from her I expect she's got it on top now so that she can't even breathe. The chief doctor told me yesterday that it would be better if she's under medical supervision. But I was so brave the whole week that I hardly recognize myself. [...] I was glad that she was at home those few days and that I could be of service to her a little. [...]

687 Hukvaldy, 15 June 1928

My dear Kamila

Such hardships that you're living through, and there's no way I can help you other than with these words of comfort. How I'd like to see your mother once more! But I fear the worst.

Just be brave! Hard advice. I too lost someone as dear to me as [your mother is] to you. I know that one has to survive it, and to keep going in full strength because it's also a duty to oneself.

Slip away for a moment when you're able to. You have here my and your little nest nicely furnished.

The writing-desk from Mr Kretschmer is magnificent. I didn't think that it was possible to make such a beauty out of that old lumber. I take great pleasure in it.

[...]

Act just like a daughter, but don't forget that you have children – and someone to whom you also belong, and who worries about you. I leave here on Monday morning [18 June]. On Tuesday I'll be in Brno and will wait for news from you. God grant that it will be good. I'll arrange everything with my sister; she'll do her best to comply with your every wish. You'll get your strength back here.

Your mother is best looked after in a sanatorium. [...] And not even in Pardubice,[1] where they treat heart ailments.

[...] If things are bad, send a telegram! I'm with you the whole time, and suffer with you.

Yours for ever

L.

1 Janáček meant Poděbrady (see p.307, fn.1).

688 Hukvaldy, 18 June 1928

My dear Kamila

I'm leaving early morning after a night where I also didn't sleep a wink.

Winter struck and it wasn't healthy to carry things in the draught in which I had to move around.

I want to have news from you soon, good news, which also spares yourself.

On the journey, although reluctantly, I'll stop off in Kroměříž. And in Brno only about twenty pages still to finish writing and then – you don't know, nor me neither.

Keep well, I love you infinitely.

Yours for ever

Leoš

Everything is prepared for you here.

689 Brno, 18 June 1928

My dear Kamila

I'm in Brno again. And how! On the way I intended being in Kroměříž at my concert. In the morning the carriage didn't go up to the station; the coachman had fought in the night from Sunday to Monday [17–18 June]. He was ashamed [to make] the journey with a broken nose.

I left at noon. I stopped in Kroměříž, I saw the deputation waiting for me at the station. I looked at them from the window of the carriage. They didn't recognize me! I didn't move. The train whistled, I fell back laughing on to my seat. Soon I no longer saw Kroměříž. You can see from that what sort of mood I'm in. I couldn't have taken the music-making and that chatter before and after.

I have thoughts only with you and your pain.

One thing is certain, that I'll bring you to Hukvaldy myself, whenever and from wherever.

I can't maroon you on an island, like Robinson [Crusoe].

I'm curious what you'll write to me.

I myself arrived here again with lumbago, with an upset stomach. All this cries out loudly now for Luhačovice and my soul cries out for you.

I'm glad that the furniture arrived both from Brno and from Prague on the same day. I unpacked it in a wintry 7° and arranged it. But it's nice and I think that you're going to like it too.

[311]

How are you now? As for your husband, [it's] as if he never existed! You poor thing, all on your own.

And that chief doctor! How can a doctor simply have news brought to him about a sick person! And then again to say that it's good that your mother is under continual medical observation! Well, well!

It's bad for the seriously ill and bad for the healthy people around them!

In Hukvaldy I was much absorbed in my own thoughts; but at least I could talk to my sister about you. That was a relief. If only you can decide soon. I know that you'll decide sensibly – and on all counts with your heart.

I've not been myself all these weeks. I don't worry about you so much now. You've now got over the first shock. One's already numbed for the next ones. I'd like to keep this letter until I get yours. Write in which sanatorium in Prague your mother is. In the Podolí one?[1]

[unsigned]

No letter came from you this morning. Could Rudin make me a rough drawing of the mirror-frame that hangs in the piano room? Here I can't agree on the form. How is it with you, my little soul?

Kamila Stösslová to Leoš Janáček, Písek, 18 June 1928

[...] Mummy's in the sanatorium, no-one's allowed to see her that professor has forbidden it they're giving her injections she's so weak she can't even speak. If you were to see her you wouldn't say that it was the same person. How everything can change in three weeks! They want to send her to Jáchymov I'm not in favour and wrote for them to bring her home. [...] I'm possibly going to Vienna on Saturday for a dress a coat and a hat I never thought what sort of clothes I'd be buying this year I don't have anything black I never liked wearing it and so I have to buy it while I'm still in one piece. I don't know how I'll get through it but rather than see her suffering [...] it's better if we will wish her that peace [...] My husband arrived from Vienna only on Saturday evening and went off early this morning.

I didn't even speak to him he's inconsiderate. [...] Believe me, his presence irritates me I'm glad that he's away. I'm happiest on my own now. And even if the worst was to happen I don't want you to come

---

1 Podolí, a district in Prague. Janáček had recommended the santorium there in his letter of 2 June (671).

to see us. [...] So don't be angry with me I know very well that you're suffering with me but to come to us is impossible now. [...]

690   Brno, 19 June 1928, at night

Kamila, my Kamila

All this that you're experiencing now is too much for you. For my part I'm frightened by your cough and by the pain in your back.

I'm now speaking calmly and with deliberation:

According to everything I judge that your poor mother will hardly recover. That you're now prepared for the worst.

Let the doctor in the sanatorium act as he thinks fit. What would they do with the poor thing in Jáchymov! Let your mother stay in the sanatorium; with you at home she'd not have the necessary nursing. And you wouldn't be able to bear all that suffering of hers.

Tell me which sanatorium in Prague she's in.

Tell me definitely when you want to go to Vienna and how long you'll be away from Písek. Don't forget to give me an immediate answer to these two questions!

It goes without saying that after the terrible moment you'll go at once to where I'll be. Nowhere else!

Answer this letter, the questions I'm asking, at once.

Be assured that I'm suffering with you and would like to be the greatest possible support. I got home with a very bad cold, but it's getting better. It was cold, windows, doors opened; a draught. I drank two glasses of cold water; now I'm treating myself with gin! What they did in Kroměříž was futile for me at that moment. With a smile on my lips I sat down when the train left the place. Much in life is pointless. What trifles we magnify and don't even permit ourselves to have serious thoughts.

[...]

The copyists will be finished tomorrow, on Wednesday, at my place.[1] With this a weight falls from me. I knew that you, among all your siblings, would take the fateful blow hardest of all. It's not always possible to take water from the body; it wasn't in the case of my daughter.[2] With my cousin now they have done so – and she takes pleasure in life again. But before that she was always eating and every

---

1 The last reference to the long-drawn-out work with the copyists on *From the House of the Dead*. Janáček indeed paid off his second copyist on 20 June 1928 (see Tyrrell 1992, 338).

2 During her final illness Olga Janáčková got dropsy and, as Marie Stejskalová reported, the doctors did not know how to deal with this (Trkanová 2/1964, 56).

day drank a glass of beer. Illnesses are various. Only leave your mother in the sanatorium. I implore you!

And find comfort in the fact that fate is blind, inexorable. No-one ever avoids it. If it's fated that your mother will die, better quickly after less pain and suffering. They can relieve her pain with injections. Only in a sanatorium is this on hand at every moment.

Write to me at once.

I'm yours for ever

Maybe Janáček's next letters were even more importunate: of the one probably sent the next day only an envelope survives (*691), and, despite Kamila's interdiction, he did visit Písek, on 23–4 June, making a trip with the Stössels and Alois Kodl to Zvíkov from where he sent a postcard to Zdenka.[1] His response on his return was also seemingly embarrassing to Kamila: only pages 1 and 3 survive; p.3, *in medias res*, is barely intelligible:

692   [undated, postmarked, Brno, 25 June 1928]

My dear Kamilka

I've now arrived and at once a few words of thanks for giving me a few happy days and that you have made me well. In your presence I would always be healthy and wouldn't long for the spa. Everything was nice. That walk in the intoxicating fragrance there beyond the cemetery. When we're alone everything around is a hundred times more beautiful.

And that trip of ours to Zvíkov!

< p.2 missing >

Well I'd like to conjure up that moment now.

And I know what still stands in your way but I also know that the way would straighten itself out then on its own; for there wouldn't be anything which could stand in your way.

Let everything be left to a good-natured fate.

So write soon then, so I'll know where you are and how long you'd be in Vienna. But I think that there's no need for you there.

< p.4 missing >

---

1 BmJA, A 3718.

693   Brno, 25–6 June 1928

My dear Kamila

Towards evening I went to have a look at the exhibition. I made a contract with the Myjava musicians for Prague.[1]

In the evening it looked like the Prater[2] in Vienna. They could have done without that. Or don't the people now want anything other than merry-go-rounds?

It was a good idea to erect a miniature railway. I also went on it. Otherwise a waste of time. [...]

(25 June 1928 at night)

[...] I'm already packing. I'd most like to pack you. You're so soft, you wouldn't get creased. I'd put you right at the top, I wouldn't put the lid down so that I could keep on kissing you during the journey. It would be hot in a moment.

You've calmed down and even begun to laugh. You see! Even through a person's tears, his character lets slip a little smile.

The only cure is a little merriment. I'm glad that I elicited it from you. Certainly we were at least a little bit happy during those few days. [...]

Brno, 26 June 1928

694   Brno, 26 June 1928, at night

My dear Kamilka

Day by day goes by – in inactivity. I'm already waiting for the Sunday of my departure. There are still live reminders of our trip; for me especially those three strawberries from your hand. Like three drops of blood. In that moment of embarrassment – and it was the strawberries that attracted you. And how we drank out of a single glass, how you put the best morsel of that 'well done' bit of goose on my plate. And, just imagine, there's my double here in Brno. He's strikingly similar to me; but – he's loathsome to me. In years he's much older than I am, and now takes a girl for his wife. On his cheek one can see only his lust, and that's hateful to me. He grins, you know; a grimace and a smile like an idiot. I love you unutterably, but something higher binds me to you, infinitely higher, bordering on sacrificing myself for you. Infinite longing for you is just one part of

1 Presumably to play at the First International Conference on Folk Arts in October in conjunction with Janáček's planned paper there (see p.268, fn.4).
2 An amusement park on the bank of the Danube.

my love for you. There's only lust on the face of that lecher.

[...]

And now, I wonder where you are? Did you go off to Vienna all the same? It's probably unlikely that you've had any news [about your mother] from Jáchymov yet.[1] If only it were good.

Just what will I do in Luhačovice without you? No-one will see me smile; I'll slink away where no-one goes. Sadness will walk beside me. I'll be there, but I'll be elsewhere in my thoughts. They'll say: that one must be ill – and I'll get ill.

I'm waiting for a letter from you tomorrow. Write to Luhačovice: *L.J. Augustýnský dům, Luhačovice*. Is your leg well?[2]

Yours for ever

L.

695   Brno, 27 June 1928, at night

My dear Kamila

It's Wednesday. Perhaps you're making preparations for that Vienna trip?

Today at my place they [the Moravian Quartet] played our quartet *Intimate Letters*. They play it with ardour as if they themselves were writing such 'intimate letters'.

Their terms are the same,[3] plus third-class rail tickets. We'll provide lunch for them. And if all were alright at your house, two of them could perhaps sleep on the ground floor? I think they'll ask you for it.

So it's fixed up.

One more thing, how is it with your mother! Is the improvement continuing?

Will you be able to get away to Luhačovice? What shall I tell them there?

I've already given you my address.

Will a letter come from you tomorrow? Will I learn something new?

I've finished all my work as if I wouldn't need to return to Brno for anything.[4] It's strange. Everything seems to be hurrying to its end all by itself!

1 Mrs Neumannová went to Jáchymov only a week later (see Stösslová's letter written before 4 July 1928).
2 Stösslová appears to have hurt her foot during the Zvíkov expedition.
3 as they would be in Brno (i.e. for the Moravian Quartet to give the première of *Intimate Letters* in Písek).
4 This fateful premonition seems to have been something of an *idée fixe* in Janáček's last days in Brno. The Janáčeks' servant Marie Stejskalová reported Janáček as saying almost the same words (see Epilogue).

It's as if I no longer were to take a pen into my hand here. And how easily everything is developing! Calm itself. And also my acquaintances, as if someone had blown them off [the face of] the earth. Well, holidays! I can't imagine my holidays in Luhačovice without you. So I stand as if by an open window, but at night, when, however carefully you look, however wide you open your eyes, you won't see anything other than sheer darkness.

I listened to their playing today. I listen. Did I write that? Those cries of joy, but what a strange thing, also cries of terror after a lullaby. Exaltation, a warm declaration of love, imploring; untamed longing. Resolution, relentlessly to fight with the world over you. Moaning, confiding, fearing. Crushing everything beneath me if it resisted. Standing in wonder before you at our first meeting. Amazement at your appearance; as if it had fallen to the bottom of a well and from that very moment I drank the water of that well. Confusion and high-pitched song of victory: 'You've found a woman who was destined for you.' Just my speech and just your amazed silence. Oh, it's a work as if carved out of living flesh. I think that I won't write a more profound and a truer one. So I end. Every day you'll hear something more from me and then from Luhačovice – what, I don't know. I won't feel like talking. I think of you healthy and content. Just sort out what to do with Rudi in good time. Don't let him grow higher than your head!

Sleep well.

Yours for ever

L.

Kamila Stösslová to Leoš Janáček, Písek, 27 June 1928

[...] Mummy wrote to me, and this has changed everything [...] It was hard for her to write to me but she begged me not to go anywhere for the time being, that there's no-one to rely on and that she wouldn't be at peace. So I wrote back immediately not to worry, that I'll be at home until she returns in good health. [...] We've got enough work and so time flies during it all. I won't even go to Vienna or anywhere at all the dress will be sent from Prague and that will do for me. There's nothing to be done and so therefore don't worry about it either, just make sure that the spa has a good effect. [...]

My dear Kamila

Once again you are left to your own devices and again endless irritation will come over you. I'm not surprised; how you can face everything! But consider *that your mother can't be ill at home*! It's in her good, surely, to be under continual medical supervision, either in a sanatorium, or in a hospital. *It can't be any other way*. Please write to me at once which sanatorium in Vinohrady[1] it is.

I, rather than any of you, will be told the truth. I'll ask the chief doctor for the unvarnished truth; I want to do so in your interest.

It's possible, surely, to arrange things at home; after all, two men and a grown boy[2] don't need you to wait on them and sacrifice yourself when they are healthy – and terribly inconsiderate! Do think of yourself a bit.

I'll write at once from Luhačovice to your mother too. Just tell me that address. Have they operated on her? That would be a hopeful sign. But everything will be a long haul whether to health or to something worse. You don't cough for a while, then it returns again so that I'd despair of you. At last be a little decisive and go. After all, Luhačovice is not the end of the earth, and you'll get a break, won't you?

Three days – and already you'd be so well as to give one joy.

I'll write to the doctor in such a way that he'll surely not deny me the truth if I ask him because of, and with respect to, your health.

That you're not going to Vienna is good. But sort things out at home once and for all and don't overdo the waiting on everyone. Can't they all eat in a pub for a while?

And don't be surprised at your mother's wishes to have you stay at home. It's for the comfort of those who come to sleep, eat, go off, sleep again, eat and go off! Take the boy with you, Otuš, who still needs you badly, and Marta will be sufficient for the sleeping, eating and going off [of the men]. *And your mother can't leave the sanatorium as long as she's not recovered*!

[...]

But I hope nevertheless that everything will take a turn for the good.

---

1 Despite Janáček's advice to send Mrs Neumannová to a sanatorium in Podolí, Prague (see 671), Mrs Neumannová seems to have gone to one in the Vinohrady district of Prague.
2 i.e. Kamila's father, her husband and their elder son Rudolf, then fifteen.

Keep well and write as I've asked you.
Yours for ever
L.

You'll also join that Mozart society.[1] We'll talk about it.

697   Brno, 29 June 1928, at night

My dear Kamila

My last letter from Brno.

You know what made me very sad? Today I was at the exhibition again. I was sorry that you weren't walking beside me, that you couldn't have chosen something for yourself from the very lovely things, that I couldn't have chosen something for you. The exhibition is magnificent; you'll have to see it.

And I'm sad too that I'm leaving and it seems to me, as if for the desert.

If my cure weren't essential I wouldn't even go there.

[...]

Today I had a day full of satisfaction. The leader of the Czech Quartet from Prague, Mr Hoffmann – came to see me – for *our* quartet *Intimate Letters*! They'll play it first in Holland. People are already speaking a lot about this work of *ours*, and nicely.

That cheered me up the whole day.

[...]

And I think to myself that if only it could be that this double life were cut short and everything were to flow only in a single stream. You know what ought to happen?

And so it gets more distant – and a year, I no longer believe this '*in a year's time*'. Something sad always comes rushing out of the blue. You immediately lose heart, and I? I'm lost in thought, I gaze into emptiness; like a spider I weave a net round about, and the wind tears it. Again and again, hopelessly.

I'm going off, and if I call you, you won't hear. As I wrote to you, I'll endeavour to learn the truth directly. Just tell me where your mother is now being treated.

In Luhačovice I'll look for a letter from you on arrival.

If only everything would change the way we wish it. Keep well.

Yours for ever

L.

1 See p.261.

My dear Kamila

And sadness waited for me in that place where you were hidden last year. I walked about the spa along the out-of-the-way paths. I took my white cap as a hat and went at once to that deserted heaven. They were surprised; you'd cancelled the room, they said. Even sadder, I went for supper. The woman was also surprised. I told her everything about your mother's illness and expressed the hope that nevertheless you'd soon arrive. Home by the back paths. I unpacked and now I'm writing to you. No letter from you was waiting for me; so I can expect nothing good from this.

I'll be living here without you for twenty-one days in a way that I've never lived in the spa before. Nothing gives me pleasure here; I didn't encounter any acquaintance and don't want to. A week ago today! I remember our beautiful trip. We all overflowed with health – except for your foot. I hope it's jumping for joy again. When I travelled here it was amazingly hot and the train jam-packed. It's said to be full here. What will you tell, what will I learn! Will you come after all?

How to tempt you here!

And your mother wanted you to come, didn't she! Isn't there a whispering campaign from your sister-in-law behind it?

I'm waiting now only for the address of that sanatorium, so as to ask about everything myself. I just beg you, write to me daily now, otherwise I wouldn't survive here.

Oh, if only I could wait for you in some quiet corner! Only with this thought will I comfort myself.

Yours for ever

L.

Janáček's letters from Luhačovice became increasingly insistent and self-pitying. From a second one sent on 1 July 1928 (*699) only the envelope remains. He wrote a postcard the next day (*700) complaining that he had not heard from her, and once again that evening, a letter that finally provoked an irritated response.

701 Luhačovice, 2–3 July 1928

My dear Kamila

Oh why don't you write? What's happened this time? You know that this uncertainty torments me more than not knowing what's the matter with you. After all a week's gone by already since you last wrote. That's not a good sign. Today an express registered letter came for me and the postman didn't leave it in the room for me. I thought that it was from you and I went looking for it. I got it only in the evening – and it was a stupid letter!

I've inhaled and lain in the carbonic spa; I've eaten meals entirely without meat. All this to add fasting to sadness. [...]

Now it's half-past eight and I'll go to sleep with the chickens and at my Kamila's hour. I've worn my feet out, walked myself off them.

And I've got nothing to look for. The path to last year's heaven is overgrown; it's full of strangers there. It's the more expensive time in the spa now; fewer visitors here. Those from the poorer classes have left. I never go across the *slanice*;[1] I'll go round it with the photographer too. I have breakfast, lunch and supper at Mrs Gutová's;[2] no-one will even know that I'm here. Tomorrow she'll send you cakes and all sorts of things. I hope you like them; I'll have a look at them tomorrow before she sends them.

As long as your letter doesn't come it's like looking into the dark forest.

The cuckoo called to me from nearby; I said that he was calling: I'm coming, I'm coming! [...] Sleep well.
(Monday, 2 July)

Tuesday, 3 July. Even today a letter didn't come from you! What should I think of it? That you've gone off? That they've brought your mother home? That she's in a very bad way? None of that would be a reason for not writing! I can't think of anything else. I'm baffled. Or haven't you had a letter from me yet and are waiting to hear that I'm definitely here?

It's really hot here. You'd enjoy the sun and the river. I'm also barely getting myself sorted out here. Instead of waiting for you, accompanying you, I stay in my room, peering out of the window.

[without signature]

Kamila Stösslová to Leoš Janáček, Písek, before 5 July 1928

[...] Today my husband wrote to me saying that mother's going to Jáchymov. He was with her, she's very weak so he drove with her around Prague which she likes so much. She was pleased that he came

---

1 The local name for the central area of the spa, a reference to the salty earth out of which curative salt waters come.
2 See Glossary: 'dairy'.

and just kept on asking after me and said she'd already like to be home. [...] And now a few words for you.

I've read your letter of yesterday several times and was sorry how you grumble about the whole world. Is everything really so hopeless with you? Were you happier before? How well you too know how to embitter a person's life! Are you just a small child that can't do without a dummy? You write as if it was my fault. Who's suffering more than me but what can I do? I'm just doing my duty. There's a time for everything for joy and for sorrow. I'm losing heart but you even more so. You've got peace you can devote yourself to treatment and all that you want, and I don't even speak about myself. Why do you take it so tragically possibly you'll still be with me so long that you'll grow tired of it. And how on earth did you live before you knew me? You're at home all year long without me so why carry on so? [...] So I hope that you'll be a changed man now otherwise I wouldn't even write this letter. I want you to be terribly cheerful and enjoy yourself as is fitting for a visitor at the spa. [...]

702 Luhačovice, 4–5 July 1928

Dear Kamila

Well, now at last I'm content. When I know that it's impossible otherwise and 'no more about it', I'm calm. Another day of that uncertainty and I'd have been in Luhačovice in vain.

Now I know that I have my Kamila again, that perhaps suddenly she'll appear and that we'll love each other madly, not so?

Yes, I need great strength for what awaits me this year. I'm gathering it in Luhačovice and perhaps I'll get rid of those rheumatic pains from all that sitting, and – from that joyless life at home. Vigour and defiance, movement, change, that's the way I like to live. It's you, your character to which I cling. Now I'd so like to hug you! Oh, if only you would once let yourself be hugged. And you always just escape like a slippery little fish!

I say to myself 'don't think about it. She doesn't want what you so long for. Why do you torment yourself, plague yourself with it? Only dreams remain for you!' But sometimes dreams come true. Will you help them come true? [...]

So sleep well. I'll imagine that you're sleeping next to me. – In that case you certainly wouldn't sleep!

[...]

(Wednesday, 4 July at night)

And today the letter came with 'a few words for me'. I wasn't happier before; I was like a tree in the field, the gale-force wind made it shake, it's a wonder it wasn't wrenched from the earth. But I thought that I was very happy at the time, then, on the contrary, moments come when the tree is shaken again. And how easily the strong wind lets itself be calmed – with a few words in a letter. I'd never grow weary living with you. And how did I live before I knew you? I didn't live at all. I was dying. How can you think that I should be 'cheerful' here as is fitting for a visitor at the spa! You give me a dummy! You ought to have said that the way I write is not like a man – but like an old woman! You wanted to say that, not so? It's true, I'm a silly child. I'm glad that you're well. Here there are few visitors this year; that was due to the Brno exhibition.

Yours for ever

L.

Luhačovice, 5 July 1928

703 Luhačovice, 5–6 July 1928

My dear Kamila

And I too have read through your last letter many times. I walked through the quiet, empty wood, I stopped at this bench or that and read it again. What serious things you wrote on a single page!

If only you could imagine what it's like to be in these lodgings of mine in Luhačovice this year! You must know very well by now that I'm completely alone. What should I be doing here, apart from this stupid treatment, were it not for those bonds between us two? I think that these bonds are too strong now, well I don't need any stronger, for me not to feel for ever bound to you. Were it not for these bonds, I wouldn't survive in this isolation. That's why I wrote to you so piningly when no letter came from you for several days. Just think, I've got nobody in the world to search for apart from you. The worst thing was when the word *hopelessness* came into my pen. In that sadness of mine I felt myself deserted. You're bound to your household as if with ropes; you don't have the strength to break them. How could *hopelessness* have not occurred to me!

Of course I know and feel that even this relationship of ours is an act of kindness to me, a refuge. I feel it especially here now, in this isolation.

You said what was it like before I knew you? Didn't I run away from home myself, always eager for at least a little sincerity? Not now; since I have you and know you, the whole world and what's in it is all the same to me. You are my light and when it doesn't shine in my room, there's darkness all around.

However, away now with lamentation!

Old woman, child, dummy to you!

Possibly, 'that I'll be with you so long that I'll grow tired of it!'[1] What silly things you say! Try being with me *a long time*, i.e. for ever! – Oh, forgive me, if I'm tormenting you again. It will never be different while I live. The isolation is terrible. Write at least *Tvá Kamila*! To lessen that hopelessness.

Yours for ever

Leoš

Luhačovice, 5 July

Tomorrow, Hus Day, I was at your place.[2]

And now in the morning I read your letter again. There are also some words of comfort there. Words of course are too little for me. But you know how to 'tell me off'! As no-one else. I'll pull myself together again. Especially when someone mocks me. And you chose such apt words: 'Don't take it so tragically!' But that hope: 'Possibly you'll still be with me', here at least I smile. It's like when you put a little speck of sugar into bitter coffee. You know that I avoid everyone here, that I talk only with the waiter? Isn't it enough that I've promised you, if instead of a long sermon you'll write me just two words: <u>Tvá Kamila</u>, it will be a miraculous cure for me. I'll recover my spirits. Without that, mud, salt water, inhalation[3] will do nothing to help if I don't see those two words. [...]

Yours for ever

L.

704 Luhačovice, 6 July 1928

Dear Kamila

Today is the fifth day of treatment, so a rest of from it all. From 7 o'clock in the morning I've been wandering around the Jestřabí forest.

You know, on that one side of a letter so many serious thoughts! I read one. 'Was I happier?', you ask. I've been reflecting on it the

---

1 An inexact quotation from Kamila Stösslová's letter written before 5 July 1928. The shorter version the next day is exact.

2 See Glossary: 'Hus Eve'.

3 A common method of treatment in Luhačovice for which a special building was erected at the beginning of the century, replaced in 1922 by a modern 'Inhalatorium'.

whole morning; I've been recollecting things. At my wedding? I wasn't happy. Just coldness, no warmth. And then that rush began. Only a rush to be able to get attached to someone, to give oneself entirely to someone. In vain. I'm sure I burnt with love, but never any response. I was like a ship at sea, without oars. Tossed about. And now I'm the happiest man. That's because of that mad, beautiful moment, when I said 'Ty' to you for the first time! My soul joined with yours. I found happiness here for the first time.

< part of page cut off > [...]

705 Luhačovice, 7–8 July 1928

My dear Kamila

Today I went out to have a little look round the places with memories for us. Miramare[1] is again in other hands and – empty.

The little place above Glücksmann, that bench, where you used to put a twig between you and me to divide us,[2] that little place not far from the stall where I got to know your blood,[3] which smelt for ever fragrant to me!

That little wood above Žofín[4] where you hid, that's no longer there. They're building a *pension* there. They'd already got it up to three floors and suddenly the earth began to move. They shouldn't have built in the place where my Kamila's feet have run! I felt intensely nostalgic for the years that have passed and their beauty! But, old woman, you mustn't cry! I am coming to myself a little; my nerves were already worn out.

Mrs Gutová asked me again if I'd had any news of the parcel.[5] That's everything today. I endure mud as hot as your sun, 40°. But the sweat pours out from me.

What's your news? What about your mother? What about Rudi? Is he already an 'apprentice'? What of Otuš? Doesn't he ask when he'll be going to Hukvaldy? Being the fifth wheel on a cart [i.e. redundant], I don't ask you this same question now.

Another week, and then I think actually that I could flee from here. But no, I'll tour the surrounding villages by car. The local museum society has asked me for the speech notation of local people. Here it's full of Hungarians, Germans and Jews, which you yourself don't like.

1 A café (see also 475).
2 See Glossary: 'Glücksmann'.
3 This incident is not described elsewhere.
4 The *pension* where Stösslová stayed in 1917.
5 She had already asked on 6 July (*704).

Well, all people want to have good health. In addition I want Mrs Kamila, but they don't have her in Luhačovice.

Tomorrow is Sunday, 8 July. You also remembered Hus's eve![1] It was beautiful; I no longer know why. Well, I don't know why at all it is that something draws one to something. You know, a flower also turns to the side where the sun comes from. From Luhačovice, Písek is in the west; possibly enough for me too always to turn to that side. At the end of the letter I'll wait to see whether a letter comes from you tomorrow; I wonder about the *signature*! Sleep well. For the night [there are] still your letters. Forgive me that I'm bitter. I love you so much – and I don't have you! –

Sunday. Will a letter come from you? Won't it come? And I think that I'll launch into my second love when I don't have my first, this Kamila of mine. And that second love? It's work. One thing I know, that no power can betray me, even if it wanted to. – And Sunday! The postman doesn't deliver the post! Mrs Gutová offered to pick it up in the afternoon. Will there be something from you?!

And my little soul, I love you unutterably! You say I've known for ages! But you don't know how very much, do you? Will there be just that signature *'Tvá Kamila'*!? I've calmed down. I acknowledge that you're right in everything. I already know 'those few words for me' by heart; especially those where you write 'perhaps[2] we'll be together so long', but minus those final words. Keep well.

Yours for ever
Leoš

By Monday 9 July the post had come bearing two letters from Kamila. They have not survived, but one seems to have been signed as requested (see 707). Janáček continued the letter he had begun writing on Sunday evening (*706), outlining various plans for meeting. He continued to elaborate these plans in his next letter:

707 Luhačovice, 9–10 July 1928

My dear Kamilka
    I thank you for that most beautiful signature.
    It's my guarantee that everything contained in it will come true.
    Everything had to happen like that, that grief before joy. And you'll

1 See Glossary: 'Hus Eve'.
2 His memory, however, was fallible. By this time, Kamila's 'possibly' ['možná'] had become his 'perhaps' ['snad'].

make up for all the grief. You have no idea how I long for you. Under that roof of ours I won't let you out of my arms. And Kamilka, I think you could come to Luhačovice as early as Sunday [15 July]. I'll stay only that week in Brno and you, either be that week in Luhačovice or get through it in Strážnice. We'd meet in Hulín and then travel together. It's not far to Hulín either from Luhačovice (via Hradiště) or from Strážnice. We'll talk about it in detail here. Leave the exhibition until the journey back from Hukvaldy.

But decide according to your own wishes. I've got no thoughts other than to make those days pleasant for you, if only they were years! So that we could forget the whole world. I'd like you to be all my joys, all my world.

Were that so already! Let these days fly now! Today for the first time I passed through the *slanice*[1] and perhaps I smiled too. How you have me in your power, how glad I am in your power, how happy I am that I'm yours! Sleep well my little dark angel! Why have you slept badly? Under our roof I'll always get you to sleep! Storms, come every night, for all I care! I'm waiting for your decision by return of post! –

I too was up at 5 o'clock and am also finishing this letter to you. Oh believe me I'm on tenterhooks here. It's like when a person is on the way to heaven – and St Peter lets him wait there still at the gate. Keep well.

Yours for ever
Leoš

708   Luhačovice, 10 July 1928

My dear passionately beloved Kamila
   [...]
If you liked it, then you can stay [in Hukvaldy] as long as you want.

Never, and no matter how long, would I have my fill of you. The longer we'll be together, the more I'd desire you. You're so beautiful, for me you're heaven, the sweet of the sweet. I don't know why it's so, but there's nothing dearer in the world than to have you.

You yourself perhaps don't feel how very dear you are to me. I can't kiss you enough; it's as if one drank a red-hot fire, always

1 See p.321, fn.1.

[327]

hotter and hotter. What is it that burns in your mouth, let alone in your dear sweet body! Can it be expressed! I think that the whole time I'll just carry you in my arms – and will never let you go. Would that it were so!

So decide as you wish. I'll wait for you here on Sunday [15 July], or on 29 July in Brno. My beloved Kamilka!

[...]

Janáček wrote once again on 10 July, but only the envelope has survived (*709).

710   Luhačovice, 11–12 July 1928

My dear pretty little Negress

You wrote that you'd write again 'tomorrow', but a letter didn't arrive today. I got a fright. If only you were here already or in Hukvaldy. I won't have peace any sooner. What a good mood you can put one into! Today I went as far as Řetechov![1] From Alojzka[2] in one go. After that I ate a fried cauliflower with a salad, macaroni with Parmesan cheese and tea as well! It was good, but I know that you're so nice that one could kiss you all the time. At Hukvaldy we'll eat every chicken, goose, duck! If I could see how you'll like it. I can't help it, someone's coral lips taste better to me. And if in that heat at the oven you were a sort of half-naked savage, everything about you would have tasted nice then. I wonder why you haven't written? I fear something bad again! So sleep well.
(11 July, evening).

Oh dear Kamila, it's good that the two letters came together; the first annoyed and the second nice. [...]

So it's decided! *You'll come on Sunday 29 July by the noon express to Brno. I'll wait for you at the station. In the afternoon we'll go to the exhibition, and on Monday 30 July at 10 o'clock we'll leave for Hukvaldy!*

So make your arrangements accordingly. I think that you'll recover in the peace of Hukvaldy. Here the spas are now so packed[3] that it's

---

1 The round trip from Luhačovice to Řetechov was described in Balhar's guide book (1914) as a 'very gentle' walk of 7.5 km.
2 See p.304, fn.2.
3 Either custom had picked up or Janáček had not been observant; ten days earlier he had commented on how few visitors there were (701 and 702).

impossible even to get in for inhalation. At the same time the heat's unbearable.

So my little soul don't get angry with me any more, I've stood up to torture here and have thought the whole time that you're indecisive and you don't think of yourself.

I'll leave here on Saturday 21 July. I'll be glad when I disappear from here. You yourself have been upset and I'll have a veritable jail here right up to the end.

[...]
Yours for ever
Leoš
12 July 1928

So 29 July and to Brno!
If you were to come here to Luhačovice I'd wait for you on 22 July.

711   Luhačovice, 12–13 July 1928

My dear Kamila

Well that annoyed letter, that was a hiding for me! You let out that you were no longer thinking even of Hukvaldy! Didn't the same thought go through my head? And could I have been myself then! Yes, I wasn't myself. I knew that you couldn't behave otherwise, but what about me, poor wretch! A greater punishment couldn't be piled on me than this year's stay in Luhačovice! I'll only believe that you're with me when you're under my roof!

Now sleep well and keep well! I won't reproach you any more with anything; better to talk about it [in person]: it will be seen at the same time that I love you unutterably – and then one can bear anything! –

And I feel now that I ought not to have written such irritated letters to you. You yourself have had quite enough to bear and I've burdened you even more!

But even you, had you been in my place here, wouldn't have remained calm. Especially when the treatment did no good, and all hopes were thwarted. [...] If only you were already under our roof. – I deserved that annoyed letter and the nice one from Tuesday [10 July] cheered me up again. It's you, my dear Kamilka, who's weighed down by more than a person can bear. From 29 July I'll take everything upon myself for you, and I want to serve you devotedly and bring you pleasant things. I'll forget about myself, since in Luhačovice I've thought too much about myself.

Such heat in the night! I threw off the coverlet [–] I'd have stripped everything off myself, opened the window – only then did I get to sleep, sleeping until 7. I'm writing to you first thing in the morning. Don't be angry with me any more! You are my Kamilka.

Yours for ever

Leoš

13 July 1928

712 Luhačovice, 16 July 1928

My dear Kamila

The heat today! I protect myself against the sun as best I can – I'm the only one here who has a white cap – but today even the forests are furnaces.

Tomorrow I'll start the cold water treatment: oxygen dissolved in water, paddle in warm water – then cold, then a shower. I'm already looking forward to it!

I've lost my desire for being photographed[1] – without you, why bother! Today in the reading room about six young ladies and students surprised me. They wanted my autograph. I said do you know me? They said yes. So I signed for them. And they were all Jewish! That's interesting. It's like that when I burn with love for my dear black girl, said to be a Jewess. But we have that God who doesn't know religious differences, the God of love!

Dr Vavrouch[2] has gone blind in his left eye because of the heat; he isn't treating patients; only those who were with him before – he continues to treat. And I was glad of the way that that cold shower fell on me. I was already up at 5 o'clock today. It's now 10 in the morning and hot again. It will be better in Hukvaldy.

The dam hasn't got any water yet;[3] I won't even go there. And today, I was standing – standing with an acquaintance from Prague, when a photographer took me.[4] I don't want to see it; I don't have anyone to 'cut off' the picture.[5] In this heat you'll go about naked even in Hukvaldy. I'll spank you whenever we meet.

1 On 8–9 July (*706) Janáček reported not having been photographed yet; by 11–12 July (*710) he reported that he had been chasing a photographer 'for miles'.
2 Dr František Vavrouch had served as a doctor at the spa since 1906.
3 Work began on a dam two kilometres from Luhačovice in 1912 but the war interrupted its progress and it was completed only in 1928.
4 The Prague acquaintance was probably Josef Jiránek (1855–1940), one of Smetana's pupils. The photograph was reprinted in Český svět, xxiv (1928), no.51 (13 September 1928).
5 See 503.

I'll begin slowly packing; it will be all at sixes and sevens. I'll be grateful for the spa, but I'll have bad memories of my solitariness. It's still lucky that we've written so much to one another, and such 'good things'! Yesterday there was no letter from you. Keep well! I love you very, very much.

Yours for ever

Leoš

713 Luhačovice, 17–18 July 1928

My dear Kamilka

You probably didn't finish reading that last wild letter! Perhaps you'll be afraid to go to Hukvaldy because of it?

Oh no Kamilka, I'll be obedient, nice — everything just left to a kind fate! And to your will.

However I was agitated by my desire for you, so enraptured, wanting you so much that I couldn't write in any other way. Answer as you want. God forbid that I should want to force you into anything. You surely know me by now, that I'm completely devoted to you. In particular don't misunderstand one thing: that I'd wish to gain you through promises. God forbid!

I know you and I know myself. It's obvious, surely, that if one day we should belong to one another, what's mine would also be yours. Tempting you would be ridiculous because it would be my duty. I wanted to add that to my last letter, so that you wouldn't get angry with me, so that you wouldn't wrong me.

Sleep well. (17 July 1928, Tuesday)

And now I'm already looking forward to your saying 'I'm coming!' And to our leaving Frenštát by car for Hukvaldy, stopping in front of the 'cottage', leading my darling Kamilka 'under our roof' and saying to her, now be in charge here, be at home here, be my sweet ruler here; I look forward to your scurrying about everywhere in your silent slippers, to the house being full of you, of your laughter, of your chatter — to my happiness and joy entering the house with you!

No letter came yesterday. Keep well

and that Zvíkov leg also.[1]

Yours for ever

Leoš

18 July 1928.

1 See p.316, fn.2.

My dear Kamilka

Today, Thursday 19 July, no letter came from you. And how I rushed to the post office! The Frenchman William Ritter sought me out here and chatted with me from 12 until 4 o'clock.[1] I gave him my letter for him to drop into the station post box so that it would still go off today from here. There are really two letters in one envelope with two stamps. Tell me if it's reached you. We spoke about Fibich–Anežka.[2] He said she was as ugly as night and held him with her claws. And I know my Kamilka, black and beautiful as the dark night with the stars in the sky. She hasn't any claws, but soft and nimble little fingers.

Ritter is probably coming to hear our quartet in Písek. Perhaps you'll even meet him in Hukvaldy. I've already done half my packing. I shall be glad to get away from here this year; apart from your letters there was only quiet sadness about me.

And I go to supper stick in hand. And it starts raining. It's raining for the first time in three weeks; but only a few drops. You know how [last year] during the rain Mrs Gutová lent us an umbrella, how you jumped in and out of the car like a little squirrel? And nevertheless I'm sorry even when I'm leaving! For the time spent here, the three weeks! Just as I'm grateful for your intimate lines! What terrible loneliness would have come over me here! I didn't feel like work, sometimes more like crying.

I've already painted your stay in Hukvaldy so beautifully in my mind that I'm almost frightened that an evil turn of events might thwart these passionate wishes. Now not even to talk of it and to have you now [with me] in the train and go off with you, to drive away with my treasure. Not to stop until in front of the gates of the house; to go in and forget about the whole world. To dance attendance as a faithful shadow on my Kamilka and serve my queen. I know that you'll feel at home and I'll be really with you in a happy home. You'll warm it and make it very dear. And let all beautiful dreams float down and come true!

Yours for ever

Leoš

---

1 In his letter of 24 March 1928 (BmJA, D 1363; see 619) Ritter mentioned that he was hoping to meet with Janáček alone, and that he had resolved to write a book about him.
2 See 534 and 540.

Janáček sent off a second letter on 19 July 1928, though only the envelope survives (*715).

716   Luhačovice, 20 July 1928

My dear Kamilka

What news will come from you? Today the last letter from here. I wrote to you about the only person who has told me that he likes me. But poor thing! Now for the third or fourth year he always tells me his life story. As soon as he begins I know that the wheel won't be stopped! He tells it in the same way to the very last detail. I smile and pay attention [to hear] whether he won't falter. He doesn't. So I hear him out, give him my hand at the dairy and we part. An invalid. He doesn't know that he keeps on saying the same thing.

And I? Since I've been writing to Kamilka it's always about one thing. I return to the same thing, but it seems to me nevertheless always in a different way – and yet I also don't lie. And there are hundreds of these letters. And they are a comfort and a need. So the time without sadness is approaching! We'll revel from morning till eve. And in the evening still more and in the night I'd like to revel most of all. Only when will my Kamilka sleep? She won't have time to, will she!

I think that I've thoroughly recovered despite this food fit for a cat! Yesterday evening: cabbage – dumplings, sheep's milk cheese – sour milk! And one isn't bad on it. One eats everything. But that fasting was necessary for me; gout would have taken root in me like masonry, unmoving, painful. I lost eight kilos! And it's not noticeable on me.

I got up my strength! Just wait, there'll be contests. Someone will win – who will submit! And it will surely be you, my little dove! Of all the treatment the best is cold water. I turned the shower on to cold; it was as if needles were pricking. And to paddle in water! Warm for a moment then cold for a shorter period! That brings one back to life. And now you, my dove, I'll wait for when you fly off, lose your way and don't return – at least not soon. I'm waiting for the post now! ... (20 July). And again a letter didn't come from you. There's something bad in this!

Yours for ever
Leoš

And when here last year we sent out portraits![1]

And that Friday–feast-day[2] of the first kiss! How poor it looked here this year! Only the forests are similarly brooding! And how many fireflies fly here in the evenings! Where do they come from, where are they born!

717 Luhačovice–Brno, 20–1 July 1928

I'm off; a letter didn't even come yesterday evening.

This torment, just like three weeks ago!
Luhačovice, 20 July 1928

My dear Kamila
I've arrived in Brno. Why didn't you write when you told me that you'd write again tomorrow?

What's happened?

How even the last two days were spoilt.

Yours for ever

Leoš
Brno, 21 July 1928

718 Brno, 21–2 July 1928

My dear Kamila
What should I think? Thursday – Friday – Saturday – Sunday [19–22 July] no letter from you!

Either your mother is in a bad way,

or something's happened to you again,

or you're now preparing for the journey,

or, or – but not one of these cases is enough for you not to take a pen into your hand and write a few lines! But already in the first weeks in Luhačovice I was much troubled by your silence. This time I'll wait calmly until you answer.

I left Luhačovice without even taking a [last] look round. No-one missed me and I, still less, left nothing there except lots of money.

In one thing I've mended my ways, I've got used to a dummy. This calm now when I can't find any more passionate words! I called as if into the distant plain, I wait longingly for an answer to be born somewhere; and it's so quiet, not a single sound. It stops me in my

1 Plate 5, for instance (sent on 27 August 1927), and Plate 11, sent with a short inscription to Kamila's cousin Malvína Mikolášková.
2 See Glossary: 'Friday–feast-day'.

[334]

tracks, I hang my head; at Radhošť I saw the sheep standing like that a while. They hung their heads, without grazing. As if they were thinking; I think, however, that they had no thoughts at all. Dullness. So sleep well. (Saturday, 21 July, Brno)

I'm in such uncertainty over you! Your last letters full of joy, and suddenly, as if cut off!

The day before I left Luhačovice a nice incident happened to me. I went beyond 'Glücksmann'[1] to say goodbye to your bench. Further on, a woman was sitting with her two- or three-year-old child, who barred my way on the path with a stick. 'I won't let you further', it cried; a little way on a servant with another child; and that child also didn't want to allow anyone to go on. I sat down on the next bench, that one of ours, and – in a while both children came to me. So I chatted to them. One was *Jenda*, the smaller one *Mařenka*. It's a wonder they didn't climb on to my lap. I learnt that they were from Bratislava. After a long while they shouted 'Daddy' and both went off towards him. I said 'I've been talking with your children!' Well, and that was the end of the fun. You know what pleased me? That those two unknown children trusted me, that they weren't frightened of me! Somebody else's children! Would it be different with 'our' children? Wouldn't it be even better? Wouldn't their Negress mother sit with me as well? That was the secret reason why I so liked the incident, and why I like retelling it.

If a letter doesn't come from you tomorrow, then there's surely something wrong with your mother! If only you hadn't taken her away from Jáchymov! Poděbrady is a spa for heart complaints, and not for such an insidious illness! I'm calmly awaiting your explanation. (Sunday, 22 July p.m.)

What am I waiting for tomorrow? That you'll tell me for certain when you're coming to Brno, that I'll learn when we'll get into the train for Hukvaldy. Will it be so?

I now sit in Brno tired rather [than recovered] after Luhačovice. Today, Sunday, I sat out in the garden. No wish to go anywhere, to travel anywhere. If only I were over the hills from here! I don't want to work and don't want to talk either.

As you know how uneasy I am when you don't write, you ought at least to have written, whatever's the matter.

I'll finish this letter after tomorrow's post.

Be well and sleep well – if everything is for the good and if you

1 See Glossary.

haven't written before my letter from Brno arrived (22 July, evening).
Yours for ever
Leoš

The letter came. Your poor mother! So I won't see her any more. You could have sent a telegram, I would have come! I want to see you here now.
Your.

Kamila Stösslová to Leoš Janáček, Písek, 21 July 1928 at night

Dear Maestro
After great grief and suffering I let you know that my beloved mummy died on Tuesday [17 July], they brought her [home] to me on Wednesday and the funeral was on Friday. I can't write any more[; more] when we'll see each other in Brno on Friday or Saturday. I want peace and I'll find it only in your presence. I greet you warmly.
Kamila

719   Brno, 23 July 1928

My dear Kamilka
I had a foreboding that something bad had happened! So she's no longer among the living, your mother who loved you so much! I'm sorry for you, your being deserted at home, your isolation. Believe me, I stand by you at every moment of need. You'll suffer most of all now. It will be deserted in the house, you'll wander around in it often. Now we have even more in common; I too am at home like a pear tree in an open field. When I come to see you, I'll lay a nice wreath on her quiet grave. I'm sorry for her; I liked her because of you and think that I wasn't a stranger to her. I'm sorry I hadn't seen her again. I didn't think that the end of it all would be so quick. With my mother it lasted years.

If there were no help for her then God was merciful to shorten her suffering.

I'm now expecting notification when I should wait for you in Brno; write soon, you'll have to spend the night here, it will be necessary to get a room for you. We'll leave on Monday 30 July at 10 o'clock; we'll be in Hukvaldy towards evening. There you'll grow calm, you'll take a rest; I wouldn't like to say that you'll forget a little. It's too heavy a blow for you. I'll try to ward off everything from you which would hurt you and add to your pain.

Now I know that you couldn't write! I can imagine what it was like at your place!

And I can also imagine you, poor thing! On the day of her funeral I had that French visitor [i.e. William Ritter] here ad nauseam. The whole of my stay in Luhačovice was a mourning, a presentiment of evil. I was glad that I left those places which without you were suddenly deserted. Everything lost its feeling, became hard, looked foreign.

[...]

Calm yourself; I'd like to have been with you in the first difficult moments. But believe me too, that [my] sorrow went through the countryside from Luhačovice to Písek. A sort of presentiment of evil that couldn't be chased away.

And we'll go together to her grave.

Write soon.

Yours for ever

Leoš

Janáček's letter of 23–4 July 1928 (*720) was concerned mostly with offering sympathy and making arrangements for the trip to Hukvaldy, a topic to which he returned at greater length in his next letter:

721   Brno, 24 July 1928

My dear Kamilka

I'd be glad if your decision about your arrival came by tomorrow. I must arrange transport from Frenštát to Hukvaldy.

I need to tell my sister all that she has to prepare; we can't turn up at the house without there being something to eat. I think that you should arrive on Saturday noon [28 July] at the latest. In the afternoon we can still buy a ball for Otuš; on Sunday it's closed everywhere here.

On Sunday we'd go out morning, afternoon and evening as well to the exhibition. You'd sleep the night; on Monday morning we'd leave Brno after 10.

You'll get this letter only on Thursday [26 July]; I'm waiting for your decision tomorrow. I think that we'll be in agreement. I won't write to you any more on Thursday; the letter would perhaps arrive only on Saturday and you'll certainly be in Brno by then.

And a tiny remark. Those letters which refer to things which only the two of us know I have burnt. The other letters I've put away in a safe. Take good care of my letters too; also that album.[1] It's not for curious people.

Just for you to be here now and for us to be already on our way together.

I'll take work with me,[2] but my only work and concern will be to give you a little bit of pleasant life. I won't have any thoughts other than to make what I see in your eyes come true for you. Or rather to make it come true for you before I notice it in your eyes. For you not to feel pain; we'll also talk together about your poor mother; we'll both be equally and sincerely sorry for her because we both loved her, because she wished us well.

Certainly there'll be a pleasant warmth in the little rooms of our dear cottage; we'll be happy everywhere; we'll dwell everywhere to our heart's content. I'll look for you in every corner like a gold ring which had been put away. And when I find you, what pleasure there'll always be from it. Your dear eyes will brighten whole rooms to gold, will frighten away every shadow; and when the evening twilight comes, we also [i.e. as in Písek] won't turn the lights on immediately. We'll remember the beautiful evenings in the Písek heaven. Let us transfer that heaven into the Hukvaldy cottage too. It will fit in there; we'll make a whole little heaven for ourselves. We'll be happy, like no-one else on earth.

From time to time we'll be sorry that your good-humoured, cheerful mother is no longer living. How hard it must have been for her, poor thing, when she learnt that there was no more help!

However, another feeling is getting stronger, that we two won't leave one another. Don't rejoice, you people who'd like to see the opposite! You'll give me handcuffs and I'll put out my hands for them and will kiss them; they give me the freedom to love you because it's impossible to do other than to love you.

Sleep well. I think that you must already be packing and getting together what you'll bring with you.

Yours for ever

Leoš

---

1 See Glossary.
2 Janáček took with him copyist's score of Act 3 of *From the House of the Dead*, and two unfinished pieces: sketches for his *Danube* symphony and for the incidental music to *Schluck und Jau*.

722 Brno, 25–6 July 1928

My dear Kamilka

Why do you delay so long? I waited confidently for a letter from you today. It's that Sunday when they don't get post in the country; therefore I have to write tomorrow, on Thursday, both to Hukvaldy and to Frenštát to order transport.

They must have a letter to hand on Saturday [28 July]; I'll have to send off the letters tomorrow.

I'll wait then for news from you tomorrow, Thursday, for certain.

Perhaps you've already got everything prepared for departure? You won't need that much, will you? I'd like to see you already away from your sad surroundings; after all, there you're like a kneaded roll which knows only a journey into the oven. I look forward to diverting you, that after a long time you'll breathe freely. Not so much binds you now to your orphaned home.

I'll get rail tickets from Brno as soon as I'm certain about your arrival; I'll have to get them on Saturday. Will you have many cases? Like that singer from the National Theatre.[1] When she travelled from Luhačovice to Zakopané? She had forty pieces. But a knight in shining armour appeared who looked after every piece. Poor thing, she nevertheless married someone else.

The railway will take us; but I just hope that the car will also be able to cope with us. The heaviest 'piece' will be our Kamilka; she'll have to be specially insured! How will you survive the journey? If well, it will be a good sign. When we've travelled together it's always turned out well so far. And I'll look after you as if you were my very own eye.

So this is my last letter from Brno; I think that you'll have it to hand on Friday [27 July]. Have you made a decision perhaps according to my advice?

On Saturday noon arrive in Brno

on Sunday look at the exhibition and

on Monday 30 July after 10 o'clock in the morning leave Brno for Kojetín–Frenštát pod Radhoštěm.

I shall see how you've decided.

I'll post this letter after tomorrow's, Thursday's, post. Sleep well! What will you dream under our shared roof!

Yours for ever

Leoš

---

1 Apparently Marja Bogucká, see p.20.

25 July 1928 at night

I got your letter. I'll wait for you on Sunday. Calm down, it couldn't be helped. In any event we'll set off from Brno at 10 on Monday. I'll get you a room for the night.

Yours for ever

Leoš

Kamila Stösslová to Leoš Janáček, Písek, 25 July 1928

Dear Maestro

In reply to your letter I inform you that we'll arrive on Sunday [29 July] at noon. [...] Peace simply peace where I'll be able to forget a little. [...] I wish her that peace, she suffered so much. [...]

What can I still ask for perhaps nothing? Just relief like a sick person and I look for this only with you. [...]

I knew it wouldn't last long. However I told you that. I also didn't believe any of what they told my father in Prague.

I'm glad now I was at home that she died with the thought that I was taking care of everyone. We'll talk about other things when we meet.

She died in Jáchymov in the street she was meant to have left already, but she wanted to stay two more days.

Everything is sad for me.

I greet you warmly.

Kamila

I won't write any more.

Kamila

Epilogue

On 1 July the master went to Luhačovice. When he returned after three weeks he seemed a broken man. During that time he had lost seven[1] kilos, he told us that was perhaps because he had kept to a vegetarian diet. We kept looking at him barely dragging himself round the garden; once the mistress couldn't resist it and told him not to gamble with his health so. I don't know how it occurred to her to add:

'One day you'll get pneumonia and then it will be the end.'

He just went on nodding his head and said quietly:

'Yes, yes.'

That was on the path in the garden — and in a fortnight it had come true.

Mrs Neumannová, the mother of Mrs Stösslová, had been ill with cancer for some time and now died. She was a good and upright woman, we all had the best memories of her. The master invited Mrs Stösslová to Hukvaldy to recuperate. They agreed that they would leave Brno on 30 July, on the very birthday of the mistress. The Stössels with one son [Otto][2] arrived on Sunday 29 July, the other lad remained in Písek.[3] The master put on his white suit and went to meet them at the station. He took them to the exhibition of Úprka's paintings[4] and then to the fair grounds which had just been built and which opened with a large Exhibition of Contemporary Culture.

He went off before noon the next day, the Stössels waited for him at the station. The mistress advised him to take a taxi. He ordered one and was preparing to leave. Into his briefcase he put the third act of the opera *From the House of the Dead*, which he wanted to look

1 Janáček wrote 'eight' (716).
2 See 681 and 684.
3 There was talk of Rudolf's going to work for Mrs Stösslová's sister in Nezvěstice (652), though it sounds from Janáček's remark that Stösslová would not be 'deserted and isolated' (659) as though he remained in Písek to start an apprenticeship (see 660, 705).
4 Jóža Úprka (1861–1940) was allegedly the model for the painter Lhotský in Janáček's opera *Fate*. His paintings, which perhaps attracted Janáček for their use of Moravian ethnographic elements, were exhibited in the summer of 1928 at the Aleš Pavilion in Marešova ulice.

through in Hukvaldy. Then he shut the piano. He stood over it lost in thought and as I went about he said quietly:

'I have everything ready, but it seems to me as if I'm never to return.'[1]

This account by the Janáčeks' servant Marie Stejskalová recording Janáček's last days in Brno concludes with his abrupt farewell to his wife, an account verified by, or probably taken from, Mrs Janáčková's own reminiscences.[2] There were fewer witnesses in Hukvaldy. Otilie Krsková, who helped out in Janáček's cottage, reported that Mrs Stösslová arrived accompanied by her husband and one of her sons and that David Stössel went off again soon afterwards, leaving her with the boy. There are no further reports of Stössel; as usual he seems to have been taken up with business. Another absentee was Janáček's sister Josefa Dohnalová, who does not figure in any of the accounts of Janáček's last days.

Kamila and the boy lived in the upstairs room specially built for her visit. The weather was good and Janáček took them for walks daily in the countryside around Hukvaldy, regularly stopping on the way back in Míčaník's hotel for a snack. There were also longer trips – to Štramberk, Kotouč and Bílá hora. Some time on Wednesday 8 August – accounts differ whether it was in the morning or after lunch – they went up the hill, Babí hůra, in Janáček's part of the forest, a climb of 580 metres.[3] On the way back they picked up laundry that Miss Krsková's mother had done for them. According to Miss Krsková, Janáček began to feel pains in his ears and throat 'for the first time' towards evening, though he did not yet have a temperature.

By the next morning Janáček had a discharge from the ear and he sent a note to the Hukvaldy doctor, Dr Emil Franta, asking him to visit him. After breakfast he felt worse, Mrs Stösslová made up a bed for him, and he lay down. Visitors included Dr Franta, his colleague from the neighbouring town, and the mayor of Hukvaldy, Jan Sobotík, all of whom urged Janáček to go to hospital. He would not hear of it, agreeing only the next day, when he was worse. After drinking tea to sustain him on the journey he walked, unaided, to the waiting ambulance, joking to the orderlies on the way: 'So bring me back well again soon!'

It is striking that neither the brief article by Robert Smetana published shortly after Janáček's death in the memorial issue of *Hudební rozhledy* nor the recollections of Miss Krsková[4] (the above account draws on both these sources) say anything about what has become the best-known event of Janáček's last days: how the Stössel boy got lost, how Janáček went off to find him, and caught a chill which turned to pneumonia. Versions by Adolf Vašek (1930) and Janáček's niece Věra Janáčková (1940), based on the witness of 'local people' and 'the doctors', suggest respectively Monday and

1 Trkanová 2/1964, 116–17.
2 Janáčková 1939, 193.
3 Smetana 1928.
4 Procházka 1948, 170–1.

Tuesday (6 and 7 August) as the day of the fateful expedition in which the boy got lost. Since Janáčková claims that it took place in Janáček's part of the forest, this sounds like the Babí hůra expedition on Wednesday 8 August. Both agree that Janáček got flushed and overheated. The account by Marie Stejskalová, again based on the witness of others, includes a rain storm and the fact that the party all got drenched. From Thursday onwards there is little discrepancy about what happened since there are reliable medical reports made by the local doctors, who visited several times that day. On Friday morning Janáček consented to go to hospital in the nearest big town of Ostrava, where the doctors' diagnosis of pneumonia was confirmed by x-ray. Although the patient was in good spirits and showed some signs of improvement on Saturday, there was a sharp deterioration in his condition that evening, his heart began to fail, and, having great difficulty in breathing, he refused further injections to strengthen it. After he had been given a sedative, he fell into a sleep at 9 o'clock on Sunday morning 12 August and died an hour later. Kamila was at his bedside – she had been taken for a relative.

It was only then that Kamila Stösslová sent a telegram to Zdenka saying that Janáček was seriously ill (while alive he had refused to let anyone contact her). But, as she was making arrangements for the journey, Mrs Janáčková heard from elsewhere about her husband's death. Her memoirs describe her feelings in some detail, especially the fact that she would be meeting Stösslová at the other end. The two women travelled together from Ostrava to the Hukvaldy house so that Mrs Stösslová could hand over keys and money. In her memoirs Mrs Janáčková made no mention of either David Stössel or Josefa Dohnalová, nor even of the boy, though she did describe how Stösslová returned the inscribed ring that Janáček had given her. What happened to Kamila Stösslová next is not known. Presumably she made her way back to Písek unaided, perhaps stopping off in Strážnice, where her husband's relatives lived. There is no record that she was present at Janáček's funeral in Brno on 15 August, a large-scale civic affair with the body lying in state in the opera house, speeches, and a performance of part of Dvořák's Requiem and the Forester's farewell from *The Cunning Little Vixen*.

The author of the first book on Janáček to appear after his death, Adolf E. Vašek (1930), drew on the letters to Mrs Stösslová and some of her recollections, discreetly omitting any mention of her name in the main text (though it appears several times in the notes). And, as Svatava Přibáňová explained in her preface (see Appendix 1), it was on Mrs Janáčková's orders that Stösslová thereafter became something of a non-person and her death from cancer in 1935 at the age of forty-three was barely noticed. The quartet dedicated to her appeared in print only in 1938, the dedication omitted. Apart from Mrs Janáčková's interdict, another reason for the low profile of Kamila Stösslová was the knowledge that Janáček's association with a Jew would do him no good during the Nazi occupation of Czechoslovakia. This attitude prevailed for almost the next forty years, with access to the letters, eventually acquired by the Moravian Museum (see Appendix 1), generally restricted. Kamila Stösslová's husband managed to escape to Switzerland; her two sons, married to gentiles, survived the war in Czechoslovakia but other members of her family, for instance her father Adolf Neumann, perished in the concentration camps. The Jewish cemetery in Písek in which Kamila Stösslová and her mother were buried was desecrated.

*

On the journey to Hukvaldy Kamila Stösslová had brought with her the album in which Janáček had recorded most of their meetings since 2 October 1927. This is a book of fine sayings and music rather than a diary but with its almost daily dated entries it does add a little more information about the last days of Janáček's life at Hukvaldy. He made a short entry on Wednesday 1 August, two days after their arrival. The next day he sent off a holiday postcard to Zdenka: 'We've arrived safely. Cheerfulness in the house. Pains from arms and legs gone. So it should be. The money arrived. Leoš'.[1] The entry in the album dated 3 August suggests that Kamila wanted to leave – her son Otto[2] recalls her annoyance at Janáček's playing the harmonium late into the night in the room immediately below them. But the next day things had been sorted out. Janáček's entries become warm and loving, and he wrote a little composition into the album marked 'passionately'. By 5 August the days were passing 'peacefully and happily', he wrote. During that day, a Sunday, he added a codicil to his will in the album whereby he assigned the interest on Kč 100,000 and the royalties of *Káťa Kabanová*, *The Diary of One who Disappeared*, *From the House of the Dead* and the Second String Quartet to Kamila Stösslová. Two sheets with this and the beginning of a little composition entitled 'Čekám Tě' ['I'm waiting for you'][3] were later cut out of the album and used in evidence in the court case brought by David Stössel in 1930 on behalf of his wife. This was to uphold the codicil, in conflict with his previous will (which left the interest on the money divided between Mrs Janáčková and Masaryk University). On appeal the courts allowed a compromise in Mrs Stösslová's favour. Another appeal was needed to regain possession of the album, restored to Kamila Stösslová only in 1934, a year before her death.[4]

Janáček wrote again in the album on Tuesday 7 August, a celebration in words and music of a 'Zlatý kroužek' ['Golden circle'] – presumably the ring that he had given to Kamila Stösslová in January 1928.[5] On 8 August he commented on how happily the days were passing and on how Kamila was continually singing to herself. There is no mention of a missing boy, of any expedition or of any illness. On 9 August, the day the doctor was summoned, Janáček did not write in the album but a feverish entry on 10 August records his sweating during the night and his gratitude to Kamila. So apart from that, the album ends in pure happiness:

And I kissed you.
And you are sitting beside me and I am happy and at peace.
In such a way do the days pass for the angels.

1 Quoted in Trkanová 2/1964, 118.
2 Private communication.
3 Partial facsimile in Kožík 1967, 254.
4 Novák 1956, 289–93.
5 See Glossary: 'ring'.

Glossary of Names, Places, Works and Topics

This glossary contains entries on recurring names, works and places; others are dealt with locally, in the footnotes or in the commentary. A number of topics are included especially where Janáček's shorthand allusions are not always immediately comprehensible and where, by reference to other citations, it is sometimes possible to piece together some of the meaning a particular term held for him.

album [*památník*, occasionally *zápisník*]   This is an octavo-size black bound book (BmJA, D 505) of 129 pages, of which 84 are written on. It was kept originally in Písek and served as a commonplace book, in which Janáček jotted down thoughts – both in words and music – during his visits there. Its character is set by the opening words ('So read how we have simply dreamt up our life') and by the first composition, a nine-bar piece for piano entitled 'Naše děti' ['Our children']. Altogether there are thirteen compositions in it, mostly just a few bars long, though one has over forty bars. Only one piece, 'Čekám Tě' ['I'm waiting for you'], has been reproduced (see Epilogue). Kožík (1967, 253) alleged that David Stössel bought the book for his wife, but this seems unlikely in view of the use it was put to. Mácha (1985, 24) stated that it was Janáček who bought it in Písek. Possibly Janáček acquired the album in Berlin: his first entry is on 2 October 1927, straight after his visit there. The intention seems to be that Stösslová should read the book during Janáček's absences: 'And you haven't read the album for a whole week! No, that won't do. There's not a word in it that's untrue. Both of us would have pined for it. There would have been nothing else but to live through it all once again!' (602). In a dramatic episode on 26 February 1928 (593–4) the album narrowly escaped being burnt by Janáček; only Kamila's pleas and tears saved it. Kamila Stösslová took the album with her to Hukvaldy at the end of July 1928 and Janáček continued to make additions to it up to 10 August 1928, two days before he died.

Augustiniánský dům ['Augustýnský dům'] [Augustinian House]   A guest-house in Luhačovice where Janáček stayed during all his visits from 1918 (see p.19 and see Plate 15). According to a contemporary advertisement, this was 'a modern, comfortably appointed house in the quiet of the forest with fifty dry, airy rooms'. It was 'ten minutes from the middle of the spa' and 'moderately priced'. That it was also 'particularly recommended to Catholic families' seems not to have deterred Janáček.

Bertramka   The villa in the Smíchov suburb of Prague where Mozart stayed in 1787, completing the score of *Don Giovanni*; it is now a museum of

Mozart memorabilia. Janáček visited it with the Stössels on 7 April 1928 (photographs were taken: see Plates 25–6), and Janáček wrote an article (see 644) which appeared in *Lidové noviny* on 20 May 1928, essentially an appeal for funds, drawing attention to the sorry state of the building.

Brno   Capital of Moravia (see Plate 30). Janáček went to Brno as a schoolboy in 1865 at the age of eleven, continuing his schooling there and most of his training; apart from short study trips abroad in his youth, and holidays in his more prosperous later years, he lived and worked in Brno for the rest of his life. In 1880, the year before his marriage and his appointment as director of the new Organ School, Brno was a town of 82,660 inhabitants, with a predominance of Germans. The Czech-speaking population of 32,142 (38.88%) nevertheless sustained a growing cultural life evident in the opening of Janáček's Organ School and of a small permanent theatre (1884), in which the première of Janáček's *Jenůfa* was given in 1904.

After the First World War and the establishment of an independent Czechoslovakia in 1918, the Czech character of the city became even more pronounced, especially with the immigration of Czech speakers from nearby Vienna, and the incorporation of the outlying villages into Greater Brno, so that at the 1921 census the population had grown to 221,758 inhabitants, of which 156,000 were Czechs (72.4% of the total). This allowed the Czechs to take control of the 'German' city theatre (1881–2), an attractive building, which became the venue for the premières of Janáček's later operas. During the last decade of Janáček's life (and the first decade of the young republic), Brno continued to grow, opening a modernistic new concert hall in 1927, the Stadion (the venue of the première of the Glagolitic Mass), and staging an enormous national Exhibition of Contemporary Culture in 1928.

At first the Janáčeks lived in a flat in the Czech suburb of Old Brno, but in 1910 they moved to a newly built 'villa' in the grounds of the Organ School, remaining there even after the Organ School became the Brno Conservatory in 1919 and Janáček's retirement as director a year later. Although Brno had always been loyal to him, and he had celebrated the town in his most famous orchestral piece, the Sinfonietta, at the very end of his life, he began to associate Brno more with the unpleasant things in life, particularly his wife, and began talking of retiring to his cottage in Hukvaldy. Less than two months before he died, he wrote: 'Brrr! Brno! That's a prison for me' (685).

Brod, Max (1884–1968)   German-speaking writer and critic, born in Prague. He was the friend and biographer of Kafka, and from the Prague première of *Jenůfa* in 1916 a staunch friend and supporter of Janáček. He translated most of his operas into German and wrote the first substantial biography of Janáček (1924).

buchta   A traditional yeast-raised cake, usually with a sweet filling (curd cheese, poppy seed, jam).

burning of letters   It is clear from Janáček's letter of 13 November 1927 (514) that he was acting under Stösslová's instructions to burn her letters as they came, but this practice started earlier since there is a reference to

Janáček's burning letters on 30 April 1927 (437) and to Zdenka's burning a letter a month later (451). There are many references to Janáček's reluctantly carrying out this melancholy task (e.g. 522, 527, 539) and few letters of Stösslová's survive from this year. From 527 it is also clear that Stösslová also burnt some of his letters, perhaps explaining the thirty-two empty envelopes that survive. Janáček's later practice seems to have been to keep each letter from Stösslová until the next one arrived (609). Later, however, he simply burnt the more personal ones, having kept them for a while: 'Now I'm reading all your letters which I haven't yet burnt. With a heavy heart, I'll sacrifice to the pure fire the most intimate, which many people would take the wrong way. I'll keep the rest' (661); 'Those letters which refer to things which only the two of us know I have burnt. The other letters I've put away in a safe' (721).

Capriccio For piano left hand, piccolo/flute, two trumpets, three trombones and tenor tuba. Janáček composed the piece in 1926 (completed by 30 October 1926) at the request of Otakar Hollmann (1894–1967), who had lost his right hand in the First World War. It was originally entitled 'Defiance', which is how Janáček often referred to it. It was first performed on 2 March 1928, the day after the Prague première of *The Makropulos Affair* (see p.216, fn.4).

carpets (Turkish) The Stössels were asked to supply carpets for Janáček's cottage in Hukvaldy. The first mention was on 9 July 1925 (330); they failed to arrive in March 1926 (*370) and were eventually delivered on 27 April 1926 (*379), when Janáček thanked Stösslová for sending them, saying that they were 'very beautiful'. He added further comments on 15 May (390). Another carpet was sent in January 1928 (569). Three more rugs or carpets were requested in May 1928 (649, 662) but seem not to have been sent.

change [small change] This topic is never properly explained, though is often mentioned, for instance in 589 (Stösslová's 'witty idea to go and get change') and in 613, where Janáček's use of quotation marks suggests that the 'change' might be a fiction. It could perhaps have been a pretext for Janáček and Stösslová to go out on their own, away from the family at Písek. The topic is even described musically in Janáček's String Quartet no.2, *Intimate Letters*, though in a slightly different and more ambiguous formulation: 'gave change to one another' (587).

children Janáček's significant way of describing the pair of paintings by František Dvořák (1862–1927), *Laškující amorci* [Dallying Cherubs] (Plate 37), which he bought from the Stössels in 1927 (502) and hung in Hukvaldy (607). *See also* Kamila's baby.

children, Gypsy *See* Gypsy children.

Cunning Little Vixen, The [Adventures of the Vixen Bystrouška, The] Janáček's seventh opera, after Rudolf Těsnohlídek's novel *Liška Bystrouška* (1920). The novel was based on a series of drawings by Stanislav Lolek (1873–1936), with which it was serialized in *Lidové noviny*. Janáček wrote his own libretto and composed the opera between 22 January 1922 and 10

October 1923. The novel describes the life of a vixen cub caught by the Forester and raised by him until she escapes, mates and raises a family of her own. Janáček, however, inflects the material to include the death of the vixen and explores the relationship of the human characters to this symbol of self-renewing nature. It was first performed in Brno on 6 November 1924 and in Prague 18 May 1925 during the Prague ISCM Festival.

Czech Quartet The quartet was founded in 1891 and until its disbanding in 1933 was one of the best-known and most distinguished string quartets of its time. Its members included the composer Josef Suk (second violin), who with the leader Karel Hoffmann remained with the group throughout its existence. It gave the première of Janáček's First Quartet on 17 October 1924 (see 263–4) and Janáček considered it for the first performance of the Second Quartet (629, 632), but in the end the honour fell to the Moravian Quartet.

dairy The vegetarian restaurant in Luhačovice (see Plate 17) run by Marie Gutová and her husband. Since building began in the spring of 1927 it was a very new addition to Luhačovice when Janáček and Stösslová ate there in August 1927 (476). Mrs Gutová seems to have taken a special interest in the couple, lending them an umbrella when it rained (714), inquiring after 'Madam' when she had left, and sending her cakes and sweets when she was unable to come the next year (701). Janáček's vegetarian diet in Luhačovice in July 1928 was presumably taken mostly in Mrs Gutová's restaurant (710, 716).

Defiance *See* Capriccio.

Diary of One who Disappeared, The For tenor, contralto, three women's voices and piano. Janáček's 'song cycle' was based on twenty-three short poems published anonymously in *Lidové noviny* in May 1916. Purportedly in the words of a young farmer, they describe his attraction to a Gypsy girl, Zefka, who seduces him and takes him off with her; the final poems are his farewell to his parents and his home. Janáček told Stösslová about the poems when he met her in Luhačovice in August 1917 and soon after his return to Brno began composing the pieces, although it was not until 1920 that he was finished. The song cycle was first performed in Brno on 18 April 1921. Janáček later confessed to Stösslová that he saw her as the Gypsy (245), and even wanted an image of her to be printed on the cover of the score (172).

diminutives of proper names Janáček used the diminutive 'Kamilka' interchangeably with Kamila (this edition follows Janáček's practice). Several diminutive forms are used for Stösslová's two sons, Otto Stössel and Rudolf Stössel.

Dohnalová [née Janáčková], **Josefa** (Adolfína) (1842–1931) One of Janáček's older sisters. She worked as a sewing teacher and, remaining all her life at Hukvaldy, became a focus of family news and reunions. In 1892, at the age of fifty, she married a local teacher, Jindřich Dohnal. The marriage did not work out (she was twenty-six years older than he was), and the couple got divorced in 1919. She was close to her brother and took his side in the family quarrel over Stösslová. She kept house for him in his Hukvaldy cottage (242) and lived there until her death.

earth trembling   The earth 'burst open' when during his visit to Písek 17–23 April 1927 (442) Janáček told Kamila that he loved her. In a later version the earth 'trembled' when Janáček used the intimate form of 'you' (*see Ty*) for the first time (550). The place appears to be in a wood (512, 531), near some rocks (512); later Janáček proposed to sow poppies there (550). A later reference (587), however, is to 'places where the earth trembled with joy'. In a much later reminiscence, the day when the earth 'shook' is said to be a Thursday (682), which would date it to 21 April 1927. The event became celebrated in the third movement of Janáček's String Quartet no.2 (see 588).

Excursions of Mr Brouček, The   Janáček's fifth opera, after two satirical novels by Svatopluk Čech (1846–1908). Janáček composed the first *Excursion*, then regarded as a whole-evening entertainment, from 1908 to 1917, going through a plethora of librettists in the process. He added the second *Excursion* at high speed in 1917, encouraged by the success of *Jenůfa* in Prague the previous year. The National Theatre in Prague felt obliged to accept the work, though took its time about staging it; after many difficulties, it was first given on 23 April 1920 under Otakar Ostrčil, Janáček's only operatic première in Prague. Brno staged only the first *Excursion* in Janáček's lifetime, on 15 May 1926. Its central character is a Prague landlord who in two drunken dreams finds himself in unlikely surroundings: on the moon, surrounded by lunar aesthetes (a send-up of 'artistic' attitudes of the 1880s); and in the fifteenth century, where the cowardly and complacent nineteenth-century Mr Brouček is compared to his more heroic forebears and found wanting. Janáček emphasized this aspect of the opera when he described it to Kamila Stösslová shortly before its première (163).

Exhibition of Contemporary Culture   Staged to commemorate the tenth anniversary of the Czechoslovak Republic. It was held at a newly built permanent exhibition site in the suburb of Pisárky, Brno, between 26 May 1928 and 30 September 1928.

fish thrashing   One of the persistent images of Janáček's frustration from 1927 onwards is that of a fish out of water, remembering the fresh water (628) or 'hurl[ing] itself about and thrash[ing] itself to death' (503). Later the fish is at least in the water, though trapped in a fish pond (510) in which it thrashes so much that a wave is formed which casts it (or by then two fish) out of the pond (515).

Friday–feast-day [*pátek–svátek*, note the rhymes in Czech] Janáček's reunion with Stösslová in Luhačovice on 19 August 1927 seems to have been a particularly joyous one: 'In my life I've not experienced more beautiful moments than those this afternoon!' (474). It was some months later, however, that he began to recall it (654, 672), even adding a few physical details: 'One Friday is the dearest of all Fridays for me. Do you remember where that table stood? That you were at it seated against the wall and I against the window. But do you remember where that low couch stood in [our] heaven? That it was near the mirror and behind it that glass case with the decorative knick-knacks?' (660). Janáček coyly did not reveal the real significance of the day until the last month of his life: it was the day of his 'first kiss' (716).

[349]

From the House of the Dead Janáček's ninth and final opera, after Dostoyevsky's *Memoirs from the House of the Dead* (in effect an autobiographical memoir of the author's experiences as a political prisoner in Siberia). Working only with a rough scenario, Janáček adapted and translated the original himself, beginning in February 1927. By May 1928 the opera was complete, though Janáček continued to work with his two copyists as they made a fair copy of his manuscript. By the end of July 1928 he had checked Acts 1–2 of their copy, taking the score of Act 3 with him on his final holiday in Hukvaldy. He died before its première (Brno, 1930), and his pupils and colleagues, puzzled by the strange nature of the opera and its sparing orchestration, revised and reorchestrated it. These revisions have been largely discarded since the 1960s. As the opera was written during the great flare-up of his relationship with Stösslová in 1927–8, Janáček told her more about the composition of this opera than about any other. He identified her as the young Tartar boy Aljeja (a breeches role; **448, 456**) and as Akulka, the heroine of Šiškov's tale (**550**).

Glagolitic Mass Janáček's mass for four soloists, chorus, orchestra and organ, is based on a version of the Old Church Slavonic text (originally written in the Glagolitic script, hence the title). It was mostly composed during his summer holiday at Luhačovice in August 1926, and was completed in autograph score on 15 October 1926. It was first performed in Brno on 5 December 1927, and in Prague on 8 April 1928. Janáček wrote a revealing description of it in his letter to Stösslová of 24–5 November 1927 (**523**).

Glücksmann ['the Glücksmann bench episode'] This is an incident from Janáček's first meeting with Stösslová in Luhačovice, August 1917, which he continued to recall, for instance on 10 March 1924: 'And you know that it was nicest when each of us told the other from the heart our worries and desires – there in Luhačovice on that path, on that bench, when you split off a branch of a shrub. It was close above the villa of Dr Glücksmann' (**231**). Four years later this is remembered as 'The little place above Glücksmann, that bench, where you used to put a twig between you and me to divide us' (**705**). Dr Edvard Glücksmann was one of the longest established medical doctors in Luhačovice, active from before 1902, when the spa was launched as a public company, and was active on various public committees in the running of the spa.

Gypsy children In an article entitled 'They caught them' and published in *Lidové noviny* on 3 July 1927, Janáček described how when Gypsies had been jailed in Písek and their children were left untended in the forest an unspecified woman took them off, fed and clothed them. Kamila Stösslová is not named, but she is clearly intended from her identification in the article with the heroine of *Káťa Kabanová* and with Akulka and Aljeja in *From the House of the Dead*. On 30 July Janáček wrote to Stösslová (**472**) proposing to divide the fee he received for his article between himself, the Gypsy children and their 'new "mummy"'. By then he had written a second piece for *Lidové noviny*, 'They've now got a roof over their heads' (published on

31 July 1927), continuing the story of the children, now being cared for in the Písek hospital. Janáček wrote two further pieces on the subject for *Lidové noviny*, the second of which ('Pepík and Jeník', 2 April 1928) describes two of the Gypsy children who had been taken into care by the town, now going to school and evidently thriving (see also 625).

heaven ['our Písek heaven' etc] Originally a code for Kamila Stösslová's home in Písek. An early reference was on 18 December 1927 (538), when Janáček proposed to send Stösslová vocal scores of his operas to lie around on the piano 'so that it can be known – that those are now rooms which can be called heaven – and in heaven a little music is also necessary'. A week later the references were in quotation marks: 'Well, wait until I write about Písek! So there'll be my dear Negress, so there'll be our "heaven"' (546). Thereafter the term was used frequently and accepted as synonymous without further ado, e.g. 'In March Prague – and a leap to my beloved Písek, which has a special heaven' (607). Later a particular room seems to be indicated: 'And now the author or authoress of these pointless anonymous letters knows well what your place looks like. Where there's "some sort of" back room. There the writer probably has our heaven in mind' (635). By the final months 'heaven' was any room where Kamila was, in Luhačovice ('the path to last year's heaven is overgrown; it's full of strangers there', 701) or in Hukvaldy: 'We'll remember the beautiful evenings in the Písek heaven. Let us transfer that heaven into the Hukvaldy cottage too. It will fit in there; we'll make a whole little heaven for ourselves' (721).

Hollmann, Otakar *See* Capriccio.

Horvátová, Gabriela (1877–1967) Mezzo-soprano/dramatic soprano (see Plate 21). She sang the Kostelnička at the Prague première of *Jenůfa* (1916) and for many years was one of the National Theatre's most useful and versatile singers, celebrating twenty-five years with the company in 1928; she retired in 1930. Janáček carried on a passionate correspondence with her soon after her casting as the Kostelnička early in 1916, and by early 1917 the relationship, conducted rather ostentatiously by both partners, had wrought so much disharmony in the Janáček household that Janáček and his wife went through an out-of-court legal separation (*see* Zdenka Janáčková). The advent of Mrs Stösslová was responsible for his waning interest in Mrs Horvátová (this was one reason why Mrs Janáčková was inclined to welcome her husband's new friend). By 1918 the correspondence had died out and later references to her in his letters are derogatary.

hotels While in Prague for the rehearsals and première of *Jenůfa* in 1916, Janáček stayed at the Imperial Hotel, a large hotel of 150 rooms on Na poříčí, near the fashionable heart of Prague. However on 5 May 1919 (*116) Janáček announced that he was avoiding the Imperial 'for the second time'. His more modest alternative was the 'Hotel–Pension U Karla IV.' [Karel IV.], by the Kinský Gardens (see Plate 28). Though this was in the less fashionable Smíchov district, it was only a short walk from the National Theatre and nearer his Czech publisher, Hudební matice. Janáček returned to the more prestigious Imperial for the première of *The Excursions of Mr Brouček* in 1920 (**164**), but thereafter stayed at the Karel IV. during his trips to Prague for the rest of his life, and Stösslová was frequently exhorted to write to him there.

Hřebíková [née Neumannová], **Helena**   Sister of Kamila Stösslová. She was married to Josef Hřebík and lived in Nezvěstice, near Plzeň. Janáček visited her family there on 10 September 1927 and thereafter issued invitations for her to come to performances of his works in Prague (**587, 618**).

Hudební matice   Music publishing organization, founded in Prague in 1871 under the aegis of the Czech cultural society, the Umělecká beseda. The Hudební matice published the second edition of *Jenůfa* in 1917 and thereafter many of Janáček's chamber, choral works and orchestral works.

Hukvaldy   A village in northern Moravia, Janáček's birthplace (see Plate 29). At the 1890 census it contained 86 houses with 551 Czech and 45 German inhabitants, a two-class school (where Janáček had been born), a church dedicated to St Maximilian, a police station, a savings bank, a steam sawmill and a brewery. The ruined castle on the top of the hill was the largest of the Moravian castles and during its heyday it withstood sieges by the Hungarians and the Prussians. Janáček, who had left home at eleven, began revisiting his home village during his folksong-collecting expeditions (from 1888), later taking his wife and daughter there for holidays. By the time of his acquaintance with Kamila Stösslová he went there regularly and wrote some of the longest of his early letters to her (e.g. **77**), with lyrical descriptions of the local countryside and even a drawing (**190**). By the end of 1921 Janáček had bought a small house there from his sister-in-law (see **186**), which served as a holiday home, and in which he installed his sister Josefa Dohnalová as housekeeper (see **242**). Thereafter he went there several times a year, both to relax and to get on with work away from the distractions of the city. He put down roots there, acquiring extra land in 1925 (**286**), and made improvements in 1928 by installing electric light (**568**) and adding on an extra floor in place of the loft (see his sketch accompanying **580** and Plate 27).

  Janáček began considering an extension to his Hukvaldy house in November–December 1927 (**519, 531**). At first he was put off by an estimate of Kč 20,000 for the work (**573**), though in the end went ahead at the even larger sum of Kč 22,500 (**597**). The work began in early May 1928 and went fast, with Janáček receiving regular reports (**645, 647, 649, 651**). By 23 May the builder's work was ready for Janáček's inspection, and he gave Stösslová a description including the dimensions of the new room (**662**). Painting and putting down a parquet floor began two days later, after Janáček's departure (**663**). Thereafter his concern was with furnishings (**668–9, 682**). Janáček had tried hard to persuade Stösslová to visit Hukvaldy several times before, most notably in July 1926 for the unveiling of his commemorative plaque (**391**), but the new closeness in the relationship, her recent bereavement, and Janáček's extension finally tipped the scale for a visit beginning on 30 July 1928, a visit which turned out to be his last.

At the time the journey from Brno to Hukvaldy was not straightforward (see Railway Map, p.xviii). It meant a train-journey to Frenštát or sometimes to Frýdek (a minimum of four hours, many more on the slow train), from where Janáček had to arrange in advance to be picked up (722). His usual transport was a carriage supplied by the owner of the local brewery, Ludvík Jung (see Procházka 1948, 159) – a further three-hour journey. Horse-drawn vehicles were common in the Moravian countryside until long after Janáček's death and having a car at his disposal was an exceptional event (see 397). When Janáček took the Stössels to Hukvaldy in July 1928 he estimated that the journey would last from 10 until 7.30 (*720).

Hus Eve   The Czech religious reformer Jan Hus was burnt to death as a heretic on 6 July 1415. For many years during Austrian (and Catholic) rule his name and teachings were suppressed, but after the creation of Czechoslovakia in 1918 Hus began to be prominently cultivated as an early Czech nationalist. On 5 July 1927 Písek celebrated 'Hus Eve' with an afternoon concert given by the Moravian Teachers' Choir under Ferdinand Vach including some of Janáček's more patriotic choruses. By chance Janáček was present, on his way back from Frankfurt, and sat unobtrusively with Kamila Stösslová at the back (Vymetal 1958, 36). That evening there was a bonfire in the Písek woods which Janáček and all the performers attended. Janáček referred to the event in his *Lidové noviny* article published later that month ('They've now got a roof over their heads') and in a letter to Mrs Stösslová one year later (703).

Imperial Hotel   *See* hotels.

isolation   Janáček commented in his letters on Kamila's 'isolation' (e.g. 442), presumably a reference to the fact that her husband was often away, or that Janáček considered her spiritually isolated from her husband. Even during the time of her mother's illness her husband seems to have been frequently absent: 'My husband arrived from Vienna only on Saturday evening and went off early this morning. I didn't even speak to him. [...] Believe me, his presence irritates me I'm glad that he's away' (Kamila Stösslová to Janáček, 18 June 1928, p.312); 'As for your husband, [it's] as if he never existed! You poor thing, all on your own' (689). Physically Stösslová was not at all isolated since the household there included her two boys, her parents and the maid.

Janáček's family   *See* Zdenka Janáčková (wife), Josefa (Adolfína) Dohnalová (sister), Věra Janáčková (niece).

Janáčková, Josefa   *See* Josefa (Adolfína) Dohnalová.

Janáčková [married name: Rosenbergová], **Věra** (1891–1967) Janáček's niece, the daughter of his cousin Augustin Janáček. Janáček got to know his niece, who lived in Prague with her widowed mother, during the rehearsals for *Jenůfa* in 1916 and was a witness at her wedding that year to Dr Viktor Rosenberg (the couple got divorced in 1921). She seems to have known Stösslová from early on and did her best to upset the relationship (75), remaining outspokenly critical ten years later (571).

[353]

Janáčková [née Schulzová], **Zdenka** (1865–1938)   Janáček's wife (see Plate 20), former piano pupil, daughter of Janáček's superior at the Brno Teachers' Training Institute. The marriage (1881) was not a happy one. They had two children, Olga (1882–1903) and Vladimír (1888–90), but soon after Olga's birth the couple separated for two years; after Olga's death there was little more than habit and convenience to keep the couple together. In January 1917, in the middle of Janáček's ostentatious affair with Gabriela Horvátová, the couple went through a legal separation, recorded by the family lawyer, whereby they were both enjoined to keep the peace, continuing to keep house together, but sleeping apart (Janáček in his office in the Organ School). Holidays tended to be taken separately, and it was during his solitary stay in Luhačovice in the summer of 1917 that Janáček met Kamila Stösslová. This led to the fading of his interest in Horvátová, and though there were tensions between Zdenka and Kamila, the Janáčeks and the Stössels publicly made up a decorous foursome for the first ten years of the friendship. If anything, Janáček's relationship with his wife improved, especially around 1925, as Janáček reported to Stösslová (318, 324). After the increase in intimacy between Janáček and Stösslová from April 1927, Janáček's marriage became more difficult when his wife discovered a letter from Stösslová signed with the intimate form (*see Ty* and 451), and from early 1928 Janáček began to consider how he might end his marriage (*see also* wife, Janáček's).

Jenůfa   Janáček's third opera, after Gabriela Preissová's play *Her Stepdaughter* (1890). Janáček composed it over a long period, from 1894 to 1903, adapting the play himself. While its setting in rural Moravia, its evocation of folk music and folk milieu suggest Czech nationalist models, the violence it depicts owes something to Italian verismo. The work itself, however, transcends all such models in its concentration on the spiritual growth of its central characters. It was first performed in Brno on 21 January 1904. After many years of lobbying, it was reluctantly accepted by the Prague National Theatre; its highly successful production in 1916 was the turning-point in Janáček's artistic life and he became famous overnight. The opera was taken up by the Viennese firm Universal Edition (which subsequently published most of his large-scale works), and over the remaining years of his life it became Janáček's most popular and best-known work. Many of the important foreign performances are recorded in his correspondence with Stösslová, beginning with the German-language première in 1918 in Vienna (which the Stössels attended).

Kamilka   *See* diminutives of proper names.

Kamila's baby   One of Janáček's fantasies was that Kamila was pregnant (see 586, 636, 640). This was shown in many ways, e.g. by his approving comments on her increasing girth, his depiction of the events in his String Quartet no.2 (582) or in his fortuitous discovery of the Komenský lullaby, which he felt might come in handy (633). The first piece of music that he wrote into the album was a little composition entitled 'Our Children'. Physical contact with Stösslová at that time was limited: the first kiss (*see*

Friday–feast-day) took place on 19 August 1927 and even by 5 July 1928 (702) embraces were not permitted ('Now I'd so like to hug you! Oh, if only you would once let yourself be hugged. And you always just escape like a slippery little fish!') Thus the whole question of 'children' lies in the realms of wishful thinking. A decade earlier Janáček went through a similar phase with Gabriela Horvátová, announcing to his wife that Horvátová was pregnant with his child and that she had even had a miscarriage, a fantasy that Horvátová encouraged, though not one his wife thought worth believing.

Karel IV. Hotel   *See* hotels.

Karlštejn   Gothic castle built by Bohemia's most celebrated king, the Emperor Charles (Karel) IV, in 1348–58. It is 33 km from Prague, on the railway line to Písek. Janáček suggested taking a trip there as early as 1925 (308), though realized this only in April 1928, a particularly happy day when Janáček and Stösslová were alone together, as he frequently recalled (627–8, 631, 633).

Káťa Kabanová   Janáček's sixth opera, after Ostrovsky's play *The Thunderstorm*. Janáček composed it from 5 January 1920 to 17 April 1921, adapting the play himself. It was first performed in Brno on 23 November 1921 and in Prague on 30 November 1922. It achieved a particular triumph when it was given in Berlin (31 May 1926), leading to the production at the Prague German Theatre (21 January 1928), where Janáček's extended interludes in Acts 1 and 2 were performed for the first time. This was Janáček's first opera inspired by Stösslová: its story about a married woman having an affair during the absence of her husband on a business trip was one with which Janáček could identify all too easily. He dedicated the opera to her (see pp.201–2), and determined that she would receive the royalties from it (568), a decision he confirmed when he added a codicil to his will on 5 August 1928 (see p.344).

Kodl [Janáček generally wrote Khodl], **Alois** (1861–1944)   Headmaster of a secondary school in Písek. He was an amateur musician, a composer of short pieces and in the 1890s had conducted the local choral society 'Otavan'. The Stössel boys went to his school (see Vymetal 1958, 36) and in this way Mrs Stösslová and, through her, Janáček came in contact with him. Kodl was a leading figure of Písek musical life, helping to organize the Janáček celebratory concert in May 1925 (*295); it was to Kodl that Janáček turned to invite the Moravian Quartet to give the première of his Second String Quartet in Písek (629, 633, 640, 645, 659). Janáček seems to have met Kodl quite often during his visits to Písek. He was one of the party on the trip to Zvíkov during his last visit to Písek in June 1928 (*693).

Kretschmer [Janáček generally used a Czech transliteration: Krečmer]   Janáček seems to have become friendly with the factory-owner Otto Kretschmer (1875–1945) and his wife Marie Louise (1891–1957) in 1926 and described their private art collection in one of his *Lidové noviny* feuilletons ('Strolls', dated Prague, 5–7 January 1927). The Kretschmers hosted a party after the Prague première of *The Makropulos Affair* (600). Among the furnishings for the extension of his Hukvaldy cottage in 1928 was a writing-desk, acquired through the Kretschmers (604), which he had repaired in Prague (618), and with which he was highly delighted (687).

Lachian Dances   A suite of six dances for orchestra, based on folk materials from Janáček's native district of Lašsko. The suite was assembled in about 1893 from dances used in earlier collections such as the ballet *Rákos Rákoczy* (performed 1891) and the *Valachian Dances* (two published in 1890). The suite became popular after performances in Brno, 19 February 1925 (as a ballet) and in Prague, 21 February 1926 (see 371). They also formed part of the Janáček celebratory concert in Písek, 2 May 1925. The dances were published by Hudební matice in 1928 (645, 661).

Libenský, Václav (1877–1938)   One of Janáček's Prague doctors, professor of pathology at Charles University, founder of the Czechoslovak Cardiological Society. Janáček first mentioned him in his correspondence in January 1924 (*229). In June 1928 he recommended Stösslová's mother going to see him as he was 'the most reliable' for internal diseases (671).

Lidové noviny ['People's Paper']   Daily newspaper of Brno founded in 1893 as the organ of the liberal Lidová strana [People's Party]. It had a particular emphasis on music and culture, and Janáček contributed over sixty articles on a wide variety of topics from its first number (16 December 1893) up to the end of his life. The paper was also the source of several of Janáček's works, including the texts for *The Diary of One who Disappeared*, *The Cunning Little Vixen* and *Nursery Rhymes*. During his friendship with Kamila Stösslová, Janáček was writing on a regular basis for the paper: in 1927 alone there were seven pieces, including three devoted to her charitable activities in Písek (*see* Gypsy children).

Love Letters   *See* String Quartet no.2.

Luhačovice   Spa resort in Moravia. The Luhačovice mineral water was first described in a treatise *Tartaro-Mastix Moraviae* (1669) and thereafter exploited systematically by its owners, the Serényi family, especially from the late eighteenth century, when a small resort began to grow up. In 1902 the spa was acquired from Count Otto Serényi by a limited company and it then rapidly developed into a fashionable Czech-speaking resort. This was due largely to the efforts of its first director Dr František Veselý and his friends such as the architect Dušan Jurkovič, who designed several buildings in a style that married Art Nouveau and Moravian folk art. Situated in the middle of fine countryside with many possibilities for walks and excursions, Luhačovice attracted leading figures of Moravian cultural life for holidays and to take cures (the waters were recommended particularly for digestive and respiratory problems). From a village of 142 homes and 945 inhabitants in 1880, it had grown by the 1921 census to 352 houses and 1850 permanent inhabitants. In 1902 it attracted 2024 registered visitors; by 1926 the number was 9559, mostly from Czechoslovakia, with food provided in ten *pensions*, eight hotels, and seven restaurants and wine bars. Janáček was among the best-known and most faithful of the visitors, spending several weeks there almost every summer from 1903 until his death (*see* Augustiniánský dům). It was mostly a time for recreation with long walks and excursions, though in August 1926 he mentions a 'schedule for treatment' (407) and in July 1928 he described his treatment (701, 705, 712). In 1926 the rainy conditions kept him indoors and it was in Luhačovice that he composed the first draft of his Glagolitic Mass. Luhačovice was crucial for him in two other respects: it provided the original inspiration for his fourth opera, *Fate* (1903–7), whose opening act is set there, and it was in Luhačovice, 1917 that he met Kamila Stösslová.

Makropulos Affair, The Janáček's eighth opera, based on the play by Karel Čapek (1890–1938). Janáček composed it between 11 November 1923 and 3 December 1925. It was first performed in Brno on 18 December 1926 and in Prague on 1 March 1928. The chief character is a woman, Elina Makropulos, who as a young girl was given a longevity potion and, when the opera opens, is already over 300 years old and fast approaching the end of her life. The action concerns her attempt to regain the potion; in so doing it portrays her weariness and cynicism that is all her long life has brought her. In his letters to Stösslová Janáček frequently referred to the opera in terms of its chief character: 'the 300-year-old' (286, 378), the 'cold one' (330) or the 'icy one' (417) etc. Occasionally he hinted that this was a portrait of Kamila herself (422, 456).

Marta Servant in the Stössel household. The first mention of her is in late April 1928 (643) and although the question of whether to retain her during the summer is discussed a few days later (645), she continued to be mentioned until late June (696).

Moravian Love Songs Janáček's work in folksong collection and research dated back to the nineteenth century, but he continued to show an interest in the subject to the end of his life. His last years were dominated by work on the publication of *Moravian Love Songs*, which he edited with Pavel Váša and which appeared posthumously (Orbis: Prague, 1930–6). The beginnings of this project can be traced back to 1905, when Janáček was entrusted with organizing the Moravian contribution to an official collection *Das Volkslied in Österreich* and began enlisting co-workers. In 1918 the Austrian folksong institute fragmented and Janáček's work was taken over by the newly-formed Institute for Folksong in Czechoslovakia (see Janáček 1955, 57–66). In late November 1927 he wrote a 'great meditation' intended as a preface (520), and on 29 February 1928 he met with government ministers in Prague over the funding of its publication (597). By April 1928 the folksongs were going to the printer (635). Janáček alluded to this again in June (685).

Moravian Quartet The quartet was founded in 1923 as the Kudláček Quartet by František Kudláček (1894–1972), then professor of violin at the Brno Conservatory, and was renamed the Moravian Quartet a year later. It continued to perform until 1959, with Kudláček still as leader. By the time it worked with Janáček, rehearsing his String Quartet no.2, it had undertaken tours (in 1925) of Germany, Italy and Vienna.

Negress   One of Janáček's terms of endearment for Stösslová (*see also* rocks).

Neumannová [née Ehrmannová], [Henriette] **Jetty** (1865/6–1928)   Mother of Kamila Stösslová. The Stössels lived with Kamila's parents in the same house in Písek, and it was presumably there that Janáček met Mrs Neumannová on his first visit in June 1924 (237). There are quite frequent, if conventionally polite, references to her thereafter, with Janáček sometimes suggesting her as a companion for Kamila on various trips to Prague. It was not, however, until her final illness that Mrs Neumannová became a recurrent topic in the correspondence. She was diagnosed as suffering from cancer on 2 June 1928, and seems to have been taken immediately to a hospital in Nezvěstice (near Plzeň), where her daughter Helena lived, for an operation planned for 6 June. Exploratory surgery presumably revealed the disease as being too far advanced, and instead the family was told that she was better. By 11 June she had been taken to a sanatorium in the spa town of Poděbrady, but within a couple of days she was brought home briefly en route for another sanatorium in Prague. There are reports of her being in Prague until 4 July, though a move to Jáchymov was planned and she died 'in the street' (presumably on a car-ride) in Jáchymov on 17 July 1928.

Janáček seems to have got on well with Mrs Neumannová, characterizing her as Kamila's 'good-humoured, cheerful mother' (721) and 'the only other person in whom you confide everything, who's a firm support for you without your thinking much about it; who cries and laughs with you' (681).

Nursery Rhymes   Originally a suite of eight songs for three women's voices, clarinet and piano, based on folk texts published in *Lidové noviny* and illustrated with humorous drawings by Josef Lada and others. It was first performed in Brno on 26 October 1925. Janáček later expanded it to nineteen items (including an introduction) for slightly larger forces, a version first performed in Brno on 25 April 1927 (433). A couple of songs appeared in the *Revue musicale* in 1926; Universal Edition published an authorized arrangement by Erwin Stein in 1927 and the full score in 1929.

Obecní dům [Municipal House]   Built 1905–11, containing one of the chief Prague concert halls, the Smetana Hall, and a restaurant, which Janáček had begun frequenting from the days of the *Jenůfa* rehearsals in 1916. The first Prague performances of some of Janáček's works (e.g. *Taras Bulba*, the Glagolitic Mass) took place in the Smetana Hall. The Obecní dům was often suggested as a location for meetings with Kamila Stösslová.

omissions, crossings-out   Not all of Janáček's letters have survived. There are thirty-two empty envelopes (and suggestions that their contents were burnt). Other letters have omissions which range from a single word blotted out or cut out, to missing pages or sections of pages. It is clear from Janáček's comments that the obliterations were made by Kamila Stösslová, evidently because he had gone too far, in his language of passion, for a married lady to accept. Some passages, however, escaped unscathed and provide an idea of the sort of thing liable to be excised: 'Ah, lips, my fiery, blood-red lips! If only I were allowed to kiss you! You'll also obliterate that? [...] And I'll be completely happy only when I really will be your shadow all the time, when that shadow will breath your warmth, when it will feel your soft hand, when you'll intoxicate me with the fragrance of your beautiful body. You'll certainly obliterate that too. But why bother when it's true' (**660**). 'So you've crossed out "mouths!" once again. [...] Surely no-one's going to understand these letters, or will only think up something even nicer there' (**620**).

Ondrúšek, František (1861–1932)   Czech painter. After a successful career as a portraitist in Germany, Ondrúšek retired to live in his native Bystřice pod Hostýnem in Moravia in 1920. Janáček was in contact with him from 1924; correspondence between the two exists from 1926, including twenty-nine letters from Janáček to Ondrúšek (now in the Kroměříž Museum). Ondrúšek painted Janáček twice, a pastel study (see Plate 32) made in Hukvaldy in June 1926 (**396**) and a large oil painting made the next year at Ondrúšek's home, which Janáček visited on 10 and 24 February 1927 for this purpose (Macek 1988, 54). Perhaps it was the 1927 portrait, still in progress, that Janáček described as 'excellent' (**423**). It was on display in 1928 at the Exhibition of Contemporary Culture in Brno (**672**) and now hangs in the Brno Conservatory.

Ostrčil, Otakar (1879–1935)   Conductor and composer, from 1920 to his death chief of opera at the Prague National Theatre, where he conducted the première of *The Excursions of Mr Brouček* and the Prague premières of *Káťa Kabanová*, *The Cunning Little Vixen* and *The Makropulos Affair*, and a new production of *Jenůfa* in 1926. Ostrčil was a sincere admirer of Janáček but nevertheless upset the composer by not wanting to stage his first opera *Šárka* (**363** and **365**).

Otava, (little) waves of the   The Otava is a southern Bohemian river, the eastern arm of the Vltava, which it joins at Zvíkov, running through Písek on the way. Janáček often compared Kamila's breasts to its waves. In some cases (**534**) the Otava waves become a metaphor for them. *See also* rocks.

Písek   Town in southern Bohemia, in which Kamila Stösslová's parents lived; the Stössels moved there in 1919. Its population of 16,306 (1921) was, even in the nineteenth century, overwhelmingly Czech-speaking. The small Jewish population sustained a Jewish cemetery, where Stösslová and her mother were buried. Písek contains a thirteenth-century stone bridge, the oldest one still standing in Bohemia, to which Janáček refers (**509, 650**). Cultural life was limited, but invigorated by the arrival of the violin teacher Otakar Ševčík in 1906 and his pupils (see p.58, fn.4). Twenty years later, local musical culture and resources were sufficient to put on an all-Janáček concert on 2 May 1925 to celebrate his seventieth birthday, an event organized largely by Alois Kodl and Cyril Vymetal. On 2 November 1927 the South Bohemian Opera from České Budějovice performed *Jenůfa* in Písek, 'in the presence of the composer and absence of an audience', as a local review put it. Travel from Brno to Písek was long (almost eight hours, with only one train a day), and Janáček generally tried to combine his visits to Písek with trips to Prague or foreign tours. Janáček planned to have the première of his String Quartet no.2 given in Písek, but his death upset this plan. *See also* Gypsy children and Otava, (little) waves of the.

post   From the time of his affair with Gabriela Horvátová in 1916 Janáček picked up the mail himself from his own postbox at the post office ('no.2') beside the Brno station. This was a walk of about half an hour to the other end of town. That he went there virtually every day is attested by his letters to Stösslová, which are inevitably franked from 'Brno 2' and from comments such as 'Day after day I go myself with a letter to the station post office. I'm there at 10 o'clock in the morning.' (652).

Prácheňské noviny, the man from   *Prácheňské noviny* was a newspaper published in Písek (Prácheňsko is a district mostly south of and including Písek), and an unspecified editor on the paper was one of Kamila Stösslová's cultural acquaintances whom Janáček met and occasionally referred to. The meeting may have taken place as early as Janáček's visit to Písek in June 1924, since Janáček refers in his letter of 10 July 1924 (242) to going into newspaper offices in Písek. In August 1927 Stösslová's friend appears to have asked Janáček to write something for the paper (*479), a request finally conceded in January 1928 (see 568); the paper published Janáček's unsigned article 'When we were in Luhačovice' on 8 February 1928.

Prague   Capital of Bohemia and, 1918–92, of Czechoslovakia. At the 1880 census, a few years after Janáček's first stay in Prague, it had 157,713 inhabitants. After independence in 1918, with the incorporation of outlying villages into Greater Prague, this had grown to 676,657 inhabitants at the 1921 census. Janáček's connections with Prague go back to his student days, when in 1874–5 he attended the Prague Organ School, but it was not until he was almost fifty that he could afford regular visits there to keep up with the novelties staged by the Prague National Theatre. His relations with the theatre were frustrating. Although a ballet of his had been performed in 1892, *The Beginning of a Romance* and *Jenůfa* (his second and third operas) were turned down by the theatre, and it was only after a wait of twelve years that the National Theatre grudgingly accepted *Jenůfa* in 1916. Thereafter Janáček's works were regularly performed in Prague, his operas mostly under Otakar Ostrčil. Janáček made frequent trips to attend rehearsals. Another reason for his visiting Prague was his work on official folksong commissions (*see Moravian Love Songs*). After Kamila Stösslová moved to Písek, Janáček used Prague as a halfway house to meet her; and from 1924, when he began to visit her in Písek, he often travelled directly from Prague, a much shorter journey than from Brno. *See also* hotels and Obecní dům.

ring   Janáček lost his ring on his way to Hukvaldy in August 1919 (127) and asked Stösslová to send a replacement. She did (20 August 1919) and he continued to wear it at least until July 1925 (the last specific reference to it, 329). On 8 May 1927 Janáček described 'the sort of ring [he]'d like to give' (443), an ambition realized during his visit to Písek in January 1928. Janáček appears to have brought with him a new gold ring for Kamila (560–1), which he described as 'our little ring' (562), and which clearly had symbolic status ('I'm your husband'). Mrs Janáčková was aware of the rings, writing in her memoirs that Janáček and Stösslová exchanged rings 'very similar to engagement rings' (Janáčková 1939, 191). During the encounter of the two women in Hukvaldy after Janáček's death, Stösslová gave Janáčková her ring. Janáčková described it (p.199) as having 'deep grooves' and bearing the name 'Leoš'.

Ritter, (Marie) William (1867–1955) French-speaking Swiss critic, novelist and writer on music. He visited Prague in 1903 and in 1904–5 lived there for a year with his Slovak secretary Janko Cadra, writing reports on Prague musical life for the *Mercure de France* and the first French book on Smetana (1907). His first written contacts with Janáček were in 1924 when he offered Janáček two librettos. Eighteen letters from Janáček to him survive, including the last letter Janáček wrote (11 August 1928), suggesting that Ritter come to see him in hospital or in Hukvaldy (see Knaus 1988). Ritter visited Janáček in 1927–8, both in Brno, where he heard the première of the Glagolitic Mass, and in Luhačovice. Janáček recounted long conversations with him in July 1928 (714, 719), perhaps in connection with the book that Ritter was planning to write about him.

rocks Kamila Stösslová liked the sun and frequently went to sunbathe by the 'rocks', presumably on the banks of the river Otava ('I'm by the water the whole time, I'm already so black that I can't even tell you', 9 July 1924); 'To burn your body with the sun and then into the cold, fierce Otava' (671). Her penchant for sunbathing explains her dark colour to which Janáček often alluded in his pet-name for her as his 'Negress'. Presumably Stösslová took Janáček to the rocks in April 1927, since he mentioned them himself soon afterwards ('If you aren't at the station I'll go straight to the rocks'; 439). Thereafter the rocks are a frequent topic of comment and inquiry. He worried about her getting too much sun (643) and was concerned for her safety (512), urging her to take the servant Marta with her (643). Nevertheless he found the idea of Stösslová's exposing herself to the sun an attractive one (648, 651).

Šárka Janáček's first opera (1887–8), to a libretto by Julius Zeyer (1841–1901) based on Czech mythology. The librettist refused to give Janáček permission to use it (he had intended it for Dvořák) and so the opera was left unperformed. Janáček salvaged it in 1918, extensively revised the voice parts and had the orchestration completed by a pupil, Osvald Chlubna. It was first performed at Brno Theatre on 11 November 1925 as a belated tribute to the composer for his seventieth birthday (352). Janáček thought highly of the work and took it particularly ill that Otakar Ostrčil did not want to perform it at the Prague National Theatre (363).

soul Janáček's favourite endearment for Kamila Stösslová. There are occasional instances in the early letters ('You, good soul, do not understand it' (36), but Janáček did not use the term much until his return from the crucial Písek visit in April 1927 (434). On 30 April 1927 (437) he used it four times in the same letter, and frequently thereafter.

Stössel, David (1889–1982) Businessman, husband of Kamila Stösslová, whom he married on 5 May 1912. He was the sixth son of the tailor Marcus

Stössel (1851–99), who had moved to Strážnice, Moravia, from Lwów. Mrs Janáčková's first impressions of him are recorded in her memoirs (see pp.6–9). He dealt mostly in antiques, of which there were evidently many entering the market after the collapse of the Austro-Hungarian Empire in 1918 and the departure of German families from the new Czechoslovak state. In January 1927 he opened a shop, the 'Galerie Vera' (selling mostly reproductions of old masters) in Karlín, Prague, which on 1 March 1927 moved into central Prague. After his wife's death and shortly before the Second World War, he sold her letters and other Janáček documents and emigrated to Switzerland (see Appendix 2).

Stössel, Otto (1916–) The Stössels' younger son. He accompanied his mother during her visit to Hukvaldy (see Epilogue). He is referred to by the diminutive forms Ota, Otuš, Otušek and Otoušek.

Stössel, Rudolf (1913–78) The Stössels' older son. He is referred to by the diminutive forms Rudi, Ruda and Rudin.

Stösslová's family, Mrs *See* David Stössel (husband), Otto Stössel and Rudolf Stössel (sons), Jetty Neumannová (mother) and Helena Hřebíková (sister).

String Quartet no.2, 'Intimate Letters' Originally called 'Love Letters', composed 29 January – 19 February 1928. This is the work most directly inspired by Kamila Stösslová. Janáček described its composition to her in 573, 576–7 and 581, mentioning its final title in 590. Originally he wrote it with a viola d'amore substituting for a regular viola (see 576). Despite Janáček's hopes that the Czech Quartet might give the première (see 629, 632), the Brno-based Moravian Quartet, to whom Janáček had already given the music (629), played the quartet privately for Janáček at his house (18 and 25 May 1928) and he described to Stösslová his impressions of the rehearsals (659–60, 664, 695). Janáček intended the first performance to be in Písek, but the posthumous première was given by the Moravian Quartet in Brno at the Exhibition of Contemporary Culture on 7 September 1928 (a private performance for critics) and publicly on 25 September 1928. The first performance in Písek took place on 2 October 1928.

trembling of the earth *See* earth trembling.

T (at the end of letters) *See Ty.*

Taras Bulba 'Rhapsody for orchestra' in three movements after Gogol's tale about the patriotic Ukrainian Cossack. Janáček completed a first version on 2 July 1915, which he had revised towards the end of the First World War, by 29 March 1918. It was given its première in Brno on 9 October 1921 and was first performed in Prague on 9 November 1924.

Ty Intimate form of 'you', as opposed to the formal *Vy.* Janáček regarded it as a crucial stage in his relationship with Kamila Stösslová when on 21 April 1927 he first called her 'Ty' and 'the earth trembled' (*see* earth trembling). Thereafter he wrote to her in the *Ty* form, and signed himself as

'Tvůj Leoš' ['your Leoš']. He set much store by her signing herself 'Tvá/Tvoje Kamila' ['your (intimate form) Kamila'] or just 'T.', and often specifically commented on it, though most surviving letters from Stösslová to Janáček are expressed in the 'Vy' form. She sometimes signed her letters with an oblique stroke (/), suggesting a more intimate ending but avoiding the unambiguous 'Tvá Kamila' (see Janáček's comment in 538). The relationship between Janáček and his wife sharply deteriorated when she found a letter from Kamila signed 'Tvá Kamila' (451), and thereafter Janáček had to burn most of Stösslová's letters.

Universal Edition   Viennese music publishing firm, founded in 1901. Its modern bias led to early contacts with such composers as Bartók, Schoenberg, Berg, Webern and Schreker among many others. From 1917 it published most of Janáček's large-scale works, including six of his operas.

vegetarian restaurant   *See* dairy.

Vymetal, Cyril (1890–1973)   School teacher and conductor. The son of a composer, he received a thorough musical training, in Písek, Prague and Munich, and from 1915 earned his living teaching music in Písek schools. He was active in Písek musical life, serving as repetiteur at the Ševčík violin school, and as the conductor of the amateur orchestra Smetana (1922–5), which performed the *Lachian Dances* at the celebratory Janáček concert on 2 May 1925. From his short memoir of Janáček published in 1958 it is clear that they had frequent contacts in Písek, for instance together attending the military band concert which provided the initial inspiration for Janáček's Sinfonietta (373). In 1928, when Janáček planned to have the première of his String Quartet no.2 given in Písek, there was a comic misunderstanding (632–3) in which Vymetal, no doubt misdirected by Stösslová, thought that the new work was for string orchestra and that he would have the honour of conducting the first performance.

Výmola, Karel (1864–1935)   Medical doctor, an ear, nose and throat specialist, from 1902 a lecturer at Charles University in Prague. Janáček mentioned planning to see him in December 1925 (*360) and tried to persuade Stösslová to see him several times in 1926 and 1927 (e.g.*370, *401), eventually taking her there himself in April 1928 (631–3).

wife, Janáček's   Janáček married Zdenka Schulzová in 1881 and although the couple went through a form of legal separation in January 1917 (*see* Zdenka Janáčková) they lived together until Janáček's death. But in the last year of his life Janáček began to see himself more and more as married to Mrs Stösslová. Writing from Frankfurt in July 1927, he described her as his 'hoped-for wife' (464). By November that year he had omitted the epithet 'hoped-for': 'tomorrow's the day where I wait [to see] what my "*wife*" will write to me' (518). Later, the quotation marks disappeared (586, 595 etc). During the time they spent in Prague together in April 1928, they took lunch 'as a "married couple"' (629), Janáček began describing her with his surname 'Mrs Dr Janáčková' (664) and wished to dedicate his String

[363]

Quartet no.2 to 'Mrs Kamila Janáčková' (667). See also Appendix 2.
writing-desk   *See* Kretschmer, Otto.

Diary of Meetings

[365]

DATES	PLACE: EVENT	DOCUMENTS
18 May	Prague: DS (without KS) meets Janáčeks during the Prague première of *The Cunning Little Vixen*.	*313, 314, *315
31 August–1 September	Písek: Janáčeks stay with Stössels on their way to Venice.	*341, *342, 343, *344
1926 19 February	Písek: Janáčeks visit Stössels briefly before the Prague concerts on 20 and 21 February.	*368, *369, 371
11–12 May	Písek: LJ stays with Stössels after his trip to London.	389–90
5 November	Prague: Janáčeks meet KS during the German Theatre's *Jenůfa*; KS 'goes her own way'.	*415, 417
1927 17–23 April	Písek: LJ visits KS, the turning point of their relationship.	428–35, LJ to ZJ 21 April 1927, 442
before 26 May	Brno: Rudolf Stössel meets Janáček briefly on a school trip.	KS 26 May 1927, 449–50
5–6 July	Písek: LJ visits KS on his way back from Frankfurt, attending an afternoon concert and an evening bonfire on 5 July, Hus's Eve.	459, 463, 465, 703, 705
?16–28 August	Luhačovice: LJ and KS meet on holiday in Luhačovice.	472, 474–6, *477, *478, *479, 480, *481, 498
1–3 October	Písek: LJ comes for lunch after his trip to Berlin. First entry in the Album. He leaves very early on 3 October.	*494, 495–6, 503
?1–4 November	Písek: LJ stays in Písek to see a performance of *Jenůfa* there on 2 November with KS and her mother, given by the České Budějovice opera. They also go to see an operetta.	509–11, 516
8–12 December	Písek: trip between LJ's meeting in Prague on 7 December and concert on 13 December.	527–8, 532–3, 537
1928 8–10 January	Písek: LJ visits Písek, leaving very early on the morning of 10 January.	551, 557–8, 560–2
21–2 January	Prague: LJ, KS (and DS?) meet for the première at the German Theatre of *Káťa Kabanová*.	560–2, *564, *566, 567, 568, 571–4
12–?14 February	Písek: LJ visits KS on his way back from a folksong commission meeting in Prague on 11 February.	583–6
24–7 February	Písek: LJ visits KS between stage rehearsals for *The Makropulos Affair* in Prague.	587–9, 593–4, 600

DATES	PLACE: EVENT	DOCUMENTS
2 March	Prague: DS hands over tie pin from KS on the day of the première of *The Makropulos Affair*.	600
8 March	Brno: DS visits LJ to get reference for citizenship; LJ tells DS 'what binds' LJ to KS.	KS 5 March 1928, 605
23–5 March	Písek: LJ visits KS after visit to Prague.	612–13, 616–17, 620, *622, 624
7–10 April	Prague: LJ arrives on 6 April and is joined by Stössels on 7 April. KS attends the première of the Glagolitic Mass (8 April) and makes various trips with LJ (Karlštejn, Chuchle races, Prague castle).	618, 620, 623–9, 631, 633, 642
23–5 April	Písek: visits KS after his folksong meeting in Prague on 23 April.	634, 637, *638, 639
23–4 June	Písek: LJ visits KS during her mother's illness and makes an expedition to Zvíkov with the Stössels and Alois Kodl.	692, 698
29 July – 12 August	Brno–Hukvaldy–Ostrava: Stössels (KS, DS and Otto) meet LJ in Brno on 29 July and travel with him to Hukvaldy the next day; DS goes off, LJ, KS and Otto go for walks and excursions; LJ becomes ill on 8 August, goes to hospital in Ostrava on 10 August, where he dies on 12 August.	710, KS 21 July 1928, 719, *720, 721–2, KS 25 July 1928, Epilogue

APPENDICES

APPENDIX I:

The History of Janáček's Letters to Kamila Stösslová

In her Czech edition of Janáček's letters to Kamila Stösslová, Dr Svatava Přibáňová wrote two untitled prefaces printed in parallel columns at the beginning of the book. That printed in the left-hand column deals mostly with biographical details of the Stössel family and Janáček's relationship to it. Much of the material contained in it has been absorbed into the footnotes and commentary of this English edition. The right-hand preface, mostly describing the fate of the letters after Janáček's death in 1928, follows here. Passages relevant only to the Czech edition (such as editorial procedure and acknowledgements) have been omitted. A few explanatory footnotes have been added.

Kamila Stösslová saved Janáček's letters from the beginning of their acquaintance. Two years after Janáček's death she made some of his letters available to Adolf Vašek for the book he had prepared[1] and allowed him to cite them in his book. Shortly after the publication of Vašek's book an article appeared in the Sunday supplement of the daily newspaper *Národní osvobození* no.253 (14 September 1930) entitled 'Z korespondence Leoše Janáčka' [From the correspondence of Leoš Janáček], whose author, under the cipher of B. V-ý, drew the attention of the public to the 'gigantic collection' of about 1000 letters which Kamila Stösslová was keeping in Písek. In this article the author also quoted fragments of letters which Janáček wrote in 1926 in London and in 1927 in Frankfurt. The article very much upset Zdenka Janáčková, who found any sort of reminder of the relationship of Kamila to Janáček hard to take; in her name a legal representative protested against further possible publication of Janáček's letters.

The article, however, prompted Vladimír Helfert[2] into action over acquiring the composer's letters for the Janáček archive; but Kamila Stösslová refused his request, not wanting to sell the letters. After her death, Helfert tried again, this time now acting personally with David Stössel, a course of action which was bound to fail owing to the court case over Janáček's estate; in addition – according to Helfert's later words – David Stössel's financial demands were unacceptably high for the Philosophy Faculty. A breakthrough came only in 1939 with the panic over war and fears about how the situation would develop.

1 See Bibliography, Vašek 1930.
2 (1886–1945), Professor of Music at Masaryk University and author of a proposed four-volume biography of Janáček of which only the first had appeared by his death.

[371]

At that time Vladimír Helfert learnt from the administrative executive of the Janáček Society, Jaroslav Raab, that Janáček's letters to Kamila Stösslová were 'on the market'. Since he wanted to keep his interest and action in the matter hidden, Helfert turned to the director of the Association of Authors' Rights, Karel Balling, with a request to act for him in the sale.[1] Through the help of Marie Schäferová, wife of the editor Otomar Schäfer, Balling started negotiating with Bedřich Hirsch, by then the owner of the estate which Rudolf, the older son of Kamila Stösslová, had pawned for a loan of Kč 20,000. On 6 November 1939 agreement was reached between the seller Bedřich Hirsch and the Philosophy Faculty of Masaryk University in Brno (the beneficiary of the Janáček estate), represented by Karel Balling. For the sum of Kč 22,000 the Philosophy Faculty acquired 713 letters and postcards (including empty envelopes) from Leoš Janáček to Kamila Stösslová, twelve letters and postcards and one empty envelope from Leoš Janáček to David Stössel, seventeen letters from Josefa Dohnalová which she wrote after Janáček's death to Kamila Stösslová, Kamila Stösslová's album, the autograph score of the *Chorus for Laying the Foundation Stone of Masaryk University in Brno* to the words of Antonín Trýb and the autograph score of the String Quartet no.2, *Intimate Letters*. Vladimír Helfert took possession of the collection on 8 November 1939 and transported it to Brno. But on 14 November 1939 he was arrested at the rector's office of the university by the Gestapo and imprisoned. Even after his temporary release in 1942 he did not return to Brno; during his imprisonment, however, he took an interest in the fate of the correspondence and in completing it: he was under the impression that a number of letters dating from 1923 remained in Prague and therefore asked Karel Balling, through his wife, for help.

After the Second World War Professor Jan Racek, as president of the commission looking after the bequest of Leoš and Zdenka Janáček, decided to transfer Janáček material from the Philosophy Faculty to the archive of the present Music Division of the Moravian Museum, an action which naturally also affected the correspondence. The literary historian Dr Otakar Fiala began to work on the greater part of the letters (shelfmark E 1–691) in 1953. His work was much hampered by the fact that the collection was not complete, and the remaining portions were handed over by Mrs Blažena Helfertová, widow of the late Professor Helfert, in stages: in July 1955 shelfmark E 1142–59, in 1957 E 1178–93 (a number of these letters had been attacked by mould) and in 1958 E 1213–18. In 1967 twenty-four letters were found in the estate of Janáček's niece Věra Janáčková-Rosenbergová (E 1398–1421). Three letters (E 1422–5), together with photographs, were bought for the Janáček collection of the Music Division from Anna Platovská in 1970 by the Czech Music Foundation.

It is not possible to be absolutely certain whether the collection of letters, especially that part which Professor Helfert wanted to study, remained complete: his Brno flat was ransacked in the final days of the war. The tragic death of Vladimír Helfert at the very dawn of freedom (he died of the after-effects of his incarceration in Terezín) deeply affected those nearest to

1 Helfert's letter of 31 October 1939 reprinted in Novák 1956, 293.

him and an inventory of the documents and correspondence was not made immediately. Thus it happened evidently that during the handling of the letters they got completely mixed up with the empty envelopes, and undated letters were not returned into their original envelopes.

Only with the preparation of this edition has it been possible to carry out a definitive sorting and to determine the dating of a number of letters, putting empty envelopes together with those letters to which they demonstrably belonged and re-assembling divided letters or fragments. This is the reason why the tally of letters in the final cataloguing does not correspond with the tally of shelfmark numbers (E) given above. At the present time (1988) there are in the Janáček collection of the Music Division of the Moravian [Regional] Museum a total of 697 letters, picture postcards and correspondence cards addressed to Kamila Stösslová and 32 empty envelopes.

[...]

Janáček's letters to Kamila Stösslová have long attracted the interest of researchers, especially after Bohumír Štědroň's first publication of parts of the letters in his study of Janáček's *The Diary of One who Disappeared*,[1] and then in the more substantial cross-section which expressed Janáček's views on a further area of his work.[2] At the conclusion of his study of *The Diary of One who Disappeared* Štědroň thanked 'my late professor Vladimír Helfert' for access to the letters. All further researchers who have worked on the relationship between Janáček and Kamila Stösslová[3] have started with what Štědroň published. [...]

The letters published here were not written for the music specialist; Janáček wrote them for a simple woman and wanted her to understand them. In his discourse he was artlessly genuine and frank, naturally also impetuous and sharp in some of his judgements. At the end of his life, however, even his remarkable vitality gave way to weariness. The collected edition of letters will make possible its use by wider groups of researchers since it not only documents the relationship between composer and the recipient, but also offers a deeper view of the essential as well as the seemingly trivial circumstances of Janáček's exhausting everyday creative struggle. [...]

SVATAVA PŘIBÁŇOVÁ

1 'Zápisník zmizelého', in *Zápisník zmizelého*, ed. Adolf Kroupa (Dr V. Tomsa, Prague, 1948), 29–53.
2 'Janáčkovy listy důvěrné' [Janáček's intimate letters], *Hudební rozhledy*, vi (1953), 608–18.
3 e.g. Jaroslav Slavický: *Listy důvěrné* [Intimate letters] (Panton, Prague, 1966).

APPENDIX 2:
Civil Court in Brno: Janáček v. Janáčková, no.3 Nc 393/28, praes. 9 September 1928

It is clear from many references in his letters that at the end of his life Janáček began to think of Kamila Stösslová as his wife. To make her so legally would have been more difficult, and in this article Dr Richard Klos, for many years legal adviser to the Czech Music Foundation (which administered the royalties from the Janáček estate), explores the probable course a divorce suit initiated by Janáček would have taken under the laws of the time in Czechoslovakia.

Janáček's marriage often came close to divorce, most of all because of his relationship with Kamila Stösslová, and especially in the final years of his life. This is attested by Janáček's letters to Kamila and by Zdenka Janáčková's memoirs. Let us assume that Janáček might have tried to get divorced legally had his death not prevented it. Let us try then to guess at the further, hypothetical evolution of his marriage, and of Kamila's. Before passing judgement we will have to assemble the important facts: those to which the law of the time would apply, and the attitudes of the participants. Without this the court would not be able to come to a decision.

Zdenka Janáčková was married as a young and inexperienced girl, carefully brought up so that one day she might become the respectable, painstaking and capable wife of a notable townsman. She gives this picture of herself involuntarily in her memoirs and it is confirmed by a witness – the maidservant Marie Stejskalová. Furthermore, Zdenka was undoubtedly of good character. A marriage founded mostly on this approach would hardly be able to satisfy the impulsive and temperamental Janáček, even if he had once been passionately in love with her. Gradually his passions for other women came into play. In the case of Gabriela Horvátová his express admission of unfaithfulness led in January 1917 to an out-of-court divorce settlement. And from 1917 Kamila Stösslová was permanently on the scene. Thus perhaps we would have later read it – naturally in the verbose language of the court proceedings. How is this corroborated or amplified by the written evidence?

While Zdenka criticized Janáček above all, though not always discriminatingly, for his relationship with Kamila and could hardly pass over the insults she received if not by word then certainly by deed, Janáček criticized her for her 'hard nature' (446) and 'cruel slander' (668), while he allegedly 'concealed all her rudenesses, [...] did nothing bad to her, even by word!' (668). Relations had of course been poor for a long time. As early as his first letter to Kamila (1), Janáček complained of his 'desolation and bitter fate'. Also in the agreement of 19 January 1917 he undertook 'to keep the peace and quiet of the home and not to hurt the feelings of the other person in a hard manner'. That he himself did not keep to this is attested by letters and by the memoirs of Zdenka and of Marie Stejskalová.

With the first couple, the Janáčeks, before the court we can perhaps assume the following approaches in the summer of 1928: the husband has embarked on divorce proceedings because of another woman at the cost of taking the blame himself; the wife is willing to consider divorce for the sake of peace, naturally with the proviso that she will be provided for in her old age (Janáček always intended to do that). She does not herself feel guilty in any respect. She considers some excesses in her behaviour towards her husband natural (and many times they are). What is curious – and the court will also consider this point – is the advanced age of the couple and the length of their marriage, however unstable. And the now considerable fame of the husband will make the trial a juicy morsel for press and public. The judge must also consider this: 'embarrassing for something like this to happen in Brno!'

We know much less about the mutual relations of the other couple, the Stössels. In 1917 Janáček told Zdenka (p. 6) about them: 'They really love one another!' Nevertheless the course of the correspondence permits the interpretation that Kamila could at least contemplate living with Janáček. We know almost nothing about the attitude of David Stössel. From the sources to which we are confined he appears to have acted correctly in the circumstances, not departing from any norm, decently seeking to provide for his family. This is how Kamila herself depicts him. Zdenka believes that he might have borrowed from Janáček, not daring however to say anything that could be construed as slander. Janáček wrote to Kamila on 8 March 1928 (605) that he had explained to her husband 'what binds me to you. The conversation ended without greater excitement.' We could judge from this that David Stössel, probably a very pragmatic man and often away from home on business (that too could weaken links), would not stand against the prospective breakdown of the marriage especially when the children were already fifteen and twelve years old. It was his attitude that would probably be crucial from a legal point of view – the attitude of the seemingly innocent husband, probably not interested in divorce.

Thus the two couples, the Janáčeks and the Stössels, would have introduced themselves to the Regional Court in Brno and the Regional Court in Písek sometime in the second half of 1928.

At that time Czechoslovak regulations for the dissolution of marriage by the court were contained in the Common Civil Code of 1811 and its supplement the Matrimonial Amendment of 1919. These laws were in force until 1950. At that time the law recognized *rozvod* [legal separation] which brought to an end chiefly the duty of faithfulness and mutual help, sharing a common household, the intimate relations of marriage etc, but the marriage continued legally to exist so there was no possibility of a new marriage; a return to the old one was easy. If the couple decided on a voluntary separation it was straightforward and after three attempts by the court at reconciliation it could take place quite quickly. This was the case, for instance, in the accord between the Janáčeks dating from 17 January 1917. If there was no agreement on this it was necessary to prove some of the grounds for divorce expressly named by the law. Then battle would be unleashed and proof was often difficult.

A year after legal separation (under certain circumstances even earlier) it was possible to sue for *rozluka* [full divorce].[1] Only when the court allowed it did the marriage really cease to exist. (So for Janáček only *rozluka* would have been a step forward.) Similarly the grounds for full divorce were enumerated (and to liven the game were formulated slightly differently from those for legal separation). Among the nine grounds was adultery, an irretrievable breakdown in the marriage (this however could not be invoked by the partner who was primarily guilty of the breakdown), and insuperable antipathy, but in this case the name of the other partner would have to be attached to the request.

How would the couples in question have fared before the court?

With the Janáčeks it is Zdenka who could have invoked some of these legal grounds; by attempting to demonstrate either her husband's unfaithfulness or his guilt for an irretrievable breakdown. But Zdenka clearly had no interest in this.

Janáček himself would have had difficulty in putting together a case on which to sue his wife, again apart from an irretrievable breakdown (itself an objective fact). But Zdenka's defence lawyer would doubtless have proved that Janáček himself was primarily responsible for the breakdown (to which Marie Stejskalová would have testified – and there were other witnesses). Janáček barred this path for himself by his own headstrong openness, not attempting to conceal his relationship with Kamila and making it virtually public. For this reason his action would not have succeeded. And divorce on the grounds of insuperable antipathy was dependent on Zdenka's agreement.

Janáček therefore had no prospect other than a voluntary legal separation and full divorce on the grounds of insuperable antipathy – again with his wife's agreement. One can speculate that he would have obtained Zdenka's agreement and, after strenuous attempts by the court at reconciling an almost fifty-year marriage, he would have gained his freedom. Undoubtedly in regard to public opinion and local prudery, the court would have tried to delay the matter as far as possible. Nevertheless, sometime towards the end of 1929, and thus after his seventy-fifth birthday, Janáček would finally have been free.

Kamila would have been practically in the same boat. In so far as she was unable to demonstrate any serious misdemeanours on the part of her husband (and our court, morever, has nothing like this in its papers), she would have been just as dependent as Janáček on the decision of her partner. Even weak indications of legal grounds for the breakdown of the marriage could hardly be found and Stössel's defence would have made mincemeat of the action. At the best it would have been possible to bring a very long and

1 Earlier Czech-English dictionaries sometimes distinguished the terms as follows: *rozvod* – divorce from board and bed; *rozluka* – divorce from the bond of marriage.

painful case whose end results would have been bought off by financial concessions to secure the agreement of the husband. Similarly the legal grounds of insuperable antipathy would have depended wholly on the good will of David Stössel. There would also have to have been negotiations over maintenance and custody of the children and for this very reason the court in Písek would have had no great interest in speed. It seems then that the Písek trial, if it were to achieve agreement and success, would have lasted even longer than the Brno one.

Thus it would have been difficult for Janáček to have entered the marriage chamber with a carnation in his lapel sooner than towards the end of 1930. And it would not have happened after dramatic battles in the court house, revelations by brilliantly clad lawyers and sensational testimonies of witnesses but after a series of tussles and private deals. A miserable prospect for the old lion.

RICHARD KLOS

Note on Sources

Janáček's letters to Kamila Stösslová are housed in the Music Division of the Moravian Regional Museum, Brno (BmJA). They are printed with details of shelfmarks and document type in Svatava Přibáňová's complete Czech edition, *Hádanka života: dopisy Leoše Janáčka Kamile Stösslové* (Brno, Opus musicum, 1990), the basis for the present English edition. The locations of other letters quoted or referred to are given in the footnotes, with the exception of the letters of Kamila Stösslová to Leoš Janáček. Some of these appeared in the footnotes of *Hádanka života*, some have also appeared in an English translation by Lewis Weiner and Gertrude Hirschler in Stösslová 1991.

The letters listed below are reproduced in the present edition by kind permission of Mrs Stösslová's son, Mr Otto Stössel. Their shelfmarks in the Music Division of the Moravian Regional Museum are given in the second column. The page numbers of their publication (or partial publication) in the footnootes of *Hádanka života* are given in the third column (– indicates that they have not been published in Czech).

31 July 1917	E739	—	after 16 June 1926	E968	—
18 March 1918	E767	—	26 May 1927	E984	211
3 December 1918	E796	53	14–15 December 1927	E988	267
before 20 August 1919	E1160	67	5 March 1928	E1197	315–16
17 October 1921	E872	91	14 March 1928	E1198	324–5
2 January 1922	E883	95	15 May 1928	E1206	—
25 August 1922	E891	99	2 June 1928	E1169	383
12 October 1922	E894	102	5 June 1928	E1170	—
11 January 1923	E898	—	after 6 June 1928	E1173	—
22 November 1923	E914	—	9 June 1928	E1209	—
9 July 1924	E922	116–120 (includes facsimile)	11 June 1928	E1222	393
			14 June 1928	E1171	—
			18 June 1928	E1210	—
25 July 1924	E924	122	27 June 1928	E1223	398
13 December 1924	E993	135	before 5 July 1928	E1194	404
20 January 1925	E938	—	21 July 1928	E991	416
1 June 1925	E906	—	25 July 1928	E1211	—

Bibliography

Edited writings and letters etc. are generally listed under the original writer, not the editor. Items are arranged alphabetically by author, then chronologically under that author. Czech diacritics are ignored in alphabetization.

Abbreviations

ed.   editor, edited by
Eng. English
JA   Janáčkův archiv, first series, general ed. Vladimír Helfert (i) and Jan
      Racek (ii-ix)
      vi *Korespondence Leoše Janáčka s Gabrielou Horvátovou*, ed. Artuš
      Rektorys (Hudební matice, Prague, 1950)
      ix *Korespondence Leoše Janáčka s Maxem Brodem*, ed. Jan Racek and
      Artuš Rektorys (Státní nakladatelství krásné literatury, hudby a umění,
      Prague, 1953)
LN   *Lidové noviny*
OM *Opus musicum*
trans. translation, translated by

Balhar, Jak. *Průvodce Lázněmi Luhačovicemi na Moravě a 75 výletů do okolí* [A guide to Luhačovice spa in Moravia and seventy-five excursions into the surrounding countryside] (F. Hložek, Luhačovice, revised 3/1914)

Balhar, Jakub et al: *Lázně Luhačovice 1902–1927* [Luhačovice spa 1902–27] (n.p., n.d. [Luhačovice, 1927])

Bednaříková, Marie et al: *Dějiny university v Brně* [The history of the university in Brno] (Universita J. E. Purkyně v Brně, Brno, 1969)

Blažek, Vlastimil: 'Vzpomínky na dra Leoše Janáčka' [Memoirs of Dr Leoš Janáček], *Hudební výchova*, xix (1938), 96–9

Československý hudební slovník osob a institucí (The Czechoslovak music dictionary of people and institutions], ed. Gracian Černušák, Bohumír Štědroň and Zdenko Nováček (Státní hudební vydavatelství, Prague, 1963–5)

Chlubna, Osvald: 'Dr Leoš Janáček: Z mrtvého domu' [Dr Leoš Janáček: *From the House of the Dead*], *Divadelní list Národního divadla v Brně*, v (1929–30), 177, 189–94

Essers, W. M.: 'Katja Kabanowa: zur Erstaufführung der Oper Janáčeks in Prager Neuen Deutschen Theater', *Die Bühne*, v (1928), no. 171, pp. 36 and 58.

Flodrová, Milena, Galasovská, Blažena and Vodička, Jaroslav: *Seznam ulic*

[379]

města Brna s vývojem jejich pojmenování [Catalogue of streets of the town of Brno with the evolution of their naming] (Muzejní a vlastivědná společnost, Brno, enlarged 2/1984)

Helfert, Vladimír: *Leoš Janáček*, i (Oldřich Pazdírek, Brno, 1939)

Heyworth, Peter: *Otto Klemperer: His Life and Times*: i, *1885–1933* (Cambridge University Press, Cambridge, 1983)

Janáček, Leoš: 'Výlety páně Broučkovy: jeden do měsíce, druhý do XV. století' [*The Excursions of Mr Brouček*: one to the moon, the other to the fifteenth century], *LN* (23 December 1917); reprinted in Janáček 1958, 52–5; Eng. trans. in Janáček 1989, 92–6

Leoš Janáček: pohled do života a díla [Leoš Janáček: a view of the life and works], ed. Adolf Veselý (Fr. Borový, Prague, 1924); annotated edition by Theodora Straková in *OM*, xx (1988), 225–47

Slavnostní promoce Leoše Janáčka čestného doktora fil. fakulty Masarykovy university v Brně 28.1.1925 [The graduation of Leoš Janáček as an honorary doctor of the Philosophy Faculty of Masaryk University in Brno 28 January 1925] (Ol. Pazdírek, Brno, 1925)

'Toulky' [Strolls], *LN* (16 January 1927); reprinted in Janáček 1958, 185–91

'Concertino', *Pult und Taktstock*, iv (1927), 63–4; Czech original in Štědroň 1973, 366–7; Eng. trans. in Janáček 1989, 108–10

'Schytali je' [They caught them], *LN* (3 July 1927); reprinted in Janáček 1958, 179–80; Eng. trans. in Janáček 1982, 108–9

'Už jsou pod střechou' [They've now got a roof over their heads], *LN* (31 July 1927); reprinted in Janáček 1958, 181–2

'Pro pár jablek' [For a handful of apples], *LN* (4 September 1927); reprinted in Janáček 1958, 47–50; Eng. trans. in Janáček 1982, 110–12

'Glagolskaja missa' [Glagolitic Mass], *LN* (27 November 1927); reprinted in Janáček 1958, 57–61; many Eng. trans., e.g. in Wingfield 1992, 116–19

'Moje město' [My town], *LN* (24 December 1927); German trans. in *Prager Presse* (4 December 1927); Eng. trans. in Janáček 1982, 41–3

'Smráká se' [It's dusk], *Venkov*, xxiii (1928), no. 31 (5 February 1928); reprinted in *OM*, vi (1974), 207–8; Eng. trans. in Janáček 1989, 115–19

'Když jsme byli v Luhačovicích' [When we were in Luhačovice], *Prácheňské noviny* (8 February 1928) [unsigned]

'Pepík a Jeník', *LN* (2 April 1928); reprinted in Janáček 1958, 183–4

'Zvoní na poplach' [Sounding the alarm], *LN* (20 May 1928); reprinted in Janáček 1958; Eng. trans. in Janáček 1989, 195–6

O lidové písni a lidové hudbě [On folksong and folk music], ed. Jiří Vysloužil (Státní nakladatelství krásné literatury, hudby a umění, Prague, 1955)

Fejetony z Lidových novin [Feuilletons from *Lidové noviny*], ed. Jan Racek (Krajské nakladatelství, Brno, 1958)

Leaves from his Life, ed. and trans. Vilem and Margaret Tausky (Kahn & Averill, London, 1982) [Eng. trans. of selections from Janáček 1958]

Dopisy strýci/Dopisy matky [Letters to his uncle/Letters from his mother], ed. Svatava Přibáňová (Opus musicum, Brno, 1985) [published under Janáček, Vincenc, 1985]

Janáček–Newmarch Correspondence, ed. Zdenka E. Fischmann (Kabel Publishers, Rockville, Maryland, 1986)

Briefe an die Universal Edition, ed. Ernst Hilmar (Hans Schneider, Tutzing, 1988)

Janáček's Uncollected Essays on Music, selected, ed. and trans. Mirka Zemanová (Marion Boyars, London, 1989)

Hádanka života: dopisy Leoše Janáčka Kamile Stösslové [The riddle of life: the letters of Leoš Janáček to Kamila Stösslová], ed. Svatava Přibáňová (Opus musicum, Brno, 1990)

Janáček, Vincenc: *Životopis Jiříka Janáčka* [The autobiography of Vincenc Janáček] ed. Jiří Sehnal; with Leoš Janáček: *Dopisy strýci/Dopisy matky* [Letters to his uncle/Letters from his mother], ed. Svatava Přibáňová (Opus musicum, Brno, 1985)

Janáčková, Věra: 'Poslední dny Leoše Janáčka' [Janáček's last days], *Národní politika* (13 August 1940); reprinted in Bohumír Štědroň, ed.: *Leoš Janáček: vzpomínky, dokumenty, korespondence a studie* (Supraphon, Prague, 1986), 168

Janáčková, Zdenka: *Můj život* [My life], written with and edited by Marie Trkanová (MS, 1939; Brno, Opus Musicum, 1993)

Jančář, Antonín: *Luhačovice: průvodce* [Luhačovice: a guide] (Olympia, Prague, 2/1988)

Knaus, Jakob: 'Poslední dopis' [The last letter], *OM*, xx (1988), no.9, pp. xxv–xxvii

Kožík, František: *Po zarostlém chodníčku* [On the overgrown path] (Československý spisovatel, Prague, 1967, 3/Velehrad, Prague, 1983)

Macek, Petr: 'Leoš Janáček a František Ondrúšek: přátelství skladatele a malíře' [Leoš Janáček and František Ondrúšek: the friendship of composer and painter], *OM*, xx (1988), 52–6

Mácha, Jaroslav: *Leoš Janáček a Písek* (Okresní knihovna v Písku, Písek, 1985)

Masarykův slovník naučný [The Masaryk encyclopedia] (Československý kompas, Prague, 1925–33)

Mika, Zdeněk, ed.: *Dějiny Prahy v datech* [The history of Prague in dates] (Panorama, Prague, 1989)

Nejedlý, Zdeněk: *Zdeňka Fibicha milostný deník* [Zdeněk Fibich's erotic diary] (Hudební matice Umělecké besedy, Prague, 1925)

Nováček, Otakar: 'Janáčkovi novopačtí přátelé . . .' [Janáček's friends from Nová Paka], *Program* [Státního divadla v Brně], l (1978–9), no.1, pp. 13–15 [on the Kretschmers]

Novák, Přemysl: 'Poslední vůle Leoše Janáčka' [Leoš Janáček's last will], *Časopis matice moravské*, lxxv (1956), 279–98

Ottův slovník naučný [Otto's encyclopedia] (J. Otto, Prague, 1888–1909)

Pala, František: *Opera Národního divadla v období Otakara Ostrčila* [Opera at the National Theatre during the time of Otakar Ostrčil]: i (Divadelní ústav, Prague, 1962), ii (ibid, 1964), iii (ibid, 1965), iv (ibid, 1970) [see under Pospíšil for vols. v–vi]

Pospíšil, Vilém: *Opera Národního divadla v období Otakara Ostrčila* [Opera at the National Theatre during the time of Otakar Ostrčil]: v

(Divadelní ústav, Prague, 1983), vi (ibid, 1989) see under Pala for vols. i–iv]

Přibáňová, Svatava: 'Nové prameny k rodokmenu Leoše Janáčka [New sources for Leoš Janáček's family tree], *Časopis Moravského muzea: vědy společenské*, lxix (1984), 129–37

   Opery Leoše Janáčka doma a v zahraničí [The operas of Leoš Janáček at home and abroad], *Program* [Státního divadla v Brně] (1984, special no.)

Procházka, Jaroslav: *Lašské kořeny života i díla Leoše Janáčka* [The Lašsko roots of the life and work of Leoš Janáček] (Okresní a místní rada osvětová ve Frýdku-Místku, Frýdek-Místek, 1948)

   'Leoš Janáček, Václav Talich a Česká filharmonie', *OM*, x (1978), 184–7; no.v–vi, pp. xix–xxiv

Procházková, Jaroslava: 'Prezident a skladatel' [President and composer], *OM*, xxii (1990), 168–81

Racek, Jan: 'Leoš Janáček a Praha' [Janáček and Prague], *Musikologie*, iii (1955), 11–50

Sajner, Josef: 'Patografická studie o Leoši Janáčkovi' [A pathological study of Leoš Janáček], *OM*, xiv (1982), 233–5

Simeone, Nigel: *The First Editions of Leoš Janáček: a Biblographical Catalogue* (Hans Schneider, Tutzing, 1991)

Sládek, Jan Václav: *Historie plná otazníků* [A story full of question marks] (Kroužek bibliofilů DK ROH Vítkovic, Vítkovice, 1988)

Smetana, R[obert]: 'Z posledních dnů' [From the last days], *Hudebni rozhledy*, iv (1928), no. 4–8 [unpaginated]

   Vyprávění o Leoši Janáčkovi [Stories about Leoš Janáček] (Velehrad, Olomouc, 1948)

Štědroň, Bohumír: 'Leoš Janáček a Luhačovice', *Vyroční zpráva Městské spořitelny v Luhačovicích za rok 1938* (Luhačovice, 1939)

   Dílo Leoše Janáčka: abecední seznam Janáčkových skladeb a úprav [Janáček's works: an alphabetical catalogue of Janáček's compositions and arrangements] (Hudební rozhledy, Prague, 1959: Eng. trans., ibid, 1959)

   'K Janáčkově inspiraci pro Concertino' [Janáček's inspiration for the Concertino], *Na křižovatce umění: sborník k poctě šedsátin prof. dr. Artura Závodského* (Universita J. E. Purkyně, Brno, 1973), 363–8

Stösslová, Kamila: 'Selected letters of Kamila Stösslová to Leoš Janáček', ed. Svatava Přibáňová, trans. Lewis Weiner and Gertrude Hirschler, *Review of the Society for the History of Czechoslovak Jews*, iv (1991), 65–99

Susskind, Charles: *Janáček and Brod* (Yale University Press, New Haven and London, 1985)

Sýkora, Václav Jan: *František Xaver Dušek: život a dílo* [Life and works] (Státní nakladatelství krásné literatury, hudby a umění, Prague, 1958)

Trkanová, Marie: *U Janáčků: podle vyprávění Marie Stejskalové* [At the Janáčeks: after the account of Marie Stejskalová] (Panton, Prague, 1959, 2/1964)

Tyrrell, John: *Leoš Janáček: Káťa Kabanová* (Cambridge University Press, Cambridge, 1982)

Janáček's Operas: A Documentary Account (Faber and Faber, London, 1992)

Vašek, Adolf E.: *Po stopách dra Leoše Janáčka* [In the tracks of Dr Leoš Janáček] (Brněnské knižní nakladatelství, Brno, 1930)

Vogel, Jaroslav: *Leoš Janáček: Leben und Werk* (Artia, Prague, 1958; Czech original, Státní hudební vydavatelství, Prague, 1963; Eng. trans., Paul Hamlyn, London, 1962, rev. 2/Orbis, London, 1981 as *Leoš Janáček: a Biography*)

Vymetal, Cyril: 'Nezapomenutelná setkání [Unforgettable meetings], *Leoš Janáček: Ostravsko k 30, výročí úmrtí*, ed. Ivo Stolařík (Krajské nakladatelství, 1958, Ostrava), 31–8

Wingfield, Paul: *Janáček: Glagolitic Mass* (Cambridge University Press, Cambridge, 1992)

General Index

[388]

Index of Janáček's Works